EQUATOR

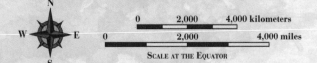

N

W E

S

| 0 | 2,000 | 4,000 kilometers |
| 0 | 2,000 | 4,000 miles |

SCALE AT THE EQUATOR

BIRDING
WITHOUT
BORDERS

BIRDING
WITHOUT
BORDERS

AN OBSESSION,
A QUEST,
AND THE
BIGGEST YEAR
IN THE WORLD

NOAH STRYCKER

FOREWORD BY
KENN KAUFMAN

HOUGHTON MIFFLIN HARCOURT
BOSTON · NEW YORK · 2017

For information about permission to reproduce selections from this book,
write to Permissions, Houghton Mifflin Harcourt Publishing Company,
3 Park Avenue, 19th Floor, New York, New York 10016.

hmhco.com

Library of Congress Cataloging-in-Publication Data is available.
ISBN 978-0-544-55814-4

Book design by Eugenie Delaney

Printed in the United States of America
DOC 10 9 8 7 6 5 4 3 2 1

CONTENTS

FOREWORD

Birds are real. If I had to justify extreme birding, that would be my first defense. Even as we dash around in a mad quest for the biggest list of bird sightings, we're keenly attuned to reality—not just the birds but also geography, weather patterns, forest types, tide schedules, and myriad other factors, because everything in nature is connected. Other people may take up hobbies to escape reality, but birding has the opposite draw. It's a deep dive into the real world.

A year is also a real thing—one orbit around the sun—and yearlong birding efforts are the epitome of extreme birding. The first "Big Years" were done in the 1890s by Lynds Jones and W. L. Dawson in Lorain County, Ohio, cooperating and competing to run up their county tallies. By the 1930s, a few birders were competing for the biggest annual list for all of North America north of Mexico. The popularity of the pursuit has been creeping up ever since, and so have the totals produced. Recent North American Big Year champs have pushed the theoretical maximum and cratered their bank accounts by flying back and forth across the continent, chasing every rarity that strayed within our boundaries.

I myself did a Big Year as a teenager in the 1970s, on a very modest budget, but the restriction of boundaries rankled. I took time out for three trips into Mexico that year, even though birds south of the border wouldn't "count." The allure of tropical diversity was irresistible. Even then, the wide world of variety beckoned more than the idea of birding within borders.

Peter Alden, a pioneer leader of international birding tours, had ticked more than 2,000 species globally during 1968. We all thought that was cool, but in that era, no one seriously thought about topping that score. World birding was hard. Thousands of tropical bird species had never been illustrated at all, and good field guides existed only for North America, Europe, and South Africa. Bird-finding publications were almost unheard-of outside the United States. Birding tours still took in relatively few destinations. For my friends and me, an overseas birding trip involved weeks of preparation, and often more research afterward to figure out what we'd seen. As rewarding as these trips were, no one wanted to cram too many into a single year.

In the few decades since that time, world birding has gone through two major revolutions, utterly changing the game.

The first big change, gradual but massive, has been the information explosion. Today, every known bird species has been superbly illustrated. Practically anywhere on Earth, we can choose among multiple bird ID guides. Thousands of "mystery birds" are now less mysterious, their secrets revealed. Excellent sound recordings make all the difference in finding elusive targets, especially in dense tropical haunts. At one time, if you wanted to see a Zigzag Heron, for example, you wandered in the Amazon Basin for a year and prayed for a miracle. Now that its voice and precise habitats are known, this weird little wader isn't hard to find.

An even bigger change is the emergence of a worldwide community. Not long ago birding was a lopsided pursuit, popular in a few English-speaking countries, plus northern Europe and Japan. Between these silos of activity, communication was limited. The rise of the Internet changed that. Listservs brought about instant communication among the continents. Social media like Facebook even broke the language barrier with the sharing of bird photos and automated translation. At the same time, local birding communities have sprung up in most nations. In the past, if you wanted advice on birding Colombia, you sought out North Americans or Europeans who had been there. Today that country has a thriving

----

birding scene, and Colombian experts know their own avifauna better than any outsider. Knowledge is now decentralized. And since birders everywhere tend to be open and sharing, travelers now have vastly more potential sources of help.

For birding the world, the biggest driver of change is eBird, the massive online database of bird sightings. Launched in 2002, eBird was limited to North America at first, going global in 2010. Its acceptance and growth worldwide have been phenomenal, and it utterly changes how we perceive the potential in distant lands. Once, when reading about Blyth's Hawk-Eagle in the Malay Peninsula and Indonesia, it would have seemed impossibly remote. Now a few clicks into eBird will display half a dozen sites where the species has been seen within the last month, and we can check how consistent it is at those sites and who the local observers are. It's no exaggeration to say that eBird has become the global hub for active birders.

As world birding has evolved, the global year list record has pushed upward. The American ornithologist James Clements ran up a total over 3,600 in 1989—just before the Internet became a factor. An intrepid British couple, Alan Davies and Ruth Miller, surpassed 4,300 species in 2008—just before eBird went global. The time was ripe for someone to push past 5,000, recording more than half the world's birds in a single year. The previous champs—Alden, Clements, Davies, and Miller—have all been friends of mine, and I watched with keen interest to see who would be next.

We could not have hoped for a better contender than Noah Strycker. This brilliant young man was already a veteran of detailed field research, already renowned for writing about birds with depth and grace; no one could dismiss him as "just a lister." In one carefully planned, continuous sprint around the globe, he shattered previous records. He also made a point of going native and connecting with local experts everywhere. The result is a thoughtful, vivid portrait of the world's birds and birders.

At this moment in history, it's easier than ever to see birds worldwide . . . and all over the planet, birds face unprecedented perils. A pessimist might say we're in the sweet spot between accessibility and extinction. I don't see it that way. Noah Strycker turned up plenty of birds on his grand tour, but more important, he met people in every land who care passionately about those birds and who will fight for their survival. Everything in nature is connected, and as the birders of the world become more connected also, the reality of the future looks brighter already.

—Kenn Kaufman
March 2017

1

End of the World

ON NEW YEAR'S DAY, superstitious birdwatchers like to say, the very first bird you see is an omen for the future. This is a twist on the traditional Chinese zodiac — which assigns each year to an animal, like the Year of the Dragon, or Rat — and it's amazingly reliable. One year, I woke up on January 1, glanced outside, and saw a Black-capped Chickadee, a nice, friendly creature that everybody likes. That was a fantastic year. The next New Year, my first bird was a European Starling, a despised North American invader that poops on parked cars and habitually kills baby bluebirds just because it can. Compared to the Year of the Chickadee, the Year of the Starling was pretty much a write-off.

So it was with some anxiety that on January 1, 2015, I looked around to see which bird would set the tone for the next 365 days. I already knew this would be no ordinary year: I'd just quit my only regular job, broken up with my girlfriend, spent most of my savings, and then, cramming all my possessions into a small backpack, made my way literally to the end of the Earth. Now, at the stroke of midnight, on top of a Russian ship in the frozen reaches of Antarctica, with a bottle of champagne in both hands and binoculars dangling around my neck, I was in a hot tub with a Scottish historian, a penguin researcher, and a geologist. What bird could possibly tell where all of this was heading?

With any luck, it would be a penguin. I'd gone to great lengths to engineer this New Year celebration just so that, right after the obligatory countdown and toast, 2015 could be declared the Year of the Penguin — which, karmically speaking, couldn't possibly go wrong. In the previous week, I'd spent a lonely Christmas night on the floor of the Los Angeles airport, traveled from the United States to the southern tip of Argentina, caught this ship, sailed across the tumultuous Drake Passage, and positioned myself for this moment, this pivotal moment when fate would set in motion the biggest year of my life, and possibly of international birdwatching history.

The goal was simple: in the next twelve months, I hoped to see 5,000 species of birds — about half the birds on Earth — in the ultimate round-the-world journey. After leaving Antarctica, I'd spend the next four months in South America, then migrate north through Central America, the Caribbean, and Mexico, reaching the United States in May. If things went well, I'd fly over to Europe, do a big U-turn through Africa, bounce around the Middle East, zigzag across most of Asia, and island-hop Down Under to ring in the following New Year. While the Earth completed one full orbit of the sun, I would visit forty countries with no days off. Nobody had ever attempted such a trip, and bird-brained experts argued about whether it was even possible to spot 5,000 species in one calendar year. By the end, the journey would surpass even my own wildest dreams. But for now, all I knew was that the clock started ticking at midnight.

✦–✦–✦

The world's most frequent fliers don't have platinum status, free upgrades, or even passports. Every hour, millions of these undocumented immigrants pour across major political borders, and nobody thinks of building walls to keep them out. It would be impossible to anyway. Birds are true global citizens, free to come and go as they please.

A few years ago, two British scientists tackled the question of how many individual birds are living on Earth — a sort of global avian census — and calculated that, at any given moment, between 200 and 400 billion feathered friends share this planet with us. That works out to something like forty birds for every human, spread from here to Timbuktu. Birds occupy almost every conceivable niche of our world, from the wild Amazon in South America to the heart of the Bronx in New York City. Even places that seem lifeless lie within their reach: intrepid birds have been recorded at the South Pole, winging over the summit of Mount Everest, and soaring across the open ocean hundreds of miles from land. As of 2015, 10,365 bird species had been identified on planet Earth, a number that only begins to hint at their sheer diversity. The smallest, the Bee Hummingbird of Cuba, could perch comfortably on the toenail of the largest, the Ostrich.

Birding is a state of mind more than anything else, which makes it hard to define. Roger Tory Peterson, generally considered the father of modern birdwatching, once observed that birds are many things to many people: a science, an art, a sport. They can even, as Peterson's friend James Fisher added with a wink, "be a bore, if you are a bore." It's a tough activity to pigeonhole, though many have tried; birding is hunting, collecting, and gambling rolled into one. Nobody can decide whether birdwatching constitutes an addiction, a release, or just a game played by khaki-clad eco-nerds.

My own interest in birds was sparked innocently enough at the age of ten, when my fifth-grade teacher suction-cupped a clear plastic bird feeder to our classroom window. When I was twelve, my dad helped me build bluebird houses and took me to a bird-watching festival in eastern Oregon. Pretty soon I was dragging home rotting deer carcasses to attract and photograph Turkey Vultures, then deferring college to go study bird nests in Panama, then eschewing a nine-to-five job entirely, introducing myself as a "bird man" whenever anyone asked.

From the beginning, the pursuit gave me a sense of purpose. By watching the skies, I began to see the world in different and unfamiliar ways, letting curiosity lead me to new places. By my mid-twenties, I'd spent more than a year and a half occupying tents in various remote corners of the world, in between avian research projects and expeditions, and accepted that there was no going back. I also had a growing, slightly uneasy sense that even if I kept it up for the rest of my life, there were just too many birds and too little time.

The feeling of urgency seems to be everywhere. Psychologists call it FOMO (Fear Of Missing Out), conservationists call it habitat loss, and Hollywood directors call it The Apocalypse. In terms of connecting with the outdoors, we live at an interesting moment. A hundred years ago, people watched birds in hopes of finding new species, but the golden age of ornithological discovery has mostly passed; virtually all birds are now thoroughly, scientifically described, and tucked away as musty specimens in museum collections. Today, people are drawn to birding for the exact opposite reason: to rediscover and celebrate nature at a time when significant chunks of society rarely venture outdoors. It's poignant that, just as record numbers of people are paying attention, the birds themselves have never faced a more uncertain future. This planet is being cleared, flattened, tilled, drilled, paved, and developed at an unprecedented rate. What that means for birds, humans, and the rest of the world is unclear.

As easy as it is to get discouraged, birders are a particularly opti-mistic, action-oriented group. They know that you won't see much if you stare at the wall all day. They also know that some experiences can't be duplicated digitally. There is a special joy in watching an actual Scarlet Tanager instead of looking at a virtual red bird, how-ever spectacular, on a phone screen. And by setting their sights on the freest creatures in the world, birders have a unique perspective about how their subjects stitch together even the farthest parts of our globe. Birds teach us that borders are just lines drawn on a map — a lesson we can all take to heart.

As my thirtieth birthday loomed, a grand plan emerged: to travel the planet, meet its most passionate birders, perhaps set a fun record, and take a unique snapshot of Earth, all in one swoop. I set out to see the world, one bird at a time.

✦ — ✦ — ✦

About a hundred passengers and forty crew had converged for this Antarctic expedition, advertised as "New Year's Eve among Emper-ors and Kings" — a reference to the world's two largest penguin species. If you're going to see the world, you might as well start at the end of it, and Antarctica seemed like the perfect beginning for my yearlong journey.

As the official onboard ornithologist on this cruise for Cana-da-based One Ocean Expeditions, it was my job to point out the penguins and other wildlife until the ship returned to Argen-tina a week after the New Year. We traveled on the *Akademik Ioffe,* a Soviet-era vessel ostensibly built for oceanographic research but rumored to have once scouted American submarines during the Cold War. The trip's passenger manifest included doctors, lawyers, business people, technogeeks, and a variety of well-traveled and well-heeled types from South Africa, Australia, the United States, Europe, and other scattered countries, about a third of whom were bucket-listing their seventh continent. The interpretive staff, by contrast, were younger, free-spirited souls like me, many of them experts in their field, who could happily spend extended periods in remote parts of the world. This was my nineteenth polar expedition in the past three seasons, and it would be my last for a while.

As midnight arrived, strains of "Auld Lang Syne" wafted up from the ship's bar two decks below while four of us soaked in the hot tub outside. The geologist, a master's student named Casey from New York's Stony Brook University, shook up a champagne bottle and popped its cork like a starting gun. Its contents sprayed freezing foam on everything in sight.

"Happy New Year!" we shouted.

A few passengers emerged from the bar to take cell phone videos of us. Most people, which is to say normal people, don't celebrate New Year's by spraying champagne at each other in a hot tub in Antarctica. I gingerly shielded my binoculars. It was hard to focus because the whole world seemed to be rocking. Maybe it was the ship moving, or the champagne, or the general mayhem, or the hundred thousand miles of unknown lying ahead. But . . . no birds! Not one! Oh, I desperately wanted to find a penguin.

The Scottish historian, a red-haired doctoral candidate named Katie, caught my eye. "Well? Do you see anything?"

In the midnight sun, the view from the hot tub, strategically perched on the ship's upper deck, was unbeatable. Thousands of sculpted icebergs, glistening in shades of cobalt, sapphire, and steel, dotted the ocean as far as the eye could see, with a narrow line of dazzling glacier faces tracing the Antarctic mainland on one horizon. An artistic friend, inspired by a similar sight, once confided to me his idea to carve a few bergs to psych out passengers of passing ships: just imagine sailing past a mansion-sized block of ice in the Southern Ocean shaped like Mickey Mouse. But my friend was forced to admit that human creativity has nothing on the brute forces of nature, especially down here. An iceberg the length of a football field weighs a million tons, about the same as, oh, the annual wheat import in Ethiopia; and in the icy waters of the southern sea, I've seen bergs several miles wide. A few years ago, a chunk broke off the Ross Ice Shelf south of New Zealand that was bigger than the entire land surface of Jamaica; it drifted for several years, interfering with penguin and ship traffic alike. In this part of the world, the ice is likely tens of thousands of years old — perfect for an aged whiskey on the rocks — and the tip of an iceberg above water truly is only about a tenth of its full size. Watching icebergs is like watching birds: the more you think about them, the more insignificant you feel, and only gradually do you begin to sense how much lies beneath the surface.

The sun hung at a low angle, casting everything in its eerie glow. In the distance, I could see Trinity Island, a fifteen-mile-wide projection of ice and rock. It was too far away to make out the Gentoo and Chinstrap Penguins I knew were nesting in its sheltered harbor. Still, with a breeding colony so close, I figured I could spot one or two strays passing by. Penguins are perfectly capable of swimming hundreds of miles, and they like to rest on icebergs.

But . . . no penguins. On top of that, the hot tub was getting cold. Outdoor hot tubs are not really made for Antarctica, and this one couldn't keep up with the frigid temperature. If we didn't hit the sauna soon, the four of us would turn into icicles.

"Do goosebumps count as a bird?" asked Nicole, the young penguin researcher, and no one answered.

In the austral summer, when phytoplankton flourishes in twenty-four-hour sunlight, the Southern Ocean is perhaps the single most productive place for life on Earth — and yet there were no signs of life at all, not a single whale spout or seal. In the so-called land of penguins, where was a penguin when you really — *really* — wanted one?

Someone said: "You're the worst birder in the world! How are you ever going to reach five thousand if you can't even find number one?"

Casey got out, then Katie. Water sloshed over the side of the hot tub and froze on the metal deck. Nicole took off. Which left just me, the self-described bird man, sitting alone in a half-filled, half-frozen hot tub in Antarctica near one o'clock in the morning, with zero penguins in sight.

What could I do? Birds are fickle souls. I picked up a towel, followed the others inside to warm up, and abandoned my carefully scripted plan to spot my first bird of the year from a hot tub at the end of the world. All around me in the narrow corridors, people straggled toward their cabins. With the ship's lights dimmed for dusk, a uniformed Russian officer soberly patrolled the bridge, and a Canadian bartender mopped up in the bar. Throughout the ship, people tucked into their bunks, and things settled down after a long and lively evening. Adventures awaited after breakfast — namely, a visit to a large penguin colony, where I was guaranteed to see thousands of the tuxedoed birds on the first day of the New Year.

But I was just too keyed up to sleep. After most everyone had ambled off to bed, I pulled on two layers of long underwear, wool socks, a pair of ski pants, a fleece sweater, a waterproof down jacket, a fleece neck warmer, a pair of insulated waterproof gloves, a wool toque, a pair of fleece-lined waterproof boots, and binoculars, and headed out. This time, instead of staking out the upper deck, with its expansive view, I made my way to the very back of the ship, where I could look down its roiling wake. Wedged on the stern deck between a winch, a large crane, coils of rope, and several inflatable Zodiac boats lashed in place, I stood sheltered from the wind by a metal dumpster storing all of the expedition's garbage, and leaned on the rail.

This was my favorite spot on the ship. Personal space is scarce on a 383-foot-long vessel occupied by 140 people, so I retreated here whenever I wanted a moment alone. Nobody ever went behind the dumpster. Plus, some species of seabirds like to follow vessels, and I often saw birds coursing the wake, occasionally hanging in the breeze almost close enough to touch. None was visible now, but at least this was a nice vantage point.

Could I really spend a whole year birding the world without burning out? I wasn't sure. From now until the end of December, I planned to do nothing else. I would be so focused that I'd skip some of the great wonders of the world — Machu Picchu in Peru and the Taj Mahal in India — just for a couple more hours of stalking birds in the nearby forests. Was that gauche? My friends love to poke fun at me for constantly chasing birds, and I admit that "taking time off" is kind of a foreign concept. But 365 days of predawn awakenings, total strangers, and nonstop, grueling travel would test the limits, sort of like a drug addict doing nothing but cocaine for a year. If it didn't completely break me down, it would leave me high as a kite.

There was only one way to find out if I could hack it, and now I was committed.

My watch read 3 a.m. Suddenly, a hundred yards out, something flickered among the icebergs. In the low light, it almost escaped detection — appearing as a dark speck skimming the surface, zigzagging on broad tacks, gradually approaching the ship.

I knew what it was before even raising my binoculars. This bird flew on stiff wings, riding intricate wind currents deflected from waves; every now and then it flapped a series of snappy beats to change direction, but mostly it just glided on air. It was the length of a football and equally plump. Its head was matte black, contrasting with immaculately white underwings and belly, and its tail was dark. But the bird's most striking feature resolved when it banked toward me and swooped low, below eye level. The upper sides of its wings were spattered with frosty black and white blobs, a crisp vision of abstract expressionism.

Many people call this bird a "pintado," literally meaning painted, because of its splotchy appearance, but in proper English I had spotted a Cape Petrel, a relatively common Southern Ocean bird that nests on remote cliffs. Although Cape Petrels occasionally spew stomach oil from their beaks in fits of foul humor, they are admired and well liked by most people lucky enough to encounter them. This tough little seabird, trying to keep pace next to the ship at three in the morning, might not be a penguin, but it was perfect.

Petrels, in their infinite grace, are thought to be named for Saint Peter and his habit of walking on water. With a blessing like that, the Year of the Petrel was off to an auspicious start.

2

The DSP

ACCORDING TO THE American Birding Association's Recording Rules and Interpretations, a bird must be "alive, wild, and unrestrained" for official consideration on a birder's list of sightings, be it a world list, year list, world year list, life list, national list, state list, county list, month list, yard list, feeder list, birds-seen-while-driving list, or any other list. In other words, dead birds don't count, and you can't rack up exotic sightings in zoos and aviaries. Any bird "under the influence of captivity" is as illegal as can be.

The rulebook has a few more interesting tidbits. Webcams are a no-no for listing. Eggs don't count until they hatch, and chickens, as domestic animals, don't count at all (except the Red Jungle-fowl of Asia, the wild ancestor of barnyard stock). You can put an injured bird on your list, but not a perfectly healthy hybrid; to be countable, a bird must have the traits of one recognized species. Heard-only encounters are fine so long as recorders "assure themselves" that they aren't listening to someone else playing a tape from the bushes, a circumstance that happens surprisingly often.

Otherwise, keeping your list is up to you. Many people assume that birders must document every sighting as if collecting evidence for a court case, but that misses the spirit of the game. As a practical matter, it would be impossible to photograph them all — birds are often too far away or flitting too quickly to get a shot — and anyway, birding works on the honor system.

Not that a few con artists haven't tried to fudge the facts. Birders even have a name for them: fakers are called "stringers," and fabricating a sighting is "stringing." In one particularly egregious case several years ago in Australia, a birder announced his intention to see as many bird species as he could in one year in his home state. He spent the first few months notching up an impressive list of sightings, started a blog, and built a following. About halfway through the year, some local experts began to get suspicious; then, in a dramatic stroke, the guy was caught red-handed: he reported a frigatebird — a tropical species rarely seen in that part of Australia — and posted a photo of it flying against a blue sky. When it was pointed out that the weather on that day was cloudy, the man broke down and, in a long and cringing confession on the regional email list, admitted that he'd actually photographed the bird on a trip to Fiji. For such blatant stringing, the man was blacklisted by the birding community. As they say, you can lose your reputation only once.

But birding scandals are rarer than a Diademed Sandpiper-Plover. It's pretty easy to tell if someone's faking it, and there isn't much reason to make it up. Adding bogus birds to your list is like lying to your diary. What's the point?

Most birdwatching transgressions involve far more minor infractions. For everyday situations, the American Birding Association (ABA) maintains a "Code of Birding Ethics," which outlines respectable field behavior and follows common sense: don't stress birds; give nests enough space; respect private property; keep your bird feeders clean. The ethical code advises birders to "be especially helpful to beginning birders" and "support the protection of important bird habitat."

The rules leave a few gray areas. For instance, if you snap a photo and later discover a bird in the image that you hadn't noticed before, can you count it? If you are standing near an international border and spot a bird on the other side, can you record it for a country in which you have never set foot? Situations like these come up constantly, and not all birders give the same answers.

Also, just because the rules allow certain birds, it doesn't mean you have to count them. Some birders count only self-found sightings, omitting any bird first identified by someone else. Others, who designate themselves NIB — "no introduced birds" — try to keep their lists pure by excluding non-native species. The thorny subject of introduced birds involves various official committees and whole swaths of gray areas. In short, established feral species are legitimate, but the word "established" has inspired heated debates. Even the term "native" is problematic.

The most contentious part of the ABA's recording rules is Rule 4, Section B, which allows birds that are heard but not seen. Despite this rule, many birdwatchers note only visual sightings and pay little attention to sounds beyond the most familiar ones. Jotting down heard-only birds can seem almost like cheating; some species that are phenomenally difficult to spot, like cryptic owls and skulking rails, are relatively easy to hear. Few people would dispute that the distant call note of a Stygian Owl is somehow less satisfying than having the bird itself stare back at you. And yet some bird species have such distinctive calls, why wouldn't you count them, even if you didn't see them?

For my Big Year, I decided to tally both seen and heard birds. The previous single-year world record had counted heard-onlys, so

I'd be applying the same standard. Also, it's better for the birds: listening has less impact than playing recordings, trampling through a bird's territory, or flushing it in a desperate attempt to get a visual. Many species are best appreciated by their sound, anyway; one might argue that you haven't really experienced a Screaming Piha until you've heard one. Vocalizations are as reliable as visual field marks, and lots of drab-looking species have lovely, distinctive songs. In wide-open environments, such as Antarctica and the Chilean Andes, it's easy to see almost everything; but in places such as the Amazon, where birds hide in thick jungles, the soundscape becomes more important. By the end of this year, I would identify about 5.5 percent of the birds I encountered — one in eighteen species — by ear alone.

Although hard to believe in this globalized age, there is no single, agreed-upon checklist of all the bird species on Earth. Instead, we have competing interpretations: the Americans versus the rest of the world. In the United States, most birders use the Clements Checklist, which is periodically updated by experts at Cornell University and which recognized 10,365 living bird species while I traveled in 2015. In Europe and other parts of the world, birders tend to rely instead on the International Ornithological Congress (IOC), a progressive committee that acknowledged 10,612 species in 2015. Some countries, notably the Netherlands and Brazil, have adopted their own, even more liberal checklists. The trouble is, birds don't always fit into neat boxes, and many so-called species blur into each other. On top of that, scientists lately have been re-evaluating birds around the world with DNA evidence, and in the past couple of decades they've proposed thousands of "splits" — dividing one species into two or more — narrowing our definition of what a species should be.

You need rules to play the game, and for my year I adopted the Clements Checklist — the American standard. It helped that eBird, the app I use to keep track of sightings, is based on the same check-list. Along the way, I would keep notes on subspecies, too, so that it would be possible to dynamically adjust the tally. These days, a list of birds is more software than hardware, and keeping it up to date presents an unending task.

+ — + — +

A week after the New Year, high in the Andes Mountains of central Chile, I went looking for an oddball animal called the Diademed Sandpiper-Plover. Two local birders from Santiago, Fred Homer and Fernando Díaz Segovia, came along to help with the search, and the three of us were switchbacking up a magnificent Andean valley at dawn.

Months before, I had asked a friend in Arizona if he knew any good birders in Chile, and he referred me to Fabrice Schmitt, a Frenchman who, after taking a teaching sabbatical in South America, had been inspired to move to Santiago to lead birdwatching tours. Fabrice replied right away with regrets that he would be on a trip to Antarctica when I arrived in Chile — but kindly put me in touch with Fred, who thoroughly embraced the mission.

"We'll meet you at the airport and dash off to hunt the birds," Fred emailed, "and then we'll rush you back with tires smoking."

Fred then called Fernando, a young Chilean biologist, who picked us up at oh-dark-thirty that morning. And that's how it went: a friend of a friend of a friend of a friend — someone I had neither met nor even corresponded with — was now taking me to see one of the world's most enigmatic birds in the world's longest mountain range.

The Diademed Sandpiper-Plover, or DSP as birders call it, is a peculiar creature, found only at high elevations in Chile, Argentina, Bolivia, and Peru. It is a shorebird that doesn't live on the shore, apparently related to plovers but with a profile more like a sandpiper (hence the hyphenation). No other bird looks much like it: the DSP, about the size and shape of a dinner roll, has a dumpy body, fat yellow legs, a droopy beak, a deep reddish collar, finely barred underparts, and an upturned white mark behind each eye — the "diademed" part — that gives it a quizzical expression. The bird looks like it doesn't mind being stared at but wonders why anyone would bother.

You won't stumble across one by accident unless you spend a lot of your spare time stumbling around desolate Andean bogs, as Fernando does. For the past few years, Fernando has been tracking sandpiper-plovers, trying to coax out their secrets. As part of a research project, he surveys likely looking habitat; for some reason, the DSP is reliably found in some bogs but not in others that look just the same, and nobody has figured out why the bird is so darned picky. Fernando also captures each bird so that he can mark it with color bands, which help identify individuals from a distance. Keeping track of all these little sandpiper-plovers is like following a soap opera, but maybe the data will unlock some of their mysteries.

Fernando drove us in his freshly washed SUV up a dusty gravel road that emerged above tree line and continued, hacked into a cliff, up a steep-sided valley. The route was so narrow in places that only one vehicle could pass. When we nosed around a corner to find an oncoming car, Fernando painstakingly reversed along the sheer drop to a slightly wider spot, then folded in his side mirrors to allow the other vehicle to squeeze by.

While we climbed, I sat in the passenger seat, my thoughts drifting back over the previous week. After kicking off the New Year with champagne and a Cape Petrel off the Antarctic Peninsula, the year's bird count had progressed slowly. I quickly ran out of Antarctic birds to see, and on January 3 — just the third day of the year — recorded no new species at all, notching my first zero day practically out of the starting gate. The pace picked up with albatrosses and other seabirds on the Drake Passage, followed by a fantastic morning at a colony of charismatic Southern Rockhopper Penguins in the Falkland Islands. But by the time our ship returned to port in Ushuaia, the world's southernmost city at the southern tip of Argentina, I'd recorded only 53 species of birds in the first seven days of the year. With the need to average 13.7 new species each day — about one bird for every daylight hour — to break 5,000 by the end of December, my score was already lagging.

A full week in Antarctica wasn't exactly strategic, because there aren't enough species on the whole continent to keep up this average. If I had scheduled the same time somewhere in the tropics, I would have seen two or three hundred birds by now, well ahead of the target pace — starting my marathon with a sprint rather than a lope. But then I would have missed the world's coldest and driest and windiest continent, with its massive colonies of Adélie and Chinstrap Penguins, spouting humpback and minke whales, impossibly blue icebergs, and unparalleled ice cap. To me, Antarctica underlined, from the beginning, that this year was not just about numbers. Any global journey that skipped Antarctica wouldn't be as cool.

Still, as our ship neared the dock, I was ready to pick up the pace. I felt light and happy. Everything lay before me — uncertainty, opportunity, and a limitless planet of birds and birders. The sun bathed the world in a hopeful light, and I had the exhilarating feeling that I was exactly where I should be, doing exactly what I should be doing. There would be challenges, but I was eager to explore. I was a little apprehensive, too. I couldn't help wondering whether the local birder I planned to meet would actually show up.

In the few hours after the ship docked in Ushuaia, before flying on to Santiago, Chile, I hoped to track down some Patagonian bird specialties in nearby Tierra del Fuego National Park. An Argentine birder named Esteban Daniels, whom I had contacted months before, had agreed to help — but now that the day had come, would he remember me? I said a round of hurried goodbyes to the ship's staff and crew, grabbed my backpack, and walked down the gangway onto Ushuaia's industrial dock. There, outside the pier's security checkpoint, awaited Esteban and a friend, a keen photographer named Rogelio "Roger" Espinosa. I was ecstatic to see them — and relieved. Over the next couple of hours, Esteban, Roger, and I stopped by the local landfill, then made our way to the park, where we found my most-wished-for bird species of the day: a pair of red, black, and white Magellanic Woodpeckers, the largest woodpecker in South America. We clocked thirty-seven new bird species — bringing my year total so far to ninety-one — before heading to the local airport in midafternoon.

After a quick flight to Santiago, I sped through immigration, skipped the baggage claim, and headed straight for Exit 3, where Fred Homer, exactly as planned, awaited in a green hat. So far, so good! Fred and I crashed at his house in Santiago, where Fernando picked us up in the early morning hours, and now the three of us were hot on the trail of the Diademed Sandpiper-Plover.

The road continued to climb, skirting around a shallow reservoir in a broad valley of rock and dirt, which was birdless except for a lone Andean Gull flying in lazy circles.

"A couple years ago I came down here," Fred said, "and, maybe three hundred meters from this spot, saw something on the road ahead. As I got closer, I realized that it was the rear axle of a lorry, implanted into the road surface. When you looked around, there were bits of lorry all over the place. I guess it went off the edge above and just fell to pieces."

All plant life ceased as we ascended into the upper El Yeso Valley, flanked on both sides by chiseled peaks in ochre and umber. The sky up here looked polarized, like the deep blue you see through sunglasses. Snowfields clung to the mountaintops, almost at eye level, and I could see bluish, crevasse-wrinkled glaciers hanging from steep slopes above us. Every so often we passed a *Vía de Evacuación* ("Evacuation Route") sign, illustrated with a friendly stick-figure image of mother and child walking in front of an exploding volcano.

Fernando turned at an unmarked junction at about 10,000 feet and followed a side track until it petered out into boulders. The three of us jumped out and walked a little farther to the only speck of green in this valley, where a snowmelt stream fanned into a bog of squishy, carpetlike vegetation.

This, Fernando said, is the realm of the DSP, and he led us straight into the bog. Surrounded by the stark landscape, Fernando looked the part of a rugged biologist: checked shirt, khaki cap, glacier goggles with mountaineering flaps around the temples, work pants, low-slung binoculars, and a slightly unkempt beard. He wasn't much older than me and shared the same bent for fieldwork in remote places. He had quit working as a landscaper to focus fulltime on bird research. Now he was in his element, scanning for movement.

Fred wandered behind us in the sunshine, smiling, enjoying just being out here. A few years ago he'd moved to Chile, after retiring in Britain from a career in financial services, and set up a bird-touring business as an excuse to spend more time watching birds. He wore a gray vest with lots of pockets over a collared T-shirt, aviator shades, and a wide-brimmed hat with braided leather accents; his trimmed beard was 25 percent pepper, 75 percent salt.

Halfway across the bog, I almost stepped on our target. Fernando pointed toward my feet, and I looked down just in time to see the Diademed Sandpiper-Plover staring up with beady-eyed

curiosity. It was completely unafraid as an animal a hundred times
its size blundered toward it, and I wondered if this behavior might
have something to do with the bird's low population. Nobody knows
how many sandpiper-plovers are out there, but the best guess is
about 2,000 individuals scattered over an area half the length of
South America. They don't have many predators, at least not in
human form, and part of the DSP's charisma is its totally blasé attitude — as if it knowingly trusts you.

An impossibly cute, fuzzy chick emerged from behind some
nearby rocks and the two birds slowly waddled off together, probing
for bugs with their droopy beaks. They wore matching green and
red plastic bands on their right legs, and the adult had a red and
yellow combination on the left. Fernando noted down the colors,
adding another data point to the DSP project — and I chalked up
species number 123 for my Big Year list.

The sandpiper-plover is listed as near-threatened because of its
vulnerable populations. In the high Andes, insidious effects such
as atmospheric disturbances and climate change could have serious
impacts on the DSP's habitat, but it's hard to tell without enough
data. Fernando hopes that more surveys will document patterns,
which might eventually help with conservation efforts. We lingered
until lengthening shadows reminded us that, despite its star status,
the Diademed Sandpiper-Plover still counted as only one species.

"It would be pointless to bust a gut to see Chile's most rare and.
beautiful bird," Fred said, "if you could, in the same duration, find
ten locally common and ugly ones that you weren't going to see
elsewhere."

He was right, of course. When all birds are created equal, no
bird is worth a significant amount of time. It's an age-old tradeoff:
you can go narrow and deep, or broad and shallow, but you can't
focus in all dimensions at once. I took one last look at the Dia-

demed Sandpiper-Plover, and we drove off to see how many ugly Chilean birds we could find.

Later that evening, Fred and I sat on his backyard patio in a leafy Santiago suburb. Fred served up a bowl of pasta and a fresh salad and poured us each a glass of red wine. The last rays of daylight caught the upper branches of a tree next to the patio. January is the hottest month of the year in Chile, and the afternoon's warmth hung in the air. We'd returned before dark to try for a Rufous-tailed Plantcutter that sometimes visited Fred's yard at dusk. As we waited, it was nice to sit back after a long day in the mountains.

"I'm not really a very serious birder," Fred said, "in the sense that I like watching birds, but I don't particularly care what the species is. I just like watching them. And, of course — today was a prime example — it takes you to some very nice places."

That's what I like about it, too. Birding is always an adventure, and it gives you focus when you travel, instead of staring yourself glassy-eyed at too many tourist attractions. Fred got hooked on birds from one of his sons, who caught an interest at a young age. Although his son's attention passed on to other things, Fred has been addicted to birds ever since.

"It was like a relay race — he handed off the baton, and I kept going," he said.

The sun was setting, its last rays of light fading from the trees. The evening air felt cool and refreshing after the blasting mountain sunshine and dust. Just then, from the corner of my eye, I caught a movement.

"Could you hand me my binocs?" I asked.

Even in the dim light, there was no mistaking this bird: chestnut crown and breast, dark cheeks, white wing bar, serrated beak. A plantcutter! The plump little bird, named for its tendency to shred and eat leaves, had returned at dusk, as Fred predicted. It peered down at us for a minute before fluttering off to its nighttime roost. I was delighted with its brief visit, the sensation heightened by sharing it with Fred, a person I barely knew but with whom I already felt a deep connection. We thoroughly embraced the moment.

"A nice glass of wine, a delicious dinner," Fred said. "Now *this* is birding!"

3

Cerro Negro

WHEN I TOUCHED DOWN in northwest Argentina, the arrivals area of the tiny airport in Jujuy (pronounced hoo-HOO-ey) was deserted. I wandered around for a few minutes with my backpack and binoculars, then walked outside and sat down on the curb to wait. The few other passengers from my flight drifted into cars and drove away, leaving me in an empty parking lot. Would anybody pick me up?

I was a little fuzzy on the plan here. A birder named Freddy Burgos had invited me to visit his province for the next four days, but because Freddy speaks no English, I had been writing to him in my shaky Spanish. As far as I could tell, using Google Translate to fill in the gaps, Freddy had suggested a camping trip, but the details were vague. Maybe I hadn't quite grasped his instructions — was I supposed to meet him somewhere? I had no idea what he looked like, what his phone number was, or where he lived. At least the weather was nice, warm and sunny. Fluffy white clouds drifted over the airport's brick facade, perfect conditions for camping — if indeed that was the plan.

Sixteen days into the year, my bird list stood at more than 300 species, right on track for my 5,000-species goal. The pace had picked up dramatically when I arrived in central Argentina two days before. In Buenos Aires I met thirty-year-old birder Marcelo Gavensky and his friend Martin Farina, a twenty-eight-year-old dog trainer and paleontology student, and the three of us dashed up to the marshy cattle country of the Entre Ríos province, about 125 miles north of the city. On our first day, we found 146 species of birds — more than I'd seen in four full days in Chile — 108 of which were new.

The grasslands were fantastically productive. Between sips of hot *mate* (pronounced MAH-tay), Marcelo proudly told me about La Alianza de Pastizal, a conservation group that encourages ranch owners to practice sustainable grazing techniques. The idea is that, with the right methods, ranchers maximize profits with fewer cows, leaving a lighter impact on the landscape: certified, ecologically sensitive beef can be sold at a premium in Europe, and the Argentine market for it is growing. Shipping overseas isn't a perfect environmental solution, but well-managed *estancias* are the key to protecting habitat in this region, which has no designated parks or reserves. We saw dozens of prehistoric-looking Southern Screamers, a few towering Maguari Storks, and scattered, ridiculously pink Roseate Spoonbills in the fields. Around one corner, a five-foot-tall Greater Rhea stalked past — South America's answer to the ostrich.

After that quick visit, I crashed for a couple of hours on the floor of Marcelo's one-room apartment in Buenos Aires, with my feet in the kitchen and head wedged under the dining table, then bid *adiós* to central Argentina and caught an early flight to the northwest. Now, low on sleep, I sat outside the Jujuy airport and wondered what had happened to Freddy.

I was about to try sending him an email message from my phone when a small bird flitted around the departures area, and I jogged over to get a better view. It had a warm, brownish body, a gray face, and wings that flashed a rufous-red color in flight. This bird was definitely something new, but what? It behaved like a flycatcher, perching and sallying after insects, occasionally hovering to go after bugs in the corners of the eaves.

I closed the email browser and opened my phone's photo gallery. Packing a six-foot-high stack of heavy reference books around the world was out of the question, so before leaving home I had painstakingly scanned dozens of field guides and saved the images as digital files on my smartphone. In an album titled "Birds of Argentina," I swiped through illustrated plates to the flycatcher section and quickly found a match: the Cliff Flycatcher, a common inhabitant of South American forests and of airport lampposts, was bird number 338. This fine specimen was still flitting around twenty minutes later when a white pickup truck sped into the parking lot and stopped at the curb. Four young people jumped out, smiling and gesturing, and one of them extended a hand.

"Noah," he called, "*yo soy* Freddy!"

He was about my height, five nine, with a squat, stocky build. His hair was straight, jet black, and shaggily cut, long enough to cover his sideburns and the back of his neck, and he had a pointy beard at the tip of his chin, perfect for stroking — as I soon discovered he loved to do. He wore a military-green long-sleeved shirt, black field pants, and hiking boots. His most striking feature was his smile; he couldn't seem to wipe it off his face.

Freddy had brought along some friends, and as they clustered around, a lot of excited Spanish suddenly went flying past my ears. They were apologizing for the delay in picking me up, something to do with groceries and supplies, and introducing themselves all at once: Claudia Martin, José Segovia, and Fabri Gorleri. I was excessively glad to be among them, reassured by their welcoming kindness.

I threw my pack into the bed of the pickup, which was piled with enough gear to outfit a mountaineering expedition. What exactly had Freddy planned for the next four days? The five of us squeezed into the pickup's double cab and peeled out. As we left, the Cliff Flycatcher sallied in front of the windshield to pick off an insect, and from the back seat I pointed it out.

"*Sí, sí,*" said Freddy, who was simultaneously driving, navigating, and eyeing our gear to make sure nothing blew out. "*Hirundinea ferruginea.*"

It took a minute to realize that this was the bird's scientific name.

"Right, a Cliff Flycatcher!" I said. Everyone looked blank.

Of course, they had no reason to use English common names for birds. Most Latin American birders don't use Spanish common names either, because they aren't well standardized; instead, Spanish-speaking birders learn the international scientific classifications, a system in Latin that scientists around the world use to understand each other. This was going to make things interesting in the field, where new sightings come fast and furious.

Freddy drove straight out of town, and as civilization receded behind us, the truck turned off the highway and began to ascend a gravel road into lush east Andean foothills. Gradually I absorbed bits of information. Freddy worked as a biologist in Jujuy, and Claudia, his girlfriend, was a botanist with an interest in all natural things. José and Fabri were students at a university in eastern Argentina and had come more than six hundred miles by bus to join us. All four of them were between the ages of twenty-three and thirty-three and shared a love of birds and adventure.

When Freddy received my first email, he thought it would be a great opportunity to go camping at Cerro Negro, a seldom-visited mountain range with some special birds. No roads lead into the high elevations there, so we'd have to hike in more than ten miles and climb thousands of feet up a tortuous pack trail. Freddy had arranged for three mules to carry our stuff so that we could spend four nights in the Yungas cloud forest and Pastizal grassland above tree line, sleeping in tents. He said he'd packed plenty of food. We made a brief stop at a village to collect a driver who would return the pickup, and arrived at the trailhead in early afternoon. The road ended at a river that sliced through dense, green forest, with bare mountain peaks visible above the valley.

Sure enough, three mules — one white and two brown — appeared with their owner, a *campesino* in jeans and rubber boots, who lashed our bundles of gear to their saddles. I hoped Freddy had packed an extra sleeping bag, because my silk liner wouldn't keep me warm at high elevations. The mule team went ahead while Freddy, Claudia, José, Fabri, and I spent an hour meandering around the river. The sun had disappeared behind a layer of clouds, which was beginning to look worrisome, but birds kept popping into view.

"*Cypseloides rothschildi,*" Freddy shouted, and I saw a cigar-sized bird with sickle-shaped wings zooming overhead. It looked like a swift, and I scrolled through the field guide on my phone, trying to confirm the scientific name and its English equivalent. Aha! — Rothschild's Swift, a nice regional specialty and year bird number 342.

"*Psittacara mitratus,*" said Fabri, which I translated as a Mitred Parakeet, another new one.

"*Empidonomus varius!*" Claudia called out.

At the same time, José, looking in the opposite direction, announced, "*Progne elegans!*"

"*Sporophila lineola,*" Freddy added.

"Ay yay yay," I said.

I tried to ask them to wait while I looked up each bird name, but it was no use. Birds don't hang around to be identified, and I did my best to keep up with the onslaught of sightings, jotting down scientific names in a notebook for later reference when we hit a big canopy flock. Almost every bird in this part of Argentina was new to me, so I appreciated the help of these local experts in identifying fast-moving targets.

A pair of Torrent Ducks occupied this stretch of river, needing no translation. I'd seen one in Chile, so the species had already been counted for the year, but I paused for a few minutes to admire how they braved the whitewater. Like most ducks, the male had strikingly different plumage than the female — he was black and white with a red beak, while she was gray and orange — and they had long, slender bodies, streamlined for life in rushing water. The birds swam effortlessly through churning rapids, using their feet to propel against the flow. They appeared to be hunting for aquatic insects, inspecting the undersides of each boulder as they went.

I glanced up to see Freddy, pants rolled up past his knees and hiking boots swinging loosely around his neck, wade into the current. He turned and waved.

"*Vámanos!*"

Time to start hiking, or we'd arrive in camp after dark. The trail entered the forest on the far side of the river. There was no bridge.

Claudia, José, Fabri, and I removed our shoes and plunged in, taking extreme care with each step. The stream was ice cold, running fast, and up to my thighs. Knee-deep water moving at just four miles per hour can knock a person off balance, and one slip on these slick boulders might send any of us floating away down the river. I'd taken the precaution of lining my backpack with a waterproof garbage bag, but didn't relish the thought of getting soaked before even starting this hike.

The Torrent Ducks swam by as if paddling on a glassy pond,

then hauled out on a rock between two waterfalls and watched while we struggled across, dried our feet, and put our shoes back on.

Dark clouds were gathering in earnest now, obscuring the peaks in a heavy blanket. I remembered that I had landed in Jujuy only a few hours ago, and had been birding with Marcelo and Martin just yesterday afternoon, more than eight hundred miles away. The ranchlands of Buenos Aires already felt like a distant memory. Freddy pointed to a gap in the trees where the trail began to climb, and we walked into the forest just as the first rumble of thunder echoed down the valley.

✦ – ✦ – ✦

Going solo and being alone are two very different things. I went solo in 2011 when I hiked the 2,650-mile Pacific Crest Trail, a backcountry route up the American West from Mexico to Canada, but I spent much of the time in company with other people. It would have been hard not to: hundreds of hikers attempt to walk the whole thing each year, and about 95 percent of them take the northerly option, as I did, to follow the progression of summer. During four "solo" months in the backcountry, I saw at least one other person every single day, and often hiked and camped with others.

On my Big Year, I was also going solo, in the sense that I planned the trip myself and that nobody traveled with me from place to place, but I didn't want to go birding alone. I made a point of seeking out bird-minded companions in each country I visited. Applying the lessons I'd learned from long-distance hiking, I went ultralight for the year, carrying only a forty-liter backpack with trail-tested gear and traveling in a steady progression to the seven continents, with no days off and no jumping around. A one-way trip requires no backtracking, so I always looked forward to new territory ahead, but I couldn't sync my itinerary with local seasons in scattered parts of the globe, so I'd miss some bird-migration hotspots and hit other places during the not-ideal monsoons.

I set some ground rules. Every bird that I would count, for the whole year, would have to be seen by at least one other person. That would keep me from getting lonely, and, as a side benefit, would provide backup witnesses for each sighting. Also, I decided, my companions should all be locals, living in the same country where we went birding together. It would have been easy to hire professional guides from international tour companies to show me around, but that didn't exactly fit my style; I didn't have the budget, for one thing, and I'd always rather go out with friends than as a client. Connecting with locals became a key part of my strategy — this would be the couch-surfing version of birding trips.

A decade ago, such a concept would have been difficult to pull off, but technology has shrunk the world so that it's now easier to call someone up in another country than to get the attention of your roommate. The Internet has revolutionized birding: what was once a leisure pursuit for the First World has suddenly become a truly international pastime. Now anyone with an interest can find all kinds of helpful information online — and, even more important, get in touch with sympathetic souls through email lists, discussion groups, and forums.

Finding all of these local birders and arranging plans with each of them was a tricky logistical challenge. After settling my basic itinerary, I started looking for the best birders in each place who might be willing to host me for a few days. First I asked friends I already knew; then I asked them for their contacts, and so on. Some people were busy, but almost everyone replied with enthusiasm when I explained the project. To find Freddy, for instance, I first contacted a birder named Ignacio "Kini" Roesler, on the faculty of the University of Buenos Aires, who said he'd be busy with a Hooded Grebe research project in January, but he passed me on to a friend named

Nacho Areta. When I emailed Nacho, he replied that he'd be on a
Mississippi Kite survey, but he gave me Freddy's email address —
and so the match was made, with the friend of a friend of a friend.

In some places I used a website, BirdingPal, where people list
themselves as willing hosts for birders traveling through their area.
These aren't professional guides, but they offer hospitality and good
company. It's fun to show off your local patch to someone who has
never seen it, and favors get returned when the roles are reversed.

I also relied heavily for my planning on eBird, an online database of sightings started by the Cornell Lab of Ornithology and
the National Audubon Society in 2002. With nearly half a billion
observations logged by hundreds of thousands of birders around
the world, the website has become an incredible resource on bird
distribution and records, used by scientists to track bird migration
and populations. eBird was a godsend for logistical planning: it
helped me identify places where I was likely to find certain species,
with up-to-the-minute reports, and showed which birders had
been most active in areas I wanted to visit. Whenever the word-of-
mouth method hit a dead end, I checked out eBird for new leads.

Crashing on couches seems like a casual approach, but setting
up all of these visits took five solid months of intense planning. By
the time I left home, I knew where I would be, and who I would
be with, on nearly every day of 2015. The roster of birders had
hundreds of names and kept growing as plans changed and the year
progressed.

Nothing can replace local knowledge — of restaurants, short-
cuts, customs, languages, secret spots, and the innumerable other
things that only residents can tap into. By going with locals, I could
instantly become an insider instead of a tourist; and by staying in
people's homes instead of resorts and lodges, I could experience
a big slice of real life on Earth without busting my bank account.
Local knowledge would certainly pay off with birds that might oth-

erwise be missed. But until the year began, I had no way of answering the question: Would it work?

Many of the people I contacted had no experience with guiding visitors; they came from all walks of life, spoke different languages, and ranged in age from their teens to their seventies. Each seemed to have a slightly different vision of what I was trying to do. Some of them wrote back immediately, while others took months to respond. In some cases, the only correspondence I'd had before landing in an unfamiliar country was through a Facebook message or WhatsApp chat. When I found myself blindly wiring money to personal bank accounts in sub-Saharan Africa and Southeast Asia, to cover expenses for upcoming trips to national parks with birders I'd never talked to on the phone and who replied to my emails in barely intelligible English, or in other languages entirely, I had a momentary panic attack. Was this a good idea? There was only one thing to do — trust and go forward.

$$+\!\!-\!\!+\!\!-\!\!+$$

Might as well have jumped in the river with the Torrent Ducks, I thought, as I slogged up the mule trail. Rain slashed down in sheets. For a while, I held grimly to an umbrella, but it was no use. Drops ricocheted off the ground, a gust of wind whipped the umbrella inside out, and wet vegetation lined the trail like the scrubbers at a car wash. At this point, it was impossible to get any wetter. I could have filled a pint glass with rainwater by wringing out my underwear.

Of more immediate concern, though, was the electricity in the air. Freddy, Claudia, José, Fabri, and I had hiked into a thunderstorm, not under it but *inside* it, and the atmosphere was charged with popping and crackling sounds as we ascended a ridge. Lightning and thunder became indistinguishable; in a cloud break I saw a bolt strike the valley underneath us, then the view snapped shut and we were left inside a swirling, horizonless world of strobe lights, reverberating concussions, and disorienting motion.

The rain pounded us. I no longer tried to step on bare ground; the rutted trail became a six-inch-deep cascade, and I sloshed upstream, hoping that the garbage bag lining my pack was at least keeping some stuff dry. Every time I looked up, wind stung my eyes, so I walked with my head down, water streaming off the tip of my nose, trying not to think of the estimated 20,000 people who get hit by lightning each year. Around a corner I almost bumped into Freddy, who had stopped to wait. He turned around, spread out his arms, looked up at the sky with a wild gleam in his eye, and said, *"Me gusta esta Cerro Negro!"* — I like it this way!

I had to admire his enthusiasm.

We arrived at our campsite, completely bedraggled, just before dark. The thunderstorm finally blew into the next valley, leaving behind a clear sky and curling tendrils of mist at sunset. Our mule driver had dumped piles of gear on a ridgetop, and we located several waterlogged tarps and tents, staked them to a grassy area, and dug into dinner. To feed five people for four days in the mountains, Freddy had packed biscuits, saltines, corned beef, tinned sardines, apples, peanuts, and candy, all of which were damp from the rain. Right now, it looked like a feast. At least water wasn't an issue — we gulped straight from a nearby stream, on hands and knees, until Freddy figured out how to drink out of a plastic shopping bag. Somehow, none of us had thought to bring a water bottle.

Thank goodness Freddy had brought an extra sleeping bag for me. After a brief *buenas noches*, I turned in early, looking forward to my first good sleep in several days. Inside my tent, I opened my backpack, untwisted the garbage bag inside, and discovered with delight that its contents were still fluffy and dry. I peeled off wet layers, put on dry ones, and promptly passed out. Weird, unidentifiable birds occupied my dreams all night long.

In the morning, groggy and slightly confused as to my whereabouts, I poked my head out of the tent flap to see an enormous Andean Condor glide by at eye level, swiveling its head as it passed. Ah, yes — Argentina. Fresh snow frosted the peaks around camp. The tent smelled like rain, the grass smelled like rain, the trees smelled like rain, the sopping clothes on our clothesline smelled like rain, and the view was magnificent. Layer upon layer of green ridges, cloaked in cloud forest, folded away in every direction. I checked my watch, but the battery had stopped; my cell phone was also dead, so there was no telling the time except by the sun, which emerged in one of the most brilliant dawn displays I'd ever seen.

The others also were stirring. Claudia strolled around camp, using her botanist's knowledge to forage for wild peaches, and suddenly exclaimed, "Oh!"

"*Que pasó?*" called José, from inside his tent.

"*Una culebra,*" said Claudia, as she leaned over to inspect something in the grass.

I wriggled into soaking wet pants, folded up the dry pair to sleep in, pulled on freezing wet socks and shoes, and padded over to check it out. A foot-long snake, marked by a repeating X pattern along its back, was curled up in a loose pretzel.

"*Bothrops,*" said Claudia, referring to the genus of pit vipers — highly venomous residents of Latin America — and motioned for me not to touch it. It was an attractive little snake with a boxy, triangular head, less than thirty feet from where I had just been resting, and it could bring down a horse. We left it well alone.

A few minutes later, as I chewed on whole sardines for breakfast, crunching their vertebrae and licking up the oil, an Aplomado Falcon kept an eye on us from its nearby perch. Freddy, munching on a chocolate bar and stroking his pointy beard, explained our plan: the next two days would be spent hiking around the Pastizal grasslands, up to about 11,500 feet elevation, searching

for seldom-seen birds with alluring names like Tucumán Moun-
tain-Finch, Maquis Canastero, and Zimmer's Tapaculo, before we
returned to be picked up at the trailhead the following afternoon.
With luck, the rain-swollen river would subside and we could wade
back across without having to swim the rapids.

Taking in the scene, I reflected on the benefits of going local.
Organized tours never visited this place; when I later asked some
professional guides about it, they'd never heard of Cerro Negro. It
was too hard to reach, too difficult as a tourist destination. But the
birds were here, and that's exactly why I had contacted Freddy — he
knew the back corners of the Jujuy province in a way that no visitor
ever could.

My system was working! I couldn't quite believe it. Two weeks
into the year, nobody had stood me up yet; in fact, I was beginning to realize that birders were excited enough about this project
to make elaborate plans and invite others along. This is what birding is all about — people with a shared passion, sometimes from
entirely different continents and maybe not even speaking the
same language, meeting as strangers, joining in a common goal,
and becoming the best of friends. When I first emailed Freddy, I
couldn't have predicted that we'd be standing on this mountain, the
five of us, with three wet mules and a killer view.

He flashed a huge grin. The day was young, and we had birds
to find.

"Okay, *vámanos!*" — let's go!

4

Over the Years

As a kid, I wouldn't have been caught dead with a "history" book, but from the time I could barely read, at about the age of three, when I received a lovely picture book called *A Year of Birds,* I couldn't get enough stories about nature and adventure. Birding has a particularly wacky and wonderful lore, in books such as *The Big Year; The Big Twitch; The Biggest Twitch; Kingbird Highway; Lost Among the Birds; Birding on Borrowed Time; Call Collect, Ask for Birdman; The Ardent Birder; Extreme Birder; The Feather Quest; Wild America; Return to Wild America; To See Every Bird on Earth* — well, you get the idea.

I learned from reading bird books that nothing happens outside of historical context. In birding as in everything, personalities and events unfold over time, one thing leads to another, and pretty soon you wake up to discover that you are part of the stream.

Historically speaking, obsession with birds has often overlapped with a healthy sense of wanderlust. Seat-of-the-pants exploits feature prominently in the resumés of most early ornithologists, including

John James Audubon, who was inspired to track down the birds of North America with little more than a shotgun and a set of paints after being jailed for unpaid debts from a failed business venture in the early 1800s. For the next several years, Audubon traveled across the continent, living rough, studying (and shooting) every bird he could find, and created beautiful, meticulous illustrations of each species. The resulting folio of portraits, *Birds of America*, eventually earned him the respect he craved, but it was Audubon's swashbuckling tales from the frontier that made him truly famous — a real American hero.

Audubon wasn't the first by any means. The Scottish-American artist Alexander Wilson, sometimes called the "father of American ornithology," released nine volumes of bird paintings, literally drawing from his own intrepid travels, before Audubon had even stepped into the wilderness. And a full eighty years before that, the luminary British naturalist Mark Catesby included 220 plates of birds and other species in his *Natural History of Carolina, Florida, and the Bahama Islands*, the first published record of North America's flora and fauna. Just imagine Catesby's impressions when he landed on Virginia soil at the age of twenty-nine, in the spring of 1712, to spend the next seven years traipsing through the colonies. His illustrations included many species never before encountered by European naturalists.

But it wasn't until the mid-1900s that watching birds became an obsession unto itself, more like a sport than an art or science, and one man did more to popularize this new activity than anyone else.

His name was Roger Tory Peterson.

This is where modern birding really begins. The son of two immigrants in western New York, Peterson studied at the Art Students League and National Academy of Design in New York City. There, in the mid-1920s, he attended meetings of the Linnaean

Society, still active today, where amateur biologists gathered to talk about birds. He soon fell in with a group of teenage bird nerds who started their own group, the Bronx County Bird Club.

At the time, the best bird-identification guides were produced by Chester Reed, who supplied the nascent movement in nature study with illustrated pocket-sized guidebooks. The first, published in 1905, *Bird Guide: Land Birds East of the Rockies*, described nearly 220 species, with one color drawing on each page. Now bird enthusiasts could carry into the field a portable reference with color pictures of birds. Reed is largely forgotten today, but his importance cannot be overstated — he essentially created the first modern field guide, which Roger Tory Peterson, along with the rest of the Linnaean Society and Bronx County Bird Club members, used while scouting for birds around New York.

After graduating from art school in 1931, Peterson pursued his interest in identifying birds in the field — with binoculars instead of the shotgun used by earlier ornithologists such as Audubon. In the meantime, partly inspired by Reed's guides, he worked steadily on his own project. In 1934, a twenty-six-year-old Peterson published the book that would change birding forever.

A Field Guide to the Birds was something entirely new — so different from any previous book that several publishers rejected the idea, and Houghton Mifflin, the company that took the chance, committed to printing only 2,000 copies. The guide included Peterson's illustrations of all eastern North American birds, arranged with similar species side by side on plates, in various plumages, with arrows pointing out each distinctive feature. Unlike Audubon's *Birds of America*, which comprised four volumes, each weighing sixty pounds, Peterson's guide could be carried into the field; unlike Reed's little bird guides, Peterson's book was complete and showed multiple birds on each page.

When *A Field Guide* exhausted its first printing in one week, Peterson knew he had a hit, but it would take years for the full impact to sink in. He would live to edit, decades later, the book's fifth edition, by which time seven million copies had been sold. Peterson-branded nature guides, covering everything from birds to mushrooms, are the world's most successful series of field guides, all because of that first bird book in 1934.

In many ways, Peterson changed the way we look at the natural world. His field mark system offers encouragement, suggesting that any thorny problem can be solved by observing it closely enough. Not only did *A Field Guide* instruct its readers, but it also reflected a revolutionary shift in perspective. By simplifying each bird into its distinctive characteristics, Peterson made it possible for anyone, not just experts, to identify complicated targets — and thus brought birdwatching to the masses.

These books made Peterson famous. But one thing was still missing in his life: the rugged adventure that had become a tradition among earlier ornithologists. Peterson traveled often, but his work kept him so busy that he could never leave it all behind. At last, he hatched a plan with British seabird expert and friend James Fisher to take an extended trip across North America in 1953. The two devised a 30,000-mile route from Newfoundland to the tip of Florida, around the Gulf Coast to southern Texas and into Mexico, through Arizona and up the Pacific Coast to Washington, ending with a flight to the outer Pribilof Islands in Alaska. They set off in April and finished in July, exactly one hundred days later. Afterward, Peterson's commentary and Fisher's journal entries became a book, *Wild America*, a classic of environmental literature full of fascinating observations on everything from birds to alligators, fur seals, and 1950s America.

Wild America rode the swell of patriotic environmentalism that swept the United States in the 1950s, with birds at the heart of the story. The two naturalists introduced their readers to places that many had never heard of, inspiring more interest in the outdoors.

And near the end of the book, in small text at the bottom of a page, an intriguing footnote appeared.

"Incidental information: My year's list at the end of 1953 was 572 species (not counting an additional 65 Mexican birds)," wrote Peterson.

"Mine was 536, plus the 65 Mexican species, plus 117 others seen in Europe, a total of 718," added Fisher.

In fine print, a gauntlet had been thrown.

While Peterson and Fisher were crossing North America, another Mr. Fisher — this one named Dean, from Michigan — was headed for a U.S. Navy cruiser assigned to the Pacific Ocean. Dean Fisher was a bird enthusiast who tracked his sightings while sailing abroad. He'd seen about nine hundred bird species when he left the Navy in 1958, and he wasn't quite ready to settle down.

So he set off in 1959 with a friend on quite an adventure: they drove from California through Mexico, skirted Panama by freighter, and continued all the way to the southern tip of South America; then shipped their vehicle to South Africa, drove across the Sahara, sailed to Spain, and drove clear across Europe to reach India; then hitchhiked around the rest of southeast Asia for a while, sailed south, and finished with a long transect across northern Australia. It took three years.

Along the way, Fisher scouted for birds at every opportunity — local parks, swamps, forests, deserts. Many species he couldn't identify, because most countries had no published field guides at that time, but he kept detailed notes. It took a while — sometimes years — to identify what he had seen, but in the end he reckoned he'd passed 4,000 birds, more than 3,000 of them on this one round-the-world trip. In the year 1959 alone, he recorded 1,665 species, an unprecedented feat. Without really meaning to, he became the world's top bird lister.

Others were beginning to explore more far-flung places around the same time. Travel and tourism surged after World War II, thanks to new technology and an increasingly mobile population, and birders started to realize how many alluring species could be found beyond their own borders. Passenger jets began plying the skies in the late 1950s, cutting an overseas trip from five days to a few hours, and it wasn't long before intrepid ornithologists booked regular trips abroad.

One of them was young Peter Alden. During his studies at the University of Arizona in the mid-1960s, Alden spent five weeks each semester leading field trips across the border to Mexico with an emphasis on birds and local culture. After graduating, he went full-time and negotiated with the Massachusetts Audubon Society to lead a series of trips to even more exotic destinations. In 1968, he observed more than 2,000 species — a new single-year world record, surpassing Dean Fisher's 1959 tally — and helped pioneer international birding tourism, which would eventually become an industry of its own.

Perhaps the biggest advocate of birding abroad in those early days was an energetic Brit named Stuart Keith, who got hooked on birds while studying the classics at Oxford. Inspired by *Wild America*, Keith moved from England to California after graduating in 1955, then took careful aim at Roger Tory Peterson's North American single-year tally referenced in that fateful footnote. In 1956, the year he turned twenty-five, Keith drove across the United States and Canada with his brother, following a route similar to that of Peterson and Fisher but taking more time, and saw 594 species of birds — a new American Big Year record.

At the time, most ornithologists thought the world held about 8,600 bird species, and Keith began to wonder how many one person could see in a lifetime. As he took birding trips and got to know other keen birders, such as Roger Tory Peterson and Peter Alden, he realized that they were wondering the same thing.

Recognizing a critical mass when he saw it, Keith cofounded the American Birding Association in 1968 and became its first president, working with a friend, Jim Tucker, to produce a magazine they called *Birding*. Despite its focus on North America, the club's members — which numbered 115 after the first year, more than 500 a few months later, and about 13,000 today — did not confine themselves to the United States. In the early days, the association was all about listing, anywhere and everywhere. Initially it was an exclusive club: to join, prospective members had to have identified at least 500 species in North America or 70 percent of the birds in their home state, and people mailed in their list totals to determine a pecking order.

By the early 1970s, Keith had become the world's biggest lister, surpassing Dean Fisher's achievements in the late 1950s, and set his sights on a landmark goal. Several well-traveled birders, including Roger Tory Peterson, had decided to try to see half the birds in the world — about 4,300 species, according to prevailing wisdom — and Keith wanted to be the first to cross the threshold. He officially passed it in 1973, at age forty-one, having spent years slogging through some of the world's most rugged and remote corners. (Peterson would also reach half, but not until the mid-1980s.) Keith became a minor birding celebrity, hailed as a "superstar" by *People* magazine.

In a tantalizing article called "Birding Planet Earth: A World Overview," published in *Birding* magazine, Keith reflected on his experiences. "Getting to 'half' was the most exciting moment of my birding career," he wrote. "For the tireless and dedicated world

birder who simply cannot rest until he has seen a kiwi and a cassowary, and for those other addicts for whom visions of jabirus dance
in their heads, we may establish 4,300 species as a possible lifetime
goal. It took me 26 years."

He also made some predictions for his own future.

"I think I can just make it to 6,000, though I may be in a wheel-
chair when I do it," Keith calculated.

As it turned out, he exceeded that goal. He continued to travel
for the next thirty years before succumbing to a stroke in early
2003 on the Micronesian island of Chuuk, during a birding trip.
The day before, he had seen a Caroline Islands Ground-Dove, life
bird number 6,600.

In his article, Keith had considered the possibility of a one-
year global birding adventure.

"This is a big subject and worth an article in itself," Keith wrote,
"so rather than treat it here I would like to invite readers to send in
some theoretical models of global routes detailed month by month.
The appropriate person to write on the subject would be the reigning world annual list champion, Peter Alden, who has several times
gone over 2,000. How about it, Peter? Could you do 3,000?"

To me, this paragraph is radical. It is the first printed reference
I can find to a world Big Year — not just an incidental one, but a
whole calendar year specifically designed to maximize species on a
planetary scale. Keith inspired others but never went for a global
Big Year himself, explaining that he preferred "to go to one area
and work it thoroughly."

Birdwatchers began to ask: How many birds in the world could
you really see in a year, no holds barred?

The birders who survived the early 1970s tend to look back on those
years with wistfulness, using words like "innocence" and "golden

age." A lot of things came together: Birders realized they were part of a larger community and began to share information with one another on a broad scale. New regional clubs made it easier to connect, and the pursuit was young enough that anyone could contribute to ornithological knowledge.

"Birding changed from a mild local pastime to a continent-wide craze," American birder Kenn Kaufman would write years later, reflecting on that era. "It is only now, looking back from a distance of two decades, that we can see how far-reaching and thorough the changes were . . . Birding for the twenty-first century was born in the brief period from 1970 to 1975."

Kaufman was a long-haired nineteen-year-old high school dropout when, in 1973, he spent an action-packed year hitchhiking long distances around the United States to chase birds — partly inspired by Peterson's *Wild America*. North American Big Years suddenly became trendy: a young prodigy named Ted Parker surpassed Stuart Keith's old record by seeing 626 species in 1971; then both Kaufman and American educator Floyd Murdoch set out to beat Parker's total two years later. It was the first time two people tried to set a birdwatching record in the same year, introducing a new element: competition.

Kingbird Highway, Kaufman's memoir published in 1997, is a manifesto of unfiltered passion. Kaufman often slept under bridges and practiced draconian frugality to survive on less than a dollar a day; one memorable passage describes Little Friskies cat food as a cheap and nutrient-filled dinner alternative. Though he set out to look for birds, Kaufman found himself swept up in the growing flock of avian admirers and, by the end of 1973, cemented a place for himself within this larger community. That he set a fresh American record of 666 species, only to be edged out by Murdoch's 669 that year, was of such diminished importance to him that he included the totals only as an afterthought, in an appendix.

Kingbird Highway had a profound effect on me when I first read it as a twelve-year-old. I was hungry for exotic stories. Here was a guy who refused to follow the typical path, a rebel, choosing instead to chase birds wherever they might lead. Such is the power of words that *Wild America* inspired a teen-aged Kaufman to start a birding revolution, and Kaufman's *Kingbird Highway* solidified my own dreams.

By the 1980s, North American Big Years were well established among hardcore birders, and it became clear that the domestic record was up for grabs. A Mississippi businessman, James Vardaman, sensing an opportunity to raise publicity for his forestry firm, hired a team of bird experts to guide him around North America for a year and ended with 699 species — showing what a "lousy birder but a great promoter," as Vardaman described himself, might do with enough money, time, and expert guidance. During his quest, Vardaman flew 137,145 miles, sometimes catching a plane just to chase one stray bird reported on the opposite side of the continent, and drove another 20,305 miles. His strategy set the tone for later efforts, when a few dedicated souls would push well past 700 species and even, in the new millennium, 750 in a year, but this willy-nilly style — ticking one rare, vagrant bird at a time after listing all the common ones, burning massive amounts of fuel for vastly diminishing returns on one continent — has completely diverged from the pastime of wandering through a forest just to see what's there.

Perhaps Vardaman was thinking of this disconnect when, in the final paragraph of his book, *Call Collect, Ask for Birdman*, he abruptly shifted his gaze to all of planet Earth.

"I will definitely start planning a World Big Year," he wrote. "But because of the distances and complexities involved, planning a World Big Year will take some years, and executing the plan will take 365 days and probably cost $700,000 even at present prices. Therefore, I couldn't make the try before 1985, and I'll be glad to turn the plan over to someone else if I can't carry it out. Is 5,000 possible?"

Heaven only knows what Vardaman had in mind with that budget estimate (his $700,000 in 1980 would inflate to more than $2 million by the time I embarked on my worldwide adventure), but at least he was thinking big. He did travel enough to net 2,800 species and a new official worldwide record in 1984, even if he never got around to a coordinated international assault.

The only person who achieved a higher one-year total in that generation was James Clements, a maverick ornithologist who literally wrote the book on birds of the world. For his doctoral thesis at California Western University, Clements authored the global checklist still used by most American birders (including me), which standardizes names for every bird species on Earth. He then operated a printing business, which allowed him to travel a lot, and in 1989 set out to see as many birds as he could, using the Big Year concept to raise funds for the Los Angeles Museum of Natural History. By the end of the year, Clements had covered more than 265,000 miles and recorded 3,662 bird species, at one point getting himself arrested in West Africa for stalking a hornbill "without permission." He raised $50,000 for the museum. Afterward, he continued to study birds abroad until he died in 2005, leaving the Cornell Lab of Ornithology the task of maintaining his world checklist.

Today, James Clements is remembered as one of birding's most passionate proponents and explorers, with a species of Peruvian gnatcatcher named in his honor, and few people even know about his 1989 Big Year. That record stood quietly for almost twenty years. By the time anyone could take a serious crack at it, birding itself was undergoing a global revolution.

+ –+– +

When Clements took his round-the-world jaunt, I was a three-year-old. I am part of the digital generation, a so-called millennial — the world's first cohort to grow up online, coming of age around the year 2000. Culturally speaking, we millennials are significantly different from the baby boomers or even Generation X: we're more progressive, less religious, more educated, less family-oriented, more urban, less political, more narcissistic, less environmentally minded, and, above all, more technologically dependent. For better or worse, my generation lives on computers and smartphones; we are children of the Internet.

So how do you explain the surging allure of birdwatching in recent years? If nobody cared about the environment anymore, you'd expect outdoor activities to slack off — but, strangely, they've never been more popular. A 2014 *Esquire* magazine headline said it best: "Uh-Oh. Birdwatching Is About to Become Cool." When, in short order, Owen Wilson plays a real-life birder in a Hollywood movie about birding, Jonathan Franzen writes an angsty feature about birds for *The New Yorker*, and rock star Geddy Lee is quoted saying "I'm a birder, believe it or not," you know something's up.

It's tempting to suggest that birdwatching is a backlash against technology, that getting back to nature responds to a deep, intangible human need, and I'd like to think that people are willingly seeking outdoor therapy to balance their new digital lifestyles. But it's probably the other way around — all this technology and connectedness has changed the way people enjoy birds and nature, engaging us in new and exciting ways. Ironically, going online is inspiring us to go outside.

For birders, the Information Age revolutionized the way we communicate with each other — through dedicated email lists, discussion groups, and websites like BirdingPal, eBird, and BirdForum. Instead of a niche activity for wealthy retirees, birdwatching has been transformed into a truly international popular pursuit.

Outside the United States and Europe, places like Brazil, India, and the Philippines are adding their own cultural twists to the appreciation of birds. In China, for instance, birding is now seen as an aspirational activity — a sign of elite class, because you must have enough money for binoculars and spotting scopes, as well as leisure time to do it. Ten years ago there were virtually no birders in the entire country, but bird groups have suddenly sprung up on most Chinese university campuses and in most major cities.

At the same time, technology has made it easier to learn about birds. Digital cameras make identification a breeze, while binoculars have become so good that manufacturers worry customers will never replace them. Field guides are available nearly everywhere, and they're increasingly available as smartphone apps. The Cornell Lab of Ornithology has an app, Merlin, that identifies the bird species in your photograph with about 80 percent accuracy. Another program does the same for bird songs: hold up your phone and it names the unseen singer, like Shazam for bird calls.

We are now at the point where it is about as easy to travel the world as it was to explore the United States in the 1970s, during the previous revolution in birdwatching.

In 2008, two British birders, Ruth Miller and Alan Davies, decided to take on Clements's record from 1989. A lot had happened in the intervening nineteen years, and they thought it was time for someone to revive the world Big Year idea. Miller and Davies took their adventure seriously, planning discrete trips to rack up as many species as they could, and they sold their house to pay for it. By the end of the year, the two had seen 4,341 species of birds together in more than twenty countries, smashing Clements's old tally and showing what was possible in this new, networked age.

I followed their progress closely and scoured their book, *The Biggest Twitch*, for insights on how to improve their global strategy. Miller and Davies flew home between each destination, skipped around, missed some key areas, and spent a whopping three months in Europe, which has the fewest birds of any of the six major continents. I wondered if someone would put together an even bigger Big Year, and how they might approach it.

That spring, I graduated from college and had my sights set on remote research stints with various bird projects. As the global economy crashed, I rode it out in a subfreezing tent in Antarctica, strapping GPS tags to penguins and tracking their movements as part of a long-term study. If you had told me then that I would be the one to assault the all-time world Big Year record a few years later, I would have laughed. But now, looking back, I can see that the seeds of a plan were already sprouting in the back of my mind.

5

The Harpy

BY LATE JANUARY, the days had begun to speed up and blur into each other. After leaving Freddy and *amigos* in Jujuy, my plan was to blitz through northeast Argentina, then spend the next three weeks racing through the birdiest parts of Brazil with a relay of excellent local contacts.

In Argentina I joined up with a gung-ho birder named Guy Cox to rattle around the Misiones province in his newly acquired 1974 Chevy camper van. Our meeting was slightly delayed on account of a broken drive shaft that had to be fixed, which gave me a morning to explore the spectacular Iguazu Falls, a two-mile-wide cataract best described as "Niagara on Viagra," as well as Iguazu's specialty bird species — a flock of Great Dusky Swifts that nest behind the falls. Then Guy and I trundled down red dirt roads to the nearby San Sebastian de la Selva forest reserve, a little-known gem where we ditched the hordes of tourists and found ourselves surrounded instead by tropical birds: antshrikes, antvireos, antwrens, antthrushes, antpipits, antpittas, and ant-tanagers.

At last, I'd reached the tropics, complete with unrelenting heat and humidity, cloying mud, brightly colored macaws, all manner of vines and fronds, titi monkeys . . . and ants. The northeast corner of Argentina forms the western boundary of a wet, muggy jungle called the Atlantic Rainforest, which stretches in a narrow belt 2,500 miles along the coast to eastern Brazil. The forest is isolated by dry savannas to the north, so it's a hotspot for endemic plants and animals: more than 150 species of Atlantic Rainforest birds are found nowhere else. Unfortunately, it is also one of the world's most degraded environments, and virtually all of the Brazilian section of the forest has been chopped down. A system of reserves protects the Argentinian side, which means that while historically only 4 percent of this forest was outside of Brazil, today about 50 percent of what's left of it is in Argentina.

Guy and I prowled the jungle, looking and listening for specialty birds. With Guy's local knowledge and incredible ear, we found many, including a gleaming blue-black-green-red Surucua Trogon on January 22 that marked my first big milestone — the 500th bird of the year. Only 4,500 to go.

I said *adiós* to Guy, then crossed the Brazilian border by taxi and flew onward to São Paulo. Brazil was a key strategic stop, but as a United States citizen, it was not easy for me to get in because of an ongoing visa spat. In most countries I got tourist visas, for a fee, online or upon arrival. But to enter Brazil, U.S. citizens must procure a travel visa ahead of time at a Brazilian consulate, which entails showing up at an appointed time with a completed application form, extra photo, valid passport, copy of a round-trip ticket, and U.S. Postal Service money order for the full price (no cash or check). This is all payback for the United States government's tightening its visa requirements for Brazil and other nations in 2001.

Of the many visas I had to get, the one for Brazil was by far the most complicated and expensive. In the end, I had to buy a second passport and hire the specialists at VisaHQ to sort out the visa morass. I would shell out more than $2,000 on visas during the year.

In Brazil I hooked up for a couple days of birding with Guto Carvalho, a birder and film producer who sold his production house several years ago to focus on special projects and conservation. Guto used to commute to Hollywood and New York to work on special effects for commercials and films. Now he travels around South America to give talks about birds, runs the annual Brazil Bird Fair, organizes regional bird fairs in other states, and operates a small editorial house that publishes nature and photography books. He had recently wrapped an animated TV series about sustainability and would be off in a couple of weeks to northern Brazil to work on a book about Amazonian bird life. Partly because of a dedicated core of birders and conservationists like Guto, a grassroots birding culture is rapidly growing in Brazil.

"Ten years ago there were almost no birders in Brazil," he told me as we left behind the lights of São Paulo near midnight, "but now we have lots of them around the country."

Guto and I visited Intervales State Park, one of the last significant remaining patches of Atlantic Rainforest. There, with the help of park guide Luis Avelino — who called out bird names in Latin — we saw more than 120 species in one exceptional day. At dinner that evening, it struck me that birding had brought together a very unlikely trio: a Brazilian film producer (Guto), a rural forest guide (Luis), and a twenty-eight-year-old bird man from Oregon (me). None of us would have had any other reason to know each other, and Luis spoke only Portuguese, yet we connected instantly and effortlessly with our shared interest in birds.

Guto passed me on to René Santos, a thirty-four-year-old birder also from São Paulo, who had a Spix's Macaw tattooed on his left shoulder, and the phrase "Extinction Is Forever" written in Portuguese on the spare tire of his seventeen-year-old Jeep. Tall and athletic, a disciple of surfing and the Brazilian martial art form of capoeira, René took me up the coast to the island of Ilhabela — literally, "beautiful island" — where we stayed at a friend's house and walked for hours through the hot, sticky lowland forest, searching for a few final regional endemics. Seeing a near-threatened Spot-breasted Antvireo was almost as sweet as the celebratory açaí ice cream, with sliced bananas and honey on top.

René dropped me at the São Paulo airport with good wishes, and I winged north, looking forward to a change of scenery. In ten full days of birding with Guy, Guto, and René across various sections of the Atlantic Rainforest, I had slept in ten different places. My few clothes desperately needed a wash, sweated out from a week and a half of slogging through the moist and mucky jungle, but I had trouble mustering the energy even to rinse them in the sink. All these quick transitions from one spot to the next — driving late, arriving in the middle of the night, getting up in the dark to start birding at dawn — were wearing me out, and sleep took priority over laundry, which wouldn't have dried anyway.

I scheduled most of my travel segments during afternoons and evenings to preserve the precious morning hours for birding, but I had no idea whether this itinerary would be sustainable. Besides the lack of sleep, I had no downtime, no alone time, and no rest. Whenever I moved to a new place, a new local birder was ready to go, and the effect was like constantly swapping in fresh horses for the Pony Express. I had another eleven months to go. Could I keep this up? Should I pace myself more? The great benefit of going nonstop is that new sights, people, and birds are always ahead, and an exhilarating jolt comes with each transition. Despite experiencing some torpor in the tropics, I was glad I had planned one continuous journey because I enjoyed the rush and didn't really want it to end. At this point, I was adjusting to the routine, relying more and more on the kinetic energy of new ground to keep me going. Increasingly, rest seemed to me a bad idea — it would break the flow, stop the roller coaster. Better to just keep riding.

After almost a month on the run, things were going fantastically well. None of the things I most feared had happened. I had not been sick. There had been no serious logistical nightmares. None of the local birders had let me down. And I was racking up birds faster than I'd dared to hope. Despite the slow start in Antarctica, by January 29 I had recorded 617 species, well above the daily average needed to reach 5,000 by the end of the year. It was early days yet, but I could feel the Big Year momentum building. The sun seemed to be shining a new light on the world, and nothing could over-shadow my happiness. Maybe it couldn't last, but so far, so good.

Then, upon landing in the city of Cuiabá in central Brazil, I received some unexpected and exciting news.

$$+ - + - +$$

Deep in central Brazil, in the sprawling state of Mato Grosso near the Bolivian border, lies an obscure range of low mountains called Serra das Araras. The landscape here is squeezed between powerful forces. To the north, the Amazon — the world's largest rainforest — runs all the way to Guyana and eastern Ecuador. To the south and east is the Cerrado, an interior plateau about the size of Green-land, with tropical savannas to rival the wide-open vistas of east Africa. And to the west, the famous Pantanal floods a seasonal wet-land the size of Spain. The headwaters of the Paraguay River trickle down from the Serra das Araras; follow the flow and you'll drift 1,700 miles across the Pantanal and into Argentina, merge with the Paraná River, and continue another lazy eight hundred miles to the Atlantic Ocean somewhere north of Buenos Aires.

West-central Brazil is a long way from anywhere, and amid this trifecta — Amazon, Cerrado, and Pantanal — the Serra das Araras doesn't get much attention from foreigners. The escarpment isn't dramatically scenic or touristy, though you can stay at a small Brazilian inn called a *pousada* with a spa and cozy rooms next to grazing cattle and a limestone mine. It's sizzlingly hot and sticky, and the access highway from Cuiabá, the nearest big city, has so much heavy truck traffic that the pavement resembles hardened Conestoga wagon ruts.

As darkness fell, I bumped down this road with Giuliano Bernardon, a young bird guide, and his sister Bianca, a biologist visiting from the north Brazilian province of Amazonas. They had picked me up after I touched down in Cuiabá on a late afternoon flight. Once we crossed the city limits, the highway ran straight as a parrot can fly. The landscape was flat, flat, flat, and it was crowded with trucks, trucks, trucks. Roadside tire shops popped up every couple of miles, evidently doing brisk business owing to the many potholes and ruts. After sunset we were left in a jarring, terrifying tunnel of oncoming headlights and black holes, and I was relieved when Giuliano decided to stop in the tiny town of Jangada for dinner and a few hours of sleep. We had originally planned to head straight for the Pantanal, but when Giuliano met me at the airport he had some good news.

"There is an active Harpy Eagle nest at Serra das Araras!" he said, before we'd even made it across the parking lot. "It isn't exactly on the way — more of a side trip — but we can be there at dawn tomorrow."

Giuliano wore a broad smile, dark beard, and mustache, and was outfitted in loose layers of khaki and a wide-brimmed hat. He explained that some visiting birders had confirmed a female sitting on the nest just a few days before, so we had a good chance of staking out the elusive eagle. It might be only one species for my Big Year total, but it was worth spending an extra morning for a chance to see the most powerful raptor in the Western Hemisphere.

Three feet tall, with a seven-foot wingspan and weighing up to twenty pounds, the Harpy is a Sherman tank with fighter-jet wings. Early South American explorers named this bird after the Harpies of Greek mythology — ravenous beasts with a bird's body and a woman's face, sent by Zeus to snatch people off the face of the Earth — and the comparison is apt. Harpy Eagles prey mainly on monkeys and sloths, plucked unceremoniously from treetops, and can take down red brocket deer and other large rainforest animals, given the chance. To do so, they have evolved enormous talons, longer than the claws of a grizzly bear, and powerful legs as thick as a child's wrist. Females are nearly twice the size of males, as with most of the world's eagle species.

These creatures are stunning to behold, with large crests and bold black-and-white plumage, and have no trouble speeding through a dense canopy at fifty miles per hour, exploding onto their targets in a burst of speed and raw power. Monkeys have learned to let go when they see a Harpy Eagle coming, preferring to drop like a stone to the forest floor rather than confront such a fearsome predator at canopy level, but by then it's usually too late. Harpies are masters of surprise and disguise, adapted to close combat in jungle environments. They are the ultimate avian predator.

Harpies are also quite rare, as they need large tracts of intact forest in which to live and breed. One pair generally requires several thousand acres of pristine rainforest, which is hard to come by. Habitat loss has threatened the species throughout most of its historic range, from southern Mexico to northern Argentina, and Harpies are now found in appreciable numbers only in the wildest parts of the Amazon basin, including northern Brazil.

Even in the most untouched, remote forests, Harpies are exasperatingly difficult to glimpse. They have evolved cryptic behaviors, skulking through the canopy rather than soaring overhead, in order not to spook potential prey — which means you either need to get extremely lucky to spot one or stake one out at a nest.

While we ate fried sandwiches at an open-air food cart in Jangada, surrounded by hungry truckers, Giuliano explained that the Harpy Eagle nest at Serra das Araras has been used for about twenty years, since the mid-1990s. Many birders have seen their first wild Harpy at this site. The eagles take two years to raise their chicks, and the nest is used irregularly — at most once every other year. A few other nests are scattered elsewhere in Brazil, but the birds aren't always present, and none of the others seemed to be active during my visit. So this would be my only real chance for a view of the near-mythical bird.

Giuliano and Bianca checked us into a small hotel and, with a brief *boa noite*, left me in my room with instructions to be ready at 4:45 a.m. for the eagle search. I dropped my backpack in a corner, sat on the bed, and switched on the TV. It had only a few stations, all in Portuguese, and I couldn't understand much. As I pulled out my laptop, propped up on a pillow, and typed some notes for the day, a Brazilian newscast droned in the background.

It felt strange to be touring the world and yet to be so detached from it. In the previous week, unknown to me, the president of Yemen had resigned, people were massacred in Nigeria, Swiss banks caused turmoil in the financial markets, the U. S. Senate approved the controversial Keystone XL pipeline, and the Ebola crisis escalated in West Africa. Before leaving home a month earlier I'd paid close attention to the global news, sensing that I'd soon be out there *inside* the headlines. But the reality was just the opposite: here in a tiny village in central Brazil, the news felt very far away indeed. Now that I was actually traveling the planet, each day deepening my connection with its great wealth of birds and birders, the media stories seemed to apply to some completely different universe — one in which I had no part. The time I spent searching for each bird was so intense — heightened by the knowledge that I would soon leave and move on — that it seemed to swallow up all the available space. Disoriented, I gradually fell into a restless sleep of uneasy dreams.

When my alarm went off several hours later, it took a minute to adjust to my surroundings. Then I remembered: Harpy day! I grabbed my backpack, stumbled out the door into the dark, and met Giuliano and Bianca. We threw our gear in the truck and drove toward the eagle stakeout, ready for action.

In light traffic at 4:45 a.m., we made efficient time, arriving at Serra das Araras just after dawn. The rutted pavement gave way to dirt, then disappeared entirely into a grassy cow pasture. Giuliano carefully picked out a parking spot amidst the cows and cowpats, and led the way on foot for the last few hundred yards.

Birds were everywhere among the clearings and forest patches as the sun rose. Lettered Aracaris, a type of small, colorful toucan, played hide-and-seek among the foliage, while Yellow-tufted Woodpeckers chased each other in playful circles around a snag. A dark Bat Falcon, no bigger than a flying beer bottle, streaked overhead. Thrush-like Wrens chattered noisily from the thickets, a Blue-headed Parrot admired the view from the top of a tall tree, and a Ferruginous Pygmy-Owl called from a distance. Almost every bird was new for my year list, this being my first morning in central Brazil, but they were all common species I expected to see again in the coming weeks. I had one target here and, as the moment arrived, I could barely contain my excitement.

A massive tree materialized in front of us. About two-thirds of the way up, in a three-way fork in the trunk, I beheld a nest the size of a Volkswagen bus — a platform of sticks big enough for me to lie down inside, had it not been inhabited by one of the world's most ferocious creatures. These eagles had built themselves a magnificent fortress in the sky. I raised my binoculars, focused on the spot, and saw, poking above the rim of the nest . . .

Nothing. No Harpies.

This was obviously the right spot, but where were the eagles?

"Hmmm," said Giuliano, after a minute of steady inspection. "Bianca, do you see anything?"

"Nope," she replied. "All I see is the nest."

The three of us stared upward. Birds twittered and sang all around us, but we were focused only on the one that wasn't home.

"They were here last week," said Giuliano, looking perplexed. "A group of birders stopped here and reported the female sitting on the nest, and even watched the male fly in with some food. So it has to be active. Let's try a different angle — maybe she's in there right now but is sitting too low so we can't see her."

We edged around the tree, maintaining an equal radius from its trunk, until we reached the opposite side. No eagles, though the nest itself, from this new angle, was still impressive enough. Imagine building a treehouse, piece by piece, without being able to use your arms! What a load of work.

"Hmmm," Giuliano repeated. "They must be around here somewhere. Let's wait awhile and see if one of the eagles turns up. Maybe they're out getting breakfast."

For one of these birds, popping out for breakfast would likely mean murdering a monkey — an indelicate thought, barbarous even. Did they ever wake up and reflect on this stuff?

We settled down on a fallen log to wait. Giuliano and Bianca sat next to each other in matching outfits: pastel green shirts, field pants, knee-high rubber boots, and sun hats. Giuliano, as a full-time bird guide, knew this site well and seemed completely at ease as he kept up a pleasant banter about birds, culture, and food. Bianca, meanwhile, had just traveled down from northern Brazil, where she worked as a bird researcher in the Amazon rainforest, and her eyes lit up every time a new species was spotted. Brother and sister picked off one sighting after another, and I scrambled to keep up.

"Scaled Pigeon!" said Giuliano, and aimed his spotting scope at a distant treetop to get a better view. Magnified thirty times, I could see the pigeon's red bill, brown body, and namesake pattern of intricate marks on the side of its neck like silhouetted snake skin.

"And an Epaulet Oriole," interrupted Bianca, pointing out an all-black bird with bright yellow shoulder patches.

A few minutes later we observed a Red-necked Woodpecker, one of the largest woodpeckers in the world, sidling up a dead tree like a feathered jackhammer, and later heard its echoing double-knock display. Then a Black-throated Saltator — distinguished by its orange bill and black face — made a cameo, and I pondered the benefits of birding in overlap zones. The woodpecker is a true Amazon bird while the saltator is confined mostly to the central Brazilian Cerrado. But here, where the two biomes meet, birds from both habitats could be seen side by side.

As the sun climbed into a fiercely blue sky, Bianca was telling me about her research in the Amazonas province, where she was about to begin a Ph.D. project studying Black Skimmers — strange, tern-like birds that drag their elongated lower bill through the water to snap up fish midflight — when suddenly she broke off and pointed to a distant line of trees. "Hey, what's that white speck?" she asked.

All three of us trained our binoculars on the spot, which appeared to be a large bird perched on a limb. It had the hulking shape of a raptor, with stooped shoulders and a fierce-looking gestalt, just far enough away that we couldn't quite discern the details. Giuliano lined up his spotting scope, took a look, and stepped back with a slow smile.

"It's . . . an . . . eagle . . ." he began.

My heart skipped. I leaned forward to peer through the eyepiece. Staring back at me was a big, mean-looking bird with a black back, all-white chest, white head, yellow eyes, black mask, and orange bill.

". . . but it's not a Harpy," Giuliano said. "That's a Black-and-white Hawk-Eagle, which is a big bonus for us! These are really rare and unpredictable — we don't have any nest sites or stakeouts for Black-and-white Hawk-Eagles, so it's lucky to come across one in the forest."

Were we lucky? I wasn't sure whether to be ecstatically happy or disappointed. The Harpy, which would have been almost twice as tall and ten times heavier, remained at large, but in any other circumstance this hawk-eagle would have made my day. It was a neat, crisp-looking bird, dressed in sharp lines and stark contrasts, and I spent a long time studying its features through the scope. The Black-and-white Hawk-Eagle preys on all kinds of animals, but its main diet is other, smaller birds, so it has to be quick and agile. Eventually, this one fanned its tail, flashing a neat barred pattern, and disappeared into the forest. It really was a rare sighting. I wouldn't see another for the rest of the year.

After my heart rate had returned to normal, I sat back down on the log to resume the Harpy Eagle vigil. An hour passed. Conversation died. The same smaller birds bounced around us — aracaris, woodpeckers, pigeons — and I watched them, getting to know them while keeping one eye peeled for a freakishly large raptor. I supposed the other birds were keeping an eye out, too, never knowing when an attack might come from above. For me, this was a fun way to spend a morning, but for the other creatures of the forest, eagle-watching was a never-ending fact of life.

Two hours passed, then three. Giuliano and Bianca looked a bit nervous, and I couldn't help checking my watch. How much time could we afford on one species, even if it was a Harpy? Strategically, spending more than an hour looking for a single bird was counterproductive. I chided myself for making these calculations;

surely anyone could see that a Harpy Eagle is worth more than the usual effort. But as we crept toward the four-hour mark, and my stomach started to worry about lunch, I wondered what else might be sacrificed if the guest of honor didn't appear soon.

✦ ✦ ✦

As much as anything, our Harpy Eagle stakeout served to remind me that birding, like so many other pursuits — crossword puzzles, police work, space travel — is a game of patience punctuated by sharp moments of excitement. The thrill comes in unexpected doses. If birds were completely predictable, it would no longer be fun to look for them. Waiting is part of the addiction: the longer you wait and the more you hope, the bigger the payoff — even if that payoff never comes.

People like me get hooked on the birding habit in part because of the random payoffs, or what American psychologist B. F. Skinner described in the 1950s as a "variable ratio schedule." Skinner showed, in his now-famous operant-conditioning experiments, that mice can be taught to press a lever for treats, but that they become much more addicted to pressing the lever if they are sometimes rewarded with big treats, sometimes with small ones, and sometimes with nothing at all. Humans share this behavioral quirk; perversely, getting rewarded every time is not as fun as hitting the jackpot every once in a while. Casinos offer a classic example of random reinforcement: they have figured out how to exploit the way our brains are wired. Imagine a slot machine that, without fail, spit out ninety cents every time you put in a dollar. What's the fun in that? Switch it up, though, so that the machine occasionally pays more and sometimes gives you nothing, and, *voilà*, the game is irresistible.

Birding is exactly the same. For each moment of excitement, the brain gets a hit of dopamine — the neurotransmitter that controls pleasure — which reinforces all kinds of habit-forming behaviors. Research has shown that the more unexpected the reward, the more dopamine is released, which makes sense in the context of Skinner's variable schedules. But that's not quite the full story, because these chemicals can flood the system long before rewards actually occur; dopamine starts to kick in when we first *anticipate* a reward. This semi-stressful state keeps us curious and engaged. In other words, chemistry makes the search for birds as fun as the discovery.

All of which is a roundabout way of validating an otherwise irrational behavior like sitting for four hours in a remote Brazilian forest in a one-sided appointment with a wild bird. As lunchtime drew closer, I kept thinking, "The Harpy Eagle could appear at any moment if we just stay here a little longer!"

$$+ - + - +$$

When the eagle came, it arrived silently, gliding directly over our heads on rigid wings. Giuliano, Bianca, and I had just decided to wait fifteen more minutes before packing it in, which felt a lot like admitting defeat.

"We need to move on toward the Pantanal," Giuliano said, in as soothing a tone as he could muster. "There are lots of other birds to find."

I could read the disappointment in his eyes, a reflection of the gutted feeling in my own chest. A Harpy might count the same as a sparrow for the Big Year, but to miss such a spectacular bird at such a promising location, after sitting for hours, didn't bear thinking about. I couldn't believe we'd blown half a day for zilch. Then, as if riding this emotional climax for its grand entrance, the mythical creature simply appeared, and any disappointment evaporated in a nanosecond.

My first thought was, "Whoa, that's a big bird!" The eagle swooped low toward the nest tree and flared into a stall, landing softly on a thick branch, facing away from us. Then it swiveled its head, fixed us with a hard stare, and turned its body around so that we could see the underside. From the front, I could admire the two powerful talons, which clutched something furry.

"It's got a snack," I said, while Giuliano aimed his spotting scope on the spot.

"Yeah," he replied. "I can't quite tell what it is. Here, take a look."

The Harpy Eagle was so big that it completely filled the scope view, so magnified that each feather was crisply delineated. I could see its black chest band, a spiky crest on top of its head, the hooked beak, and black and white bars on the wings and tail. The overall coloring was of charcoal, ash, and ink, and the bird's eyes were deep black without highlights. Size and plumage indicated an adult male, relatively small compared to a female — as if you could call it anything but enormous. There was nothing subtle in the expression of this Harpy.

Close inspection showed that the bird was holding some kind of animal with a long, striped tail hanging loosely underneath.

"What do you think of the prey?" I asked, swapping out with Giuliano and Bianca for extended looks through the scope.

We ruled out the local monkeys, which have plain-colored tails, before deciding that the only possible match was a coati, a raccoon-like animal widespread in the American tropics. This particular coati was past caring about its fate; it had already been partially consumed and seemed to be missing its head. Evidently the male Harpy Eagle had eaten half its lunch before transporting the leftovers, perhaps intending to share it with his mate. But where was his mate? Off hunting on her own somewhere? Hidden inside the nest? The male seemed uncertain, swiveling his head back and forth as if looking for her. He made no move to eat. He perched quietly, waiting for her to appear. How ironic, I thought. After we waited four hours for this eagle to show up, he was now waiting for someone else.

For such a large bird, he was oddly inconspicuous. If I hadn't seen him swoop overhead, it would have been easy to miss the shadowy shape sitting under the canopy, partially concealed by layers of foliage. The Harpy is a sneaky surprise-attack artist, and the half-eaten coati in his talons had probably not known its fate until the last instant.

After our allotted fifteen minutes stretched into an hour, the male eagle showed no signs of budging from its perch, and the female eagle showed no signs of appearing. I reluctantly let Giuliano fold up his scope.

"We have a long drive ahead," he said, "and a few other species to look for before dark."

Still, I hesitated. I hated to just walk away from one of the world's rarest, most spectacular birds, as if I'd won the lottery, shrugged, and returned the ticket. But you can only stare down a monster for so long before it starts to seem tame, and I liked the idea of keeping the memory wild. We had stayed long enough.

Giuiliano, Bianca, and I retraced our steps, high on the Harpy and dopamine, to begin the journey toward the Pantanal and, for me, the rest of the world. On January 30, the Harpy Eagle became one more species on my list — number 657. With the better part of six continents and eleven months remaining, I had a long, long way to go.

6

Gunning It

AT 16,000 FEET of altitude, the ratio of oxygen in the air is almost exactly the same as it is at sea level — about 21 percent — but atmospheric pressure is reduced by half. The low pressure is what upsets your system. When you take a deep breath at 16,000 feet, you're inhaling only half the usual amount of oxygen, so your heart and lungs have to work twice as hard to keep up.

This thought flitted through my hypoxia-addled brain as I gazed down on the country of Peru from Ticlio Pass, high in the Andes Mountains east of Lima, on Valentine's Day, the forty-fifth day of my Big Year. Colorful ridge lines spidered away in pastel shades of red, yellow, and brown, with hardly a scrap of vegetation clinging to the rocks. Lingering snowfields and glaciers dotted surrounding peaks like dirty specks of frosting, and the sky was impenetrably, obscenely blue. The whole riotous scene seemed to be celebrating my good fortune in passing the 1,000 species mark of my Big Year. I had been inching toward this milestone for the past few days, and finally got it with a fluffy Pied-crested Tit-Tyrant. It took twenty-two days to see the first 500 birds of the year and twenty-three more days to add another 500, and I liked the way things were adding up. I laughed, a little too hard, and got a concerned look from Carlos Altamirano, a young Peruvian birder I'd met just a few hours earlier.

"You feel okay?" he asked.

"Never better!" I replied.

In fact, my head ached and my stomach churned indelicately — typical symptoms of mild altitude sickness. At high elevation, the oxygen-starved human body pumps more blood to the brain in an effort to compensate, and those dilated vessels cause the head-ache. Meanwhile, blood is diverted away from your digestive system, which means the stomach becomes less efficient. I'd landed in Lima, at sea level, less than twenty-four hours earlier, not nearly enough time to acclimate to a change of more than three vertical miles.

Never in my life had I been so high. Ticlio Pass is above the level where skydivers typically jump from planes, higher than most helicopters can safely fly. A rock dropped from this height would fall a third of a mile before striking the summit of Mount Whitney, the tallest mountain in the Lower 48 states. At this spot, I was more than twice as high as any particle of the entire continent of Australia, and I sure felt like it.

Dizziness swept over me as Carlos snapped a picture to mark the occasion.

"*Feliz Día de San Valentín!*" he said, grinning.

In the photo, I am smiling in front of the Andes Mountains, standing alone with feet shoulder width apart and hands stuffed deep in the pockets of my black down jacket. My shoes and pants are visibly dirty, my hair is sticking up, and binoculars dangle loosely around my neck. Behind me, an empty road snakes around several hairpin bends before disappearing down the mountainside. It is a portrait of a man who, for the past 45 days, has done nothing but look at birds and who, in the back of his mind, knows that he will spend the next 320 days doing nothing but the same.

What I didn't know, at that moment, was just how crazy things were about to get.

+ – + – +

Months earlier, when planning the logistics for South America, I had earmarked a full twenty-one days to cover Peru, a country bigger than the combined areas of Denmark, Italy, Switzerland, Portugal, Romania, the Netherlands, Austria, Hungary, and Poland. For birders, it is an exciting part of the world to visit: you've got everything from desolate coastal deserts to the snow-capped Andes to the Amazon, with all kinds of elevational gradients and tropical diversity in the mix. About 1,900 bird species have been recorded in Peru, of which nearly 150 are endemic — that is, found nowhere else. Compared to the rest of the world, these numbers are staggering; the United States, for instance, has fewer than half as many species in an area eight times as big.

But traveling here can be hazardous, especially off the beaten path. Virtually all foreigners who visit Peru head straight for Machu Picchu, the fifteenth-century Inca city that is now swamped by more than a million tourists each year. It would be nice to see those ruins, but on this trip I had to focus on the birds. Awaiting me were tanagers to chase through the cloud forest, owls to spotlight in the jungle, and hummingbirds — including one very special hummer called the Marvelous Spatuletail — to stalk among the Andean valleys. Three weeks would scarcely be enough to scratch the surface of Peru's bird life, and that's not even considering the difficulties of getting around this country.

Things have improved since the *Sendero Luminoso* ("Shining

Path") period of guerrilla revolt, severe economic turmoil, and political unrest in the 1980s and 1990s, but Peru is still a raw, developing nation. It produces more cocaine than any other country, except possibly Colombia, and has all the trouble that goes with the drug trade. Outside major cities, you're lucky to find pavement. Some regions have no roads at all. In the deep Peruvian Amazon, there are still a couple of native tribes relatively untouched by civilization, including the reclusive Mashco Piro of the Madre de Dios region — an area I planned to visit — who figured in a sensational murder in 2011.

Birds don't stick to tourist traps, of course, so I needed someone local to help navigate this complicated landscape — someone who lived in Peru and understood its culture and birds. I contacted a couple of guides at ecotour companies, but they were less than helpful. Others didn't reply at all. In the end, I realized there was only one man to turn to: the bird-crazy Swede of Peru, the man who, when I mentioned his name to several friends, came across as a modern-day warrior, post-punk rocker, and international birding legend.

His name is Gunnar. It rhymes with "lunar."

I'd heard a few rumors about Gunnar Engblom, and had even come close to meeting him several times, but he was like a ghost, popping up in unexpected places, then disappearing back into Peru. Two months before the beginning of my year, I was at a birdwatching festival in Texas when someone at a party turned to me and said, apropos of nothing, "Did you know that Gunnar Engblom showed up here today but was immediately detained by the authorities?" It was simply assumed that I knew who Gunnar was and that I would want to know that he had been detained by the authorities. I chalked it up to idle cocktail conversation and forgot all about it until months later, when I met Gunnar for the first time. After I asked him about it, the subject morphed into a fascinating story about something else, and I still have no idea what happened at that bird festival in Texas.

Some tales are true, some exaggerated, but everyone in South America seems to know Gunnar. Originally from Sweden, he first traveled to Peru as a thirty-year-old biologist in 1990 — the year that monetary inflation hit 12,000 percent — and returned for several months each year before moving permanently in 1998 to Lima, where he's flourished ever since. He quickly fell in love with the country's birds and began to pursue them with singular zeal, developing a reputation for new discoveries and for bravery in treacherous situations.

Once, in the early days, following patchy information, he took a public bus across the Andes and found himself escorted off by armed guerrillas at a checkpoint. This was serious: two British birders had just been captured and executed by Sendero Luminoso soldiers, their bodies never recovered, and kidnappings were common at the time. Gunnar, crouched on the side of the road, explained that he was broke and just looking for birds.

"They pointed at my binoculars and demanded for me to hand them over," he told me. "But they were nice binoculars, and I didn't want to lose them! So I said no, but they could have my camera, which was basically a piece of crap. I told them it was a really valuable camera and that I'd donate it to the cause as a supporter."

After a lengthy interrogation, the guerrillas became so baffled by this Swedish man's babbling about birds in accented Spanish that they just let him go.

"The best part," Gunnar said, "is that I was wearing a T-shirt that day of Che Guevara" — the Marxist revolutionary instrumental in the Cuban Revolution. "Just imagine!"

These days, insurgency is less worrisome than plain old logistical chaos, which Gunnar confronts with practiced equanimity as he guides visiting birders around the country. Strikes, strandings, accidents, and natural disasters are part of daily life in Peru, but Gunnar is not a man given to panic. He can put together any trip, on any budget, and now runs a full-time business outfitting custom itineraries for birding expeditions.

When I sent him a message to explain my mission, Gunnar replied immediately and enthusiastically.

"I am the right guy to talk to!" he wrote. "I love these kinds of challenges, and am glad to be involved. Time is money for most people. Time is lifers for birders. Count on me for Peru!"

He was as good as his word, and soon drafted a schedule on a shoestring for my proposed dates, encompassing every corner of Peru. Only later did I realize quite how ambitious the itinerary was: Gunnar intended to wring every possible second from our twenty-one days in his adopted country, targeting endemic birds all over the map. This wasn't a regular tour — it was a saturation patrol. He would personally accompany me for most of the trip, and we would rendezvous with local experts in each region. Gunnar also found an American birder from California, Glenn Sibbald, an environmental scientist from Sacramento, who would join us for the full three weeks; Glenn's extra company, cost-sharing, and good humor turned out to be an enormous bonus. All around, it seemed like a great, if potentially exhausting, plan.

And so, after leaving Brazil — the memorable Harpy Eagle with Giuliano and Bianca in the Pantanal, plus another ten days with other excellent birders in Belém/northeastern Brazil and in Itacaré/east-central Brazil — I touched down in Lima with high expectations. When I landed, I found a brief message from Gunnar: "Just back from a successful and disastrous day trip. Lots of good birds. I will meet you in Santa Eulalia Canyon at 5pm."

He had arranged for a local birder to pick me up with a driver, and they waited diligently with a sign at the airport. We did a little birding in urban Lima and then took off out of town. As we ascended toward the 16,000-foot Ticlio Pass that afternoon, one single-lane switchback at a time, my head swam with the altitude and I began to wonder what, exactly, I had gotten myself into.

As promised, Gunnar met us at a roadside gas station where, after some transfers of people and belongings, he jumped into the driver's seat of our van. Carlos, the birder who had just taken me across Ticlio Pass, sat shotgun while I occupied the back seat with Glenn, who had arrived a few days before. The four of us rolled out.

I was glad to be heading to lower elevations after spending much of the day around Ticlio, though the idea of "lower" was relative. For the first days in Peru, Gunnar had planned an assault on the central highlands for a few key endemic birds. We wouldn't quite reach 16,000 feet again, but the Andean valleys in this region were known for their hardy, high-altitude residents, and we'd sleep a couple of nights above 13,000 feet. My head still ached, and I hoped my system would acclimate quickly.

I had little time to size up my new companion before we hit the road again. Gunnar was in his fifties and had kept the sinewy physique of a long-distance runner — in fact, he was training to run the Boston Marathon in a couple of months, hoping for a competitive time — and he bristled with energy. He sported graying stubble, a gap between his front teeth, and a baseball cap with MORE BIRDS embroidered across the front. I liked him immediately.

"Here's the plan," he said, as the van slalomed around slow-moving trucks, pedestrians, farm animals, and potholes along a cliffside, guardrail-less road. "We're heading for a place called Andamarca and a bird called the Black-spectacled Brushfinch — a super-endemic species, first described to science in 1999, that is known only from a small part of the Cordillera in central Peru. We have a good chance to see one, but Andamarca is kind of far from here." He paused to glance at his watch. "I think we can just make it if we drive into the night, sleep in the van, and then get up at sunrise."

Carlos, Glenn, and I nodded. It was worth a shot. I wouldn't see a Black-spectacled Brushfinch anywhere else.

Gunnar explained that he had spent the past two days scouting with a group of birders and that they'd had some great sightings, but had gotten their vehicle stuck on a remote, muddy road while trying to cross a landslide.

"The spot was so narrow that we couldn't open the doors against the cliff on one side, and there was a sheer drop on the other," he said. "It took us a while to get things sorted out, and we lost a lot of time. But don't worry, we're not going to try that road today — it's been ruled out!"

Instead, we turned off toward the Upper Andamarca Valley and rattled onto a single-lane dirt track hewn into the side of a mountain. Gunnar knew the route and kept his foot down, driving us onward with unstoppable enthusiasm, but as the sun set it became clear that we had a long way to go before reaching the brushfinch stakeout. When darkness descended, a heavy fog settled on the landscape, shrouding everything in black drizzle. The road snuck around sharp bends without signs, folding us ever deeper into the mountains; I had the surreal impression of dramatic scenery in the dark and a gaping void on the downhill side. No other cars passed us and, after a while, I lost all sense of direction. We pressed on for hours into the night until my eyelids drooped, conversation died, and I slumped against my seatbelt.

Finally, just after midnight, Gunnar murmured, "Okay, this is it! The brushfinch spot!" We had entered a precipitous valley covered in cloud forest, though all I could see in the headlights was mud and drizzle. A light rain fell as Gunnar gingerly parked on a wide spot and switched off the engine. There were no lights, no stars, just swirling mist and the vertiginous sense that a couple of feet from our wheels the world dropped into a bottomless abyss. The four of us reclined our seats as far as they would go, closed our eyes, and drifted off after a very long day.

I stirred awake a couple of hours later to the sound of steady rain drumming on the van's roof. Outside, dawn was dissolving into gunmetal skies, and a chill had seeped under my layers of clothing. Gunnar, Carlos, Glenn, and I were each curled up, awkwardly propped in our respective positions, and we awoke with groans and stretches.

"Hey, can we run the heater for a bit?" asked Glenn. "It's freezing in here."

Gunnar grunted from the driver's seat, groped around for the key, and turned it in the ignition. Nothing happened.

"Hmm," he said, after a few seconds of silence. "I think we might have a dead battery." He tried a couple more times, but the van stubbornly would not start.

"Oh well," he said, apparently not too bothered. "We might as well go for the brushfinches now and deal with this later. Dawn is our best shot for finding these birds, and it's already getting light outside. Let's go!"

The four of us eased out of the cramped van and stood for a minute in the rain, stretching, taking in the spacious Andean view. In the moody light, I could better appreciate our position. We had parked next to a ravine where a waterfall gushed across the road surface and abruptly disappeared over the edge of a cliff. Lush, wet forest clung to the mountainside, and through a break in the mist I could see farms scattered far below us on the valley floor. Everything dripped from the rain, which was now slashing down.

BirdLife International lists the Black-spectacled Brushfinch as endangered based on its tiny range and threats of habitat destruction; it is known only from five single localities, and the population seems to be shrinking. It's a neat-looking bird, about the size of a potato, gray and black with orange on the back of its head. On close inspection, it's possible to see a bright white mustache stripe and the namesake black smudge around each eye. These birds prefer damp forest with patchy openings between 8,200 and 11,100 feet elevation. They aren't particularly secretive but they tend to stay inside cover, either scratching on the ground or sitting in bushes, so they can be hard to spot.

Gunnar and Carlos led the way, walking slowly along the road while scanning for movement. A pair of White-capped Dippers foraged energetically for aquatic insects below the waterfall, plopping their plump bodies into fast-rushing water to snag their prey. Scarlet-bellied Mountain-Tanagers, dressed in blood and ink with sapphire accents, streaked across openings like bursts of static electricity. Several types of hummingbird, including a Velvetbreast, Starfrontlet, Metaltail, Sunangel, Violetear, and the exquisitely named Shining Sunbeam, buzzed around colorful flowers, tiny droplets of water glistening on their iridescent feathers.

Locating the brushfinches took more than an hour, by which time I was soaked and shivering. Finally, Carlos pointed out a pair of the birds teed up in a bush, their feathers matted and disheveled but nicely showing the distinctive field marks. After a minute, they disappeared back into the forest, leaving us to exchange damp high-fives for number 1,027. It was a muted celebration, but I was happy that we hadn't come all this way for nothing.

Our attention soon returned to the van, which was now stranded with its dead battery between a cliff and the waterfall — no space to try a push start. What to do?

Just then, a little white car appeared around the bend, navigating slowly toward us through the rain and muck — the first vehicle we had seen since the previous day. Gunnar waved and approached, conferred with the driver for a moment, then gave a thumbs-up and a smile.

"These people are going to help us with our dead battery," he said.

The car stopped behind our van, and its driver, a five-foot-tall man with friendly features, got out. The rest of his family stayed put, preferring to keep out of the pouring rain. I counted at least seven bodies sardined inside, squished against the windows; they sat quietly, patiently, and watched us with round, curious eyes.

The man didn't have jumper cables but he did have a screwdriver, which he used to remove the battery from our van. Then he removed the battery from his own car, which he left running, and switched batteries. This had the desired effect: our van started right up, and his little sedan was able to charge the flat battery. He didn't bother to switch them back — "They're the same size!" he said — and cheerfully drove off with his family, leaving us to wonder what might have happened if they hadn't passed by.

The generosity of this man, whose name I never knew, moved me. Time and again during the year, people like this — utter strangers — would generously bail me out of tight situations. Why did they do it? I could be a criminal, for all they knew, yet they noticed a need and took the time to do what they could, be it switching a dead car battery, pushing a van out of the mud, or offering food, transport, or a place to stay. Acts of kindness from strangers continually surprised, buoyed, and humbled me, and just saying thank you never seemed to capture the fullness of my gratitude.

Gunnar got back in the driver's seat.

"Okay, we nailed the brushfinch," he said. "Let's go!"

The exchange had cost us less than an hour, and we were in good spirits despite being soaked through. We left the Andamarca Valley, navigating across an exposed flank of the Andes, with the rain still falling out of a gray sky and birds flitting here, there, and everywhere.

✦ — ✦ — ✦

Two days later, Gunnar, Glenn, and I arrived in Huánuco, a city of nearly 200,000 in east-central Peru. Carlos caught a bus to return to his house farther north, with plans to rejoin us in a few days closer to his home territory. Huánuco is said to be a delightful colonial city — "the soul of the Andes, dressed in jungle," according to Peru's tourism board — but I had no time for urban distractions. We rolled into town at 11 p.m. after another long drive on some of the world's most dangerous roads. Then Gunnar announced that we would be leaving again at 2:30 a.m.

I was used to getting up before dawn, but 2:30 was pushing it, especially after several days of very little sleep.

"Gunnar, why not 3:30?" I asked, in a slightly exasperated tone.

He looked sympathetic but wouldn't budge.

"Tomorrow is our Golden-backed Mountain-Tanager quest," he replied, "and we have to be in the elfin forest at dawn. The road up there is pretty sketchy, so we'll need at least two hours to make it."

This point was inarguable — I simply had to see that rare mountain-tanager — and so we checked into a hole-in-the-wall hotel for a couple hours of rest, setting our alarms for a ridiculous hour.

When Glenn and I staggered downstairs at the appointed time, Gunnar was sitting in the lobby with his laptop propped open, making last-minute arrangements on the hotel's Wi-Fi.

"I just booked us a flight back to Lima for this afternoon," he said, in a chipper mood. "That should give us plenty of time to reach the mountain-tanager spot, with extra birding along the way."

I rubbed sleep out of my eyes and thought, this guy is inhuman.

He's booking same-day flights at two in the morning. How does he do it?

We set out in quiet anticipation, leaving the dim streets of Huánuco for a rural track that began to switchback steeply up out of town. As the road climbed past potato fields and open pastures, its condition rapidly deteriorated until Gunnar, in pitch darkness, was navigating around fallen boulders, eroded channels, and sudden drops. Glenn and I bounced in our seats in a state of stoic acceptance, resigning our bodies to whatever might befall us. Driving in Peru, especially at night, is best done with a certain dispassionate attitude, somewhere between nonchalance and apathy.

I tried not to think of the grisly statistics. Broadly speaking, in Peru you are nearly ten times as likely to die in a traffic accident as in the United States. The website TripAdvisor, in an article about how to rent a car in Peru, begins by saying, "It's not a good idea to drive in Peru. Driving in Peru should be considered an 'extreme sport.' The main rule here is that the bigger you are, the less you follow the rules."

The U.S. State Department officially advises against driving in Peru, "particularly at night or alone on rural roads at any time of day," and the British Embassy emphasizes the point: "Driving standards in Peru . . . are poor, with stop signs and traffic lights frequently ignored. Drivers overtake on either side, with little concern for pedestrians or oncoming traffic. Crashes resulting in death or injury take place almost every day."

Bad roads are an unavoidable hazard of traveling in developing countries, especially when trying to access remote birding destinations, and I well knew the risks of spending so much time on them. Several prominent birders have perished in traffic accidents, including the late Phoebe Snetsinger — the first person ever to see 8,000 species of the world's birds — who completed her life list in 1999, when her van rolled off a highway in Madagascar.

Vehicle crashes are the number-one killer of travelers worldwide, far ahead of headline-grabbing terrorist attacks, plane crashes, and epidemics; according to the U.S. State Department's careful records, more than one-third of all Americans who don't make it home are involved in a car, train, or boating accident (a combined 3,104 deaths just between October 2012 and June 2015). And on a global scale, more than 90 percent of all crashes occur in low- to middle-income countries, where infrastructure and safety standards are lacking. Statistically speaking, driving a car — especially in a country like Peru, at night, while sleep deprived — is the most dangerous thing you can do.

Already I'd seen some horrific accidents, including a gasoline tanker that had jackknifed, flipped, and exploded on a highway in central Brazil on the same day I saw the Harpy Eagle. We had passed that stretch of road early in the morning without incident, and then, returning a few hours later, found the blackened, burned-out wreckage blocking traffic in both directions. Apparently its driver had fallen asleep at the wheel, probably at the exact same time that I was enjoying the eagle nearby. "We just have to remove the body," said a guy in an orange vest. "Then we can push the truck off the pavement."

Dwelling on such incidents wouldn't help anything, so I willed myself into composure on these long drives. Deep down, car accidents remained my biggest worry, a fear that would become only too real a few months later in northern Tanzania. But there wasn't much I could do about it, other than digging out long-disused seat belts from all kinds of vehicles. (In Argentina a taxi driver once admonished me, "Oh, you don't need that! I am a very safe driver!") Life always carries risk, and on the road I tried to sit back and enjoy the ride.

After a couple of hours of ascending switchbacks, Gunnar announced with excitement that we were nearing the top of the climb — just in time, because streaks of dawn were beginning to smudge the eastern horizon. The road had become a rough, rocky, muddy, two-wheel track cut into the mountainside, and it finally gave out in a flat, muddy area on a saddle, just below a beautiful patch of elfin cloud forest. As Gunnar initiated a three-point turn to park the van facing downhill, the van's wheels suddenly skidded, spun around, and dug in. We had arrived, and we were stuck.

Glenn jumped out to assess the situation. As he walked around the back of the van, I heard a shout.

"Hey, we seem to be missing something!"

Gunnar reluctantly switched off the engine and we disembarked. In the dim light of dawn, I could see Glenn's silhouette standing behind the van, and I walked back to join him, stepping carefully around muddy spots. He pointed silently. The entire rear bumper assembly was gone, apparently ripped off by a rock during our rough drive in the dark. The van's shape looked funny without it, like a horse without a rump.

No wonder most birders who visit this spot opt to hike the last five miles, I thought — but I couldn't have done that. It wouldn't have left enough time to come up here.

"Well, I guess we'll look for it on the way down," Gunnar said, scratching his head. "And we can push the van out of the mud later, when it gets light. Let's go for the birds first."

Without much discussion, the three of us grabbed our binoculars for the short walk up to the forest. Suddenly, I was glad for the early wakeup: we still had to find this tanager, get the van unstuck, and drive back down the mountain in time to catch an afternoon flight from Huánuco. Thanks to Gunnar's unwillingness to sleep past 2:30, we still had plenty of time.

Golden-backed Mountain-Tanagers have been seen in only a couple of places in central Peru, where the species is restricted to high elevations in the eastern Cordillera. Even apart from its rarity, the bird is a real stunner: vivid yellow and black, with a shining blue cap and fine reddish streaks. Locals call it the *Ave de Oro* — literally, the Golden Bird — and, given a good view, you can't mistake one for anything else. Not many birders have had the chance because it lives in such remote terrain, and I was one of these lucky few.

The Golden-backed Mountain-Tanager also has an interesting history. The first person to describe one for science was the legendary Neotropical bird expert Ted Parker, who is widely regarded to have known more bird vocalizations than any other human (he died in 1993 in Ecuador, in a plane crash, during a bird survey). Parker's report of finding the bird, on his very first trip to South America, was published decades later from handwritten notes, and it's a gripping account of hiking up this same mountain with camping gear. It took him three days to see it, upon which he wrote, "In the early morning light its intense golds, blues, and velvety black colors against the lichen-covered limbs melted in to create a memory that will always be with me." This discovery was one of Parker's first and most lasting ornithological achievements.

Here, I was walking in Parker's footsteps. As Gunnar, Glenn, and I hiked up to 11,500 feet in the cloud forest, my body sensed the thin air; a cool mist rose, and birds started to become active with daylight.

Gradually, our list of sightings grew. A hummingbird called a Blue-mantled Thornbill, flashing its iridescent green and purple gorget, buzzed around some low vegetation next to the trail. Brown-backed Chat-Tyrants, little bigger than poofy Ping-Pong balls, called noisily from exposed perches, and Gunnar spotted a lethargic Barred Fruiteater, patterned in dark shades of green and black, sitting inconspicuously in the canopy. Then a fast-moving flock of small birds swept through, and the pace picked up: Pearled Treerunners and noisy Citrine Warblers joined a brilliant Yellow-scarfed Tanager, endemic to Peru. I almost missed a couple of

tiny, drab, brown birds skulking in the undergrowth — the enigmatic Pardusco, a super-local species, known only from these highlands, classified in its own genus.

All of it was marvelous — the fresh air, new birds, beautiful
landscape. Even if we didn't find the marquis mountain-tanager,
just being in this place was worth the hassle. On top of the eastern
Cordillera, in the mists of the cloud forest, the bustle of Peru's cha-
otic cities felt very far away.

The trail crested a ridge and dipped down the other side,
plunging into a steep set of switchbacks. Gunnar bushwhacked
confidently across a meadow to stay high, traversing at right angles
to the trail, until we reached an isolated stand of gnarled, wind-
sculpted trees. The vegetation here was stunted in the face of harsh
elements, just above tree line — hence the name "elfin" forest. This
was the realm of the Golden-backed Mountain-Tanager, and Gunnar, Glenn, and I settled in to wait.

I was prepared for a long vigil, but this morning the birding
gods decided otherwise. I'd been standing quietly for less than
ten minutes, overlooking the patch of trees, when Gunnar whisper-shouted: "There, right below you! In the big tree at three
o'clock!"

Sure enough, something moved within the foliage and hopped
into plain sight. Even with my naked eye, the black-and-yellow
body was strikingly obvious, and through binoculars the view was
simply magnificent: I could see the bird's little blue cap and even
the fine red streaks on its underparts as it foraged from limb to
limb, at one point approaching close enough for a photo op. We
watched for several minutes in complete silence, each enjoying the
experience on his own terms. For me, the combination of rarity,
good looks, inaccessibility, and beautiful surroundings would rate
this Golden-backed Mountain-Tanager, species number 1,112, as
one of the best sightings of the year.

We lingered for a while, sifting through other birds in the area, before calling it a morning. As always, I could practically hear the clock ticking, and we had a long journey to reach Lima by evening. Someday, I thought, it would be nice to return here with a little more time to explore and relax — a feeling that was starting to seem familiar during my travels.

Three weeks is a criminally short amount of time to spend birding in Peru, and this abbreviated timeframe meant that I was rushed at every stop, always running from one place to the next without any rest. Might as well get used to it. I still had to cover the northern part of the country, the Amazon, the white sand forests near Iquitos, and the southeast, not to mention the rest of South America and the wide world.

First, though, our stuck van had to be extricated. When we walked out of the forest an hour later, Gunnar climbed confidently into the driver's seat while Glenn and I positioned ourselves at the bumperless back end to push.

"I hope this doesn't spray mud all over us," I said, "or we won't be very popular when we get to the airport."

But when Gunnar turned the key, the engine wouldn't start. He leaned out the window and smiled.

"Guys, I think we have another dead battery!"

Our van must have developed some kind of electrical problem that drained off the power. This was worrying, especially on a remote mountaintop.

Then I walked around the passenger side and noticed something else: both right tires were flat! Rock punctures hissed from the front and back, and we had only one spare.

"Uh," I said, "I don't think we're driving out of here."

We stood for a moment and contemplated the situation: stuck in the mud with a missing bumper, a dead battery, and two flat tires, in the middle of nowhere, with a flight to catch in a couple of hours.

What to do?

"We start walking," Gunnar said.

The three of us gathered our things — I picked up my back-pack, Glenn carried a more unwieldy suitcase, and Gunnar had two big bags, one in each hand — and started briskly hiking down the mountain, unsure what lay ahead.

At least a few birds were around. We paused to admire a Many-striped Canastero singing from a tuft of grass, its streaky brown-and-white plumage blending in with the habitat. A little farther down, a Red-crested Cotinga watched us pass. But I was anxious; hiking all the way down this road would take all day if we couldn't find help, and then we'd miss our flight out of Huánuco. All I could think about was the wasted hours, the missed flight, the lost birds.

"Maybe we'll find our bumper," Glenn said.

In the clear light of day, I could see just how rough this road was that we'd ascended in the dark; jagged rocks and potholes presented a fearsome surface even to walk on. We had been lucky to make it to the top and see the Golden-backed Mountain-Tanager before running into trouble.

After a couple of miles with no signs of civilization, the three of us rounded a corner to discover about a dozen Quechua farm-ers sitting in the shade, eating potatoes for lunch. Most were kids, and they looked up with the expressions one might expect upon the sudden appearance of three gringos heading toward them with air-port luggage — kind of like, say, a meteorite flying into their potato field.

Gunnar didn't miss a beat.

"*Hola,*" he said, walking right into the group. "*Alguien quiere una naranja?*"

He set down his bags and zipped one open to show that it was completely stuffed with dozens of fresh, ripe oranges, and he started handing them out. The kids' expressions changed from surprise to delight: it wasn't a meteorite that had crashed into their midst, it was a fruit stand.

"Gunnar, were you going to carry those oranges all the way down the mountain?" asked Glenn, looking incredulous.

We had bought a large bag of them at a roadside stall a couple of days ago, and I'd been wondering what Gunnar meant to do with the fruit, as he had way too many for us to eat. They must have weighed twenty-five pounds.

"You never know when a few oranges will come in handy!" said Gunnar, looking pleased.

The farmers invited us to join them for lunch. We sat down and ate boiled potatoes and oranges while they stared at us, whispering to each other and giggling. I could imagine that this visit would provide entertainment long after we had gone. The potatoes were delicious.

After a while, Gunnar explained our predicament and pointed to several dirt bikes parked nearby. Could we get a ride down the hill? This request sparked a fresh round of giggles, but soon enough three kids volunteered to take us far enough for a taxi transfer. Our bags were carefully tied to the dirt bikes and we climbed on, two to a saddle.

My driver was a quiet seventeen-year-old named Rolando who had seven siblings and lived next to a potato field. I rode right behind him, crotch to crotch. On a dirt bike, there is no such thing as personal space — it was common in Peru to see four or five bodies zooming past on one motorcycle — and I wasn't sure of the etiquette. Would it be weird if I clasped him around the waist, or should I rest my hands on his shoulders, or maybe try something else? In the end, I grabbed the seat on either side of my thighs and hung on tight, trying not to lean too far when we banked around corners.

He politely asked why I was visiting the area and I tried to explain, in broken Spanish, that I was traveling around the world for an entire year just to look at birds. It's a big project, I said, to set a world record. I love birds: *me encantan los aves*. Birds are amazing, I added, for clarity.

Stone silence.

Sometimes, and this seemed to be one of them, my adventure existed so far beyond the bounds of a person's everyday life that it simply could not be comprehended. I ran into this reaction repeatedly, especially in very rural areas. A few weeks later in Guatemala, for instance, I tried the same explanation on a local indigenous girl and said that I'd started the year in Antarctica. After a few seconds, she replied, earnestly, "Is that in Guatemala City?" But this can happen anywhere, and it's not always worth getting into the full story. Just before this Big Year, when I had my last haircut in the United States, at a regular salon on a Wednesday, the hairdresser asked brightly if I had the day off work. What should I say — that I was about to set off on an obsessive, forty-one-country world tour of birdwatching, hence the need to shave all extraneous hair? Sure, I replied. Just running a few errands.

At the bottom of the mountain, we hopped off the bikes and said our *muchas gracias* while Gunnar tipped the kids a few Peruvian soles for their help. They buzzed off, looking happy to head home. Gunnar then ordered a taxi by cell phone, describing in detail which dirt road to take, and called some other poor soul to go deal with our injured, abandoned van. Soon enough we were on our way to the tiny Huánuco airport, with barely enough time to catch the afternoon flight back to Lima.

When we finally arrived at the open-air check-in counter, tired and dusty and sweaty and hungry, there was some confusion. I couldn't figure out why the ticket agent wouldn't hand us our boarding passes; she talked too fast for me to catch the drift. It was only when Gunnar stepped in, with his usual calm in the face of trying circumstances, that I understood.

"Our flight has been canceled," he said. "The plane didn't make it in today. We might as well have stayed on that mountain."

✦ — ✦ — ✦

Then I got sick.

It happened a couple of days after our antics in the highlands. That canceled flight meant spending a night in a hotel without electricity, then a ten-hour drive to Lima the following day, where Glenn and I arrived at the Jorge Chávez International Airport exactly eighteen minutes before our connecting flight to Chiclayo took off. We sprinted through security and just made it, sinking low into our seats to avoid the glares of other passengers. Meanwhile, Gunnar stayed home in Lima, planning to fly up and join us the following day, and Carlos — the young Peruvian birder from Ticlio Pass — met Glenn and me when we landed up north.

Here was the plan: Carlos, Glenn, and I would begin an ambitious west-to-east transect across northern Peru, a diverse region with several hundred possible bird species. Most organized birding trips dedicate about two weeks to this route, but we had scheduled just six days for the whole shebang, which gave little room for error. Gunnar would join us for some sections. We even had a driver, Julio Benites, who could handle the long days and cook meals in the field.

I had visited this region once before, a few years earlier, so I knew many of the birds and places already — the first familiar ground since Argentina, weeks ago. My most-wanted bird here was the Marvelous Spatuletail, a spectacular hummingbird with peculiar tail streamers that is found only in one remote valley. I hoped to rack up a lot of species, as each day we'd be in completely new territory.

Things started well. On the first day in northern Peru I added thirty-seven new species, including some nice "Tumbesian" birds native to the dry, coastal plain shared by Peru and Ecuador. At a place called Chaparrí Reserve, a community-run conservation project east of Chiclayo, local birder Juan Julca kindly pointed out Tumbes Sparrows, Tumbes Tyrants, and a dapper-looking Elegant Crescentchest skulking through the scrubby woodland. Then we stayed up after dark to search for Peruvian Screech-Owls and Scrub Nightjars by spotlight.

That evening, though, it was difficult to write my daily blog entry — a task I never failed to do, no matter how long the day had been. "Edging on hallucinatory sleep deprivation," I noted. "Maybe that will help me see more birds?"

I'd now been in Peru for a full week and had averaged less than four hours of sleep each night, without any chance to catch up. Gunnar had driven us hard, wanting to reach every possible species in our allotted time. I appreciated the effort but wondered how long I could take this grueling schedule — it was physically wearing me down and I was having trouble concentrating. I was becoming a pro at power naps, even while sitting upright.

The next day I hit the wall.

It was probably inevitable. Carlos, Glenn, Julio, and I stopped at a place called Abra Porcuya for a picnic lunch, along a rural road with good access to foothill forest. All of a sudden, even though it was a warm, sunny day, I started shivering and couldn't quit. My throat hurt, and I had the dizzy feeling that if I didn't sit down, I'd vomit.

Carlos spotted a bird called a Piura Chat-Tyrant and I lifted my binoculars, but my arms were shaky. I knelt down on the roadside and tried not to think about my queasy stomach.

"I don't think I can keep walking," I mumbled.

Glenn suggested we abort the afternoon's plans and proceed

straight into Jaén, the next town. At first I protested, but it was no use — my system had decided to force the issue, and now I had a fever. Julio pulled up the van, I climbed in and reclined my seat, and we drove onward in silence.

It should have been a two-hour trip, but halfway to Jaén, traffic was backed up on the two-lane road, apparently because of an obstruction ahead. Julio didn't hesitate: he pulled into the opposing lane and zoomed past more than a mile of parked cars until we reached the scene of an accident, where a bus had collided with a tractor on a blind curve.

"I have a sick person and we are going to the hospital!" Julio yelled at the people directing traffic. (We were, in fact, going to a hotel.)

When the flipped tractor was cleared, we rocketed ahead of the jam on a blessedly traffic-free road.

In the next few miles, I couldn't help but notice two large billboards placed by the Jaén health ministry along the highway which said, in large letters, *"Cuidado . . . ¡El Dengue es Mortal!"* — "Be Careful, Dengue Fever Is Deadly!" The billboards featured a picture of a mosquito on a red drop of blood and were written in a dramatic font suitable for a horror movie.

When you have just contracted a mysterious fever, signs like this are not encouraging. Sprawled in my seat, I wondered what I was in for. I hoped that it wasn't dengue — which often manifests as severe joint pain, hence the disease's nickname, "breakbone fever" — but it was too early to tell. Dengue fever is serious in tropical areas around the world, especially in South and Central America; hundreds of millions of people are infected with dengue by mosquitoes each year, and the incidence is growing, which is why even on the hottest, most humid days I covered myself in clothing that I had treated with mosquito-repelling pyrethrin.

Dengue was just one of a suite of tropical diseases on my radar in 2015. Before leaving home, I had read up on all of them. Chikungunya, another mosquito-borne virus, first introduced to the Americas in 2013, had infected more than a million people in the Caribbean region by the end of 2014; like dengue, chikungunya usually presents a painful fever and has no specific treatment or vaccine. Malaria kills up to a million people each year, mostly in Africa, and I'd packed a supply of antimalarial pills that I would start taking each day later in the year to ward that off. Leishmaniasis is really creepy, caused by a flesh-eating parasite spread by sandflies, and I actually knew someone with a large, open wound to show for it. Chagas disease can lead to sudden heart failure ten to thirty years after being transmitted by the bite of a tiny, blood-sucking "kissing bug"; more than eight million people are probably infected with Chagas, though most Americans have never even heard of it. The West African Ebola outbreak of 2014–2015 had fewer than 30,000 total cases (and 12,000 deaths) — a blip by comparison — but I was worried about Ebola, too, as I was headed to the African continent in a few short months.

On the plus side, I figured I didn't have yellow fever, because I had been immunized against it. And I probably didn't have tetanus, diphtheria, or pertussis — potentially life-threatening bacterial diseases — because I had gotten a Tdap vaccine, along with a polio booster, a flu shot, and a hepatitis A vaccine, in one ghastly pre–Big Year medical visit that ended with me, and my lifelong blood-injection-injury phobia, in a dead faint. I had to be revived by three nurses with smelling salts.

It's easy, when you're far from home, to panic when you get sick, and I tried my best to keep calm. After all, the likelihood of contracting a scary disease is small compared to many other things that could go wrong. I had come down with a flu, that was all, and I tried not to think of all the diseases described as having "flu-like symptoms."

When we reached the town of Jaén, Carlos's phone rang. It was Gunnar, calling from Lima to check on our progress. He had been planning to fly up and join us that afternoon but said he'd missed his flight because of heavy traffic, so he would try to catch us the next day.

Carlos handed me the phone.

"Hey Gunnar, I'm not feeling well," I said.

"How bad is it?" he asked. "Did you see a Henna-hooded Foliage-Gleaner?"

"No," I said. "I really need to lie down now."

"Always got to be one of those days," he said, philosophically. "Listen, you still have time to try for a few birds near Jaén this afternoon. I know a great spot. Just head out by the Utcubamba River —"

"Gunnar, I can't talk now," I said, suddenly violently dizzy and nauseated.

I hung up and handed the phone back to Carlos.

"You should rest," he said, looking concerned. "Are you sure you don't want to go to the hospital? You're very pale."

"I just need to lie down for a while," I said. "I'm sure it will be fine."

We checked into a hotel, where I splurged on an air-conditioned room all to myself.

"I don't want to keep you up with coughing and all that," I explained to Glenn. Mostly I just wanted to be alone. Despite my efforts to keep calm, I was already wallowing in self-pity.

Once sealed in my room, I jacked up the AC, curled into the fetal position on the center of the bed, shut my eyes, and tried to dismiss the feeling of having been run over by a garbage truck. Chills came in waves, shaking my body, which ached from head to toe. The emotions came pouring out, too; I suddenly felt wretchedly homesick, lonely, and scared. Several times I crawled into the bathroom on all fours but couldn't throw up. Sweat soaked the sheets, leaving me shivering uncontrollably under a mountain of soggy covers. Making matters worse, I felt vaguely guilty for being so miserable, because when you are living the dream, as I clearly was, you are supposed to be happy. The hours ticked slowly by.

My fever lasted well into the night. Carlos and Glenn checked in a few times, but otherwise I lay immobile for hour upon hour, thinking dark thoughts. I had been pushing hard without a break since the beginning of the year, with early starts and late nights almost every day. My system had maxed out. Glenn and I had talked about it a couple of days ago, and his words came back to me now.

"A lot of people assume it's a sprint," he said, "but nobody can sprint hard for an entire year. That's crazy. Your year of birding is more like an endurance event, and it's not even a marathon. It's more of an ultramarathon, so long and complicated that it's impossible to reach the finish line without approaching it in sections. You can't peak too early; you have to pace yourself."

Now, sacked out and staring at the ceiling, Glenn's point struck me hard. I'd finished several marathons in past years, enough to understand the importance of pacing. Professional athletes know that world distance records are usually set with negative splits — in other words, the second half of a race is run faster than the first half — and I supposed that this Big Year might be just the same. Expending too much energy during the first couple of months could set an unsustainable pace. It was still only February and I had a long way to go, the equivalent of being just four miles into a 26.2-mile marathon. Yet I could already feel the exhaustion setting in after so many long days without rest. Perhaps getting the flu was my body's way of telling me to cut it some slack.

With my energy at its lowest ebb, one bright thought came shining through: I knew for certain that I would not quit. My main worry from the start had been the possibility of getting burned out on my favorite activity. Now my sagging spirits were soothed somewhat by the sharp realization that burning out was not going to be a problem. If I could remain enthusiastic during the worst moments, then I could be sure that birding wouldn't get stale. My sense of purpose was still strong. I just had to believe that my body would bounce back. Really, the most frustrating part of getting sick was that it kept me from looking for birds.

The following morning, I wobbled downstairs with binoculars ready. Carlos stood by the front desk and looked up with surprise.

"What are you doing up?" he asked. "You look terrible."

"Yeah, but I'll feel a lot better if we can find some birds today," I said, with a half smile.

I'd been in bed for eighteen painful hours and hadn't eaten anything in more than a day, but the fever had broken and I could stand up without vomiting. Might as well go birding.

Carlos tried to dissuade me, but then, surprisingly, Gunnar walked into the room — apparently he had managed to catch a late flight from Lima and had arrived during the night.

"Ready to rock?" he asked, grinning broadly.

"Let's go find a spatuletail!" I answered.

Our posse trundled out of Jaén, a little worse for wear but glad to be on the road again. If anything, I was now more committed: a case of the flu only made me want to see more birds.

The Marvelous Spatuletail spot was another two days' drive eastward, and by the time we arrived there I was feeling well enough to walk in the forest. I had a hacking cough that threatened to break my ribs, but a course of Azithromycin was helping with that, and as long as I could function enough to continue birding, the quest was on.

We parked at the Huembo Reserve, near the town of Pomacochas in the Utcubamba Valley — the only valley where you can reliably find a Marvelous Spatuletail — late in the afternoon. Huembo is a conservation success story, a ninety-six-acre sanctuary set up by the American Bird Conservancy and the Asociación Ecosistemas Andinos (a Peruvian conservation organization) as an easement with the local community; a small shade-grown coffee plantation supplements entrance fees to protect the land from deforestation. Several feeders are always kept full of nectar for hummingbirds, and some benches have been arranged for birders to sit on while waiting for the star of the show to appear.

This particular star is worth biding time for. Even without its bizarre tail feathers, a male Marvelous Spatuletail is unmistakable: tiny, fierce-looking, with a spiky purple crest, green throat, and a flashy black line down the center of its body. But it's the bird's tail that sets it dramatically apart, earning it the distinction of "world's most spectacular hummingbird." (Practically all of the world's 342 species of hummers are gorgeous, so tread lightly with such superlatives — but this one has my vote.)

Uniquely in the bird universe, spatuletails are born with only four individual tail feathers: A pair of stiff, pointy feathers in the center, flanked by two wildly elongated, curved shafts that cross over each other to end in round, shiny blue paddles. The effect is like two butterflies fluttering behind the bird's body, each one moving independently of the bird itself. When it gets excited, a male spatuletail can whip these paddles back and forth over its head in a frenzied display, waving them like semaphores to attract the attention of a nearby female. (You can't make this stuff up; check out the videos on YouTube.) Otherwise, he seems content to carry his strange tail around like a miniature turbocharged peacock.

As with the Golden-backed Mountain-Tanager, this bird is both stunning and rare — a knockout combination. Marvelous Spatuletails are restricted to the eastern slope of one remote valley in northern Peru, occur in low numbers, and are thought to be declining; the species' total population is estimated at fewer than 1,000 individuals. At the Huembo Reserve, Gunnar, Carlos,

Glenn, and I sat down on a bench to watch dozens of humming-birds, of ten species, swarm like bees around several sugar-water feeders. The sight was mesmerizing.

"Bronzy Inca," Gunnar said, when an unusually drab hummer darted in for a sip.

"Long-tailed Sylph!" exclaimed Carlos, gesturing toward a hummingbird with shimmering tail feathers longer than its own body.

"Ooh, and a woodstar," I said, pointing out one that flew like a bumblebee. "Maybe a White-bellied?"

"*Sí,*" Carlos confirmed. "Good call!"

So many hummingbirds surrounded us that they demanded full attention, and after nearly an hour I realized that I was completely captivated — for the first time in three days, I had forgotten all about the flu. These hummingbirds were as good as a swarm of antibodies.

It's amazing, I reflected, what we will do for our passions, and what our passions will do for us. At home I might still have been flat in bed, but here I was in remote Peru, barely even aware that my body was out of whack. The crisp mountain air, good company, and onslaught of birds offered a healing combination, and the real star hadn't even materialized yet.

I was beginning to wonder if he'd keep his appointment when the male Marvelous Spatuletail, species number 1,235, zipped out of nowhere, briefly lit on a twig to scan the scene, and moved in aggressively for his turn at the feeder. The effect was like a rock star stepping onstage. His little tail paddles bobbed along behind, floating like a twin escort of pea-sized helicopters while he slurped down sugar water. Light scattered from his iridescent head and throat patches, sending neon beams of green and violet into space. When you're so small and quick, predators aren't a big worry, and this bird flaunted himself like he owned the forest.

"Dang," Glenn said. "That is some crazy, crazy bird."

It is impossible to put into words what washed over me just then: euphoria, transcendence, a sense of things coming together. I was ecstatic and pensive, filled with adrenaline. The hummingbird was magnificent, but its allure owed as much to desire as beauty. Because I had spent so many years scrutinizing this bird in books and magazines, it almost didn't seem real in three dimensions.

There is something metaphysical about the human connection with nature, and we each find our own points of contact. For me, that afternoon, the Marvelous Spatuletail represented something far beyond a single bird. It distilled the whole experience of Peru, incarnated in avian form — all of the rough, raw material of an entire country compressed into one bright and shining diamond.

✦ ✦ ✦

I spent two more weeks with Gunnar and crew, continuing to have adventures and misadventures. On a single day in Manú National Park, we survived two major landslides, a broken transmission, a flat tire, and a lost driver's license, and twice had to be towed out of the mud before an agricultural workers' strike completely shut down the road. We suffered torrential rain in the Amazon, endured the aftermath of a bus accident in the highlands, and briefly got lost in the forest one evening as darkness fell. I developed a bacterial lung infection that persisted for weeks afterward, despite two courses of antibiotics, and I couldn't ever catch enough sleep.

And just when we thought that was it, Peru had one last surprise. Immediately after Gunnar dropped me at the airport, he was mugged at a stoplight in Lima while sitting inside a taxi on the way home, and lost all of his birding gear.

"All of a sudden there was a violent sound and the crash of glass splattered all over the back seat of the cab," he recalled. "Before I realized what was happening, a dark-clad man reached in the window and grabbed my backpack containing practically all my working material. I was stunned."

In that instant, Gunnar lost both his cameras and telephoto lens, laptop, iPad, and GPS, among other things — particularly devastating because of the three years' worth of photos on the computer's hard drive. I felt terrible about the robbery. It was an awful way to end three wild weeks of birding.

"In Peru it is best to count on things not going as you hope and be happy when they do," once quipped John O'Neill, an acclaimed ornithologist and artist who has discovered more than a dozen species of birds within Peru since the early 1960s. That's the nature of traveling in such a rough and beautiful country: you take the ups with the downs.

Gunnar likes to reference O'Neill's quote when things take unexpected turns.

"The gods know I have learnt that lesson after years of living in Peru," he said. "I never get worked up or get despair in these situations. Eventually things work out with some patience. Stay flexible and reassess the situation."

Whatever Peru cost us in wear and tear it more than paid back in birds. By the end of our twenty-one days, I had recorded 784 species in the country, more than I would see in any other nation during the year. Of those, 488 were new additions, and 242 turned out to be unique — not seen anywhere else. I left Peru with 1,468 birds on the year list, amped up by a huge boost in sightings. It could not have been done without the help of generous Peruvians and the unflappable genius of Gunnar Engblom.

7

An Angel of Peace

LATE AT NIGHT, while waiting at Lima's spacious Jorge Chávez International Airport for the plane to Ecuador, I remembered something Gunnar had mentioned a few days earlier. A young Dutch birder had announced his intention to spend 2016 birding around the world, and Gunnar was curious about my reaction. This was the first I'd heard of it. I had been so focused on strategizing my Big Year, and then so busy traveling off-grid during the Big Year itself, that I didn't know anything about it. Now, sitting quietly at the gate, I pulled out my laptop and snooped around.

From what I could tell, Gunnar was right: a man named Arjan Dwarshuis was indeed plotting a round-the-world birdwatching trip the following year. He seemed to live in Amsterdam and to spend most of his time out birding — he was almost the same age as me, just four months younger — and he had posted a map on his personal website, with an itinerary spanning about twenty countries. In Africa and the United States he'd arranged long road trips, and in various places he apparently had convinced friends and family to join him. It sounded like fun, though I didn't think he could reach his goal of 5,000 species of birds with the route he had chosen. He appeared to be in it for the experience, and I hoped we might run into each other. It would be like meeting my Dutch twin.

I'd always assumed that someone would come along and challenge any mark I set, even if this guy didn't do it. For me, finding 5,000 birds was the game, but the real adventure was in the people I would meet, the places I would visit, and the stories and memories I would accumulate along the way. The third month into my Big Year, I wasn't thinking too hard about the world record anyway, which was still thousands of birds away and months in the future, even if I got that far. Still, it was unsettling to imagine that the very instant I finished my own year, someone else would embark on a global tour and conceivably challenge my record. What if he was inspired by my quest to up his game? After all, he'd have the benefit of my successes and failures, like following a blueprint, and he could alter his strategy to squeeze out more birds.

Slightly annoyed, I shut my laptop. Then, annoyed at feeling annoyed — what was this, a competition? — I boarded the plane, flew to Ecuador, and forgot, for the moment, all about it.

＋－＋－＋

Ah, Ecuador: home of the Incas, fried guinea pigs, the world's highest capital city, the farthest point from the center of the Earth, and, acre for acre, the highest biodiversity of any country — all within an area smaller than the state of Colorado.

For birds, Ecuador offers nothing short of a tropical paradise. Virtually every habitat is represented, from coastal deserts to snow-capped peaks to the Amazon basin, and more than 1,700 species have been recorded — 16 percent of the world's birds on less than 0.0006 percent of its land surface. For birders, conditions are just as alluring: unlike neighboring Peru or Colombia, Ecuador has a long history of conservation, is relatively stable and safe, has a well-developed infrastructure, and is small enough to cover efficiently. If you want to see the most species of birds in the shortest amount of time, Ecuador is without doubt the best place to do it.

The importance of natural diversity in this tiny nation cannot be overstated. It's even written in the constitution: Ecuador is the only country in the world to recognize "Rights of Nature" — the idea that ecosystems have inalienable rights, just like people do — at the highest legal level. "Nature, or Pachamama, where life is reproduced and occurs, has the right to integral respect for its existence," states Article 71 of the country's constitution, in accordance with the Ecuadorian concept of *Buen Vivir*, which emphasizes harmony with other people and nature above material development.

This constitution was passed in 2008 following the election of Rafael Correa, a former economics professor who campaigned for president on a popular socialist platform. It didn't stop Correa from auctioning 12,000 square miles of Amazon rainforest to Chinese oil companies in 2013, or from overturning a ban on the sale of shark fins, but at least he pays attention to the environment. I once bumped into him, almost literally, when he visited the Galápagos Islands before being sworn into office during the fall of 2006. I was there on a study abroad program with the university where he used to work. He looked at me and said, "I used to teach here, but now I'm the elected president!" Correa remains the only national president I've ever met in person, for better or worse.

After the nonstop intensity of Peru, Quito felt immediately friendly and familiar. In past years I had spent about eight months in Ecuador, on three separate trips — more than any other country outside the United States — and now I looked forward to revisiting some old haunts and familiar birds.

It was pleasant, for a change, to arrive in a place where I didn't feel overwhelmed by everyday details. The constant exposure to new destinations in Peru often gave me the impression of wandering through a museum, and, more than two months into this adventure, I was beginning to worry that my sense of discovery would dull into complacency before I reached the end of the world. New discoveries make us feel good, but we sometimes forget that the main prerequisite for novelty is ignorance — and it's no fun to be oblivious all the time. One of the biggest risks of moving too fast is that you always stay a beginner, and I wanted to dig deeper than that, to soak everything in and keep advancing. Time was an unaffordable luxury while racing from place to place, which meant that I sometimes felt like a blind sprinter. The best antidote was familiarity: because I had spent time in Ecuador before, I knew what to expect here, which meant I could settle in and focus on the real highlights.

My plane touched down at Mariscal Sucre International Airport at two in the morning. By dawn, I was in the cool, misty, high-altitude cloud forest at Yanacocha Reserve, above the city of Quito, with a local birder named Manuel Sánchez. I remembered this spot from my first, mind-boggling trip to South America with a group of young American birders in 2005. I returned to Ecuador in 2006 for the university study abroad program, which included three months in the Galápagos, and came back in 2012 to spend a season at the remote Tiputini Biodiversity Station in Amazonian Ecuador tracking Wedge-billed Woodcreepers with radio telemetry.

This time around, I wouldn't be visiting the Galápagos — too far, for too few species — but instead planned a quick assault on the most diverse parts of Ecuador: the northwest cloud forests, the Andean slopes, and the Amazon lowlands. You could spend a lifetime in these areas without seeing every bird, but I had little more than a week to track down as many species as possible, helped by several locals who thoroughly knew the territory.

Manuel and I wandered slowly down the trail at Yanacocha, enjoying the cool air near 11,000 feet and the forest birds. Hummingbirds stole the show, highlighted by an iconic Sword-billed Hummingbird perched in the mist. Although I'd already seen one in Peru, I took a few minutes to admire this individual as it, in turn, admired us from the safety of its high vantage. The Sword-bill has such a long bill — adapted for probing certain tubular, hanging flowers — that it must preen itself with its feet and usually holds its head upright to rest, like someone who is balancing a javelin on the tip of their nose. No other bird has a bill exceeding its own body length; I snapped a few photos of the distinctive silhouette. Other hummingbirds, including a shimmering Golden-breasted Puffleg and a dazzling little Rainbow-bearded Thornbill, species numbers 1,478 and 1,479, lured us farther down the trail.

As we walked, Manuel, who wore glasses, a scruffy beard, a plaid shirt, and a warm coat, talked passionately about conservation. A native Ecuadorian, he had studied science communication at Edinburgh University before returning to Quito to guide ornithologists and work in ecotourism, and he was only a couple of years older than me. Like me, Manuel decided to pursue birding full-time, and believes that watching birds is a powerful tool for sustainable development. He is part of a new generation of Latin American conservationists who are working hard to preserve nature by getting people inspired about their birds. It's a tough career path, but Ecuador — with all its natural riches and constitutional commitment to the environment — presents a better chance than most places. And Manuel isn't the only one to take advantage.

"Have you heard of Ángel Paz?" I asked, as an Andean Pygmy-Owl called in the distance.

Manuel stopped and looked as if I'd just asked a question so utterly obvious it almost didn't bear answering.

"Of course," he said, speaking slowly. "All the birders in Ecuador know him. That guy is an absolute legend."

✦ — ✦ — ✦

A few years ago, reports began to surface of a man in rural Ecuador who, improbably, had figured out a way to attract antpittas — which belong to one of the skulkiest and trickiest families of birds in the New World. Taxonomists recognize about fifty species of antpittas, collectively limited to South and Central America. All of them are plump, long-legged, short-tailed, and upright-standing, shaped like eggs on legs, and they are secretive. Most of the time, antpittas hop on the ground within thick vegetation; the conventional way to see one is to listen for its call and then try to sneak up on it. Birders love them and dread them in equal measure.

The largest of the family is the Giant Antpitta, an enigmatic species that stands up to eleven inches tall and weighs ten ounces. Despite its size, the Giant Antpitta is despairingly difficult to observe. It lives only in primary cloud forest with dense understory and is known from just a few scattered locations in Ecuador and Colombia. Nobody knows its population (the best estimate is a couple thousand individuals), its nesting cycle, or exactly what it eats. It's a spectacular bird, for those lucky enough to catch a glimpse: salmon orange with fine black barring, a bluish cap, long legs, and large, watery, inky black eyes.

The man who first befriended the Giant Antpitta is Ángel Paz — literally, "Angel of Peace" — and his story is as unusual as his name. In a former life, about a decade ago, this particular Ángel worked as a logger in northwest Ecuador. His father purchased a beautiful tract of cloud forest on a flank of the Andes, and Ángel moved in to start chain sawing.

"The faster you cut down trees, the more money you make," he told me with some pride. "I used to be one of the fastest tree cutters in this region."

The forest on his property hosts a display site, known as a lek, of an iconic and easy-to-see bird, the Andean Cock-of-the-rock — neon orange with black wings and a fluffy crest. The birds gather at the lek each morning so that females can view the males' elaborate courtship rituals and magnificent plumage. About a decade ago, someone advised Ángel to charge tourists admission to view the birds. He built a trail to the spot and, sure enough, people paid to see the spectacle. Ángel decided to leave the trees alone in that part of the forest.

One day, while Ángel was walking with a birdwatching group on his trail, a plump creature hopped out of the undergrowth and turned its dark eyes on the visitors, who promptly freaked out.

"That's a Giant Antpitta!" one exclaimed.

After everybody calmed down, they told Ángel: "Forget the cock-of-the-rocks. If you can show this bird to birders, they will pay double."

Ángel had seen the bird before but didn't think much of it. In fact, the bird sometimes followed him around when he was cutting trees, apparently attracted by disturbed grubs, and wasn't particularly shy, though it usually stuck to dense cover. Ángel called it Maria, an endearing local name for many types of small birds in Latin America. He began to methodically stalk Maria, trying to figure out her habits.

He offered the bird food, unsure what it might like to eat. He started with pieces of spaghetti and meat, but Maria didn't have a taste for human delicacies. So he scrounged around for worms, and, lo and behold, the bird gobbled them down. He began bringing fresh worms to the same spot each morning so that Maria would get used to the gifts, and eventually he trained Maria to come when he called.

At the time, most birders would have scoffed at the idea of hand-feeding a wild Giant Antpitta. Books emphasized the species' secretive and elusive nature (rightly so), and few people imagined that one could be habituated to handouts. But Ángel didn't read birding books; he was a logger who saw an opportunity to make a little extra cash. Maybe, looking back on it, the idea of feeding an antpitta wasn't that far-fetched, as antpittas have been known to shadow large mammals inside the forest, apparently to scavenge disturbed insects.

When word got out, amazed birders began showing up to see for themselves, and Maria's fame quickly spread. It seemed too good to be true: a species that had traditionally been regarded as near-mythical was suddenly real and viewable — guaranteed even — within a couple of hours' drive of Quito.

Soon, so many people were visiting Ángel that he quit logging, planted a few blackberry crops, and spent his time hanging out with birds and birders. He found that he could make a better living by leaving the forest intact than by cutting it down; as long as the birds stuck around, he'd have a steady income from entrance fees. Gradually he learned about the other species on his property and became an expert in showing them to visitors. He put up fruit and hummingbird feeders, constructed new trails, and, each morning, kept his worm-feeding appointment with Maria.

I arrived at Ángel's property, along with another Ecuadorian birder, Edison Buenaño, four days after leaving Manuel at Yanacocha. Edison and I had connected after I took a quick trip to eastern Ecuador for some Amazon specialties, during which I had gotten thoroughly rained on. As we parked in front of Ángel's house in the cloud forest, I reveled in the anticipation of what was sure to be a standout morning.

Ángel stepped into his driveway to greet us as Edison and I hopped out. He was dressed in pastel greens with a camouflage down vest over a khaki shirt, a military green baseball cap, and binoculars around his neck. He smiled warmly.

"Bienvenidos a Refugio Paz de las Aves!" he said.

Without much chitchat, the three of us headed straight into the forest. Ángel took us first to where it had all started: the Andean Cock-of-the-rock lek. I'd seen these birds before but couldn't pass up the opportunity to watch their displays at close range. Just after dawn, we walked quietly along Ángel's trail to the spot where male cock-of-the-rocks postured, hopped, bobbed, and contorted in a mesmerizing combination of color, motion, and sound. As their grunts and squawks filled the air, I marveled at how these birds had been returning to the exact same tree for many years. Cock-of-the-rocks are polygamous; the gorgeous males compete for the attention of passing females, and after mating, the females fly off to build a nest and raise their chicks alone. The birds use lek sites like this one for generations, as long as they remain undisturbed.

After a few minutes, I realized that I was alone with the birds — Edison and Ángel had slipped away. Completely transfixed, I stayed put to watch the cock-of-the-rocks in full swing. A male perched in front of me, snapped his bill, flapped his wings, arched his back, bowed deeply, croaked, bobbed his head, did several pushup-like maneuvers, and crowed in my face. Even within the understory of this dense forest, in the muted light of dawn, his electric orange feathers glowed like a fluffy, misshapen light bulb, and he made a popping noise to signal the start of each display. It was all very flattering to me, but a few seconds later I noticed that this bird had higher hopes: a maroon-colored female sat inconspicuously in a tangle of foliage, watching intently as the action unfolded. Two other males danced nearby, seemingly trying to outdo each other's moves. If a female likes what she sees, she'll land next to a male and peck his neck and they'll mate on the spot, but this one didn't seem impressed by any of them. She flew off a minute later.

Just then, I heard a different sound.

"Psst! Noah — over here!" whisper-shouted Edison.

I turned around to see him gesturing from a patch of foliage inside a small, lush ravine.

"Come, very quietly!" he called.

Leaving the cocks, I tiptoed down. As I approached, trying not to slip on the slick mud and sopping vegetation, I could see Ángel standing behind Edison, staring at something on the ground.

"It's not an antpitta," Edison said, "but look at this! Ángel is feeding a family of Dark-backed Wood-Quail!"

Sure enough, several chunky, grapefruit-sized birds were pecking at the ground, almost at Ángel's feet, partially hidden by damp leaves. He tossed something in their direction, and one of them immediately gulped it down.

"A bite of banana," Edison said. "These wood-quail don't like worms."

Ángel looked up and smiled.

"*Sí?*" he said.

"*Sí, sí, sí!*" I replied, hardly believing my luck.

Wood-quail are as infuriatingly cagey as antpittas, and I never expected to see one here. Evidently Ángel had expanded his hand-feeding operations. Chalk up a nice bonus for the Big Year.

"Okay," said Edison, translating for Ángel, who speaks no English. "Let's keep moving — we still have to see Maria. This was just the warmup."

We retraced our steps to take a different trail, this time switch-backing sharply uphill. The path was covered by damp leaves, but Ángel had maintained it well, leveling its surface against the slope and placing stairs on the steepest sections. We tunneled through thick, damp brush in a dim understory where little light pene-trated. The forest dripped from fog and mist, the only noises the muted calls of distant birds.

Walking in a cloud forest is a hushed experience, almost like hiking through a landscape of freshly fallen snow. The foliage absorbs sound, wraps you in its embrace, and dampens conversation. As we approached the antpitta spot, nobody spoke; except for my own breath, I was struck by how profoundly quiet this place was.

The calm was shattered by Ángel, who stopped us above a switchback, surrounded on all sides by tangled undergrowth. With-out warning, he cupped his hands around his mouth, took a deep breath, and shouted at the top of his voice: *"MARIA! MARIA! VENGA VENGA VENGA!"*

I was so startled that I almost lost the significance of this moment. A few seconds later, a plump bird hopped placidly into the open, stood on the path a few feet in front of us, and cocked its head expectantly.

"Hola, Maria!" said Ángel, looking pleased.

"The famous Giant Antpitta!" said Edison, like a sports com-mentator.

"Holy moly," I said.

Ángel opened a container he'd been carrying in his pocket, reached in, grasped a juicy earthworm between two fingers, and expertly flicked it at the bird's feet. Maria stared at us for a moment with big, black eyes, then bent over, pecked up the worm, and swal-lowed it whole.

Ángel tossed several more worms and Maria ate them all with clinical efficiency. The bird was so close that I could see its toenails, the tiny hook on the tip of its beak, and the bristly orange feathers at the base of its forehead. It seemed unafraid, expectant, perhaps a bit curious, though I had difficulty reading any expression into its shadowy eyes. Who knew what this bird thought of us? There was no telling, and once the worms were done, the show was clearly over. Maria took one last glance at us, hopped back into the vegetation, and disappeared.

"Wow!" I said. "That was incredible!"

In two minutes, I'd snapped dozens of photos of Maria posing on the trail, in three-quarter profile with one leg half bent, like a model showing off her best angle. It was the closest encounter I'd ever had with any antpitta, and this one happened to be the rarest. It hardly seemed fair to count as only one more species for the year (number 1,607).

"*Gracias*, Ángel," I said, at a loss for words.

"Oh, we're not done yet," said Edison, with a knowing nod.

Our *tête-à-tête* with the celebrity now over, we continued along the trail where, in short order, Ángel showed us five additional species of antpitta: Chestnut-crowned, Yellow-breasted, Ochre-breasted, Moustached, and Scaled. The first three quickly hopped in for worms, just like Maria had. The Moustached was too shy to come close — still in training — and the Scaled, apparently having already eaten its breakfast, preferred to sit on a branch and sing at us.

It was like I'd arrived in heaven, suddenly finding myself in a celestial forest made of clouds, with an Ángel who called rare, colorful birds out of the bushes left and right. Maybe, I reflected, as we retraced our steps for a hearty late breakfast cooked by Ángel's wife, this was closer to a fairy tale than a religious experience. Ángel was a real-world prince of the forest, communicating with its shyest animals. My impression was solidified when he casually pointed out a roosting Lyre-tailed Nightjar, a pair of roosting Rufous-bellied Nighthawks, a Rufous-breasted Antthrush, and an Olivaceous Piha along the path.

Ángel has named some of his favorite birds: besides Maria, there's Andrea the Chestnut-crowned Antpitta, Esmeralda the Yellow-breasted Antpitta, and Shakira the Ochre-breasted Antpitta, a tiny creature with a peculiar habit of twitching its chest from side to side.

For Ángel, too, the whole thing must seem rather like a fairy tale. Once upon a time the woodcutter set out to cut down his forest, but now he is richer than he could ever have imagined, precisely because he left the trees intact. His property hosts more than 2,000 birders each year, all hoping to see the antpittas, and everyone pays an entrance fee. When Edison and I visited, Ángel had just finished construction of a beautiful new house, with extra rooms for birders upstairs, decorated with hand-carved antpitta artwork and surrounded by lush plantings of flowers. From the balcony you can overlook most of his property: a few blackberry fields backdropped by a solid green canopy of cloud forest, stretching all the way to the horizon. In this place of life and warmth, I wondered why anyone should desire more.

It's a fantastic true story, one of the best examples of small-scale conservation success I'd ever seen. The worm-feeding idea has spread, too; in recent years, others have started promoting antpitta attractions in Colombia, Peru, and elsewhere in South America, channeling even more ecotourism dollars into local habitat preservation.

Ángel doesn't even have to advertise. He's so busy that advance reservations are necessary to secure a place on the daily tour. When he discovered his wings, Ángel found his life's work. Every morning, even if nobody shows up — a rare occurrence these days — Ángel Paz walks into the forest with a can of worms, cups his hands around his mouth, and greets the bird that changed his world.

"Maria! Maria! Venga venga venga!"

8

Flying Free

As MARCH PASSED into April, a restless urge to fly north swept over me. Millions of migratory birds in the Neotropics — hawks, sandpipers, warblers, grosbeaks, tanagers, orioles — were now on the move, beginning their grand annual migration across the hemispheres, and I could sense their haste to chase the spring.

Ornithologists have a special word for the migratory instinct of birds: "Zugunruhe." It comes from the German words *Zug* (move, migration) and *Unruhe* (restlessness, anxiety), and it is mostly an academic term — used in somewhat-obscure scholarly works such as "Zugunruhe Activity in Castrated Bramblings," published in the journal *IBIS* in 1961. Researchers have shown, under controlled conditions, that caged songbirds try to hop, flap, and jump in the same compass direction as they would naturally migrate. Birds become visibly restless during migration season, changing their patterns of sleep and physical activity. In other words, birds are programmed to move.

Poetically, spring is the season of renewal — a

cleansing of winter with the promise of a brighter life ahead. Birds hustle north in the spring, covering ground twice as quickly as when they make the return trip in the fall, as if they can't wait to reach summer. Migrants of any species go for the same reasons — territory, mating, and food — and so, evolutionarily speaking, long-distance travel is the ticket for better living.

Migration is one of the great wonders of the bird world, having been remarked upon since the days of Homer, who wrote that cranes disappeared to battle Pygmies at the far end of the Earth, and Aristotle, who believed, among other things, that redstarts turn into robins during winter. The reality, that more than half of North American bird species fly long distances twice each year, is even stranger than these fictions, and birds continue to surprise us. Researchers still haven't resolved how migration evolved: Did temperate birds fly south, or was it tropical species that went north? And modern tracking technology has revolutionized our notion of how birds connect far-flung parts of the globe. Scientists recently discovered that Bar-tailed Godwits nesting in Alaska fly directly to their wintering grounds in New Zealand, taking a mere nine days to complete the 7,500-mile one-way trip without ever stopping to rest.

With spring arriving in the Northern Hemisphere, it was time for me to migrate, too. During the first part of the year, I had stayed within South America, from Argentina to Colombia. Now I felt the magnetic pull of Zugunruhe. On April 13, after 103 days and 1,977 species of birds in South America, I left the continent in a contrail and headed north. Central America sits at the midsection of a geographic hourglass, funneling birds on the wing, and I was swept into this flow like a leaf in a stream.

This was no time to rest. I spent three weeks tracking down the birds of Colombia with a sharp group of local birders, then put in a solid five days with an awesome guide named Guido Berguido in Panama, where I hit the number 2,000 milestone with a male

Shining Honeycreeper. After a strategic one-day foray into Jamaica with some research friends to see their endemic birds, I landed in Costa Rica, where I met local birders Roy Orozco and Johan Fernández in the capital city of San José. Here would be my main chance to pick up a wide variety of Central American species, and I was stoked to explore the country with these new friends.

I'd connected with Roy through BirdingPal. When I asked if he might like to spend a week with me in Costa Rica, he responded with thoughtful enthusiasm.

"I will be happy to help you," he said. "This could be an opportunity for a new big experience, and the chance to make a new friend who shares the same passion as I do."

In the same message, he sketched out a rough itinerary and suggested that his bird-obsessed friend Johan might join us for the week.

"We can be flexible," Roy wrote, "and stay wherever we end up each evening. Instead of reserving rooms in lodges, we'll look for little places in towns where the three of us can sleep for about $30 per night. Each day we can plan the next move over dinner, following a general route."

The plan couldn't have suited me better. Costa Rica, bordering both Atlantic and Pacific Oceans and squeezed between North and South America, sits at a crossroads of bird distributions; in one day you can visit dry forests, cool mountains, and tropical jungles. Long-distance migrants flood through each spring and fall, boosting local bird populations, and many spend their winters here. About nine hundred avian species have been recorded within Costa Rica's borders, an impressive diversity for a country less than half the size of Tennessee.

Costa Rica is also an extraordinarily nice place to visit, especially if you're keen on the natural world. I fell for this country years ago, during four invigorating months of banding birds at different sites operated by the Costa Rica Bird Observatories. The locals, calling themselves *ticos*, are friendly and laid back; their standard greeting, *pura vida*, means "pure life," and it is as much a philosophy as a way of saying hello.

No other Latin American nation, and perhaps no country anywhere, has done more to promote an environmentally friendly image. In 1949, following a civil war that left few people happy, Costa Rica constitutionally abolished its army — an unprecedented move at that time for any nation — and redirected all military spending toward health care, education, and environmental protection. This bold move marked the beginning of a strong economic rise, and today the country leads Latin America in health and education indicators. Life expectancy is now longer than in the United States. For years, Costa Rica's citizens have ranked number one in both the Happy Planet Index and the World Database of Happiness. Nearly 25 percent of the land is protected in reserves and national parks (by percentage, the world's highest conservation rate), and Costa Rica has more trees per capita, and per square mile, than any other nation. In the past thirty years, the amount of forested land here has, unbelievably, increased — in fact, it has more than doubled since the 1980s — thanks to tree planting and other anti-deforestation measures, partly financed by a tax on gasoline. The national government has pledged to become the world's first carbon-neutral country, and, as of 2015, Costa Rica was 81 percent of the way there.

Taken with a plate of *gallo pinto* (stir-fried beans and rice) and a dash of the ubiquitous Lizano sauce, all of these things combine for a unique and delightful cultural experience. No wonder tourism is Costa Rica's largest international trade, earning more than coffee, banana, and pineapple exports combined. Two and a half million foreigners entered the country in 2015, about one tourist for every two residents, and more than half of those visits were eco-based.

Costa Rica's modern economy would wither without the national parks; it's a win-win for business and for conservation.

Roy, Johan, and I headed straight out of town. Roy had his sights set on a mountain called Cerro de la Muerte to search for highland birds in the isolated Talamanca Range. Despite its name (which translates as the "Summit of Death," for the perilous crossing before the Inter-American Highway was built), this area teems with life: dozens of endemic birds occupy the Talamanca highlands, from the Fiery-throated Hummingbird to the Volcano Junco, and Cerro de la Muerte offers the most convenient access to them.

As we left the city, I got acquainted with my new companions. Roy, thirty-five years old, originally from the town of Quesada in north-central Costa Rica, had graduated as a natural history tour guide. Johan, thirty-one years old, studied natural resource management and discovered his passion for birds while guiding tours. Both of them lived with their young families near Manuel Antonio National Park on the Pacific Coast and took great pleasure in showing the local birdlife to visitors.

"Do you think we'll see a quetzal?" I asked.

Johan laughed.

"Everybody wants a quetzal," he said. "Yes, we have a good chance at Cerro de la Muerte."

"Excellent," I said. "Because you can't go to Costa Rica without seeing a Resplendent Quetzal!"

The scenery became greener and steeper as the highway rose into lush forest, and the air cooled noticeably. For every 1,000-foot gain in elevation, the temperature drops by more than three degrees Fahrenheit; climb 5,000 feet and suddenly it's fifteen or twenty degrees colder. By the time we'd reached the turnoff for Cerro de la Muerte, at nearly 11,000 feet, we were cloaked in a chilly drizzle.

It had taken just an hour and a half to reach this spot from downtown San José, and I marveled at how quickly we had ascended into a completely different world. How many urbanites ever ventured up here? On my travels, I am consistently amazed at how easy it is to access splendid natural places from most large cities, and yet how few people take advantage. Drive an hour or two in any direction from almost any city center, in any country, and you can reach real, remote nature with hardly a soul around.

Roy directed us onto a side road where he thought we'd have a shot at a Timberline Wren — an obscure, diminutive member of the wren family at home in the mountaintops of eastern Costa Rica and western Panama. We stopped at a wide spot and the three of us climbed out into fresh, misty air.

Birds twittered unseen from the cloud forest. It proved to be quite a challenge spotting anything in that heavy vegetation, but gradually we teased out sightings. A curious Yellow-thighed Finch (number 2,180), jet black, flashed patches of neon-yellow feathers from its upper legs as if wearing miniature, fluffy shorts, then ducked for cover. A pair of Black-and-yellow Silky-Flycatchers (number 2,182), patterned in the same colors as the finch, flitted through the canopy. Nearby, a teensy Volcano Hummingbird (number 2,189) perched like a gemstone on a flowering bromeliad, catching the light with its purple gorget. A jeweler might say the hummer weighed twelve carats — a costly gem fit for royalty — but here it entertained us for free.

Johan bounded confidently ahead, calling out names and moving quickly. His face was round and friendly, with short stubble on the chin and thin sideburns. He wore khaki pants and a long-sleeved field shirt, and his binoculars hung from a loose shoulder harness, dangling almost to his waist. When he smiled, his eyes squinted into tiny smiles of their own, and his whole being radiated with cheerfulness.

Roy was quieter, more methodical and more thoughtful. He often stopped to inspect some tiny detail, perhaps on a frog or a leaf, and he observed birds with kindness and patience. He seemed to know every species of creature in the forest and was interested in all of their interactions — not just their names, but how each one fit into the bigger picture. I noticed that Roy walked slowly, paused frequently, and breathed with more difficulty than the altitude might warrant, but he didn't mention it. His body was thin and angular, bundled in warm clothes that hung loosely.

Johan found the Timberline Wren within a few minutes, directing our gaze to a perky brown bird clambering in the undergrowth. A close look revealed its stubby tail, cinnamon brown back, and characteristic white eyebrow, which separated this wren from the similar, more widespread Ochraceous Wren at lower elevations. It was impossibly cute, and I watched it quietly with Roy for a few minutes until a peripheral flash of green distracted my attention.

"Hey, I'm just going to check something out," I said, and jogged off in the direction of the movement.

I could have sworn I'd glimpsed another bird — a bright green one. Around the next curve in the road, a noisy flock of Sooty-capped Chlorospingus worked through the midcanopy, but I ignored these commoners. I got that feeling, almost by instinct, of picking up something unusual in my field of vision, and now I scanned the forest with a sense of anticipation. The chlorospingus flock disappeared after a couple of minutes and I stood alone, wondering what else lurked nearby. With Johan and Roy out of sight around the bend, I didn't want to stay too long and risk missing some goodies.

A few slow heartbeats passed. Then, like a mirage in slow motion, a glistening-green creature detached itself from its green surroundings and fluttered to an open branch in front of me. It banked as it landed, giving a perfect view: this bird had a red belly, white under the tail, black wings, and a small yellow beak. The rest of its body was emerald and jade, subtly iridescent in the cloudy light, with a metallic golden sheen. A fluffy crest covered its head, and long green feathers drooped over the wings like frilly shirt-sleeves. But the most striking feature was the tail (technically, the uppertail coverts), which stretched almost three feet, dangling like a soft, bright green train below the bird's body.

"I've got a quetzal!" I shouted, and Roy and Johan appeared around the corner, relief evident on their faces. We would have had a tough time missing this bird in Costa Rica, and they were glad to nail it down so soon.

The Resplendent Quetzal is Central America's most famous bird, found from western Panama to southern Mexico. It's not par-ticularly rare, but to see one you must spend time in the mountains between 5,000 and 10,000 feet, where the quetzal inhabits mature cloud forests with plenty of fruiting trees. The male is spectacular — "the most beautiful, all things considered, that I have ever seen," once wrote the legendary ornithologist Alexander Skutch — and was traditionally worshiped by the Aztecs and Maya, who associated the bird with the snake god Quetzalcoatl. Today, it is the national bird of Guatemala and namesake of Guatemalan currency, the "quetzal," and you can find quetzals in many places throughout Central America. Because so many tourists visit Costa Rica, with its easy access to national parks, the Resplendent Quetzal has become particularly representative of Costa Rica's highland forests.

As I watched, the quetzal flew a short distance and retreated into a tree cavity. A second later, its head emerged to spy on us, with the tip of its tail still sticking out of the hole.

"It's on a nest!" I said.

"Wow," Johan said. "Wow, wow, wow!"

Roy watched in silence, soaking in the details. He knew this bird very well from long study. His attention didn't waver as he observed the quetzal's behavior, and his manner conveyed contentment.

"The female must be around here somewhere," he said. "They both incubate the eggs, usually one or two in the nest. She might be foraging on wild avocado fruits nearby."

A few minutes later, the quetzal pulled his head inside the cavity, leaving only the end of his tail visible.

"The tail is so long that they have to wrap it around themselves and dangle it out the entrance," Roy said, "or else they risk damaging the feathers."

I tried to imagine what it would be like to carry around something like that — an extra, inescapable part of the body that must constantly get in the way, but that also makes life more interesting and beautiful. Did the quetzal sometimes wish he could cut his tail loose, and just be a normal bird?

Standing next to me, Roy looked as if he could read my thoughts. All of us carry our own burdens, of course, even if they're not always as obvious as the tail of a quetzal.

+ — + — +

That evening at our hostel, I opened my laptop, found an anemic Wi-Fi network connection, and settled down to catch up on email. Top priority was to confirm arrangements with my local contact in Guatemala, where I would land in a few days.

By now I was used to staying connected on the road. Maintaining my online *Birding Without Borders* blog was the toughest part. Every day, I wrote a new entry and, using some of the wimpiest Internet signals on the planet, contrived to send the text and a selection of photographs to my editors. The National Audubon Society hosted these updates on their website and posted each entry as quickly as possible, with an updated species list, map of my travels, and accompanying photos, so that people could follow my progress. Despite the rigors of blogging after long and exhausting days of birding, I never tired of having this amazing connection with the world, and I usually managed to find adequate Wi-Fi somewhere — at hotels, airports, restaurants, and even gas stations.

Using a combination of email, text messages, WhatsApp, Facebook, and Skype — mostly from my phone (with an international voice and data plan) and often while on the road in a car, taxi, or bus — I kept in touch with upcoming birding partners as well as family and friends. Though I spent a lot of time in remote places, I passed through civilization to get from one birding spot to the next, so I wasn't exactly lost in the wilderness.

Even so, as the year unfolded, I was increasingly glad to have made most arrangements before starting out, as it would have been nearly impossible to plan and coordinate everything along the way. When I hit the road at the beginning of January, I carried a spreadsheet with dates, itineraries, and local contacts for every country I planned to visit during the entire year — as well as a detailed flight itinerary and a wad of plane tickets, which I had purchased with the expert help of an agency, AirTreks, that specializes in round-the-world travel. Some details would change en route, and I could be flexible, but planning ahead meant that I was able to stay focused on birding without stressing over the logistics.

At regular intervals, I tried to check in ahead of time with the birders at the next destination so that all would be ready when I arrived, but that wasn't always possible. Some of my contacts spent as much time on the road as I did. Others barely had Internet access and replied to my messages weeks or months after I sent them. My system of birding with locals required a certain leap of faith: once I'd made plans with people, I just had to trust that they'd show up at the appointed time and place. A couple of birders had to cancel for personal reasons, but I expected that; what I couldn't get over was just how smoothly things were going so far.

Now I had a funny feeling that something was wrong with my guy in Guatemala. I hadn't heard from him in a while, which seemed a little odd because I'd be landing there the following week. I wasn't seriously worried because I knew he was one of the best birders in the country and often led tours for visitors. Months ago we'd hashed out an itinerary including Tikal and the highlands, and I looked forward to our five days together.

His name was Hugo Enríquez. I was particularly excited to meet Hugo because I'd interviewed him in 2011 for a regular feature in *Birding* magazine, where I work as associate editor. He was suggested as an interviewee by the magazine's editor, Ted Floyd, who had run into him on a trip in Guatemala.

"Hugo is at the vanguard of a fascinating new development in birding," Ted told me, "namely, the emergence of outstanding local guides in great birding destinations in Latin America."

That was enough for me. I got in touch right away.

We did the interview by email, and the final product ran several pages, presenting a personal account about bird conservation in Guatemala, from tourism to science and research, including the plight of the Resplendent Quetzal, which is threatened by habitat loss. Among *Birding* interviews, this one stood out. Because the magazine focuses on North America, only three out of more than fifty interviewees over the years have lived outside the United States and Canada. Hugo's perspective, as a young and brilliant birder in a country where birding presented a relatively new pursuit, was different and fascinating.

I felt I knew Hugo, even though I had never met him in person. So when I planned a stop in Guatemala during my Big Year, four years later, he was first on my list.

"That would be great going out to the field with you!" he had replied immediately. "Let me know everything you need."

In a few messages back and forth, Hugo had drafted a plan for us to fly to Tikal, spend a day birding there, and drive back to Guatemala City via some highland sites with several key endemics. We would stand a good chance of finding a Horned Guan, one of Central America's most elusive and oddest-looking birds, and we'd see some amazing scenery. I inked him in, booked plane tickets into Guatemala, and moved on to other logistical hurdles. It would be a thrill for me to finally have the chance to meet Hugo after corresponding with him for several years. In birding, this sort of thing happens all the time — you can connect via the Internet with like-minded souls all over the world and then wait a long time for a face-to-face encounter.

Now the situation had become urgent. With our meeting just a few days away, I hadn't heard from Hugo in months. I sent him a message: "Let me know how to meet you when I arrive. Will you pick me up at the airport?"

As I continued through my inbox, the lack of contact and my imminent arrival in Guatemala kept nagging at me, and I decided to try to find another way to reach Hugo. I opened a browser window and Googled his name.

It took a minute to process what appeared. The first result of my search was a recent post from the *10,000 Birds* blog, which often covered news of interest to bird fanatics. The post was titled, "Requiem for a Bird Guide."

"Oh my God," I said, in a tone that made Roy and Johan look up sharply.

With a sense of unreality, I started reading.

"We've lost a truly great bird guide," the post began. "Hugo Haroldo Enriquez Toledo has died, apparently as a result of injuries suffered in an automobile accident."

The walls suddenly closed in. Everything within me and around me seemed to stop. The article offered few details except that Hugo was survived by his wife and six-month-old son, and that the accident had happened a few months ago. As the news sank in, chills ran through me. No wonder he hadn't returned my recent emails. How could I have missed this?

"That's the guy you were going birding with in Guatemala?" asked Johan, looking over my shoulder.

"Yes," I said, blankly. "I sort of knew him, but we'd never met in person."

Roy, Johan, and I stared at each other, unsure what to say. Neither of them had known Hugo. In a weird way, I felt embarrassed — realizing that the man I had been pestering about a birding trip next week had lost his life months ago. I'd been so caught up in South American birds that I hadn't checked the news, and now I wasn't sure if I would have found out anyway.

When people die unexpectedly, they can't say goodbye to every friend and acquaintance. The family tells those who need to know, and from there the news goes out like a puddle on a hot day: it slowly seeps into deep cracks and then evaporates, leaving just the memory behind.

That night, I couldn't sleep. Hugo's accident was terrible; learning about it after all this time only made it worse, and I felt bad worrying about my upcoming trip. What if I hadn't Googled his name? I imagined landing in Guatemala City, expecting to see him there, only to find nobody waiting. And what else was I missing? This year I had consciously decided to put life on hold while I chased birds around the world, assuming that everything else could wait. As the clock ticked during my Big Year, was it right to ignore everything else?

For me, birding is part of life, not separate from it. I know Hugo felt that way, too, because when I interviewed him for the magazine, I asked him about the qualities of an ideal birder.

"The best local bird guide is a friend, fellow, and field partner," he said. "A person with patience and joy."

Those are words to live by. By all accounts, Hugo was a kind, generous, and passionate part of our planet. I regret that I missed my chance to meet him. His death reminded me of how quickly life can disappear, and how precious few are our days on Earth. If anything good can come from the passing of a friend, it is the renewed appreciation for those still with us — and the deeper resolve to live every day with purpose, patience, and joy. May Hugo Enríquez rest in peace.

Roy woke me up early to see a unique bird spectacle.

"Let's go," he said, quietly. "Johan is sleeping in today, but you and I have an appointment to keep before breakfast."

The three of us were staying at Rancho Naturalista, one of Costa Rica's oldest and best-known birding lodges. We'd arrived late the previous evening after several hours of searching for nocturnal birds on the flanks of a nearby volcano. Johan scored lovely views of a Bare-shanked Screech-Owl with his spotlight, but by the time we reached the lodge, had a quick dinner, and sacked out, it was past I a.m. Now, feeling hung-over after a long night of owling, I struggled out of bed and followed Roy into the predawn darkness.

We didn't go very far. A hundred yards from our room, Roy pointed at what looked like a billboard in the forest surrounded by benches. Closer inspection revealed a vertical white piece of cloth, several feet across, tacked to a wooden frame with a roof to keep it from getting wet. Floodlights on each side illuminated the cloth, which glared bright white in the dark forest.

"What is this, an interpretive sign?" I asked. "It's totally blank."

Roy smiled.

"It's a moth trap."

The cloth was liberally covered with insects: bees, wasps, flies, beetles, and other creatures of the night crept around its surface in a macabre horror show. Among them were moths of all sizes, shapes, textures, and colors, some as big as my hand. A few of the moths had gorgeous and intricate patterns, like fancy butterflies, and I spent a while snapping photos of the prettiest ones. The diversity was huge; some mimicked thorns and leaves, others were bright green and blue, and still others had huge, sweeping antennae like little aliens.

"They are drawn to the lights," Roy explained.

"Like a moth to a flame," I said, automatically.

Was it worth getting up early just to see some moths? Most of these were drab, brown, buggy-looking, perhaps scientifically undescribed. There are 10,365 species of birds in the world and nearly 20,000 butterflies, but moths are a black hole — scientists estimate 160,000 species worldwide, and many don't have names yet. Moth identification often requires microscopic examination of their genitalia and barcoding their mitochondrial DNA, and even then it's sometimes impossible to tell species apart. Moth experts are a different breed.

"Just wait," Roy said, reading my thoughts. "The show hasn't started yet."

We settled on a bench to wait for dawn. Gradually, as the sky lightened from black to gray, birds began to stir and call from the surrounding forest; I heard the distant croaking of a Keel-billed Toucan, then the spaced-out notes of a Scaly-breasted Wren tuning up nearby. As soon as enough light penetrated the understory to see shapes and movement, I realized that birds were materializing all around us, and the whole setup suddenly made sense.

"They're coming to eat the moths!" I said. "This is all for the birds, isn't it?"

Roy grinned.

"It's a different kind of bird feeder," he said.

The party kicked off at sunrise: a pair of burly Red-throated

Ant-Tanagers darted in low, their dark red feathers almost invisible in the undergrowth, and perched next to the illuminated cloth. Each one grabbed a fat moth, retreated a safe distance, and efficiently dismembered its breakfast. Then a White-breasted Wood-Wren, no bigger than a golf ball, moved in to snatch a brown moth, and a Canada Warbler appeared, its white eye-ring and flitty movements giving it a surprised, nervous air. The warbler delicately picked off an insect next to the lights and flew off with it.

When a Brown Jay showed up, the other birds scattered. The jay hardly hesitated as it confidently approached the cloth, scanned the menu, and chose the largest, most beautiful moth in sight.

"Not that one!" I cried — it was one of the pretty moths I'd photographed earlier — but the jay was hungry. It seized the fist-sized insect with one foot, pinned it to a branch, and used its beak to rip off the wings, which fluttered to the ground like colorful shrapnel. The moth's body was too big to consume at once, so the jay ate it with fastidious bites.

I watched, spellbound, as birds lined up for their turns. A Bright-rumped Attila, streaky brown with a devilishly red eye and fearsomely hooked beak, snapped up a moth and flung it apart, sending scales flying in every direction. Then a Yellow-bellied Flycatcher seized an insect in midair, and I reflected that this bird, weighing less than half an ounce, would soon migrate several thousand miles to seek a mate and nest in the boreal forest of Canada. It needed all the fat it could store to make the journey.

Roy was scanning intently, and I asked if he was looking for anything in particular.

"*Sí,*" he replied slowly, but before he could elaborate, his eyes lit up. "There!" he said, pointing underneath the moth feeder. "You see that small flycatcher? Not the Yellow-bellied . . . Yes! It just hopped onto the branch. Do you see it?"

I focused my binoculars on a plump little bird with a gray head, stubby beak, and ochre-colored underparts.

"Yeah," I said. "Got it."

Roy looked extremely pleased.

"Tawny-chested Flycatcher," he said. "That's the bird I was most hoping to see here this morning. It's a range-restricted species. Very nice!"

Like the other smaller birds, the Tawny-chested waited for larger patrons to eat before making its move. It perched quietly in the shadows, which afforded us great views. Then, in a flash, it swooped toward the white cloth, snatched a moth, and vanished into the forest.

"It comes most mornings," Roy said, "but you never know. Some days, maybe it sleeps in, like Johan. I'm glad the flycatcher was hungry today — now we can go have our own breakfast."

The action died out after the dawn rush, and Roy and I meandered over to the lodge's open-air terrace to meet Johan. Breakfast was served on a colorfully striped tablecloth: fresh orange juice, pancakes with strawberry syrup, a variety of fruits, fried eggs, coffee, and bread. As we sat down, I kept my eye on several sugar-water feeders around the terrace that were thronged by hummingbirds — White-necked Jacobins, Green-breasted Mangos, and Rufous-tailed Hummingbirds. Whether you prefer insects, pancakes, or nectar, I thought, everyone must eat breakfast.

We were joined by Lisa Erb, the longtime manager of Rancho Naturalista, who knew all about my Big Year.

"Did you get the flycatcher?" she asked.

"Yes!" Roy and I said in unison.

Lisa beamed. "Good!" she said. "Maybe later we can go find a Sunbittern, but first enjoy the food. It's all fresh and local."

I was glad to meet Lisa, who has been a fixture of the Costa

Rican birding community since her parents opened the lodge in the mid-1980s. At that time, specialized lodges hardly existed, but she had a vision for a birder-friendly accommodation in the Caribbean hills. Rancho Naturalista has flourished over the years and now includes more than a dozen cozy rooms, giving birders easy access to surrounding mid-elevation forest. Lisa, who wears long blonde hair and cowboy boots, is a perpetual bundle of energy; when not discussing birds, she's apt to gush about horses, food, and local events with a sharp sense of humor.

"Did you see Roy's paintings?" Lisa asked.

"No," I said. "He didn't mention them."

I looked at Roy, who gave a self-conscious smile.

"Well, we have two," said Lisa, who stood up and beckoned me to step inside the main room of the lodge.

"Here's a King Vulture," she said, proudly, "and over there is a pair of Scarlet Macaws."

The framed paintings were luscious oils on canvas in a hyperrealistic style.

"Wow, I had no idea he was such a serious artist!" I said.

The King Vulture perched facing away, its wings spread to catch the sun, while the macaws were depicted in a misty forest. The details of each were executed almost photographically, with a naturalist's attention to plumage and structure, but the compositions had a balanced, painterly feel.

"He paints a lot of birds, wildlife, and Costa Rican images," Lisa explained. "We're lucky to have these two pieces."

With that, she excused herself and I returned to finish breakfast with Johan and Roy. We were in no rush to leave this relaxing spot. I felt a great sense of contentedness — Lisa and her friends had carved out a little slice of Eden here.

"Roy, when did you get so good at painting?" I asked. "Those pictures in there are incredible."

"*Gracias*," Roy said. "I've always liked to draw. Painting is part of my appreciation of the world, I guess."

Johan caught my eye as if there was something more, but didn't say anything. The three of us sat for a luxurious half-hour, mostly without speaking, drinking in the scene.

This year, I was learning to treasure these moments, when the world stopped turning for an ever-so-brief rest. My hectic birding pace meant that I rarely had time to take a deep breath. Somehow, the busier your calendar, the faster it goes; it seemed like only yesterday that I'd been sipping champagne on a ship in Antarctica, but the year was already almost a third over. Not for a moment could I forget the time — or the 13.7 new species I had to average each day to reach 5,000 by the end of the year. The harder I ran, the more time sped up, like living each day in fast-forward. But even on a Big Year, I had to hit pause once in a while.

"Hey, Noah, let's walk down to the hummingbird baths," Johan suggested, "before Lisa takes us to see the Sunbittern."

"Hummingbird baths? Sure," I said.

"It's just a short trail," he said. "We might find a few other birds on the way. Roy, are you coming?"

"I think I'll stay and wait for you guys," Roy said. "Go ahead — I'll be here when you get back."

Johan smiled, stood up, grabbed his binoculars, and led the way into the forest. I ate the last bite of pancake and followed along, curious what we might see. Past the moth trap, which was now picked clean, the trail switchbacked through dense forest before dropping into a steep, wet ravine.

"Sometimes hummingbirds like to bathe in the stream below us," Johan said, "but this is a good area, close to the lodge, to see many different species."

He walked slowly, listening for rustling sounds and vocalizations while we descended a steep section.

We stopped to watch an Orange-billed Sparrow, a surprisingly cryptic bird for its striking appearance: black head with a white eyebrow and throat, olive green back, bright yellow shoulders, gray underparts, and the namesake neon-orange beak. It scratched quietly in the leaf litter, so unobtrusive that, had it sat still, I never would have seen it.

"Hey, Johan, why does Roy often seem like he has trouble breathing?" I asked.

"You noticed that he's very thin, too, right?" Johan asked. "Roy has had a difficult time in the past few years."

We watched the sparrow catch some type of small insect.

"Almost ten years ago," Johan continued, "in 2005, Roy was diagnosed with cancer — a type of leukemia. He fought it, but it left him with about fifty percent of his natural lung capacity. That's why he moves slowly now, and why he stayed back instead of walking on this steep trail."

"That means he was, what, in his mid-twenties?" I asked.

"Yes," Johan said. "It's hard to believe, isn't it? Obviously, it changed things. When he was diagnosed, he was almost completely sedentary for about two years. That's when Roy started painting a lot. Now he can be a guide, too, as long as he takes it steady."

I wondered whether this might have kindled Roy's all-encompassing interest in the natural world, and his fascination with the interconnectedness of various plants and animals of the forest. Many birders focus mostly on identifying species, but Roy took a grander view. His artwork depicted not only birds but also frogs, fish, ants, butterflies, snakes, caimans, sloths, monkeys, jaguars, flowers, trees, and landscapes. He painted people, too: kayaking, surfing, dancing, and playing musical instruments. His natural subjects were realistic, but Roy painted people in a looser, freer style, with bright colors flung across the canvas in energetic drips and spatters. All of the images were colorful and uplifting, capturing Costa Rican life in its full, vibrant *pura vida*.

The trail ended at a set of benches overlooking a shady stream, which had several shallow pools.

"These are the hummingbird baths," Johan said. "The hummers usually come here in the afternoon, maybe to rinse off that sticky sugar water."

We sat for a minute while nothing stirred. Then, like a tiny mirage, a Crowned Woodnymph appeared over one of the pools, hovering inches above the water. It was violet-blue and green, iridescent on its entire three-inch body. After a little hesitation, it dipped into the water once, twice, then zipped away again, having bathed entirely in midair.

The whole bath took just a few seconds. There was something magical about it, as if catching a fairy in an unguarded moment. I wondered how few people on Earth have ever watched a hummingbird bathe — a rare treat. We retraced our steps to the lodge. Lisa appeared and checked her watch.

"Just give me a minute," she offered, "and I can take you to look for a couple of staked-out birds nearby — including that Sunbittern. We'll be quick, because I know you guys need to keep moving."

While Lisa ran off to grab her keys, I pulled out my phone to check email on the lodge's Wi-Fi network and found a message from John Cahill, a young birder in Guatemala. I'd never met John but knew who he was. His family had moved to Guatemala when he was five years old, and he'd grown up learning the birds of his adopted country. Now nineteen, John was so obsessed with birds that he had dropped out of high school to do his own Guatemala Big Year in 2014, recording an impressive 651 species while spending all but twenty days of the year in the field.

"How is the Big Year?" he wrote. "Are you planning to be in

Guatemala? I'd love to show you some of the regional endemics and get you a step closer to 5,000!"

Reading John's email gave me goosebumps. Less than a day had passed since I'd learned of Hugo's death in a car accident, and soon I'd be arriving in Guatemala with no one to meet me. John had no idea that I had been planning to go birding with Hugo there. It really felt like Hugo's spirit had reached out and guided John to me. I silently thanked Hugo for sending this gift: now I had a new plan for Guatemala and a new friend to meet.

In the good company of Roy and Johan, I spent several more days exploring Costa Rica's rich birdlife. When it was time to say *adiós*, I had seen 413 species in the country — 158 new for the year — and averaged an incredible 22.5 new birds per day. My year list stood a little over 2,265 species, and I had reached an interesting milestone: I had found half of the birds in the entire Western Hemisphere before even setting foot in North America.

Costa Rica was followed by five whirlwind days with John in Guatemala — mostly in the highlands, where we saw more Resplendent Quetzals and actually got erupted on by a volcano. The Big Year rolled on, as life does, while millions of birds migrated north, as they do every year, flying free to chase the spring.

A couple of months later, in June, while I was tearing through Europe, Roy sent me a short message. He was in high spirits after taking a trip with friends into the Darién Gap in eastern Panama to look for nesting Harpy Eagles. Not only had the group seen the Harpy, but they had also observed nesting Crested Eagles — an even rarer raptor that I had missed. Roy was so happy that his report brought tears to my eyes.

A year after that, I heard that Roy celebrated the birth of his second daughter, then was diagnosed with cancer again, this time in the mouth. He underwent an eight-hour operation to remove most of his jaw, but didn't pull through. I learned of his passing from Lisa Erb.

"We are all very sad here in Costa Rica to have lost such a great naturalist, guide, artist, and friend," Lisa said. "His wife told me that his trip with you was a very special moment for him."

Lisa sent me a photo of the three of us — Roy, Johan, and I — smiling on the terrace at Rancho Naturalista. In the picture, Roy is wearing a T-shirt that says, "Caution: This person may talk about birds at any moment." When I looked at the photo, memories of my days with Roy in Costa Rica came flooding back.

Life's tragedies often come with blessings. With death, there is also life. The same month that I heard about Roy's death, Johan emailed me with the exuberant news that he was to have a second child, a son.

"Regards, my good friend," he said. "Just want to share with you that my wife Lauren is pregnant — it will be a baby boy and we are going to call him Noah! Noah Felipe Fernández Roman."

"Congratulations!" I replied. "How did you decide on the name?"

"We like your name," he explained, simply. "When someone asks him about it, Noah will have a great story to tell."

9

Home

AFTER AN EXHILARATING five-month run in South and Central America, I began to admit to myself the possibility not only of reaching the goal of 5,000 birds by the end of the year, but of substantially exceeding it. Barely a third of the way through the year, at the beginning of May, I was averaging 19.5 species a day — well above the 13.7 average needed to hit 5,000. If I could keep up this pace — and oh, how I hoped I could — the final tally might be a lot higher than anyone, including me, had guessed it could be.

But I tried not to think too hard about numbers as I left Central America and continued my northward migration to Mexico. To play the long game, I had to focus on small increments. And now I was entering the difficult "long middle" of this project — too far from either the start or the end to contemplate more than one step at a time.

I had a satisfying two weeks chasing the specialty birds of Mexico, divided between the southern state of Oaxaca and a lengthy transect across the north end of the country. In Oaxaca I met up with Eric

Antonio Martínez, an astute local birder who once led bird walks for tourists from cruise ships. He introduced me to eye-popping endemic birds as well as their gastric equivalent — the mouth-watering endemic black *mole* (pronounced "MO-lay") that is the signature dish of Oaxaca, rich in chocolate, sesame, peppers, and spices. One afternoon, atop the majestic ruins of Monte Albán, the ancient Mesoamerican city that stands on a flattened hilltop above Oaxaca, Eric and I watched a Slaty Vireo while the calls of Rock Wrens echoed from the pyramids. I wondered whether these birds had sung during the human sacrifices that occurred here 2,000 years ago.

Afterward, on the Pacific Coast in Mazatlán, a birder friend of Eric's named René Valdés hatched a bold but unexpected plan for us: we would drive straight across northern Mexico rather than hang around a resort town where bikinis outnumbered birds. That way, I could fly to the United States from Monterrey and have the chance for a few northeast Mexican species on the way. A few years ago such a road trip would have required crossing nearly impenetrable terrain, but René explained that an extraordinary new highway had just been pushed through the mountains, and he was chafing to explore its birding potential.

Until recently, traveling between the cities of Mazatlán and Durango meant braving the "Devil's Backbone" — an accident-prone, tortuous road across the rugged Sierra Madre mountain range. The landscape is so rough that when the road was constructed in the 1940s, mules were needed to carry supplies for the workers. Deep in the barrancas — steep gullies isolated by sheer topography and thick forests — lawlessness and wilderness have generally prevailed; for the past decade, the region has been largely controlled by drug cartels of the Sinaloa and Durango states, and traveling through the area was traditionally slow and dangerous.

But with the completion of the $2.2 billion superhighway in

late 2013, the Devil's Backbone was dramatically tamed. What had been a heinous eight-hour journey now takes just two and a half hours, much of the trip spent zipping through sixty-two tunnels and across 135 bridges. It is among the most amazing engineering feats of a country that knows a thing or two about engineering, all the way back to the pyramid-building age. The new four-lane freeway maintains an even 5 percent grade through unimaginably wild canyonlands, mostly by brute force; in one forty-five-mile section, a full eleven miles are tunneled through solid rock. At its crux is the cable-spanned Baluarte Bridge, which connects the states of Sinaloa and Durango and, at a vertigo-inducing 1,300 feet above the ground, is now the highest bridge in the Western Hemisphere — tall enough to fit the Empire State Building underneath with room to spare. It took more than a thousand workers several years just to build the bridge, in an area so remote that the first surveyors had to ride four hours by horseback to reach the site.

René and I set out from Mazatlán on May 16, and we rolled into the Sierra Madre with no traffic, no delays, and not a pothole in sight. The surface was smooth as glass, a welcome change from months of bumping around the teeth-jarring roads of rural South America. As we entered the mountains, the road seemed to lift off; its surface rarely stayed at ground level, and I had the feeling of swooping and diving around each obstacle like a bird in flight.

René told me that, soon after this highway was opened, most of the copper wiring was stolen from its tunnels, so security guards had to be posted at strategic spots. The road was also patrolled by federal police, who had rarely ventured up here before and who hoped to use the new access to combat illegal drug activities. For years these mountains were an unregulated haven for marijuana and opium poppy farms; Durango had become a flashpoint of conflict between the rival Sinaloa Cartel and Los Zetas gang, and

Durango City was briefly named one of the ten most dangerous cities in the world for its grisly murder rate. Besides speeding up commute times, the national government believed that this highway would bring modern development and the long arm of the law to an unruly region.

We stopped at several places to look for birds, not knowing exactly what we might find.

"This is all new territory for birders," René said. "We're still exploring what might be out here."

At the Baluarte Bridge, we parked and hiked down a gravel spur and watched a pair of Military Macaws fly gracefully through the canyon, their long green bodies mere specks beneath the bridge's lofty span. A Zone-tailed Hawk soared in a nearby thermal zone, and a Happy Wren sang happily from a thicket.

Down the road, at another side track, René and I stopped again to explore the scrubby forest on foot. A few minutes in, we rounded a corner and abruptly came face to face with two men armed with rifles. The men asked why we were walking there. René talked with them briefly and they continued on their way. Afterward, René told me that guns are technically illegal in Mexico except for hunting rifles, and that these guys were probably farmers out looking for game. A few minutes later we started hearing shots, seemingly at random, from several different directions; one went off uncomfortably close, right under a nearby tree. What the heck? We couldn't see anyone and I started to get nervous, but then realization dawned: the tree was covered with a vine that bore some type of air-filled fruit, and the fruits were exploding in the midday heat. Every time one popped, it gave off a sharp sound like a gunshot.

We arrived in Durango City — still a dusty cowboy town in the style of John Wayne and Clark Gable — by late afternoon, in time for a little birding in the surrounding hills. René wanted to find a Striped Sparrow, a Mexican endemic, and we had good looks at several before dusk, along with some old North American friends such as Acorn Woodpeckers, Western Bluebirds, and an Eastern Meadowlark. As darkness fell, we patrolled a dirt road among the pine trees, hoping to find a couple of nocturnal birds before calling it a day.

The Striped Sparrow put my year list at exactly 2,499 species — one short of the halfway mark. This was the best possible news, for it meant that my strategy for the year was working even better than I had planned. I originally expected that I would reach this milestone before leaving the Americas, and I hadn't yet touched United States soil. With a couple hundred more new species waiting for me in the States, I was feeling optimistic when, with my high-powered LED flashlight aimed into the dark Mexican forest, I spotted a speck of red eyeshine on the ground.

Spotlighting for animals at night, you're looking for their luminous eyes. Eyeshine is technically an effect of the *tapetum lucidum,* a layer of tissue behind the retina of some vertebrate animals that reflects light, allowing the eye's photoreceptors a second chance to process incoming signals. This gives nocturnal species their superior low-light vision, and the tissue is highly visible: if you direct light at an animal with a *tapetum lucidum,* its eyes will seem to glow in the dark. The color varies by species, and you can often guess the type of animal by its eyeshine. Cat and dog eyes glow iridescent green; horses and cows are blue; fish are white; and coyotes, rodents, and birds are red. (Primates, including humans, don't have a *tapetum lucidum,* so you won't see any eyeshine by spotlighting a person. The redeye effect in powerful flash photos is a reflection of blood vessels at the back of the eyeball.)

"René, do you see it?" I asked.

Instinctively, he leaned over my shoulder. To see eyeshine, you have to line up your own eyes with the light source.

"Yes, it's probably some type of nightjar," he said. "Let's see if we can get a little closer."

The two of us snuck toward the red glow, which was at ground level in an open area of the forest. As we approached, I began to make out the outline of a bird sitting on bare dirt. It had the typical shape of a nightjar, as René had predicted: horizontal, angular, with a chunky head at one end and a short tail at the other.

Nightjars, in the family Caprimulgidae, are a unique group of birds represented by about a hundred species on six continents. All of them are nocturnal, eat insects, are cryptically patterned, lay their eggs on the ground, and can be frustratingly tough to encounter. Some people call nightjars "goatsuckers," for the old folk tale that these birds steal the milk from goats at night (yet another bird myth promoted by Aristotle and later reinforced by Pliny). Several types are possible in northern Mexico, so we'd need a good look at this one to distinguish its field marks. Would we be able to get close enough?

René and I dropped to our knees and crept toward the nightjar, which sat unmoving on the ground. I kept the flashlight beam aimed at it, trying to discern the patterning of its plumage. It had a stocky shape with a hint of white in the throat, blackish cheeks, and buff-barred wing feathers, but mostly it just looked brown, like pretty much all nightjars do.

I snapped a fuzzy photo, crawled closer, snapped another photo, and wormed toward the bird until it was just a few feet away. Still, René and I couldn't decide if it was a Buff-collared Nightjar or a similar-looking Common Poorwill. I pulled out my phone, opened an app with the Mexican field guide, and compared the two illustrations side by side with the bird sitting in front of us. It didn't seem to mind.

"It looks all brown," I said. "I don't see any orange color on the nape."

"Ye-e-es," said René, sounding uncertain. "A Buff-collared Nightjar should have some color around its neck. But I dunno, it might be hidden by the feathers."

I inched forward until, to my surprise, only about a foot remained between my nose and the bird's bill. It still made no move to fly, apparently hypnotized by the beam of the flashlight. I'd heard that nightjars could sometimes be lulled in this way, but had never tried it before. Slowly, I reached out my left hand and, holding my breath, lightly stroked the feathers on top of the bird's head while it sat absolutely still, unblinking and unflinching.

My photos might show enough for a positive identification, I thought, but there was one way to be absolutely sure. Gently, I closed the fingers of my hand around the bird's body, using a technique I'd learned handling hundreds of bird species as a researcher for projects in various countries. The bird's head poked between my index and middle finger while its body rested comfortably in the palm of my hand, protected from sudden movements or injury. It didn't struggle when I picked it up, and it felt like palming a fluffy tennis ball off the ground.

René leaned in to inspect every feature. With my free right hand, I carefully extended one wing, spread out the tail feathers, and examined the underparts while the bird stayed frozen. Its eyes were open, and I could feel its heartbeat with my fingers, the only confirmation that it was alive.

"It's definitely a Common Poorwill," René concluded. "The patterns on the neck, wing, and tail are distinctive."

I looked up at him and smiled.

"That's it, then!" I said. "The 2,500th bird!"

To hold this halfway mark in my hand, as a living, breathing creature, underscored how little its number conveyed the thrilling, real-life experience. For a few more seconds I examined it, enjoying the rare privilege of such a close encounter with a fascinating species. The Common Poorwill is the only bird in the world known to enter torpor for extended periods; in some places, poorwills have been shown to maintain a catatonic state, like hibernation, for several months during winter. Maybe that explained this bird's extraordinary calmness.

To set it free, I uncurled my fingers so that the poorwill balanced on my flattened palm. When I switched off the flashlight, I could feel it there, letting its eyes readjust to darkness. After a minute, the bird seemed to awaken from its trance; its little feet scratched against my skin, and then, with a soft flutter, it spread its wings, took flight, and disappeared quietly into the Durango night.

✦ — ✦ — ✦

Two days later, on May 18, I landed in Houston, Texas, with shaggy hair, a farmer tan, and a thick coating of Mexican dust on my clothes. It was strange to think that my Latin American leg was already over. I handed my passport to the immigration officer and watched him flip through the stamped pages: Antarctica, the Falklands, Argentina, Chile, Brazil, Peru, Ecuador, Colombia, Panama, Jamaica, Costa Rica, Guatemala, Mexico.

"Doing a bit of traveling, huh?" he asked. "What have you been up to in all these places?"

"Birdwatching," I said, hoping he'd just let me through.

"Huh," he said, not looking up.

I'd lately discovered that a disheveled, single male traveler with a backpack and a passport full of stamps tends to raise eyebrows at immigration points, and I'd honed my story. Oddly, the sillier it sounded, the more people seemed to believe it, and so, instead of vague explanations like "I'm a tourist" or "traveling to see friends," I just told the truth. When asked, I offered that I was trying to set a world record of birdwatching. Most border officers couldn't think of any follow-up questions. Who would make up such a ridiculous cover story?

I had learned my lesson the hard way in Jamaica, the only place during the year where immigration really detained me. On the entry form, I put "writer" as my occupation. When the officer read the form, he jumped right in with questions.

"What kind of writer are you?" he asked.

"I write books," I said.

"Well, what kind of books?" he pressed.

"Books about birds," I said.

"What birds? Can I see one of your books?"

"All kinds. I write about all kinds of birds. Sorry, I don't have any books with me."

"Hmm. What are you doing in Jamaica, then?"

"Looking for Jamaican birds."

The man became increasingly suspicious, asking a litany of questions. He read every line of my form, and eventually jabbed at a line near the bottom with his index finger.

"You haven't listed a local address," he said.

"That's because a friend is picking me up and I don't know where we're staying," I said.

"You must have a local address. You can't pass. Step back, sir, please. Next!"

Brusquely kicked out of the immigration line, feeling embarrassed and denied entry into Jamaica on my first attempt, I wandered around in limbo while everyone else from my flight was checked through to customs. Eventually, I found a wall advertisement for a luxury hotel and copied its address onto my form. Then I scribbled out "writer" and, in its place, wrote "BIRD MAN" as my new occupation.

When I approached the counter again, it was the same man, but he acted like he hadn't seen me just half an hour ago. Instead of asking questions, he smiled, scanned my form, stamped it, and filed it.

"Have a great visit!" he said, and I walked straight through.

So that was the trick. You just have to fill in every blank, and the wilder your responses the better. After that lesson in Jamaica, I wrote down random hotel addresses on immigration forms — often ridiculously expensive, five-star establishments — and always called myself a "bird man." Nobody, anywhere, ever said a word.

The United States official in Houston was no different. Snapping shut my passport, he slid it briskly across the counter.

"Welcome home!"

+ — + — +

It was sweet to hear those words at a border crossing. For the next week and a half I'd be in my home country. I would even spend a couple of nights in my own bed before moving on for the rest of the year. As I walked past the baggage claim into a warm Texas afternoon, I could feel parts of me relaxing that hadn't unclenched in nearly five straight months in Latin America.

Somehow, down south, I could never let go of the feeling of being on guard. In the front of my mind, I was always aware of the logistics; in the back of my mind, I was always ready for something to go wrong. Because few of the places I visited were familiar, each day presented a series of little decisions that, at home, I don't even think about: Where is the nearest electrical outlet? Can you rinse your toothbrush in the sink? What's for breakfast? How do you adjust the showerhead without electrocuting yourself? Collectively, all of these small questions keep you engaged, but they are also taxing, and they prevent you from settling into a routine.

The farther I traveled, the more on edge I felt. I always knew how far away I was from home, both physically and figuratively, even if on an unconscious level. This is something innate to all of us: as humans, when we explore the far horizons, we need a base to return to. Nobody can be a true nomad forever, as alluring as that might sound; we all crave a place of our own.

I hadn't quite realized how much I'd missed home until I walked under an airport sign that said, "Welcome to the USA." That sign made me excessively happy — not from patriotism especially, but from a sense of letting go, knowing that, for the next stage, I'd be on well-known territory. I didn't even care that it was Texas, which might as well be a foreign nation to me. Outside the Houston airport, I looked at the big cars, the road signs in English, the steakhouses, the sprawling gas stations, and even the hitchhikers with the giddy feeling of coming home after a long sojourn in the wilderness. It was as exciting to visit my own country now as it had been, months ago, to leave it.

I had no time to slow down, though. This border crossing began a new phase — a sprint across the United States and Europe, with little space to rest. For the next three weeks I'd board a flight, on average, once every two and a half days during the short, intense northern summer.

When I set up my itinerary I'd intentionally planned a mad dash through North America and Europe. It simply wasn't worth more time. Ironically, the three continents with the most birders have, by far, the fewest birds: the United States, Europe, and Australia each host fewer than half as many species as South America, Asia, or Africa. Diversity concentrates in the tropics, so, strategically, I focused my efforts on the most species-rich areas. It's also easier to get around with First-World infrastructure, making it possible to blitz from one bird to the next in the United States and Europe, slashing the time needed for these destinations.

My United States leg would be short and sweet: after two days in Texas, I'd scheduled two days in southeast Arizona, two days in

Southern California, several days at home in Oregon, and one day in New York before flying to the Eastern Hemisphere for the rest of the year. It seemed laughably short, but numbers drove my itinerary. I was aiming for specific bird targets, and I would move lightly and quickly to get them.

At the Houston airport I was met by Michael Retter, a friend who had recently moved to Dallas and had volunteered enthusiastically for a two-day road trip in his adopted state. He was waiting when I arrived, and, as the afternoon light faded, we jumped in his car.

"We've just got time," he said, "to see one good bird before it gets dark! Did you see a Worthen's Sparrow this morning, by any chance?"

"Uh, yes, I did," I said, "outside of Monterrey."

"Good!" said Michael. "Because I doubt if anyone has ever seen a Worthen's Sparrow" — endemic to northeast Mexico — "and a Red-cockaded Woodpecker on the same day. That would be a neat trick!"

Michael explained that he'd reached Houston a little early, so he'd stopped to scout a patch of pinewoods near the airport while my plane was landing. There he'd found a Red-cockaded Woodpecker — an endangered species of the southeast United States — and, because this might be my only shot at seeing one this year, we were now headed back to see if we could locate it again.

While we drove toward the stakeout, Michael outlined his ideas for the rest of our route around Texas: First we'd hit the pinewoods for a few species like this woodpecker, then slide down the central Gulf Coast to pick up some key shorebirds. After that, we'd hightail it to the hill country of central Texas for two endemic nesters, the Black-capped Vireo and Golden-cheeked Warbler, before perhaps streaking down to the southern tip of the state for any remaining targets. It was a lot for two days, but the freeways around here had a posted speed limit of eighty-five miles per hour, and Michael was willing to drive all night if necessary.

"Excellent!" I said. "Let's go for it!"

Texas is a great birding state with well-established hotspots, and it was just a matter of connecting the dots to find each species. But my must-see list here was a little unusual, as Michael observed. The birds that people typically look for in Texas were mostly ones I'd already seen: either Mexican specialties that barely make it across the border (which I'd already found in Mexico) or long-distance migrants that accumulate along the coast during spring (which I'd already seen on their wintering grounds in Central America). On my shopping list were locally common birds that normally wouldn't seem very exciting: Blue Jays, Tufted Titmice, Carolina Wrens, and other backyard residents. I had already recorded the rarities elsewhere — in the places where they were common.

But the Red-cockaded Woodpecker, which isn't common anywhere, presented an exquisite exception. These woodpeckers are persnickety about where they live, digging cavities only in the trunks of live, mature, longleaf pine trees in scattered patches of savanna forest between Texas and the Carolinas. That pickiness hasn't helped their populations adapt to a shifting landscape, and today the Red-cockaded Woodpecker is listed as an endangered species. Their nesting areas are now heavily managed and monitored to protect the birds that remain.

Michael's woodpecker spot was a ten-minute drive from the international terminal, and we arrived just before sunset.

"These birds can be sort of lazy," he warned as we walked into the forest. "Each evening, they climb into their tree cavities to roost for the night. Sometimes they go to bed early. I hope we're not too late."

He pointed at a tree with a garish white stripe of paint around the base of its trunk.

"It's easy to find Red-cockaded Woodpecker nesting sites because many of them are marked," he said. "Researchers paint the trees to help monitor populations."

The two of us stood a hundred yards away and watched quietly. Luckily, our timing was perfect: right after sunset, a bird swooped in, landed on the tree, and announced its presence with a loud *queeck* like the sharp sound of a squeeze toy.

The woodpecker was small, less than nine inches from bill to tail, and intricately patterned with black and white over its entire body. Its cheeks were bright white, helping distinguish this bird from other small black-and-white woodpeckers like the Downy and Hairy. It hitched vertically up the bark, moving in jerky spasms toward the entrance of its cavity. In the distance I could hear one or two others *queeck*-ing back and forth; the Red-cockaded Woodpecker is unusual for living in social groups, with multiple roosting sites on each territory, and I supposed they were bidding each other goodnight after another long day of pounding their heads on pine trees.

With one quick heave, the woodpecker dove into its hole. Its head appeared at the entrance for a few seconds, as if taking one last look before going to sleep, then retreated inside.

"That's it!" said Michael. "Come on, we have a ways to go tonight."

With a sigh, I turned to follow him out of the forest. The woodpecker was at home, but I was just passing through. Even in my own country, I seemed to be a visitor, never quite satisfied with where I stood at any given moment. As long as there were more birds to see, I had to keep flying on and on and on.

✦—✦—✦

When I did finally reach home, I couldn't settle. In my original plans, I'd allowed several days at my house near Eugene, Oregon, as the only rest stop during the year. In late May, almost at the midpoint of my round-the-world journey, I thought it might be nice to hang around home for a little while.

I had a few jobs to do, anyway: get a haircut, get my teeth cleaned, pick up my duplicate passport with visas for Africa and Asia in it, buy a new cell phone, replace my watch battery, purchase new shoes, swap worn-out clothes for replacements, spray my gear with mosquito repellent, and scarf down my mom's fresh-baked chocolate chip cookies. Those tasks took half a day. But then, accustomed to birding every single second, I couldn't help feeling restless. After one night in my own bed, instead of taking it easy, I called up a couple of friends, Dan and Anne Heyerly, and asked if they'd like to go birding for a couple of days.

I'd known the Heyerlys since I was about twelve years old, attending meetings of the Southern Willamette Ornithological Club in Eugene. Dan, a retired real estate appraiser, and Anne, a pharmacist, met through the group and were married a few years later. When I was a teenager they often took me on local excursions, encouraging my interest, and they had done as much as anyone to help guide my passion for birds. Now they liked to vacation in far-flung destinations such as India and Morocco on hardcore birding trips, wearing matching field gear and keeping their lists together. As friends and fanatical birders, they were closely following my progress.

"What are you missing?" asked Dan, getting right to the point.

"And do you think you'll reach six thousand by the end of the year?" pressed Anne.

She had been running some calculations of her own and thought I had a good chance of hitting 6K.

I'd already drawn up a list of bird targets in Oregon, and

I thought I might add fifty species in my home state. For once, I could enjoy being the local expert. It was fun to plot out routes on familiar turf.

"I could use a few coastal birds like Greater Scaup and White-winged Scoter," I said, "and it would be nice to see a Tufted Puffin, since I won't find one anywhere else. As for the final tally, who knows? I guess six thousand is possible!"

The three of us decided to hit the central Oregon coast, where a longstanding puffin colony would give us an almost guaranteed sighting of the charismatic birds. From Eugene it was a two-hour trip to Newport, a small city on the rocky shores of the Pacific Ocean, where we'd start working our way north to the puffins.

As we drove, I told Dan and Anne about my most recent stops in Arizona and California, which had been productive but tiring. In Arizona, birder friends John Yerger and Scott Olmstead of Tucson joined forces to exhaust nearly every possible species in two days, even venturing into the famed California Gulch, a remote canyon on the United States–Mexico border, to nab a skulking Five-striped Sparrow. Dan and Anne nodded with appreciation — they'd been there, too. Then, in Los Angeles, I spent two crazy days birding with a colorful cast of characters: a NASA asteroid physicist named Lance Benner; an entrepreneurial nonprofit CEO named Dave Bell; and a twelve-year-old superbirder named Dessi Sieburth, who had just been named the American Birding Association's "Young Birder of the Year" in an annual competition that I had also won as a teenager. Despite our differences, we shared an all-consuming passion for birds, and we stayed up each evening talking about little else.

Increasingly, as the Big Year rolled on, it seemed I was gaining a little celebrity, among birders at least. Word about my project had filtered out, and now I was being recognized each time I arrived in a new place. People told me they were following the blog, and many asked about my recent adventures. It was fun to be feted, but some-times tiring. After a full day in the field, I often stayed up late as the guest of honor, adding to my deficit of sleep.

Dan, Anne, and I spent an easygoing day on the Oregon coast, hitting some scenic spots typical of our beautiful state. These places were all rooted in me from a lifetime of attachment, and I noted all the familiar details of the lighthouses, rocky promontories, shallow bays, and miles of towering sea cliffs. Sunshine lit up the landscape, and hardly a breath of wind licked the water. Lush, green forest lined pristine sandy beaches, unspoiled by development, where seals and otters frolicked in the sparkling breakers.

It was one of those idyllic summer days that people visiting Oregon hope to experience. After months of traveling, I had wor-ried that my sense of awe would get jaded, but now I marveled anew at the natural assets of my home state — which, in 2015, was named the most popular state in the United States to move to. Having wit-nessed the whole range of spectacular scenery lately, I was glad that, for sheer magnificence, the Oregon coast compared favorably with just about anywhere.

Near the peaceful seaside town of Pacific City, Dan, Anne, and I stopped to look for the puffins. We set up our spotting scopes on a beach and aimed at offshore Haystack Rock. Tufted Puffins, like awkward clowns with enormous orange beaks and yellow head plumes, nest in burrows and cracks in the rock, where they can be seen flying and perching during the summer. Each year, pairs return to raise their chicks in the same burrows they used the pre-vious season.

As we stood there in the late afternoon sunshine, I thought back to some of the other places I'd stood so far — from Antarctica to the top of the Andes, the Amazon to the Mexican wilderness. It felt just as satisfying to be here, where I knew the birds like friends

Birding the world requires a stack of field guides far too heavy to pack. I scanned all of these into digital files for reference during the year. Bob Keefer

ABOVE: With relatively few bird species, Antarctica was not exactly a strategic addition to the itinerary, but this Big Year wasn't just about numbers. Who could skip the world's coldest, windiest continent—and its friendly Gentoo Penguins?
Noah Strycker

RIGHT: If you're going to see the world, you might as well start at the end of it. Working as a seasonal onboard naturalist, I kicked off the new year by driving a Zodiac in Antarctica.
Courtesy of Noah Strycker

ABOVE: Birding by mule team in Argentina proved a winning game plan for picking up Aplomado Falcons, Tucumán Mountain-Finches, Maquis Canasteros, Zimmer's Tapaculos, and other incredible birds in the back corners of Jujuy province. Noah Strycker

MIDDLE LEFT: The most powerful raptor in the Western Hemisphere, Harpy Eagles are rare residents of the South American rainforest. After a loooooong wait at this nest in Brazil, I was rewarded with spectacular looks at a three-foot-tall Harpy with a seven-foot wingspan. Noah Strycker

BOTTOM LEFT: Following a breakdown in the central highlands of Peru, Quechua potato farmers saved the day. Seventeen-year-old Rolando ferried me down the mountain on his dirt bike. Courtesy of Noah Strycker

ABOVE: In a year of highs and lows, this was definitely the highest point: Peru's Ticlio Pass, at 16,000 feet. Traveling here from sea level in less than twenty-four hours was a little rough, but the birds were worth some altitude sickness.
Courtesy of Noah Strycker

MIDDLE RIGHT: Torrential rains, landslides, floods, accidents, and breakdowns were just part of the Big Year experience. In remote Peru, the van became mired in mud with two flat tires, a dead battery, and a missing bumper—all at once.
Noah Strycker

BOTTOM RIGHT: The Giant Antpittas of Ecuador are notoriously secretive. The fame of this one, named Maria, quickly spread when birders learned that a local logger/farmer named Ángel Paz had trained it to come to his call.   Noah Strycker

TOP LEFT: Big Year transportation included plane, car, taxi, bus, jeepney, motorbike, quad bike, sleeper train, bullet train, ship, speedboat, ferry, Zodiac, outboard canoe, raft, bicycle, and foot power—but by far the most unusual was "La Brujita" (literally, "The Little Witch") in Colombia, which turned an old railway into a highway using special carts powered by motorcycles. Noah Strycker

MIDDLE LEFT: In a magical moment near Durango, Mexico, this Common Poorwill—the year's 2,500th bird—posed for up-close views. Noah Strycker

BELOW: Eternal summer sunlight allowed twenty-four-hour birding in Iceland. The home of the country's president proved a good spot for watching swans, ducks, geese, and other waterfowl. Noah Strycker

TOP RIGHT: Keen birder Kalu Afasi enjoyed a bird's-eye view on a hanging walkway at Kakum National Park in Ghana. This treetop trail system transformed the once-obscure forest into a premier eco attraction. Noah Strycker

MIDDLE RIGHT: On safari, even the birds can be enormous. This Southern Ground-Hornbill stopped traffic in South Africa's Kruger National Park. Noah Strycker

BELOW: The year was not just for the birds. In Africa, other wildlife—including these lions in the Serengeti of northern Tanzania—often stole the show. Noah Strycker

TOP: A pair of Sri Lanka Frogmouths, looking like plush toys in a clump of dead leaves, counted as record-breaking species number 4,342.
Noah Strycker

MIDDLE LEFT: It was especially satisfying to set a new Big Year world record in record-crazy India. Bishop Kuriakose Mor Eusebius, in full regalia, was on hand to mark the occasion with a selfie.
Courtesy of Noah Strycker

BOTTOM LEFT: This Siberian Crane, species number 4,863, drifted off course to a farmer's field in Taiwan, where it lingered for a year and became a celebrity, complete with souvenir stands and its own government-sponsored security guard.   Noah Strycker

TOP LEFT: The world's third-largest bird after the Ostrich and the Emu, the Cassowary is a murderous-looking creature. This one had two chicks in the forest outside of Cairns, Australia. Noah Strycker

TOP RIGHT: Not seen alive since the mid-1980s, this Golden Masked-Owl was discovered on an oil palm plantation on the island of New Britain in 2015. Noah Strycker

MIDDLE RIGHT: The last bird of 2015, near midnight on December 31, was this Oriental Bay-Owl in the Assam province of northeast India. This may be the first-ever photograph of a wild bay-owl in India—an exciting way to wrap up the Big Year. Noah Strycker

BOTTOM RIGHT: After ten months on the road, I celebrated my 5,000th species, a Flame-crowned Flower-pecker, with local birders on Mindanao Island in the Philip-pines. Noah Strycker

and where my friends were birders. When this year ended, I knew I'd be content to come home.

"I've got one!" shouted Anne, peering through her scope. "It's flying clockwise around the back of the rock."

Dan and I watched the right side of the stack, where, sure enough, a football-shaped black bird with a neon-orange beak rocketed into view. This Tufted Puffin, my 2,701st species of the year, flew on stiff, paddle-shaped wings, flapping so hard that it seemed it could barely stay aloft. Those wings become flippers underwater, and puffins are one of the most elegant swimmers in the bird world, but it was hard not to laugh at the bird's clumsiness in the air.

A man on the beach stopped, stared at us with a curious expression, and asked what we were looking at.

"A puffin!" I said, keeping my eye glued to the scope.

"Oh, that's cool," he said, casting his gaze offshore. "I see them out on the water sometimes, when I'm on my surfboard."

He paused, surveyed the scene, and murmured, mostly to himself, "This place is incredible, isn't it?"

Just then, behind the puffin in my field of view, I saw a spout of water rise above the horizon — a whale taking a breath against the gathering sunset. In these calm conditions, it was easy to spot the blow from a great distance, and I watched the whale surface a couple of times in quick succession.

"Yes," I agreed, with a huge grin. "There's no place like home."

10

Missed Connections

I SHOULD HAVE KNOWN that my worst flight nightmare would come true in the United States. After months of smooth sailing with any number of dubious-looking airlines in Latin America, the wheels finally came off in New York. There, courtesy of United Airlines, I experienced the real-life embodiment of the nine circles of travel hell.

I couldn't seem to get out of the state. My first flight from Ithaca was delayed, then canceled, because the crew failed to show up. Rather than rebook me onto a flight with a later departure, the ticket agent stuffed me into a taxi bound for a completely different airport, where I waited out the rest of the afternoon, only to learn that a second flight was delayed, then canceled, because of thunderstorms. After that, in exasperation, I caught a Greyhound bus to New York City, arrived in the pelting rain at 2 a.m., crashed for a couple of hours at a Manhattan hotel, and managed to fly out the next day. By then I had been delayed for twenty-seven hours. It was a short, infinitely short, period of time in the space of a whole life, but an excruciating epoch within the confines of the Big Year.

None of this seemed to bother United in the least. Didn't they realize that time was of the essence? I had become a slave to time, and my blood was boiling. The airline that boasts the most flights to the most destinations around the world had offered me no flights to any destination, and in so doing had landed me with my second zero day of the year. Wasting time in airports wasn't quite what I'd envisioned for my last stop in the Western Hemisphere.

At least the previous day had gone well. After leaving home in Oregon, not to return until this year was over, I'd landed in Ithaca to meet Tim Lenz, a full-time programmer for the Cornell Lab of Ornithology's website, eBird, which I was using to track my sightings for the year. Tim spends his free time birding his brains out and knew where to find the species I sought in New York, partly because he'd catalogued them all in eBird. He was wiry, precise, and about the same age as me.

The two of us were near Cayuga Lake, looking for common birds such as Upland Sandpipers and American Black Ducks, when Tim received a WhatsApp message on his phone.

"Wow," he said, suddenly at full attention. "It looks like someone just reported a Brown Pelican flying over the lake. That's, like, the first inland record for New York! We've got to go see that bird!"

"Nice!" I said, and then I paused. "But, Tim, I just saw thousands of Brown Pelicans on the Pacific Ocean last week, where they're supposed to be. I don't need one for the year list. I do need to see American Black Ducks today because it's my last chance . . ."

Tim looked stricken. In this situation, it wasn't immediately clear which should take priority: a mega-rare species in New York for his life list or an ultra-common addition for my Big Year list.

"But it's a Brown Pelican!" he protested. "Do you realize how unusual that is? This might never happen again!"

I sympathized. In Oregon, whenever a rarity is reported, I leap to see it without a second thought. That's the nature of birding. You have to go for it because you don't know if it'll ever happen again. Still, for me, for the Big Year, this pelican sighting was a distraction.

"Maybe we can do both?" I suggested. "Do we have time to race over for the pelican, then go find some black ducks?"

"Yes!" Tim said. "Let's go for it!"

He pulled a big U-turn on the highway and, in moments, we were speeding toward Cayuga Lake on our new mission.

As we drove, Tim's phone blew up with WhatsApp messages from other birders on the pelican trail. Because Ithaca hosts Cornell University, with its famous Lab of Ornithology, the city is packed with birders — and all of them were now looking for the same Brown Pelican. Sightings were reported in real time via instant messages. Someone saw it flying south along the lake; someone else reported it a few miles away. The bird, for its part, apparently was roaming aimlessly around the forty-mile-long lake, probably wondering where it had taken a wrong turn from the ocean, unaware that its cover was blown.

A message pinged from Marshall Iliff and Tom Schulenberg, two of Cornell's elite birders, who suggested we head for a yacht club along the lakeshore. They were stationed up the lake and had just watched the pelican fly over their heads.

"It should pass by there in a couple of minutes if it continues straight," they said.

Tim got us to the marina in a hurry, and we ran onto the docks, scanning the skies. No pelican. How fast can a Brown Pelican fly? We stood there, trying to make hypothetical calculations of speed and distance, when Tim saw a speck on the horizon.

The long bill, dumpy body, and prehistoric-looking wings — even in distant silhouette — confirmed that we had our quarry. As the pelican approached, we raised our cameras like anti-aircraft gunners. The bird lumbered directly overhead, bomber style, giving full-frame views.

Tim was ecstatic.

"No way!" he said. "A Brown Pelican on Cayuga Lake!"

In another minute, it had disappeared in the direction of downtown Ithaca, where the WhatsApp reports kept coming. Someone reported it over the farmers' market, then a student on the Cornell University campus ran out of class and managed to see the bird fly over.

"That's quite a tick for the campus list," said Tim, with a connoisseur's appreciation.

We eventually found the American Black Ducks, for my benefit, but I couldn't stop thinking about that pelican and what it represented. On any scale smaller than the world, a Big Year is all about chasing rarities: if, say, you decided to limit your Big Year to New York State, then this Brown Pelican, or any other rarity, would be a must-see. Drawing the boundaries at the state line automatically puts you in reaction mode, with the imperative to tear off in any direction to witness one lost bird at a time. I have nothing against this sort of birding — I do it all the time — but some critics liken such pursuits to ambulance chasing, and at best it is a game of diminishing returns. Once you've seen all the common birds in a given area, it takes a lot more work and expense to find new ones.

The best way to avoid chasing rare birds is to take on the whole planet. You can go where each bird is supposed to be instead of waiting for a lost vagrant to show up on your doorstep. The world is the only scale that doesn't reward rarity hunts. I liked the idea that, by thinking globally and birding locally, I was helping to reinvent the Big Year as a way to appreciate the most common birds in their proper habitats. It seemed almost subversive, akin to a graffiti artist who paints murals instead of spraying his initials everywhere.

Well, it would be, I thought, if I could ever escape from New York. The global approach didn't work so well if you couldn't get out there.

Waiting for my flight, I'd watched the clock in despair as my next planned layover, in Iceland, shrank. By the time I finally saw New York City receding through my airplane window, the prospects in Iceland didn't look good: instead of a much-anticipated day and a half there, I'd now have only a few brief hours, and those hours would fall, naturally, in the middle of the night. With my new connection, I was scheduled to land in Reykjavik at midnight and take off again at 7 a.m.

My heart sank when I first saw the flight times. I figured Iceland was a write-off. But then I remembered something: at the height of summer, the sun stays up in the far north. It was June now, almost the longest day of the year. In Iceland it wouldn't get dark at all, which meant that, theoretically, I could still do some birding there on my short layover.

I contacted Yann Kolbeinsson, whom I had planned to meet in Reykjavik.

"Here's the deal," I said. "I'm supposed to land at midnight. I know that's a crazy time to go birding, but are you up for pulling an all-nighter? Otherwise I'll try to find a taxi and drive around for a couple of hours."

Yann quickly replied.

"Don't worry!" he said. "I'll pick you up when you get here, and we'll find as many birds as we can."

And that's just what happened. I arrived in Reykjavik a few hours later and found Yann standing in the moody, low-angled light of the midnight sun. He was a little taller than me, with brown hair and friendly features. In his pickup, we headed into the tundra surrounding the airport, just outside the city, to see what birds were around.

When I thanked him for meeting me so late, he brushed it off. Only later did I learn that Yann had driven five hours from his house in northern Iceland to meet me in Reykjavik, and then, after birding with me through the night, took a nap in his truck in the airport parking lot, drove five hours back home, and went straight to work the following day.

"It was worth it," he said, "to help with your Big Year! I wouldn't miss it!"

The land was treeless, volcanic, almost devoid of life, but Yann knew where to find the birds. We stopped at several points along the rocky coastline, where Iceland Gulls and Arctic Terns hovered over rafts of Common Eiders. Then, at about 3 a.m., we walked to a cliff with a colony of seabirds, including a Thick-billed Murre and, by great good luck, one Atlantic Puffin — a counterpart to the Tufted Puffin I'd seen in Oregon, and an iconic symbol of Iceland. The puffin crouched on a ledge outside its nesting crevice, its brightly colored bill sticking out like a navigational beacon.

I wondered how these Arctic birds get any sleep in the constant light of summer. They seemed to stay awake at all hours, catching naps whenever they felt tired. A few of the seabirds were snoozing where they perched on the rocks, but many others were energetically flying around, in defiance of the clock. I could relate. It had been days since I'd had a good night's sleep in a bed.

As my watch ticked toward 5 a.m., Yann and I scoped a large, marshy area on the outskirts of Reykjavik where Eurasian Wigeon, Whooper Swans, and other waterfowl gathered in large numbers. It was the most bird-filled spot we visited, and the greenest. Behind the wetland, an impressively large white building with a red roof stood alone on the flats.

"That's the presidential palace," Yann said.

"Wow," I said. "Imagine the yard list!"

The sun was rising again behind a veil of clouds, and its dusky light brightened into a new day. At sixty-four degrees of latitude, just a couple of degrees from the Arctic Circle, I had reached my farthest north for the year. It seemed fitting to celebrate this mark by staying up all night.

From here, things could only go south. I still had a long way to go, people to meet, and birds to see. This brief interlude in Iceland would later seem like a strange dream, sandwiched between North America and Europe, but for the moment my spirits were soaring.

By the time Yann dropped me off again at the airport, just before my connection to Norway, he had shown me thirty-six new bird species in less than seven hours. All of them were common in Iceland but rare elsewhere, which proved the point all over: you can wait forever for birds to come to you, but it's more sporting — and more logical — to go where they are.

The delay hadn't been too costly, thanks to Yann's help. We might have seen a few more species given an extra day, but in just a few hours we'd cleaned up practically every bird I'd hoped to find. After the Iceland all-nighter, on the 160th day of the year, my list stood at a respectable 2,786. I boarded my flight on Icelandair, where the mood lighting evoked the aurora borealis, the executive seats were called "Saga Class," and the attendants were all blonde, and sank deeply and gratefully into my seat. As the barren lands of Iceland slipped under the wings, I closed my eyes, imagined the president in his palace surrounded by ducks, and let sleep carry me softly into the eastern sky.

✦ ─ ✦ ─ ✦

My only other significant airline snarl of the year came between Spain and West Africa, after a quick tour of the birds of Europe. In Norway, I joined a friend, Bjørn Olav Tveit, author of *A Bird-watcher's Guide to Norway*, whom I'd randomly met a few years earlier at a birding spot in Oregon, where he happened to be vacationing.

In Turkey, in the shadow of gigantic Easter Island–type statues near the top of Mount Nemrut, I chalked up the 3,000th bird of the year, a Tawny Pipit, with an enthusiastic young birder named Emin Yoğurtçuoğlu. And in Spain, Gorka Gorospe generously introduced me to some of the country's wealth of birds and presented me with a clever Big Year T-shirt he had designed himself. Nearly halfway through the Big Year, with the Americas and Europe under my belt and three-fifths of the way to my goal of 5,000 species, I still couldn't quite believe that my plans from a year ago were running like clockwork. Not a single local birder had left me stranded — in fact, birders around the world were embracing the spirit of this Big Year, going all out to contribute whatever they could.

But things went awry on the journey to Africa. When I checked in for what should have been an easy hop, I discovered that my flight to Ghana had flown the previous day. A day late and more than a thousand dollars short, I spent the rest of that afternoon haggling with agents before making a haphazard series of connections from Spain to Ghana by way of Germany and Ethiopia. It wasn't pretty, but it got me there.

As it turned out, the reroute wasn't a total loss. Faced with a painful five-hour layover in Frankfurt, Germany, during the daylight hours, I wondered if I might salvage some birds there instead of cooling my jets at the airport. When I opened Facebook on my laptop and typed "my friends in Frankfurt" in the search bar, a few names popped up, including one I recognized immediately: Peter Kaestner.

I'd long known about Peter but had never met or corresponded with him. Among world birders, Peter is legendary. For the past thirty-four years, he had worked for the U.S. State Department in more than a dozen countries, including Namibia, Colombia, Malaysia, Guatemala, Egypt, Papua New Guinea, Brazil, India, the Solomon Islands, and Afghanistan, specifically requesting postings in bird-rich destinations. As a strategy for observing a lot of birds in a lifetime, it's hard to beat, and by the mid-1980s Peter had seen a representative of every bird family in the world — the first person ever to do so. At one point he boasted the world's second-highest life list, and with more than 8,500 species, his is still ranked among the top ten. He even has a bird named in his honor: the Cundinamarca Antpitta, which I'd heard in April in Colombia, also known as *Grallaria kaestneri*.

I'd no idea that Peter was now posted in Germany, where he served as section chief at the U.S. Consulate General. It would be a thrill to meet him. I dispatched a short note before boarding my flight to Frankfurt, only half expecting a reply. A couple of hours later, when I touched down in Germany, I switched on my phone to find a text message: "We're waiting outside!"

Surprised and delighted, I ran out of the terminal and found Peter, who had come straight from work, dressed in a suit and running shoes. He had brought his wife, Kimberly, and they ushered me into their car.

"How long have we got?" Peter asked, as we pulled away from the curb.

"Just a couple hours," I said, and explained that, on this short layover, it would be difficult to find even one bird in suburban Frankfurt that I hadn't already seen.

"I think our only reasonable target here is the Gray-headed Woodpecker," I said, "which I missed everywhere else."

"Hmm," Peter said, and conferred with Kimberly. "Let's try a patch of forest near here, where we might run across a woodpecker."

We spent an hour rambling through a woodsy park, but there was little activity in midafternoon. The fresh air was welcome, though, and it was fun to talk to Peter and Kimberly, who had been following my progress.

"I'm glad to meet you," Peter said after a while, "because a world Big Year is something I've thought about but never taken seriously. But look, these woodpeckers are a slim chance. Isn't there anything else we can look for?"

"Well," I considered, "I suppose there is one other bird in Frankfurt, but it's hardly worth pursuing."

"Which one?" Peter asked quickly. "We might as well try."

"You're going to laugh," I said, "but I haven't seen an Egyptian Goose yet this year, and I think there is a feral population here. Right?"

Peter winced.

"Yes," he said, "Egyptian Geese are everywhere downtown. If that bird stands between you and a zero day, then we might as well go count one now."

With my time rapidly running out in Europe, the three of us drove to Frankfurt's historic center on a semiwild-goose chase. Technically, because Egyptian Geese have been established in Germany for years, I could count them, but they aren't native to Europe. Birders regard these introduced populations as trashy, and I would soon see plenty of wild Egyptian Geese in Africa. But it was still a tick — and one new bird today, mathematically speaking, would be infinitely better than zero.

It was absurdly easy to find the geese, which were loafing in an urban park on the Frankfurt riverfront when we pulled up.

"Ugly birds," Peter said, "but there you go!"

The three of us spent a few more minutes wandering downtown, admiring the more rarified sights of Frankfurt: the Frankfurt Cathedral, the famous Römer building, and a Monet exhibit. It was difficult to grasp that tomorrow I'd wake up south of the Sahara. These transitions between places and cultures always seemed strange, but they were getting to be strangely routine.

With a quick selfie in front of the cathedral, my United States–Europe leg wrapped up. Peter and Kimberly wished me well as we returned to the airport. I had one goose and two new friends to show for my serendipitous layover in Germany, and I was bound at last for Africa.

11

Kalu

PRACTICALLY NO ONE VISITS West Africa during the wet season, for good reason: the week before I arrived in Accra, the bustling capital of Ghana, severe flooding killed more than 150 people in the city. The coastal rainforest that grows like a sweat stain around the crook of Africa holds some of the world's greatest biodiversity and dozens of endemic bird species, and it generates a tremendous amount of rain. Because of my linear itinerary, I had no option but to visit during the monsoon. And so, on a dark and humid morning in late June, I pushed my way through the crowd in Accra, soaking in my first impressions of a wet and wild country.

From out of the horde of taxi drivers and hangers-on emerged a man who seemed to know me. He put out a hand and beamed.

"Noah, welcome to Ghana!"

"But how did you recognize me, Kalu?" I joked.

In this throng, my blond hair stuck out like a neon sign.

"Come, let's go find our driver," he said, and led the way toward a busy parking area.

I'd contacted Kalu Afasi months ago after finding him through the BirdingPal website, but we'd exchanged only a few emails, so I was glad to see him now. He was thirty-eight years old, thin but athletic looking, with close-cropped hair and toned arms. He wore a T-shirt, loose khaki pants, and scuffed white tennis shoes.

"I waited for you here yesterday," he said. "I guess you were delayed?"

"Yeah, sorry about that," I replied. "I sent you a message, but maybe it was too late. My flight was canceled, so I spent yesterday in Germany, of all places."

"Don't worry! We are here now! It is all good! Here, let me introduce you to our driver, Yaw."

A smaller man appeared from a parked 4x4 and insisted on loading my backpack into the trunk, which was full of water jugs and other gear.

"He's called Yaw, which means 'born on a Thursday,'" Kalu said. "So if you forget, you can just call him 'Thursday.'"

I laughed, but Kalu seemed to be fascinated with birth days of the week. He asked which day I was born on, and I admitted I wasn't sure. Later, when we met a man who said he was born on a Saturday, Kalu looked chagrined.

"Bad luck," he said. "On Saturdays you must get up early to work on the farm because there is no school. That is not a good day to be born."

The three of us, under Yaw Boateng's steady hand, merged into Accra's congested traffic and navigated south under a dirty gray sky.

The road was jammed with tiny hatchbacks, beat-up passenger vans, and buses, many of them painted red and yellow. On both sides of the street, wooden stalls under umbrella canopies sold charcoal, cell phones, plantains, desk fans, toilets, sound systems, dresses, eggs, shoes, cement bricks, mattresses, electrical plugs, ice cream, bicycles, T-shirts, plastic containers, and anything else one might pop out for. Every so often we passed a dense market of fruit, vegetable, and meat stands doing a thriving open-air business. Many people balanced objects on top of their heads — pineapples, bowls, gas cans. Most were brightly dressed: schoolchildren wore crisp uniforms, women had flowing fabrics and flip-flops, and men sported spotless white shirts as if defying the red earth beneath their feet. Goats, dogs, and chickens dodged traffic, and extensive mud puddles attested to the recent rains. The air was thick with humidity, wood smoke, exhaust, and the heavy smells of sewage and cooking.

The country of Ghana, wedged between Côte d'Ivoire, Burkina Faso, and Togo, is a tall rectangle sitting on the horizontal part of Africa's western coast. Among its neighbors it is a small but relatively stable nation and has been popular for birders because of its accessibility and diversity. In a short trip, it's possible to reach the ocean, mountains, wet and dry forest, and even, in the northern part of the country, wide savannas and grasslands.

Kalu sat shotgun, twisting in his seat to talk above the engine noise.

"I was happy to receive your first email," he said, "because hardly anyone comes to Ghana this time of year. And I like your project. To travel the world and look at birds, what an amazing journey!"

"It's good to be in Africa," I said. "This is the only continent I have never visited before, so everything is new today."

"Especially the birds!" said Kalu.

"Yes," I agreed. "Almost all of the birds here will be lifers for me."

He looked pleased.

"We will see how many we can find in eight days," he said. "Basically, our plan is to start in the wet forests in the south — that's where we are heading now — then work our way north to the interior. I think maybe we can get three hundred species."

"Just hope it doesn't rain too much," I said.

"Don't worry about the weather!" Kalu replied. "We can't control it, and these days we can't even predict it. For the past few years, the wet season has been very strange; nobody knows when the rains will come. The climate is changing here."

I'd heard versions of this story in an unsettling number of places this year, and many of the birders who accompanied me had complained about unpredictable seasons. It was difficult to tease out other effects, like deforestation and overharvesting, but my view of global climate change had shifted lately after hearing enough local people talk about it. It wasn't just something for academics and politicians to argue about; these changes were already affecting those who depended on the land and environment.

We rode in silence for a while as Yaw piloted our 4x4 away from the city's congestion. Busy street scenes gradually gave way to open fields, skinny cows, palm trees, and kids on motorbikes.

I gazed out the window and thought about the coming months. After Ghana, I was scheduled to visit Cameroon, South Africa, Madagascar, Kenya, Tanzania, and Uganda before moving on to Asia. For me, all of these destinations were new, and Africa felt like the most exotic place I had yet traveled to. Its people, culture, landscape, and birds were so different from anything I'd ever experienced that I wasn't sure what to expect. The feeling of hyperawareness had returned after a relaxed stretch in the United States and Europe. For most of the rest of the year, I'd be passing through rural, tropical developing countries, and now I slipped back into the vigilant mindset I'd cultivated earlier in Latin America.

One of the benefits of returning to the tropics, I reflected, would be a more regular schedule. Each day near the equator includes a glorious twelve hours of darkness, which meant I could start catch-

ing up on the sleep that I'd sacrificed during the long days of northern summer. Also, because of Ghana's bumpy roads and diverse
forests, the pace of travel would slow down. Kalu had arranged for
us to stay in the same hotel, called the Hans Cottage Botel (yes, with
a B), for the next two nights, and I appreciated the chance to sleep
in the same bed twice for the first time in nearly a month — and
maybe even rinse out my grimy, sweat-stained clothes.

For my first session of African birding, we stopped on an
unmarked gravel road through scrubby fields, at a place called the
Winneba Plains.

"Let's spend a couple of hours walking here," Kalu said.
"Tomorrow we'll reach the forest, but this habitat has a few species
we won't see anywhere else."

The two of us wandered down the track while Yaw stayed with
our vehicle. Birds appeared everywhere, many with unfamiliar
names: gonoleks, tchagras, and whydahs. A Guinea Turaco, dressed
in green with black and white eye shadow, took flight with a star-
tling flash of red wings, swooping across the path in front of us. I
struggled to keep up, reveling in the feeling of being a little overwhelmed. Even the most common birds, such as Bronze Mannikins
and Pied Crows, were fresh and exciting.

"Oh, look, look!" said Kalu, flinging his arm to gesture at a
large bird lifting above the grass. "A Black-bellied Bustard!"

We watched the bustard fly with laborious wingbeats until it
dropped behind a distant set of bushes. It looked distinctive, the
size and approximate shape of a peacock, minus the tail, with white
wings and a dark body, spindly neck and long legs.

"That is the bird I was most hoping to see here," Kalu explained.
"Bustards are so good at hiding in the long grass, sometimes they
are tough to find. Good thing it decided to fly just now!"

After two hours, we had recorded thirty-eight species, thirty-
six of which I'd never seen before. As my introduction to Africa,

Ghana was giving me a crash course. It felt almost like being a beginner again.

✦ - ✦ - ✦

That evening at dinner, I asked Kalu how he first became interested in birds. We ate at a restaurant with no walls. I faced a large bowl of fufu: a ball of pounded cassava dough floating in a soupy mixture of vegetables, spices, and chunks of gristly goat meat. Instead of utensils, I had been given a smaller bowl of tap water to cleanse my fingers.

"Just use your right hand," Kalu said. "Break off a piece of the dough and dip it in the broth. Delicious!"

I soon got the hang of eating soup one-handed, without a spoon — messy, but tasty.

Kalu took a bite, delicately rinsed his hand, and launched into a fascinating story.

"I am originally from Nigeria," he said, "where my father is a traditional king of sixteen villages. He is a very powerful man. I have a brother and sister, but I am the oldest, so I was supposed to become the next king there."

He paused.

"But I don't want to be a village ruler — too much drama! And can you imagine a king who watches birds all the time?"

Another pause.

"Anyway, when I was younger," Kalu said, "I wanted to do something else. So I started playing football, what you call soccer. Eventually I joined a Champions League in Nigeria, and then, sixteen years ago, moved to Ghana to play for a professional Champions League here. My dream was to join a national team — in fact, I was going through the process of becoming naturalized in Burkina Faso to play for their national football team, but that fell through. I never quite reached that level, but I did play professionally for a few years, and traveled all over Africa for matches."

Kalu was not particularly interested in birds until one day, sitting down in an Internet café here in Ghana, he signed up for a website that connects pen pals. The site matched him with a sixty-two-year-old birdwatcher from Denmark who had been making regular birding trips to Ghana since the 1990s. The two corresponded, and Kalu joined the Danish man on his next visit to Ghana.

That wonderful trip was an eye opener. Kalu's Danish friend taught him to examine field marks and identify each species, and he gave Kalu a book with illustrations of common African birds. Kalu, inspired, started going out on his own, and became so obsessed with birds that he missed physical therapy appointments and football practices, and got suspended from the team.

"When we were training on the beach, I'd be off looking for birds," he said. "That's how I got suspended."

Kalu decided to retire from football and become a birdwatching tour guide. He had too many injuries — a shoulder that often popped out of its socket, bad knees — and saw a new opportunity in birding. He saved his paychecks, bought a pair of binoculars, and then, when he figured he had enough, told the football team that he wanted to quit. It wasn't a smooth transition. Because he was still under contract, the football club took him to court to keep playing. And when his family realized what was happening, they organized a surprise "intervention" at Kalu's house to ask if he was going crazy.

"They couldn't believe I was looking at birds all the time," he said.

The next time the Danish man came to Ghana, Kalu joined him again, this time as a bird spotter. The Dane was so impressed that, when he returned home, he listed Kalu's name and contact information on BirdingPal — where I had discovered him — and Kalu started receiving requests to help other visitors. He was hired by an ecotour company for a while, learned the trade of guiding tourists, and eventually decided to go out on his own. He is now a full-time guide specializing in birdwatching tours, booked solid through the high season from October to May.

His family saw that it was good business and now they support Kalu's new profession.

"When did you last go back to Nigeria?" I asked, goat soup running down my forearm.

"It was two years ago, to help with a tricky situation," Kalu said. "Recently a lot of people in my village have converted to Christianity, including my father. Nearby, we have a patch of forest that has never been disturbed because, according to traditional beliefs, it is home to the gods. Nobody would dare hunt anything in that forest. But now people think that the devil lives there, and they want to burn down the forest to get rid of the devil. They also destroyed some nearby shrines that were more than a thousand years old."

Kalu looked serious.

"You don't have to believe in it anymore, but why destroy those things? Just leave them. They could be interesting for tourists! And the trees have nesting hornbills, which need large cavities. Burning them down would only hurt the wildlife."

We concentrated on our soup for a while, using the fufu like Indian naan bread to scoop up the meat and vegetables. In Africa, as I would soon discover, it is traditional in many places to eat with your hands, and the food is typically simple and delicious: plain starch, meat, and veggies.

"Well, it's great to hear that you can make a living from birding here," I said.

"Yes," Kalu said. "Of course, it hasn't been so easy this year because of the Ebola crisis. Five of my tours were canceled, almost my whole season — a year's work. I am calling this the 'Year of Ebola.'"

Several months had passed since the outbreak, which killed 12,000 people in West Africa in late 2014 and early 2015. Before my Big Year started, I thought I might run into Ebola in Africa. As it turned out, throughout the epidemic, the country of Ghana did not record a single case — the United States had more Ebola than Ghana did — but the scare crushed tourism across the entire region. People in countries as far away as Kenya and South Africa later told me that they had trips canceled, too, even though they were thousands of miles away.

"It's all Africa to the outside world," one person commented. "Like we're just one big, messy country."

Traces of the Ebola epidemic were still evident. The airport in Accra had a temperature scanner mounted in front of the immigration line, checking for fever among incoming passengers, but at this point it was a formality. Kalu told me that, during the height of the epidemic, he had been so "angry at Ebola" for wiping out his business that he signed up for Ghana's volunteer task force and attended emergency preparation trainings; if the disease had crossed Ghana's borders, he would have shuttled patients to the hospital and helped fight it on the ground. But that never happened, and the tour business dried up.

"A million people die of malaria every year, but nobody cares," he said. "Ebola was front-page news."

With that, he stood up.

"But enough of me talking. We will have an early morning," he said, "so we should both get some rest. Tomorrow, weather permitting, will be a fantastic day!"

✦─✦─✦

When most people picture Africa, they imagine the dry savannas of the east and south, but the rainforest in southern Ghana lies worlds away from those landscapes. Wet, brooding, and nearly impenetrable, the West African jungle is a tangled mess — more *Heart of Darkness* than *The Lion King*.

At Kakum National Park, it's hard to see the forest for the trees. The dense vegetation here reduces visibility so that you might be surrounded by exotic wildlife and never know it. Lush rainforests like this are a challenge: even though diversity is high, it's possible to walk for hours and not glimpse a single bird. Sunlight barely penetrates to the ground, and the trees are so tall that canopy-loving species stay hidden above a curtain of foliage. The calls of invisible birds seem to mock any attempt to lay eyes on them.

In 1995, to help visitors experience this jungle without a Kurtz-like breakdown, Ghana's Wildlife Division came up with a bright idea: working with the United States–based group Conservation International, they constructed a series of hanging walkways 130 feet off the ground at Kakum National Park, like a trail system in the sky. They built sturdy observation platforms around seven of the tallest treetops and linked the platforms with cable and rope bridges for a heightened perspective of the forest. The 1,100-foot-long walkway was opened on Earth Day, instantly transforming a once-obscure forest into a premier eco-attraction.

"It gives us a bird's-eye view," Kalu said, as we climbed into the canopy with a park guard before sunrise. "Now the birds have nowhere to hide!"

Mist rose gently while moisture dripped from millions of green leaves; thick clouds scudded and swirled, and I could feel humidity pressing down like a moist blanket. Just a day ago I had posed in front of the Frankfurt Cathedral with Peter Kaestner, but Europe already felt like a distant memory.

The morning chorus of birdsong was in full swing, and in the half-dawn, Kalu pointed out a few species by ear.

"Hear that constant *oop, oop, oop*? That's a Yellow-throated Tinkerbird in one of the treetops . . . And there's a Tambourine Dove calling down below us, the accelerating series of low-pitched *pu-pu-pu-pupupupu* notes . . . In the distance, a Klaas's Cuckoo — the sound quickly rises and falls."

I noted each of these auditory detections, though I hoped we would be able to get visuals, too. All of them were new for me.

As the sky brightened into day, birds began to appear. A pair of enormous shapes skimmed overhead and Kalu shouted, "Black-casqued Hornbills!" The hornbills, a bulked-up counterpart to the toucans I'd seen in South America, flew slowly over the treetops, showing off their protruding beaks and black bodies with white tail tips.

A subtle movement in a vine tangle caught my attention, and out popped a tiny bird with a streaky head and yellow belly: a Tit-hylia, Africa's smallest bird species (hummingbirds aren't found in the Eastern Hemisphere). I propped my binoculars on the railing of the observation platform to absorb eye-level views, more than a hundred feet high. Looking down past my feet, I couldn't even see the ground.

We passed slowly from one platform to the next, crossing a series of hanging spans. Each bridge had a single board, about eight inches wide, to walk on. Metal cables functioned as handrails, and ropes were knotted into a safety barrier about waist high. The length of each span varied, but most were about a hundred yards — enough to vibrate like a wobbly slackline — from tree to tree.

I had climbed several canopy towers in other places, including Ecuador and Costa Rica, but none could compare to this system of walkways. It continued on and on, tiptoeing and swinging across the forest, draped through the treetops like a string of Christmas lights. The bridges were unstable viewpoints, so Kalu and I, shadowed by the silent park guard, spent most of our time spotting birds from the platforms in between. When a flock moved through the canopy, we used the walkways to follow along.

Kalu pointed out a small shape hitching along a gnarly limb overhanging one of the bridges.

"That's a Melancholy Woodpecker," he said. "See how it's mostly green, streaked underneath, with a stubby tail?"

I snickered. "That's a funny name," I said, as I watched the woodpecker pick off a stray grub. "Almost as good as the Shining Sunbeam, or Wandering Tattler, or Oleaginous Hemispingus."

"There are some strange bird names in the world," Kalu agreed. "Just wait until you hear the Jackass Penguins in South Africa."

"Or the Diabolical Nightjar in Indonesia," I said. "That one sounds scary — its other name is Satanic Nightjar."

Kalu thought for a moment, then exclaimed, "Don't forget boobies and tits!"

"Yes, yes, all right," I laughed. "Let's keep our eyes on this pecker."

The Melancholy Woodpecker, for its part, didn't seem particularly downcast. With a sharp rattle call, it took wing and darted away through the canopy.

A squall swept through near midday, shutting down bird activity, and Kalu reluctantly announced it was time to go. In a few hours of hanging out, we'd recorded more than fifty species of birds from the Kakum walkways, almost all of which were new to me — a phenomenal experience. The three of us descended carefully to the mud at ground level, where Yaw was waiting with the 4x4 at park headquarters. Kalu and I thanked the guard and waved goodbye. We rolled out, heading north, while a steady rain soaked the forest.

I'd agreed to cover our expenses in Ghana, but Kalu had an issue with his bank and couldn't accept wire transfers or PayPal.

"Don't worry," he said, "we can get cash from ATMs."

At home I'm the sort of person who swipes a credit card for every tiny purchase, but credit doesn't go far in the world's rural corners, so I had lately become accustomed to using cash everywhere. I carried multiple debit and credit cards and survived on ATMs. This strategy worked fine, but sometimes it got a little farcical.

In Colombia, for instance, I forgot to look up the exchange rate before visiting an ATM, where I needed to withdraw a few hundred dollars. Feeling lazy, I decided to make a rough calculation from the price of a Coke, which was posted at the next-door market. The soda was listed as two thousand pesos — wait, two *thousand*? If that was about fifty cents, then four hundred dollars would be . . . more than a million pesos! Hoping that I wasn't about to bankrupt my account, I punched in a 1 followed by six zeros. It worked out to $340.

I hadn't had a chance to hit an ATM in Ghana before Kalu whisked me into the forest, so after leaving Kakum National Park I reminded him of this errand.

"Yes," he said, "I know of one machine in Cape Coast, where we can stop this afternoon."

By the time we reached the city, Ghana's sixth-largest metropolis, rush hour had clogged the streets with every imaginable type of transport, from cargo trucks to mule carts. Motorbikes flowed around larger vehicles like sand in a sieve, and cows and goats wandered through traffic at about the same speed. Near the city center, thousands of people blanketed the sidewalks, spilling out of markets and open-air buildings.

In the midst of this activity, Kalu stopped us on a busy corner.

"Just around the block," he said, "is a Barclay's Bank with an ATM on the sidewalk."

"Great!" I said, and jumped out of the 4x4. "Be right back."

I walked briskly around the corner, out of sight, where I found the machine as described. Hundreds of people milled up and down the street, in and out of shops and stalls, practically shoulder to shoulder.

The ATM took my card but, like many I'd encountered, it had a small transaction limit: 800 cedis, or about US$200. I stuck my card back in, making multiple transactions, while it slowly dispensed the entire amount in grimy 20-cedi notes. By the time I had withdrawn several thousand cedis, people on the street were staring at this foreigner with a growing mountain of cash in his hands.

A man tapped me on the shoulder, and I looked up at a well-armed bank security guard.

"Is everything okay, sir?" he asked.

"Yes, fine!" I said. "But you don't have a plastic bag, by any chance?"

Unsmiling, he produced a black garbage sack from one pocket.

"Thanks a lot," I said gratefully, and stuffed the piles of notes inside.

Feeling like a drug dealer, I walked back around the corner and handed the heavy bag to Kalu.

"This is all yours," I said. "It should keep us going for a while. Just don't spend it all in one place!"

"Thanks," Kalu said, and hid the cash under his passenger seat. Then he straightened up and said, "Hey, Noah, I want to introduce you to my friend Cobby. We just bumped into each other on the street while you were at the ATM."

"Oh!" I said, suddenly aware that another man, a little shorter than Kalu and wearing a polo shirt, was standing next to us. "Hi, Cobby. Good to meet you."

As we shook hands, Kalu explained that Cobby Kwabena Tawiah had lately become interested in birds.

"Birdwatching is a great activity," Cobby said. "Kalu told me all about your trip, and I am very envious of your journey. I hope you have a good experience here in Ghana."

"Yes, we have already seen some amazing birds!" I said. "This morning on the Kakum walkway was incredible."

"I am glad to hear it," Cobby said. "I should really be going. It's good to see you, Kalu, and safe travels." He walked away and disappeared into the crowd.

Kalu and I climbed into the 4x4 and, mission accomplished, drove out of Cape Coast. As we navigated through traffic, Kalu said, "I am glad to see that Cobby is okay, because he recently had a frightening experience while watching birds."

"What happened?" I asked.

"Two weeks ago, Cobby was exploring by himself in a remote area, looking for new birding spots," Kalu said, "when he was suddenly surrounded by people from a nearby village who demanded to know what he was doing. They didn't believe his explanation about watching birds, which just made them more suspicious."

One of these villagers, Kalu told me, had accused Cobby of being "a kidnapper," and pretty soon a hysterical mob had formed, wielding machetes and sticks. Cobby calmly answered their questions: he was carrying a Swiss Army knife on his belt to cut vines and protect himself from animals, not as a weapon. And no, he hadn't asked the village chief for permission to walk there.

"You're a kidnapper!" the mob shouted, and they gave him three choices: either kill him on the spot, take him to their chief, or go to the police to settle the matter. Cobby picked the third option, but the villagers decided to go to their chief instead.

When the chief heard Cobby's side of the story, he was suspicious, too. So the chief issued a challenge: to prove that he was a birdwatcher, Cobby must produce three people within a half-hour who could vouch for him. Otherwise, he would be lynched as a kidnapper.

Fortunately, Cobby had cell service and, with the villagers watching closely, he called the Hans Cottage Botel near Kakum National Park, where a friend answered, and he explained the situation. Two people there headed out immediately while somebody else called Cobby's wife, telling her to call the police and hurry along, too.

When all of these people converged on the village, the police were angry and wanted to arrest the chief.

"But I am the one who just saved this man's life!" protested the chief. "I gave him a chance to prove himself!"

And so Cobby escaped a near-death experience.

Kalu said that when Cobby got home he was pretty shaken up. "I went to his house to console him and offer sympathy. See, I told him — birdwatching isn't easy!"

"Wow," I said. "That's quite a story."

"It is one of the dangers of exploring new territory," Kalu mused. "I've had similar experiences in Ghana, but less scary."

He laughed.

"That kind of thing would never happen in Nigeria, by the way," he said. "In Nigeria, people leave strangers alone. Because they don't know you, you might be anyone — even an angel — and it would be terrible to be responsible for harming an angel. The women will take turns cooking for you near their homes, for fear of interfering with something they don't understand. Nigerians treat themselves and their friends in all kinds of ways, but they are very afraid of being inhospitable to strangers."

Kalu and I spent the last day of June at Mole (pronounced MOH-lay) National Park, in the interior of Ghana. The landscape at Mole is classic Africa — flat, dry, thorny — and here, after a week in dense rainforest, I caught my first snatches of some of the continent's better-known creatures.

The Mole Motel, where most visitors stay, is perched on a sweeping escarpment overlooking a waterhole. First thing in the morning, when I stepped bleary-eyed outside my room, I nearly knocked into a passing baboon. Vervet monkeys, warthogs, and kob (a deerlike animal) prowled the hotel's grounds.

"This place looks like a movie set!" I said.

"No, you've got it backwards," Kalu replied. "The movies are supposed to look like this."

The two of us were joined by a park guard named Robert Tindana, dressed head to toe in green khaki and outfitted with a rifle, and a friend of Kalu's named Ziblim Illiasu. At twenty-eight, Illiasu was less than a year younger than me and had been birding for about three years, partly inspired by Kalu.

"It makes you crazy," Illiasu said, when I asked him why he liked watching birds. "And it's such an adventure!"

He told me that he had never met another birder his own age.

"This is very inspiring for me," he said, wonderingly. "I thought they were all really old."

After a quick breakfast, we all crowded into Yaw's 4x4 pickup for a full morning on the park lands. Red dirt roads spidered into the bush. Kalu picked a route that looped between several waterholes and an area of dry flats, where he hoped to find a few specialties.

Birds abounded: bushshrikes, babblers, and sunbirds sang from the scrub; a Rose-ringed Parakeet flew over; and African Palm-Swifts fluttered against the sky. We had great views of a pair of Oriole Warblers, their scalloped black heads contrasting with olive green bodies. At one small waterhole, a Lesser Moorhen — the only one I would see all year — emerged long enough to allow a close study of its yellow bill, distinguishing this bird from the much more widespread Eurasian Moorhen.

Almost every species was a lifer for me, and I did my best to keep up. Some names, like the Red-cheeked Cordonbleu — a tiny, pastel-blue songbird — were evocative, but others challenged the limits of memory. One family of drab skulkers, called cisticolas, was especially confusing: each species looked similarly brown, so they had all been named for their sounds. In Ghana I recorded Whistling, Winding, Zitting, Singing, Siffling, and Croaking, and that was just the beginning; I'd soon add the Trilling, Wailing, Piping, Chattering, Rattling, Wing-snapping, and Rock-loving Cisticolas, among a dozen other species. If Snow White's seven dwarves were born identical twins, they'd still be a cinch to keep straight by comparison.

Near the end of the morning, before returning to the hotel for lunch, we stopped at one last waterhole. Robert, the park guard, led us quietly through a stand of trees where the view opened into a wide, shallow lake.

I caught my breath. At the water's edge, like a living sculpture, stood two enormous African elephants — the first wild elephants I'd ever seen. They were just a few hundred yards away, facing us with long, curving tusks. One slowly filled its trunk and hosed gallons of water down its mouth, swishing its tail at the flies. They didn't seem to mind us watching from this distance, and we halted until the elephants moved off with slow, loping strides.

"Wow," I said. "For a minute, I forgot all about cisticolas!"

"Yes," Kalu laughed. "But, you know, we wouldn't have seen the elephants if we weren't looking for birds."

Robert explained that poaching is not a big issue at Mole National Park, partly because of regular guard patrols, and that these elephants live a relatively peaceful, unthreatened existence. Later, elsewhere in Africa and Asia, I'd see so many elephants that they would almost seem normal, but I luxuriated in this first encounter.

Illiasu and Robert bid goodbye after lunch, and Yaw, Kalu, and I hit the road again, heading south toward Accra. My week in Ghana was nearly finished. Tomorrow the calendar would flip to July. Exactly six months had passed since the New Year, and with half the world still ahead, I had seen 3,334 species of birds, including nearly 300 new ones in Ghana. If I maintained this pace, I would surely exceed my goal of 5,000.

For now, I settled down to watch the colors of west Africa slide past in a vivid stream: red dust, black soot, flowery dresses, straw-yellow roofs, green foliage, bowls of ripe fruit balanced on shaven heads. Judging by the roadside shops, Ghana was quite a God-fearing country. As we drove through a city called Kumasi, I noted the Saint Computer Service, By His Grace Phones, With God Carpentry Works Shop, God Is in Control Sewing and Decoration, the Sweet Mother Bar, and — leaving nothing to chance — the Holy Driving Institute. I pointed out a store called the Nothing But Christ Electrical Shop to Kalu.

"Do you go to church?" I asked. "It looks like the faith is strong here."

"Of course!" he said. "Most of my family are born-again Christians, but some of them keep the old ways. I myself believe in voodoo and magic."

"Really?" I asked, intrigued. "Like what?"

"I have seen things," Kalu said. "For instance, one time I saw an empty boat on the earth with a man standing next to it, making paddling motions with his hands. The boat moved on its own — that was magic."

He went on to explain that, living in Accra, he had to attend church so people wouldn't think he was too weird for being a birder.

"I just don't like hearing about hell and everything all the time," he said. "I want to die quietly one day and rest in peace. So, as a compromise, I joined a Mormon church and have been going there every Sunday for years."

"Is that much different than other churches?" I asked.

"Oh, yes," Kalu said. "The Mormons don't have dancing, partying, and endless sermons — a man just tells us calm things each week. By the end of the service, I am so relaxed! They don't yell in my face, or force me to give money."

His friends, he added, often asked about these services; they would see people go in but couldn't hear any drums or singing.

"People wonder what happens inside, because it doesn't seem much like church to them," he said.

Kalu asked politely if I was religious.

"I don't go to church, if that's what you mean," I said. "But I believe in the power of nature. Everything is connected, and we are all part of a larger whole. For me, I guess watching birds is as much a religious experience as listening to a preacher. Birds can teach us a lot about the world and our place in it."

"Amen," Kalu said.

A minute later, just beyond the Blood of Jesus Sewing Center and the End Time Cold Store, I saw a strange vision: a full-grown man stood tall on the roadside, facing traffic, without a stitch of clothing. The naked man stared at us, his eyes widening when we passed.

"Whoa, did you see that?" I exclaimed.

"Yes," Kalu said. "That was a madman."

Then he flashed a mischievous smile.

"In Ghana," he said, "we have a saying that might as well apply to birders: not all madmen are naked!"

12

The Karamoja Apalis

IN BIRDWATCHING, size doesn't really matter. That is, the length of a life list does not necessarily measure the caliber of its author. In fact, the opposite is often true: you can build a big list by seeking new birds instead of observing the same birds repeatedly — as many of the world's top listers do — but the result is that you'll have only a passing understanding of what you have seen, in the same way that someone who spends an hour at John F. Kennedy International Airport in New York City watches a lot of planes but can't possibly grasp all the nuances of the city's culture. It takes time to get to know birds, and time is a luxury that often goes by the wayside in the listing game.

Expertise comes from focusing on a single region or taxonomic group, or even just one species. There is no such thing as "the greatest birder in the world" — and even if such a determination could be made, it probably wouldn't be the guy with the most notches on his binocs, me included.

Here's an example. A couple of years ago, I took

part in an organized group tour of Ecuador for a few days. The trip was led by one of the country's most experienced guides, who had an encyclopedic knowledge of the 1,700 species found there. Several of the tour's participants had recorded many more birds than that — one man had a life list approaching 8,000 — but when I asked them about certain species, they couldn't remember them without checking a spreadsheet. The guide pointed out every single bird. He set up a spotting scope and people lined up to peer through it, hardly bothering to try spotting birds on their own. The best birder in this group wasn't one of the high listers; it was the guide, who had spent a lifetime studying the birds of one country.

So what does a list measure, if not expertise or talent? Some argue that a list is only a metric of the depth of one's pockets and the free time to empty them. Those critics have a point, but I think a list is grander than that: besides reflecting how many places a person has traveled, it measures the desire to see those places and those birds firsthand. A list, in other words, is a personal account of dreams and memories. It conveys poetry and passion and inspiration.

$$\dagger - \dagger - \dagger$$

My year list was growing by leaps and bounds, but in Africa I started to lose my grip. Everywhere else, I'd had at least a basic knowledge of the birds in each region, but here, on the one continent I'd never touched before, everything was brand-new. I traveled too fast to prepare thoroughly, which meant that I was forced to learn the birds as I went. My capacity for absorbing names and field marks was stretched to the limit.

With Kalu's guidance, I encountered a total of 318 bird species in just over a week in Ghana, 295 of which I'd never seen before in my life. Learning the bird names became an all-consuming task. I mixed up my cisticolas; I confused my camaropteras and eremomelas; I puzzled over the Copper-tailed Starling and Bronze-tailed Starling.

Typically, for long-distance birding trips, I study for months in advance. To know what to expect, there is no substitute for home-work — poring through field guides, listening to tapes, reading trip reports, printing out checklists, and researching locations. Then, when I land in a new place, I have a map in my head of what I'm looking for, ready for the treasure hunt.

Now, though, I struggled to keep up. Studying the birds of one country is different than taking on the whole planet. It wasn't pos-sible to know every bird ahead of time, so I did my best to figure out the African species along the way. By the time I left the continent two months later, I'd have a pretty good handle on its bird life, but the first forays were overwhelming.

My strategy of connecting with locals really paid off in unfa-miliar surroundings. In Africa I depended heavily on the expertise of my hosts. Some were full-time guides, others had day jobs, still others were students, and a few were retired, but they all had one thing in common: they lived there, and they were willing to share with me their sheer love of birds. This network of birders literally meant the world to me. Without it, I would have found fewer spe-cies, made fewer friends, learned less about each place, and had a lot less fun.

The purist, hoping to level birding's playing field, might sug-gest that guides shouldn't be allowed on listing endeavors at all — that any bird first spotted by someone else shouldn't count. As appealing as it sounds, the logic of this idea quickly breaks down, and not just because it ignores the camaraderie that is such a huge part of the enjoyment of birdwatching. I once thought that a "self-found" Big Year would be a noble enterprise, but gradually real-ized that imposing this limitation would be a recipe for ignorance and loneliness of planetary proportions. Refusing to use guides is like starting a business without an accountant, or writing a book without an editor: it suggests that you'd rather be incompetent than learn from others.

Still, I generally avoided group tours of the sort I once experienced in Ecuador. It would have been easy enough — though way beyond the modest book advance that was financing this trip — to contact one or two international bird-tour businesses and have them arrange everything. Several excellent companies advertise birding trips on all seven continents, with stables of expert leaders, efficient office staff, and knowledgeable ground agents. They are happy to craft bespoke itineraries, and some will even rustle up tourmates if you don't have a vanful of friends.

But my Big Year wouldn't work with the usual birding-tour strategy. For one thing, I had specific and sometimes unusual targets in each destination, skipping the birds I'd already seen. I had to move fast — on average, twice as quickly as organized tours do. Though it sounds strange, I also had to miss a lot of birds, an approach that champion birder Stuart Keith once aptly called "worldwide cream-skimming." Finally, for the kind of journey I envisioned, it just didn't seem appropriate to use big companies. I wanted one-on-one time with local characters and visionaries in far-flung places, and I was willing to sacrifice a few species for the sake of that. I knew I couldn't live like a local while surrounded by other foreigners on pre-packaged tours, so I made a rule from the start: all of my guides had to live in the country where I joined them.

The grassroots strategy worked better than I had dared hope, and I stuck to it through virtually the entire year. I scheduled only two group tours, in South Africa and Tanzania, to save money: in both cases, companions would dramatically reduce the cost of exploring the big national parks, which were geared toward groups on safari. I'd still have local guides but would be joined by other birders on each leg — several independent travelers in South Africa and a group of American friends in Tanzania — for a more formal tour experience. In these places, for the first time this year, I'd be part of a lister crowd. I just hoped they could keep pace.

✦ – ✦ – ✦

My mid-July arrival in South Africa came at 1 a.m. on a redeye from Cameroon to Johannesburg. Throughout seventeen days in the West African wet season, in a wide river of humanity, I'd seen exactly two other white people — a pair of missionaries in a remote village in Ghana — and it felt strange to be surrounded by white faces. Was this reverse culture shock? I'd gotten so used to being a minority that I only noticed when I no longer stuck out.

The past nine days in Cameroon had been an intense journey into the heart of darkness. I'd seen some amazing birds, including an odd species called a Gray-necked Rockfowl, which attaches its mud nest to the vertical walls of rainforest caves. And I'd witnessed wonderful places, from the coast to the misty slopes of Mount Cameroon, the tallest mountain in West Africa. But conditions in Cameroon were challenging and dispiriting. When I arrived, the man I'd contacted, Benji — the only local birder I could find in all of Cameroon — told me he'd spent the expense money I wired ahead without making any reservations for us, and he asked for a loan to cover our trip, which he never paid back. A large man without front teeth, Benji said between cigarettes that tourism had crashed in Cameroon after Boko Haram guerrillas invaded the northern part of the country, and that he was surviving by selling knickknacks at a botanical garden in Douala. I felt sorry for him, but also chagrined that he'd applied my entire Cameroon budget to his personal debts.

The roads, muddy from monsoon rains, were a nightmare. We had breakdowns, delays, detours, more breakdowns, and more delays. I slept in buildings that in other countries would have been condemned; most had no other guests. For the better part of nine days we got along with no electricity, running water, or toilet paper while eating everything — mostly rice and goat meat for breakfast, lunch, and dinner — with our hands. Washing clothes was out of the question, so the whole time I wore the same mud-and-sweat-soaked shirt and pants, which in the heavy humidity never dried out. Birding in Cameroon is hard enough without trying to do it on a shoestring during the wet season, and it was heartbreaking to know that despite all our efforts I missed a lot of birds. I left Douala while heavy rains flooded the city; my last memory is of an outdoor market where sellers and customers sloshed around in three feet of water and mud. Four months later, in October, hundreds of U.S. troops deployed to north Cameroon to help fight the guerrillas in what would become a long and indeterminate occupation.

I caught a little sleep on the floor of the Johannesburg airport before Wayne Jones, the leader of my South African tour, appeared in crisp attire and a clean white van to pick me up at 6 a.m. The other five participants had arrived the previous day and were waking up at a nearby hotel. Appraising my ragged appearance, Wayne said, "Let's get you to the hotel to freshen up — you can grab a quick shower there before we head out."

"Is there hot running water?" I asked.

"Of course — it's a hotel!" Wayne said.

For once, I was glad to be on an organized tour. The constant struggle of Cameroon had worn me down, and I needed a mental break. For this South African stretch, I wouldn't have to worry about anything except finding birds. The tour had been organized by Rockjumper, the world's biggest birding tour operator (by set departures), which is headquartered in Johannesburg. I couldn't wait to relax a little and hang out with a convivial group of birders.

Soaping up in the gloriously steamy shower, I wondered who they might be.

Wayne, tall and slender with short hair and a craggy smile, lived in Johannesburg and worked full-time leading tours for Rock-jumper. After this tour he'd be headed straight to Namibia, rotating with other assignments in places like Ethiopia, Kenya, and India. We were now in his home territory: eastern South Africa, home of Kruger National Park and all its natural wonders.

As Wayne drove the van, I gradually got to know the rest of the group: Martha Miller (a curriculum specialist) and Janine Gregory (an economist) from Canada; Brian Rapoza (an environmental teacher) and Alan Mitchnick (a biologist) from the United States; and Klas Magnus Karlsson, a quirky high school physics teacher from Sweden and my roommate for the week. Janine had been talked into the trip by Martha on the strength of cute safari animals, but the rest of us were serious birders.

We were all excited for what the next few days would bring. Kruger National Park, on the border with Mozambique and Zimbabwe, is the size of Israel. More than five hundred species of birds have been recorded within its borders, but the park is famed for hosting the "big five," supposedly the most difficult African animals to hunt — the lion, leopard, elephant, buffalo, and rhinoceros — along with other safari creatures: cheetah, zebra, giraffe, wildebeest, hippo, hyena, impala, rhebok, steenbok, blesbok, eland, kudu, hartebeest, suni, topi, oribi, duiker, nyala, sitatunga, klipspringer. This is South Africa's flagship reserve, visited by more than a million tourists a year, outfitted with two dozen safari lodges and hundreds of park rangers. At night everyone must stay within designated camps surrounded by high fences — if you're not back by 5:30 p.m., you'll pay a stiff fine — and then the park becomes a reverse zoo, with free-roaming animals surrounding the locked-up humans.

And birds! Some, like the Southern Ground-Hornbill and Kori Bustard, are as big and charismatic as the furry animals. Birds of the African savanna are relatively easy to see; if South America, with its thousands of species, is known as "the bird continent," then Africa is "the bird watching continent" for its raw spectacle. On safari, you don't have to spend hours stalking cryptic species through slimy jungles, because the birds sit in plain view.

Kruger's park rules forbid people to exit their vehicles lest a predator suddenly leap from the bushes, so everyone drives slowly around a network of one-lane roads, circling like the White-backed Vultures that soar overhead. As Wayne piloted our van into the park, we leapfrogged between traffic jams with good results: at one group of cars, a pride of lions emerged from the bush within spitting distance, and at another pile-up a zebra carcass seethed in scavenging hyenas and jackals. A passerby rolled down his window to direct us to a nearby group of white rhinos. Later, joining three other cars at a wide pullout, we watched two leopards lounging in the grass, barely visible on a hidden sandbank.

Each time we stopped, other vehicles appeared behind our van's bumper, their occupants straining to see what we'd spotted. It was like pointing at the sky on a crowded street — pretty soon everyone is looking up. As soon as Wayne hit the brakes five cars would stack up behind us, hoping we'd spotted a big cat. When they realized it was just a dove, or a kingfisher, most people drove off, embarrassed or annoyed, as if they'd been duped. Eventually, we hit on a solution that worked pretty well: whenever anyone got close, one of us rolled down the window and flashed a copy of *Birds of South Africa*. We called this ploy "flipping them the bird."

Never mind the big animals, the birding was fantastic. Flocks tumbled through the bushveld, and whenever our group came across one of these concentrations chaos erupted inside the van.

"Green-winged Pytilia!" shouted Wayne, stopping abruptly on

a desolate stretch of dirt road. "Look for the little red-and-green bird on the ground, just underneath the shrubs on the left."

"I see a Chinspot Batis, too!" Alan added.

"Oh, what's that bird next to the batis?" exclaimed Martha. "It's bright orange-yellow underneath!"

"Sulphur-breasted Bushshrike," Wayne said. "Does everybody see it?"

I found myself wondering how I could get more excited about a Cape Crombec — a beige-gray bird less than five inches long — than a whole herd of zebras, and remembered something Kalu had said in Ghana: "We wouldn't have seen the elephants if we weren't looking for birds." His words resonated more deeply the more I considered them.

My year list was helping me appreciate our Earth at different scales. Sometimes it's easier to absorb a large canvas, like Kruger, by examining it one small detail at a time — the difference between breezing through an art exhibit and stopping to ponder each piece. I felt more intimately connected to this landscape through the intricate plumage of a Miombo Wren-Warbler than the sight of a thousand wildebeest, because the wren-warbler required closer attention. This pursuit of birds, with prolonged focus and effort, was like a portal to the world, from the tiniest detail to the biggest panorama.

In a park full of tourists on safari, I was glad to be in a group of birders. All day we discussed nothing but our shared obsession. Nobody called us idiosyncratic for traveling halfway around the world, to one of the most spectacular big-game wildlife extravaganzas, to stare at diminutive petronias and tit-flycatchers. Cocooned inside the van with Wayne at the wheel and a nonstop stream of birds outside, we were fully immersed. If a flow state is bliss, then in this company I experienced pure contentment.

Later, adding up the day's sightings, I discovered that the Gray

Go-away-bird (named for its "Go 'way!" catcall) was bird number 3,500 — a new milestone, and I hadn't even realized it! That number hardly captured the thrill of exploring Kruger National Park with a van of happy birders. It was true that my list motivated me to explore the world and measure progress, but the list itself was no more descriptive than a phone book — a crude proxy for riches beyond numbers or words.

+ – + – +

In late August, in northern Tanzania, I wrapped up my African safari with several days in the Serengeti. The landscape here is much different than the bushveld of South Africa: wide open plains, baobabs, silhouetted acacias, the kind of long vistas where your eyes can get lost with your soul. East Africa is deservedly famous for its savannas, and the Serengeti epitomizes this landscape — in the local Maasai language, the word means "the place where the land runs on forever." The Serengeti's reputation can transcend even its own expanse: in a list compiled by *USA Today* and *Good Morning America*, it was chosen as one of the "New Seven Wonders of the World," alongside polar ice caps, Mayan ruins, and "the Internet."

By now I was on a first-name basis with the African megafauna. I had spent the past couple weeks in South Africa, birding first with Wayne Jones and then for a few days around Cape Town and the Western Cape with two sharp young birders, Ethan Kistler and Callan Cohen. I followed that with a great run in Madagascar, with Jacky Ratiantsihoarana, and in Kenya with a bird expert named Joseph Aengwo. Now, in Tanzania, I was joined by three friends from Oregon who hadn't yet experienced a full-on safari: Harv Schubothe, Kelle Herrick, and David Heath. The four of us met a local birder named Anthony Raphael and a driver, Roger Msengi, who packed us into a modified Land Cruiser, and our group rolled straight toward the Serengeti.

It was a relief that everyone had arrived OK. To help share the costs of the Land Cruiser, driver, and accommodations, I had recruited other birders for this leg — the only place where I went out of my way to sign up birding companions — and was delighted that the three Oregonians had agreed to come along. But when I wired thousands of dollars for the trip months ahead of time, a hacker cleverly diverted the funds to an account in Uganda. I never got the money back despite an extended bank investigation. The Tanzania outfitter's ground agent sent me a series of messages admitting that the company's email had been hacked, unfortunately, but blamed me for sending the money to the wrong place and insisted that I wire more (to their proper account this time) or the trip would be canceled. The whole costly business left such a bad taste that I would have canceled if I hadn't already convinced three of my friends to join me.

As it turned out, maybe I should have canceled anyway.

The reason was serious: after a productive stretch elsewhere in South and East Africa, I had just about run out of birds. With a sinking heart, I realized that I'd already seen almost all of the northern Tanzania species in Kenya and other countries. The bird life of East Africa had seemed so diverse that, when plotting my route, I hadn't thought twice about scheduling weeks here. Now, locked into a twelve-day trip, it was obvious that the pace of new sightings would dramatically slow down. There was nothing I could do about it.

Such is the tradeoff of planning ahead: a fully booked itinerary allows more time in the field instead of working out the logistics en route, but it also permits less flexibility. For the most part, I was committed to arrangements I'd made nearly a year ago, before leaving home. Back then, lacking a blueprint or optimal schedule to follow, I had laid out a logical route based on my best guess. During the Big Year, as I was learning, I couldn't easily change plans without letting people down, and I was keenly aware that many local birders had gone out of their way to give their time as guides and hosts. If I'd badly overestimated my time in Tanzania, I would just have to make the most of it.

As the days progressed, the number of new species dwindled. In twelve days in Tanzania, I found only 80 new birds — on several days, just one — dragging down my daily average for the year. Nonetheless, I hit a huge milestone — my 4,000th species, a Mountain Gray Woodpecker in a shade-grown coffee plantation — and savored the sights and sounds of this beautiful country. Tanzania abounds in big wildlife and landscapes, from the Ngorongoro Crater — by some measures, the world's largest caldera — to Mount Kilimanjaro, the highest mountain in Africa. The actual Serengeti was like a movie of itself: the place where millions of wildebeest migrate across crocodile-infested rivers, the land that inspired *The Lion King*, and the home of Maasai warriors. Fossils discovered near Serengeti National Park suggest that some of the first humans lived on this spot. Two million years later, this landscape remains timeless.

+ – + – +

The bird I got most excited about in Tanzania was the Karamoja Apalis. The name evokes nothing for most people, perhaps not even for most birders, and that's exactly why I wanted to see one: it's a birder's bird, an aficionado's tick. In a country with a reputation for large wildlife, I held out for a tiny, obscure creature.

The Karamoja Apalis is quite small, less than five inches long including a slender tail, and weighs less than two nickels. It's not much to look at, pale gray above and whitish below, with white patches on the wings and a diminutive bill. It vaguely resembles a New World gnatcatcher and is somewhat related, though the Apalis genus is closer to the cisticola family. But whatever the bird's shortcomings in appearance, it makes up for with rarity. This species is one of Africa's most range-restricted birds, known from only a few sites in Uganda (in the Karamoja region), south Kenya, and northern Tanzania, where it is confined to patches of whistling thorn woodland. It wasn't found in the Serengeti until the 1990s and is still hard to see; to encounter one, you must know where to look.

We set out for an eventful morning on the Serengeti Plains. In short order, our group found a leopard up a tree, a cheetah on a kill, and a pack of thirteen lions napping in the shade of an isolated acacia tree. To see the three big cats in one session was quite a trick, and I was as excited as everyone else (I counted twenty-seven safari vehicles parked bumper-to-bumper at the lion spot), but we were on the lookout for birds, too. I added several new species before lunch, including a Fischer's Lovebird, Red-throated Tit, and Temminck's Courser — an odd species of big-eyed, droopy-billed shorebird that prefers to nest on freshly burned grassland.

In the afternoon, after a quick stop at a picnic area where Gray-headed Social-Weavers nested in a small colony, Anthony suggested we try for the apalis.

"It's in a more remote section of the park," he said, "away from most of the tourists."

"That sounds great!" I said, and Harv, Kelle, and David readily agreed.

"We can see other birds along the way," Anthony said, "but the apalis is the main target."

Roger navigated our open-roofed Land Cruiser down a series of dusty dirt tracks, occasionally crossing streams and shoving through thorny acacia limbs, while tsetse flies — the big, blood-sucking insects responsible for transmitting African *trypanosomiasis*, better known as sleeping sickness — swarmed around us. The tsetses were slow and easy to swat, though one managed to crawl up my pant leg and chomp down. It felt like a horsefly bite. When I reflexively smacked it, the fly's body exploded, smearing my pants with blood. Contracting sleeping sickness in Tanzania carries a low risk, but I didn't want to push my luck; the disease involves a brain parasite that, left untreated, results in neurological symptoms and eventually death.

It took half the afternoon to reach Anthony's stakeout. By the time Roger stopped our Land Cruiser and turned off the engine, we hadn't seen another vehicle in hours, which made a nice change. We disembarked next to a patch of thorny forest and began to look for little gray birds.

The Karamoja Apalis prefers whistling thorn, a type of acacia tree that grows in sparse woodlands. This tree produces hollow, gourdlike thorns, which are occupied by symbiotic ants that help defend against herbivores. Because appropriate stands of whistling thorn are found only in places with the right soil, the apalis has a very limited range.

Finding this bird is mostly a matter of tracking down the right habitat. Once on the scene, it didn't take us long to spot a Karamoja Apalis — species number 4,028 — flitting among thorny branches. I snapped a few photos, put my camera down, and watched for a while as it grabbed several small insects, probing delicately, somehow managing not to skewer its eyeballs on the thorns.

This bird was a real find, but greater satisfaction came the next day, when I signed the guest book at one of the park lodges. Flipping through the pages, all the notable sightings seemed to revolve around lions, leopards, and cheetahs, punctuated by the occasional hyena or elephant encounter. I didn't even hesitate. In block caps, I wrote "KARAMOJA APALIS!!!!!" and went away with a grin stretching from one ear to the other.

On the way back to Arusha I slouched next to Harv while Roger drove. Anthony occupied his usual spot in the passenger seat, and Kelle was in the back. David had left us to take a separate transport for Pemba Island, waving goodbye as he hopped into a different vehicle. As we drove along a deserted stretch of straight, paved highway that afternoon, we jabbered happily about our latest sightings and looked forward to the next stops.

In an instant, with a sound like a cannon blast, the back right tire of the Land Cruiser blew out at seventy miles per hour and the vehicle, shuddering violently, left the pavement. It happened too fast for me to process, except that Harv and I hung on to each other as we hit the ditch. Roger didn't try to swerve; instead, he guided us across the opposing lane, down an embankment, and into the bush alongside the road, where we came to rest in a cloud of dust. Luckily there was nothing to hit and no traffic.

After a shaky moment, all of us climbed out to inspect the exploded tire, a heavy model designed for off-roading. Harv and Kelle hugged.

"I'm glad you're okay, buddy," Harv said to me.

We were a silent and sober bunch. I couldn't help thinking what might have happened if not for Roger's capable hands at the wheel.

Within a few minutes Roger had replaced the tire. We were off again, the near-miss receding behind us, and the next bird somewhere ahead on the long Serengeti horizon.

13

A New World Record

On AUGUST 23, while I was in northern Tanzania, a new post appeared on the website of Arjan Dwarshuis, the Dutch birder who had announced months earlier his aim to travel the world for a Big Year in 2016. I had periodically checked Arjan's blog since learning about him from Gunnar Engblom in Peru in March, but aside from a couple of minor clarifications, Arjan hadn't posted much. The last update on his site was more than three months old when this new post popped up.

"I've been very busy with planning my world big year," he began, "and I am very, very pleased to say that the flights for the first three months are booked!"

He added that he'd convinced friends to join him for parts of his trip, and that he was looking forward to getting started in a few months. The next paragraph snapped me to attention.

"As Noah Strycker is doing extremely well on his world big year and will surely set an incredible, very hard to beat record, I had to step up my game," Arjan wrote. "And so I did . . ."

The post went on to explain, in detail, Arjan's projected Big Year itinerary, set to begin the instant mine ended, at midnight on December 31. My jaw dropped as I read further. He had scrapped his original twenty-three-country map in favor of a route remarkably similar to mine: in all of South, Central, and North America, he now listed exactly the same countries I had visited, with added layovers in Suriname, the Dominican Republic, and Cuba. His route was also similar in Africa and Asia, tweaked here and there to squeeze out a few more birds; most of the differences involved cutting adventurous destinations (Antarctica, Cameroon, Myanmar) and streamlining the number of days in places where I'd seen fewer species. Just like me, he announced that he would travel continuously for the whole year, contribute to a carbon offset program, track his sightings on an Internet database, and post regular updates with a blog. It was like reading about my own project through the words of someone else!

Should I be flattered, uneasy, or excited by this development? I wasn't sure. One thing was certain, though: I had some serious competition. Arjan would follow a bird taxonomy favored by Europeans, different from the Clements Checklist that I was using on eBird, so he would play literally by different rules and could count a couple hundred species not recognized by Clements. Also, with a leap year, he would have an extra day. But his biggest advantage, I reflected, would be the benefit of hindsight. Having watched my whole effort unfold, he could learn from my successes and mistakes, and he clearly meant to go after whatever record I set.

Ah, well, I thought, you never can tell what the future will bring. If this guy was inspired to repeat my quest, so much the better — it would focus more attention on the world of birds and birding. Maybe we would even cross paths somewhere.

But that was getting way ahead of things — I hadn't even reached the record yet myself! As September approached, my time in Africa was winding down. After Tanzania, I spent twelve days in Uganda, where a phenomenal birder named Livingstone Kalema helped me track down 517 species of birds — including one of the country's most-wanted birds, a Green-breasted Pitta, in the wild tangles of vines and greenery of the Kibale Forest, and incidentally my very first pitta. When I left Africa, my Big Year totaled more than 4,200, inching closer to the 4,341 species mark set in 2008 by the British couple, Ruth Miller and Alan Davies. They sent a nice message on Facebook when I was within striking distance: "Hi Noah, you are going like a train! Congrats. You must be on for 5,000 plus?"

With four months remaining, I was pretty sure of reaching my goal of 5,000 species, but I couldn't afford to slack off — not with somebody ready to challenge any bar I set — and I began to feel the first vague stirrings of a possible 6,000 species by year's end. For now, I'd be satisfied with a new world record. Looking east, I set my sights on Asia.

The people of India are record fanatics. About 10 percent of all Guinness World Records applications come from India, and the country has its own set of record books: The *India Book of Records*, not to be confused with the *Indian Achiever Book of Records* or the *Limca Book of Records*. Indians go to extraordinary lengths to be recognized by these authorities — sometimes literally, like the man who hasn't cut his fingernails since 1952 or the one with the Guinness record for longest ear hair (5.19 inches).

On the whole planet, I couldn't pick a better place than India to set a Big Year world record, and it looked like that was just where it would happen. When I landed at Cochin International Airport in Kochi on September 13, in the bird-rich south India province of Kerala, my list stood at 4,243 species, just 98 short of Ruth and Alan's total. With more than a thousand species of birds to choose from in India, 80 percent of which I hadn't yet seen, I figured I would pass that number within a week.

For most of this year, I hadn't dwelt on breaking the existing record, as my goal from the outset was to see 5,000 species, half of the birds on Earth — a nice, round, individual challenge, not measured against the efforts of others. This was such an intensely personal quest that I hated to define it by someone else's idea of success; birding, after all, is not usually a competitive activity.

But a Big Year is still a competition, and as I edged closer to the world record I couldn't stop thinking about it. Buzz was building, too, with an upsurge of visits and comments on my daily blog at Audubon.org, messages of encouragement on my Facebook page, updates and discussions on online birding forums around the world, and requests for interviews from home and abroad. I responded as best I could, but it was hopeless; I couldn't keep up with the virtual world while living so large in the real world.

Actual and virtual reality intersected briefly in an unexpected way just before I arrived in India, during a day of birding squeezed into a layover in the United Arab Emirates. Two top-notch birders — Mark Smiles and Oscar Campbell — kindly showed me around the sand deserts on the outskirts of Abu Dhabi and Dubai while we baked in a slow oven of hundred-degree heat. The three of us found well over a hundred species of birds that day, including a rare find — a Green Warbler, crawling under a bush near an irrigated field, that was completely out of place, having been recorded in the UAE only about ten times.

The gilt-edged UAE made for a surreal layover, sandwiched between rural Uganda and India. I cast my eyes up, up, up the Burj Khalifa — the world's tallest building — while traveling on a twelve-lane freeway packed with luxury cars. As we watched the sun set over the Oman border fence that evening, Oscar mentioned that he'd just received an interesting email.

"Hey, some birder said he's doing a Big Year next year," he said, "with a goal of seeing five thousand species, just like you!"

"That wouldn't be Arjan, would it?" I asked.

"Yeah, that's his name," Oscar said. "Do you know him?"

"We haven't met," I said, "but I know who he is."

I had the increasing feeling that this Dutch guy was breathing down my neck — not just planning a similar adventure, but strategizing to go after me personally, and I had not even set a record yet! He was also starting to contact some of the same birders that I had connected with. In the UAE, of all places, people were saying hi to me for him. It was odd.

"Anyway," Oscar said, "you should have the world record wrapped up pretty soon."

"Yeah, but the record is sort of beside the point," I said, "though it will be satisfying to beat it. I'm still going for 5,000, which is a long way off."

"The record is important, though," Oscar said, "because people will get excited about it. All you have to say is that you broke a world record, and anyone can understand what that means, even if they have no idea what birding is."

He was right, of course. No matter what the original goal, all eyes — including mine — were now on the existing mark of 4,341 birds.

A couple days later I landed in the tea plantations of the Western Ghats mountain range, near the south Indian city of Munnar, with a gregarious birder named Harsha Jayaramaiah who seemed to know everybody in the country. He and his friends had generously organized among themselves to save money during my stay by sharing accommodations, food, and transportation. Their gift meant a lot to me, for it cut my total expenses to about $15 a day — the lowest of the whole year and well under my typical daily expenses of about $200 — while allowing me to enjoy the welcome hospitality of local birders. On my second day in India, I was just thirty-nine birds short of the record, which meant I'd probably pass it in another day or two. Harsha thought we might add a few more species in these mountains, including the Broad-tailed Grassbird — a skulky brown thing found only in grassy patches at high elevations in the Western Ghats. He couldn't locate a grassbird on short notice, though, so we stopped at a tourism office in Munnar for help.

Harsha asked to see a friend who knew about the bird, and sure enough, a man came out to give us some tips. When I thanked him, the man asked about my trip.

"Well, I hope to set a world record in the next day or so," I said, "for the number of birds anyone has ever seen in one year."

The man's face lit up like a light bulb.

"A world record?" he asked. "Are you going to submit it to the *Guinness Book of World Records*?"

"I did submit an official application, eight months ago," I said, "but I haven't heard back."

"That is strange," the man said. "They should reply in a few weeks."

"That's what the website says," I said, "but they can take as long as they want. Being in the Guinness book wasn't my main goal, anyway. I just want to see as many birds as I can."

"But how can you prove it?" the man pressed. "You will need evidence!"

"Birding doesn't really work like that — it's a personal adventure," I said, and the man looked dubious. "But I do have witnesses for every bird I've seen this year, and I've photographed a lot of them, too."

"Hmmph," he said, waggling his head. "Any record attempt must be documented. I had a friend who made it into the Guinness book earlier this year, and he had to provide all kinds of evidence."

"What was it for?" I asked.

The man glowed.

"Breaking iron rods with the bare fist!" he said, triumphantly.

It was obvious that he took this record very seriously. When Harsha and I left a few minutes later, on a mission to see the grass-bird, the man was still sitting at his desk, fanning himself in the stuffy tourism office, lost in happy remembrance of his friend's colossal achievement.

World records carry the mystique of perfection — a Platonic ideal of the material world. They are easy to understand and elegantly simple. Logically, there can be only one largest animal (the blue whale) and lightest element (hydrogen). Everybody knows that Mount Everest is the tallest mountain on Earth, and the altitude of its summit — a somewhat random artifact of geology — is less significant for its exact elevation (29,029 feet) than as the ultimate benchmark against other lofty heights. Superlatives help define our universe by precisely measuring its outer limits, giving context for everything else.

For most of history, all world records were intrinsic: they existed, by virtue of physics or happenstance, whether or not anyone noticed. The world's oldest tree (a 5,062-year-old bristlecone pine in the White Mountains of California) didn't set out to achieve distinction; it has merely stood longer than any other tree. Like-wise, the cheetah isn't consciously trying to be the fastest land animal when it sprints at speeds exceeding seventy miles per hour — it is more focused on its prey. Such records, born of chance or necessity, have little to do with recognition.

Only in recent years have people begun to equate world records with achievement. The notion of being the best is seductive, especially in an increasingly quantitative culture, and it's a quite modern concept. The ancient Olympic games originated as part of a religious festival honoring the Greek god Zeus, which went dormant in AD 393; their revival in 1896, more than 1,500 years later, dispensed with everything but unadulterated competition, leading to the multibillion-dollar spectacle we have today in which racewalkers and trampoliners are judged as solemnly as foreign policy. These days, we worship humans who run, jump, ride, swim, throw, wrestle, skate, ski, and curl better than other humans. It's not really logical, when you think about it: Michael Phelps and Usain Bolt are international celebrities, but the also-rans who finished a hundredth of a second behind them remain largely anonymous. And yet world records — or "WR," in Olympic parlance — are worth gold.

Practically speaking, our record-setting obsession aligns with two recent societal developments: enough leisure time to pursue non-survival-related activities, and the ability to know what other people are doing in distant places. It's hard to train for the decathlon if you work at a backbreaking job for eighteen hours a day, and equally difficult to proclaim a world champion without transcontinental communication.

Our greatest authority on world records started, according to legend, with a barroom dispute about birds. In the early 1950s, Sir Hugh Beaver, then the managing director of the Guinness Brewery, attended a shooting party in Ireland and got into an argument about which was the fastest game bird in Europe — he believed it was the golden-plover, but his friend maintained that the Red Grouse was speedier, and no reference could provide a definitive answer. Shortly afterward, Sir Hugh hired two journalists to research facts and figures for a collection of superlatives, first published as the *Guinness Book of Records* in 1955. The book quickly took on a life of its own; by 2015, *Guinness World Records* was the best-selling book of all time, with more than 100 million copies in print.

Sir Hugh Beaver intended his book as a reference, but it has morphed over time into a more interactive treasury. With no categorical restrictions imposed, people devised increasingly esoteric ideas, spurred on by the prospect of personal glory. Instead of describing the world as it is, the book has become the repository of humanity's sweeping desire to stand out from the crowd — a vision of the world as it might be, with sufficient ingenuity.

And so, while Guinness today lists the "fastest bird (diving)" as the Peregrine Falcon — once clocked in a stoop at 242 miles per hour — its database brims mostly with obscure human achievements. The latest triumphs are added in an endless, dizzying stream: largest display of origami elephants (78,564), most traffic cones balanced on the chin (26), largest sushi mosaic (608.16 square feet), and, my personal favorite, "most apples held in the mouth and cut by a chainsaw in one minute — self (blindfolded)," a terrifying stunt performed by an Australian man who calls himself The Space Cowboy. Each year, more than 50,000 people apply for new records.

I love all kinds of hijinks, but what does a world record mean when practically anything goes? Most people agree that running the fastest marathon is a stunning feat, but these other records, like hurling light bulbs or eating cars, are something else — a form of self-expression, perhaps. According to Guinness, each attempt must be measurable, verifiable, and breakable.

Searching for "bird" on Guinness's website returns more than 1,000 certified records, many of which are held by birds themselves: the Wild Turkey has the strongest gizzard, the Dusky Grouse has the shortest migration, and the Lake Duck of Argentina has the "largest reproductive organ for a bird" (its retractable spine-covered penis has been measured at 16.7 inches).

Birdwatching feats are conspicuously absent, probably because

Guinness considers them unverifiable. In my case, the Guinness Records Management Team sent their final decision nearly a year after I'd submitted my application: "Unfortunately, we are afraid to say that we cannot accept your proposal as a Guinness World Records title. Every record must be measurable and we feel that it would be difficult to provide an accurate measurement for your proposal."

This is why we have a Guinness record for the highest score on the Angry Birds video game, but nothing for those who pursue real, live birds.

Different people have their own reasons for striving toward a goal, and the psychology of record-setting is complicated. In a recent TED talk titled "The Puzzle of Motivation," viewed on YouTube nearly 20 million times, the analyst Dan Pink showed that external rewards have a surprisingly weak effect on all kinds of performance. After reviewing a pile of literature, Pink concluded that autonomy, mastery, and purpose — self-determination in the context of a larger focus — are much more powerful, and that real motivation comes from within. It's not the record that makes people pogo-stick up Mount Fuji, in other words; it's the personal desire to prove oneself and contribute to the world.

This is a subtly different way of viewing achievement that applies well to ambitious feats like Big Years: the end result may not be the reward, but the journey isn't exactly it, either. You need a goal, or at least a direction, to discover a true sense of purpose.

At least for me, journeys with a mission are far more rewarding — whether running a marathon or birding the world. It doesn't really matter what I'm seeking, only that I am inwardly driven to find it. Never was this truer than during my Big Year. My hope of seeing 5,000 species, and breaking the existing record in the process, motivated me to go out into the world, look for new birds every day, and celebrate and share what I found.

+ – + – +

Two days later, on September 16, Harsha and I arrived at the Thattekad Bird Sanctuary, a lowland forest patch along the Periyar River, at first light. With twenty-seven species to go to the record, we met a local birder named Sanu Sasi, who knew the area's birds like the back of his hand. The three of us entered the sanctuary in lively spirits.

Soon after dawn, a convoy of vehicles pulled up: the Ezhupunna Birders, a group of about a dozen young and enthusiastic bird lovers, had heard about my quest and wanted to help. They had driven two hours from the city of Kochi, having risen early to make the trip, and spilled out in a gaggle of smiles and handshakes.

With more than a dozen eager pairs of eyes in the forest, the birds had little chance of hiding. A Malabar Trogon, cherry red underneath with a black head and a thin white border encircling its neck, surveyed our group with apparent amusement from a high branch. Sanu pointed out a couple of Flame-throated Bulbuls, greenish yellow with black heads and orange throats, while Dark-fronted Babblers squeaked and rattled from the nearby undergrowth. Several White-bellied Treepies, a flashy and long-tailed member of the crow family endemic to southern India, called noisily from the forest, eventually affording great views while crossing a gap between trees. The birding was so brisk that I could barely keep up, and the morning hours flew by with more than twenty new species.

By noon, I was counting down single digits: a tiny Heart-spotted Woodpecker, black and white with a spiky crest and practically no tail, put me within ten species of surpassing the record; and after several more sightings, a White-rumped Needletail, a type of swift, sliced the gap down to five. But then, with the record dangling so close, activity stalled. In early afternoon a discouraging, drizzling rain began to fall, birds stopped singing, and it seemed that we might not reach the hoped-for number that day after all.

The Ezhupunna Birders reluctantly clocked out for lunch, wishing luck to Harsha, Sanu, and me. With rain pounding, we held a quick strategy session under the shelter of a leaky, unoccupied hut. Sanu suggested that we look for some common water-loving species near his house a few miles away, so we spent the next couple of hours in a downpour, tramping back and forth across a grassy field; one by one, we managed to see a White-rumped Munia, a White-breasted Waterhen, and a flyover Gray-fronted Green-Pigeon, endemic to this part of India. Now I was one tantalizing species away from tying the world record.

"Hey, I just saw a Common Iora!" yelled Harsha, who was staring at a patch of low trees a couple hundred yards away. "Come on, I think it just zipped out the other side."

The three of us sloshed across the field to catch up with the bird, my heart pounding with excitement and exertion, but the iora — a sparrow-sized, yellowish green songbird with black-and-white wings — proved flitty and elusive. I couldn't get my eyes on it. We couldn't give up the search, even though it seemed a little ridiculous: the Common Iora is one of the most familiar bird species in India, yet right now it seemed like the single most important bird in the world.

Finally, after a frustrating half-hour of peekaboo, the iora danced onto a branch right in front of me, and Sanu, Harsha, and I splashed high fives.

"That ties the record of 4,341 birds," I said. "We just need one more to break it!"

Sanu and Harsha caught each other's eye.

"Yes, we've been saving one for you," Sanu said. "Come on, we will return to the Thattekad forest for your next species — it's a special one."

"Just don't look at anything else until we get there," Harsha said. "We don't want an unremarkable bird like the Common Iora to pass the world record!"

As we made the ten-minute drive back to the bird sanctuary, the rain lightened into swirling mist. I stared at my feet in the back seat, water puddling around my shoes, wondering what Sanu had staked out for us. Harsha called the Ezhupunna Birders, who had finished their lunch, and they met us at the entrance to the forest, along with several other people I didn't know, in anticipation of the big moment.

My stomach gnawed with hunger — I hadn't eaten all day — and my skin was soaked through, but none of that mattered. All I could think about was the imminent milestone. Here I was on Day 259 of my Big Year, a once-in-a-lifetime adventure that had already taken me on a splendid journey through Antarctica, South and Central America, the United States, Europe, Africa, and India. I still aimed for 5,000 birds, but hurdling over the world record was admittedly exciting. Heightened energy sparked in the air.

Sanu led the way into the forest on foot. At a spot where the trail crossed a small creek, he stopped quietly and gestured toward a dense group of trees.

"Do you see it?" he whispered.

"What?" I said. "A bird?"

Harsha laughed.

"It's no fair if we point it out," he said. "You have to find this one yourself!"

They eyed me while I scanned the thick foliage, my adrenaline kicking in. Nothing moved, not even a breath of wind. The air hung heavy, the light muted by an overhanging canopy and mist. What should I be looking for?

I felt the sense of being watched, and turned around to see . . . what was this? A TV camera and crew had somehow materialized out of nowhere.

"They're from an Indian news station," Harsha said, "and they want to show your expression when you see the record-breaking bird!"

Behind the camera crew loitered the Ezhupunna Birders and several others, all of them watching expectantly. That moment was so weird that I'll never forget it: about twenty people staring at me while I stared blankly into the trees, hoping to spot the bird that would officially break the record. Birdwatching is not usually a spectator sport.

Then I saw it: a clump of dead leaves that, on closer inspection, wasn't vegetative at all. I raised my binoculars with a sense of fate. Clinging to a horizontal branch in the midcanopy, partly obscured by foliage, a pair of bizarre-looking birds snuggled together. They were brown with rufous accents, fluffed out in a round ball, with their eyes squeezed shut and wings tucked into soft plumage; their heads were so large that they seemed not to have necks, and their bills were the same width. The effect suggested something between a decomposing clod and a plush toy.

"No way — it's a pair of Sri Lanka Frogmouths!" I exclaimed, with a huge grin. "They're roosting here for the day, aren't they?"

"Yes," Harsha said, as he grasped my arm. "The Sri Lanka Frogmouth is an excellent record-breaking bird, nocturnal and not easy to see! Lucky for us, Sanu knew where to find these ones."

Sanu shook my hand, too, and then everyone was hugging and clapping backs and smiling.

Surges of euphoria, relief, and disbelief swept over me, and my heart swelled with gratitude and tenderness for all my fellow creatures — people and birds alike. In the midst of the merrymaking, I just stood there, savoring it, observing the scene as if detached from my own body. Through it all, the sleeping frogmouths seemed oblivious. We studied them for a few minutes, then left them in peace. Some of the birders said goodbye, but Harsha told me that he had arranged an after-party at the house of nearby bird guru Eldhose K. V., a well-respected, even-tempered character who had spent many years studying the south Indian birds.

A few of us carpooled over there in a jovial, stately caravan. I was invited in with a couple of other guests while a dozen other birders stayed outside, watching the White-cheeked Barbets vie with Malabar Gray Hornbills on a fruit feeder in the yard. A table had been set for tea in a small room. As I entered, things took an interesting turn: a man dressed in a floor-length red robe rose from a chair.

"Greetings," he said, extending a hand.

"Noah, this is Kuriakose Mor Eusebius, a bishop from Kothamangalam," Eldhose said, with elaborate politeness.

The bishop wore a dark beard, a tight-fitting cap, a high collar, and a gigantic crucifix around his neck. He explained, in soft tones, that he had driven quite a distance, and I couldn't help but wonder what had brought such a distinguished guest to take tea with me.

"Are you a birder?" I asked, unsure what else to say.

"I have an interest in all living things," the bishop replied, "and I heard about your world record. I predicted you would pass it this afternoon, in spite of the rainy weather."

"Well, thank you for the blessing," I said, humbled by his words.

We sat down at the table with Harsha, Eldhose, and a reporter who introduced herself as Preetu Nair. She quietly scribbled notes in a small notebook while our little group sipped tea and chattered about birds.

It was an oddly formal and starched way to celebrate a bird-watching record — nothing like what we do in over-the-top America — but why not? Over the next hour, as I enjoyed my tea, scarfed delicious tidbits, and fielded questions from Harsha, the bishop, and Preetu, my initial elation began to subside and deepen into a warm glow. As far as I was concerned, all was right with the world. We rejoined the other birders outside, and, many selfies later, everyone dispersed for the evening. Only then did I realize that it had been a very tiring day.

But it wasn't quite over yet: after dinner, I was fortunate to meet one more fascinating character, named Ben Mirin — perhaps the world's only birdsong beatboxer. Ben, younger than me, happened to be traveling in India on a grant from National Geographic to perform compositions of local bird songs through beatboxing, and he had been texting Harsha during his visit.

"It helps kids get interested in the birds around them," said Ben, who had scheduled shows at several schools in the area. "I record bird sounds in the wild, then use those audio clips to make beats that kids can relate to."

He did an enthusiastic demonstration, sounding less like a human being than a drum machine accompanied by bird sounds.

"I heard about your Big Year today from Harsha," he said, "and just thought I'd drop by. Congrats on the world record!"

As he said goodbye, I supposed that Ben's mission was about as wacky as my own. The world record had brought some interesting characters out of the woodwork.

The next morning, feeling slightly hung-over on excitement, Harsha and I stopped for breakfast at a street café in a rural town. As we entered, something caught my eye: a newspaper stand prominently displayed the day's headlines.

"Let's grab a paper," Harsha said.

On the front page of the *Times of India*, the world's largest English-language newspaper, my photograph was plastered underneath the headline, "Thattekad Birds Help Noah's Record Flight."

"That must have been the reporter at Eldhose's house," I said. "I didn't realize she was from the *Times of India!*"

The short story, with a special quote from the bishop, offered a straightforward account: "A reluctant smile dawned on the face of ornithologist Noah Strycker . . . Drenched in heavy rain and watched only by local bird watchers, [he] had set the world record for spotting [the] maximum number of birds [in] a year."

It was official, then. India — so crazy for records — proclaimed a new world record.

14

Hit and Miss

ON THE AFTERNOON of October 10, meteorologists noticed a disturbed area of low pressure over the remote Enewetak Atoll, which lies between Micronesia and the Marshall Islands in the Pacific Ocean. The next day, as denser air rushed in, weather forecasters in Japan upgraded the disturbance to a tropical depression, and on October 12 the system intensified into a tropical storm. When it tracked west toward the Philippines, the storm was christened Lando, and by October 17 it had graduated into a full-fledged super cyclone, equivalent to a Category 4 hurricane, with winds exceeding 150 miles per hour and a glaring, twenty-five-mile-wide eye visible on satellite images. Lando bore down on the Philippine island of Luzon, where more than 50 million people dreaded its landfall.

As the super typhoon blew toward the Philippines, I was perched seven hundred miles to the north, in the mountains of central Taiwan, with Wayne Hsu, the Director of Conservation and International Affairs at Taiwan's Chinese Wild Bird

Federation. After a long and productive day of birding, Wayne and I sat in a hotel room, examining Lando's updated forecasts on my laptop.

"You're going to the Philippines tomorrow, right?" Wayne asked.

"Yes," I said, "almost exactly where that typhoon is headed, to Luzon Island."

"It's supposed to hit tomorrow," Wayne said. "They're projecting several feet of rain and sustained winds over a hundred miles per hour when it reaches land."

"And my plane is scheduled to arrive there a couple of hours later," I added.

I felt more interest than stress about this development. If typhoon Lando slammed into Manila tomorrow, its impact on my travel plans would be trivial compared to the chaos for those who lived there. Besides, worrying about it wouldn't help, and I had more immediate concerns — like how to squeeze out a few last birds during my waning hours in Taiwan.

At that moment, my species list stood at 4,854 birds, fewer than 150 shy of my goal. For almost ten months, I had imagined the moment when I would hit 5,000: what it might feel like to reach such an ambitious milestone, and how relaxing to know that nothing could take it away. I had even, at the suggestion of a friend, considered getting the 5,000th bird tattooed somewhere on my body. The breakneck pace had not let up since setting the world record in India, and I now found myself within striking distance of the big 5K. Perhaps I could pass it in the Philippines next week, if I ever got there. Meanwhile, I had Taiwanese birds to snag.

To that end, Wayne spread out a map of northern Taiwan. We had just spent two days with Wayne's friend Kuan-Chieh "Chuck" Hung and a bunch of local birders who were tracking my Big Year through eBird. Word was definitely out by now about my adventure, and increasingly on my travels I encountered groups of birders, rather than just one or two. For me, these meetings never got old. It was energizing to share the world's amazing array of bird life with local people who knew their birds and their patches well. Everybody pitched in to find as many of Taiwan's twenty-six endemic bird species as possible during my short visit. We'd scored nearly all of them, including two fancy mountain pheasants — the Swinhoe's, which is electric blue, purple, and white with a long tail; and the Mikado, which is the country's national bird, depicted on the thousand-dollar bill and known in Taiwanese as the "Emperor of the Mist." We'd also seen the endemic Taiwan Blue-Magpie, an elegant creature dressed in blue, red, and black with an exquisitely long tail, flying against a cliff in the Dasyueshan Forest after a spectacular, misty sunrise. Now, with just a few possible birds remaining, Wayne and I tried to figure out a logical route.

"Here's where we are, in the mountains of north-central Taiwan," Wayne began, gesturing at the map. "And your flight to the Philippines tomorrow, if it takes off, will depart from Taipei, on the northern tip of the country. But the only endemic bird you haven't seen yet is the Styan's Bulbul, which lives down south, so to find one we would need to make a long drive, then catch a domestic flight to Taipei for your international connection."

"I suppose that's possible, but it's a lot for one bird," I said, "especially for a bulbul that looks basically like other bulbuls I've already seen in Asia. Is there another option?"

"Well, ye-e-es," Wayne said, as he uncapped a pen. "I've been thinking about it, and I believe I have a plan."

He spent the next few minutes drawing dotted lines, precisely annotated with times and places, until the map resembled the schematics for a sophisticated heist. The new route sacrificed the bulbul, but we'd have a chance to encounter a much more charismatic celebrity if all went well. By the time we turned in for bed that evening, I looked forward to an eventful day on the morrow.

October had been rewarding so far. After leaving India, I continued east, first to the country of Myanmar — formerly called Burma — where local birder Gideon Dun spent a week showing me some of the area's less-traveled sites. In Myanmar, "less-traveled" really means something: the nation was essentially off-limits to foreigners from 1962 to 2011 during an oppressive military dictatorship, and only recently began opening up. Along with his brother, Moses, Gideon is a former hunter who played in a rock band before taking up birdwatching. Gideon and I rode his motorbike through the mountains, prowled for birds around the breathtaking thousand-year-old temples of Bagan — one of the world's best-kept archeological sites — and waited out a flash flood after thunderstorms ripped through the hills one evening. Myanmar produced birds, but it gave the added impression of an expedition into the unknown.

From there, I moved to an entirely different environment in the Sichuan province of south-central China, where Sid Francis, a British expat obsessed with Eurasian birds and Chinese culture, hosted a wild road trip through frosted peaks, high ridges, and pristine river valleys. Sid and I topped out near 15,000 feet at Balang Shan Pass, admiring Golden Bush-Robins and Giant Laughingthrushes in two inches of fresh snow while prayer flags flapped and fluttered in a light breeze. By the end of the week, I came away with 215 species of birds and a new appreciation for China's natural riches — not something you generally read about in headlines.

I'd originally planned to fly straight from China to the Philippines, but a chance encounter in South Africa earlier in July inspired me to squeeze in this quick visit to Taiwan. In South Africa I'd stayed a couple of days in Cape Town with Callan Cohen, a full-time guide who one evening invited a friend to dine with us. That friend turned out to be Adam Welz, a campaign director for the anti-poaching organization WildAid, who knew Wayne Hsu, partly because Wayne had worked with Greenpeace in Asia. I was instantly persuaded to visit Taiwan — and now, three months later, here I was.

Wayne got us up early on my last day in Taiwan. We met a group of birders at the mouth of the Bazhang River, on the southwest coast, where we intended to scan for shorebirds before moving north on a tight schedule. A couple of minutes after arriving, though, Wayne suddenly started shouting something about a whale.

"It's on the beach!" he said. "Right at the mouth of the river!"

"A whale on the beach?" I replied, in confusion.

"Yeah, just aim your scope at that black thing," Wayne said, gesticulating. "You can see the flippers and tail sticking up."

Sure enough, I focused on the unmistakable silhouette of an enormous whale carcass on the sand about a mile away. It lay on its back, a dark shape with one pectoral fin jutting in the air, well and truly beached.

"Huh," Wayne said. "This must be the same sperm whale that washed up two days ago, a few miles north of here. The Taiwanese coast guard towed it out to sea to get rid of the carcass, but I guess it floated back to shore."

He snapped a photograph to post on Facebook, and within a few minutes a local news site had picked up the story.

"Look, my picture is in the paper!" said Wayne, showing us the grainy image under a Taiwanese headline on his phone's screen.

"Hey, wasn't there an incident with an exploding whale carcass in Taiwan a few years ago?" I asked, recalling a dim memory.

"Oh yeah," Wayne said, "A big male sperm whale washed up near Tainan — it was fifty tons, the largest whale ever recorded in Taiwan — and died on the beach before anyone could save it."

He told me the story ended badly after researchers, hoping to do a post-mortem, loaded the carcass on a flatbed truck and transported it through the city. A buildup of decomposition gases caused the carcass to explode, showering people and cars in blood and guts. Which maybe explained why this time the coast guard had tried to tow the carcass out to sea.

Wayne and I put the whale business behind us, said goodbye to the other birders, and hurried into Tainan just in time to catch a train — and not just any train.

"We could fly to Taipei," Wayne explained, "but it's faster to go by rail."

I'd never taken a bullet train before, so it was exciting to board this futuristic-looking high-speed rail. My last experience on a train, in India, had been on a cramped sleeper car out of Delhi, which ran like a polluted cattle cart. By comparison, this one felt like a sleek jet plane on rails, if not a rocket ship: inside, it was designed exactly like a commercial airliner, with an aerodynamic exterior contoured like a fuselage.

Once beyond the city limits, the bullet train glided along its track with a soft hum, picking up momentum almost imperceptibly. On a straight stretch, I used the GPS on my iPhone to gauge our speed.

"Holy cow," I exclaimed. "We are going a hundred and eighty-eight miles per hour!"

"Yeah," said Wayne, with a wry smile. "That's why the train is faster than dealing with airports."

His phone rang, and he had a quick conversation in Mandarin while I watched the scenery fly past in a colorful blur. Wayne told me, with obvious relief, that a birder he knew would meet us in Taipei.

It took us just an hour and a half to reach Taipei, nearly two hundred miles to the north, where Wayne and I stepped off the bullet train to find Hunter, a kind man who had volunteered to spend his Sunday afternoon with us, waiting with his car. The three of us drove out of the city but didn't get very far. On the outskirts of Taipei, on the shoulder of a busy highway surrounded by suburbs, we stopped to pay homage to a unique celebrity.

Wayne filled in the details. Nearly a year earlier, in January 2015, a young Siberian Crane had appeared briefly on Pengjia Islet off the north end of Taiwan, having drifted off course during its migration. This bird caused a stir in the birding community — the Siberian Crane is a critically endangered species with a global population of just 3,000 individuals, most of which migrate each year from Russia to eastern China, and it was the first time one had been seen in Taiwan. Pengjia Islet is under military control and cannot be visited by ordinary citizens, but the crane didn't stay there long. Incredibly, three days later, it was spotted again in a farmer's field outside of Taipei, within a short radius of several million people.

Pretty soon, the "little white crane," as it came to be known by the Taiwanese, was splashed all over the news. Thousands of curious people turned out to see it. The crane usually stayed in one particular field alongside a well-trafficked road, where it found a good supply of food, and it didn't seem to mind onlookers. When it dodged attacks from a stray dog and a passing hawk, local government officials feared for the bird's safety; they recognized this graceful crane as an ambassador of goodwill toward Taiwanese–Siberian relations, and so they assigned it a full-time security guard. Someone installed a webcam to let people watch from home, and a Facebook page with 13,000 fans posted updates. When members of a film crew inadvertently flushed the bird while filming in the area for an unrelated TV drama, they were duly fined for environmental disturbance, and schoolchildren formed a human chain to keep people at a safe distance. Volunteer observers began logging the crane's daily activities, hoping to figure out how to help it rejoin its flock. In the first couple of months, this one crane had an esti-mated 60,000 visitors.

Now, nearly a year later, the bird showed no signs of leav-ing, and it had become a bustling local attraction. When Wayne, Hunter, and I arrived, we found several dozen photographers stalking the bird next to a souvenir stand selling crane-themed knickknacks. Bright yellow signs in Mandarin and English warned "Caution! Drive Slow: Crane Crossing." The crane itself took no notice; it paced around its favored field with the slow elegance of a ballet dancer, occasionally bending down to grab a morsel with its serrated bill.

The bird stood a stately five feet tall, entirely white except for a maroon-red face, pink legs, delicate black wingtips, and yellow eyes.

"It has lost the colors of youth," Wayne said.

When the crane first arrived it was in juvenile plumage, less than one year old, with rusty feathers over most of its body. Now it was completely snow white like an adult.

Siberian Cranes can live to be eighty, if all goes well. But this bird might not have a home to return to. Almost all Siberian Cranes winter along the Yangtze River in China, and their preferred wet-lands were recently destroyed by construction of the Three Gorges Dam, the world's largest and most notorious hydropower project. That dam was an environmental catastrophe in many ways, and wild Siberian Cranes might eventually go extinct because of it. In a way, this crane was lucky to be here.

We watched for half an hour while the bird steadily paced back and forth, shadowed for a while by a friendly Little Egret. Did it miss the company of family and mates? I watched the bird's yel-low eye through my spotting scope, but its expression remained enigmatic.

Then, remembering Lando, I checked my phone. To my surprise, my redeye flight to Manila had been confirmed.

"It looks like I'm flying straight into a typhoon tonight," I said.

"Guess we should get going, then," Wayne said. "But I'm glad you had a chance to see this crane — it is the most famous bird in Taiwan!"

With one last, lingering look at the crane, we stepped into Hunter's car and headed to the airport.

As it happened, that Siberian Crane stayed near Taipei for another few months. In May 2016, a year and a half after it had arrived, observers noticed the young crane becoming visibly restless. It made several short flights around the north coast of Taiwan, at one point taking shelter in a Taipei subway station while satellite news trucks broadcast its movements on local TV. Then, one day, it disappeared. Nobody knows whether it managed to rejoin its flock in China, or went to Siberia, or simply flew out to sea, searching for companions, unsure which direction to fly but compelled onward by the overpowering, universal instinct to return home.

✦ ─ ✦ ─ ✦

Super typhoon Lando swung north at the last minute to make landfall about ninety miles north of Manila, hammering northern Luzon Island with sustained 115-mile-per-hour winds and torrential rain. Nine million people lost power, more than a hundred thousand took refuge in evacuation shelters, tens of thousands of homes were damaged or destroyed, and forty-eight people were killed. One city reported 51.9 inches of rain in twenty-four hours — more than four feet.

In Manila, warnings remained at Signal 2 throughout the typhoon, predicting only that "some coconut trees may be tilted" and "many banana plants may be downed." So, while the worst of the storm raged to the north, my plane lit on the runway of Manila Ninoy Aquino International Airport on a blustery, wet morning. It was unsettling to think of the chaos so close by, yet so far away. My most stressful moment came when an attendant, citing stingy carry-on restrictions, forced me to check my backpack, from which I had not been separated all year; I actually kissed it upon being reunited in Manila.

Despite the typhoon, Nicky Icarangal, a veteran Filipino ornithologist, was ready and waiting, to my great relief. Nicky had planned an action-packed week for us — four islands in seven days — but, as our first stop was supposed to be northern Luzon Island, which was now being pummeled by wind and rain, that itinerary was blown away. Nicky shook my hand and marched us over to the domestic terminal. In a few minutes, he explained, we'd take off toward the southern Philippines, where we'd be out of Lando's grip. Nicky had arranged for us to visit Mindanao, the country's second-largest island after Luzon, to search for the rare, endangered, and spectacular Great Philippine Eagle.

Nicky presented a stocky, trim, and tidy figure with dark, close-cropped hair and a patch of stubble on the tip of his chin. He wore hiking boots, a long-sleeved field shirt tucked firmly into khakis, and a watch tightly fitted to his right wrist, and he carried a duffel bag along with a mysterious hard, black, plastic case. He seemed to know everyone in the little domestic terminal, moving effortlessly through crowds at the check-in desks and nodding to acknowledge each acquaintance.

After checking his duffel, Nicky stopped at another counter, in a quiet corner of the airport, to hand over the plastic case.

"My toy," he said, a bit mysteriously, by way of explanation.

I was already dreaming of what the next days might bring. The Philippine Eagle, by length the largest eagle in the world, tops the most-wanted list for every birder who visits the Philippines. It's often called the "monkey-eating" eagle for its propensity to prey on macaques, but this predator hunts just about anything; it has been known to take down pigs, dogs, and the occasional deer. The eagle stands more than three feet tall with a light belly and a loose, shaggy crest, and is most often observed soaring above the canopy of unbroken jungle. It is Asia's counterpart to the Harpy Eagle I'd seen in Brazil eight months before. Finding both species in the same year would be a real coup.

The Philippine Eagle is rarer than the Harpy, though; with only a few hundred individuals left in the wild, these raptors are critically endangered. They require large tracts of intact forest to survive — each breeding pair is estimated to defend a territory of at least fifty square miles — and, as logging has accelerated in recent years, the eagles have declined. Today they are found in only a few scattered areas, with their last stronghold in the mountain forests of Mindanao Island.

Nicky and I were headed into the heart of that territory. I was amped to see an eagle, but also slightly concerned about what I might be getting myself into. During my Big Year, Mindanao was in the news for all the wrong reasons: armed guerrillas, militias, Islamic extremists, and outright criminals were active there, vying with each other in a messy and complicated resistance. The Philippine military, quietly backed by the United States, engaged in secretive operations to combat these groups, occasionally boiling into the international spotlight. At one point, CNN reported that 120,000 people had evacuated their homes to flee the fighting in Mindanao. This was nothing new — conflict has been ongoing since the 1970s in the southern Philippines — but it was worrying for a foreigner. Just four days before I arrived on Mindanao, the U.S. State Department issued a stern warning against nonessential travel to the region, citing a long list of terrorist incidents. "Exercise extreme caution," it read.

To see the Philippine Eagle, birders have traditionally visited Mount Kitanglad, an inactive 9,500-foot volcano in north-central Mindanao, but in February 2015 a group of birdwatchers got caught in the crossfire there, apparently between government special forces and the New People's Army, a communist rebel group. The birders managed to escape, but their guide was shot in the arm, and access to Mount Kitanglad had been dicey ever since.

To be on the safe side, Nicky decided we would try a different site, the Cinchona Forest Reserve, on the other side of the mountain's summit, where a pair of Philippine Eagles had recently nested.

"Don't worry," he said. "We will stay with a park guard who is friendly with the rebels, so they won't mess with us."

I tried not to dwell on the many recent kidnappings in the south Philippines, including a pair of Swiss and Dutch birders who were abducted on the nearby island of Tawi-Tawi in 2012. The Swiss man escaped in 2014 during a shootout, but the Dutch birder was still being held captive, more than three years later. The U.S. State Department had listed at least fifteen separate kidnappings during the first nine months of my Big Year, including four tourists abducted from a Mindanao resort a couple of weeks before I arrived. One of them, a Canadian, was beheaded several months later after a failed ransom effort.

We landed in Davao City, the bustling metropolitan center of Mindanao, in bright sunshine. Nicky picked up his luggage, then walked to a counter near the airport exit, where a uniformed man handed him the black plastic case. With precise, practiced movements, Nicky opened the case, took out a handgun, loaded it, and tucked the weapon under his waistband.

"Okay, let's go!" he said.

Mindanao offers a birder's paradise, not just for the eagle but for a host of other endemic species such as the Mindanao Bleeding-heart, a reclusive forest dove that looks like it's been stabbed in the chest, and the Black-and-cinnamon Fantail, a charismatic little songbird that sounds like a squeeze toy. Of nearly two hundred birds endemic to the Philippines, more than one hundred can be seen on Mindanao, and about fifty are restricted to this island and its outliers, making this area one of the world's richest for endemism. My skin prickled to get into it.

After driving for a couple of hours into Mindanao's rugged interior, we stopped along a muddy road where a house in a state of disrepair stood alone in a small clearing. I assumed the building had been abandoned until Nicky announced brightly, "Welcome to the Cinchona Forest Reserve headquarters!" Two men emerged to greet our arrival, and I was soon introduced to Emiliano "Blackie" Lumiston, the park's guard and caretaker, and his son, Ramil. Emiliano wore camouflage, sported a crewcut dyed blazing pumpkin orange, and smoked while we talked. He didn't speak English, so Nicky translated.

"Blackie is part of the Kitanglad Guard Volunteers," Nicky explained. "It's an indigenous organization that patrols the forest, helping protect this area against intrusions. Mount Kitanglad was declared a protected area in 2000, but it's under pressure from illegal logging and exploitation. The KGV has stopped a lot of development here in recent years."

Emiliano smiled warmly when I shook his hand.

"I'm glad to hear it," I said. "The birds need all the help they can get!"

"For the indigenous people, Kitanglad is a sacred site," Nicky said. "They know this place better than anyone. Even though they are poor, they are the forest's best protectors."

As a full-time guard, Emiliano was also an expert on the Philippine Eagle, my most-wanted bird in these parts. He told us that the local pair of eagles had finished nesting a couple of months before, but they were still hanging around. Our best chance would be to watch the skies from a nearby overlook where the birds could often be seen soaring over the forest canopy.

The four of us — Emiliano, Ramil, Nicky, and I — mounted two motorbikes to climb a narrow dirt track that no car could follow. Several miles above the headquarters, we reached a spot with a magnificent view: from a bare hilltop, the forest spread out like a flowing green carpet, with tendrils of mist swirling above it. Emiliano made a sweeping gesture toward the landscape under our feet, and Nicky said, "We will wait here all afternoon, if necessary. The eagles like to fly over this valley."

I checked my watch. It was just before noon, which meant we had about seven hours of daylight. With patience and luck, sometime before dusk I'd have an eagle in my sights.

We cheerfully settled into our vigil. Each of us remained mostly silent, lost in our own thoughts, while we continuously scanned the horizon. My mind drifted as an hour passed, then two hours, and I found myself daydreaming about the end of my journey. After ten months on the road, I was nearing the home stretch, but somehow I wasn't quite ready to be done.

And I wasn't even sure where, exactly, I'd be for New Year's Eve. For months now I had nurtured a secret plan, hatched with a couple of South African birders, to attempt to beat the world Big Day record on December 31 — to try to see more than 350 species of birds in a single day, more than anyone had ever recorded in one twenty-four-hour period. As a grand finale to my Big Year, setting two world records at once would be pretty epic, and we thought it might be possible in South Africa — especially with the help of a friend's private jet to cover the territory. I could fly from Australia to South Africa on December 30, meet the team, and go hard until the New Year.

But in early October, another crew of birders in Ecuador stunned the birding world with an announcement: after weeks of careful scouting, they completed a Big Day across the Andes and recorded 431 species of birds in twenty-four hours, smashing the existing single-day record.

"It's like beating the world marathon record by an hour!" enthused one of their team.

The South Africans were so impressed that they gave up — even with the jet, it wouldn't be possible to surpass the Ecuador tally in South Africa, which has fewer birds — and so, reluctantly, I canceled my New Year's Eve plans with them. I'd have to finish the year elsewhere.

"Hey, Noah, do you see that bird?" asked Nicky, and I snapped out of my reverie.

He was pointing downslope, toward a distant ridge. When I scanned with my binoculars, I quickly picked up what he'd spotted: a speck was rising slowly over the canopy, like a piece of dust floating in a lazy air current.

"Got it," I said, not quite sure what I had got.

All four of us immediately locked on. The bird was far away, at least a mile or two from our position, soaring against a backlit sky. I couldn't even see it with my naked eye, and the binoculars didn't help much. It was clearly a raptor, but which species? Nicky and Emiliano held an animated discussion.

"We think it's an eagle," Nicky said, finally, "but it's so far away that we're only ninety percent sure. Unfortunately, Emiliano says that it's in an inaccessible area, so we can't take the motorbikes any closer. Maybe it will fly over here for a better view."

The bird soared in broad circles, giving tantalizing looks as it banked in the thermals. I could make out its flat profile, bulky structure, and powerful flight, but that was about it. After ten long minutes, I watched the speck descend and vanish behind the ridge.

"I'm confident that was a Philippine Eagle," Nicky said, "but it was a terrible view."

Emiliano spread his hands in a gesture of helplessness: he'd found the bird all right, but today it did not cooperate. We'd waited all afternoon for a circling speck.

The eagle did not reappear. When night eventually fell without another sighting, the four of us returned to the dilapidated house. I crawled into a sleeping bag on a floor of rotten wood and lay there in the dark, turning over the day's events in my mind, pondering what I'd seen at the overlook.

Nicky and Emiliano were probably correct: the distant silhouette was likely a Philippine Eagle. But it had been so far off that I couldn't catch its field marks, not even the overall brown-and-gray colors. I might never have another chance to observe this bird — by the time I could return to the Philippines, it might be extinct in the wild — and tomorrow we had to look for Mindanao's many other species, because I'd soon be moving on. My heart ached. I wished, as I had so often lately, for more time.

When I closed my eyes, I knew that I would always remember exactly how empty it felt, that day on Mindanao Island, not to see a Great Philippine Eagle.

Next morning, Emiliano woke us before dawn. He wanted to show me the Philippine Eagle nest, even though it was no longer in use, which required a short hike through the forest. Nicky agreed — we'd have a chance for a few birds I wouldn't find anywhere else.

After a hasty breakfast, we set out on a faintly marked trail leading straight uphill. Emiliano's son, Ramil, went first, clearing the way with a machete, while Nicky and I hung back, listening for birds. Nicky had an impressive ear, identifying each unseen singer as we walked along, occasionally stopping to zero in on one.

"Hear that?" he said. "That's a Stripe-breasted Rhabdornis.

And — oh! — a Cinnamon Ibon. That's a good one, endemic to the mountains of Mindanao."

We wangled views of the ibon, a diminutive songbird in its own genus. With this sighting, I realized that I was very close, very close indeed, and my heart beat faster.

"Hey, Nicky," I said, after a quick count, "that rhabdornis was number 4,995. Only five more birds to go!"

As Emiliano led us deeper into the forest, approaching the eagle nest, we added several birds in quick succession: Island Flycatcher, Mountain White-eye, and, in a clearing, a noisy Tawny Grassbird. When a dull-green Mountain Warbler flitted in the midcanopy, Nicky slapped me on the back.

"That's number 4,999," he said. "Next one is the big five-K! Let's hope it's not some drab flycatcher . . ."

A mixed flock of birds moved into the branches above us, and Nicky and I craned our necks to look straight up.

"I see flowerpeckers," he said. "Are you looking at the one with red undertail coverts?"

"Yep," I said. "Glossy black above, white below, dark face, and a red cap."

"It's a Flame-crowned Flowerpecker!" Nicky exclaimed.

"Number five thousand!" I said.

We watched for a minute until the bird had flitted away.

"That's a great milestone bird," Nicky said. "Endemic to the Philippines, and a tough one. Congratulations!"

"A Flame . . . crowned . . . Flowerpecker," I repeated, slowly emphasizing the syllables as I considered the bird's name.

Nicky, Emiliano, Ramil, and I took a triumphal selfie, each of us with five fingers raised, one digit for every thousand birds. The stress of 299 days in thirty countries lifted: whatever happened now, I'd reached my mark. For me, accomplishing this personal objective was the sweetest feeling, better even than passing the world record in India. The number of birds mattered less than the satisfaction of achieving what I had set out to do — a task that ten months ago had seemed almost too overwhelming to contemplate.

Emiliano stopped at the end of the trail and pointed up into a large tree.

"That," he announced, "is the old Philippine Eagle nest."

I carefully climbed a viewing platform that been built in an adjacent tree. It was a rickety structure of tied-together branches now beginning to decompose, but it afforded a point-blank view of the nest, wedged solidly into a fork. The photographers must have had a field day when the eagles were here, I thought, burning with envy.

As I stood there, pondering the ghost of eagles past, Nicky's voice called up from below.

"Hey, weren't you going to get a tattoo of your five-thousandth bird?"

"Yes," I said, "but I think it's best if we forget all about it."

"Why?" said Nicky.

"There's only one place for a Flame-crowned Flowerpecker tattoo," I said. "And I just don't think I'm man enough."

15

Birds in Paradise

As NOVEMBER CAME and went, I had the eerie feeling of time accelerating — the days rushed by too quickly, like living in fast-forward. The end of the year, which for so long had extended into the distant horizon, suddenly loomed large. I swept through Southeast Asia in what seemed like the blink of an eye, hurtling toward a finish line that appeared disconcertingly close. I wanted to put on the brakes, but my internal clock had other ideas.

Since the beginning of the year, my sense of time had veered all over the map, literally and figuratively. At the start, way back in Antarctica, the days passed so slowly that I hardly thought about the future. Toward the middle, time seemed to crest a rise, then to hasten downhill, relentlessly picking up momentum into the home stretch.

We all feel the steady acceleration of time as we age, partly because each passing season becomes a smaller proportion of our lives (which explains why a summer in college feels as long as a whole year at age 75), and partly because we experience fewer new things as we get older and therefore generate fewer vivid memories to mark the time. People often experience this effect on a more compressed scale when they are on vacation. The so-called "holiday paradox" can be explained in terms of novelty: the more new experiences we have, the denser the timeline becomes.

During my Big Year, I experienced the holiday paradox in a big way. As I developed routines, each new month moved faster than the last. Time also sped up because I had so little to spare; it really does fly when you're having fun, and I was so busy that, every time I glanced at a clock, the minutes and hours leapt forward. But at the same time, looking back, the beginning of the year seemed like an eon in the past.

Time melted in my grasp and fled before I could touch it, "gone in the instant of becoming," as the psychologist William James said more than a hundred years ago. I wanted to savor every moment, but found my own consciousness too slippery to hold. And so, as time flew like a bullet train, I hung on to my binocs as tightly as I could, enjoyed each fresh memory, and began to look ahead toward the New Year.

+ - + - +

A few months into my Big Year, Joseph Yenmoro, who works at a dive resort on the island of New Britain in Papua New Guinea, took a group of Japanese tourists on a firefly-watching excursion. Joseph is a scuba guide, but after more than a decade of entertaining visitors to Papua New Guinea he's learned about the above-water wildlife, too, including birds. He has wide features, a toothy smile, and round cheekbones, and is now the most experienced birder living on New Britain. That evening, as Joseph drove through an oil palm plantation, he saw something interesting fly across the road.

He'd spotted a shadowy shape there several times after dark and always assumed it was a Rufous Night-Heron, a common nocturnal species. This time, though, the shape landed on a fence post, and Joseph realized it wasn't a heron at all. It was an owl.

"Oh, my God," he said to the Japanese tourists. "That's a Golden Masked-Owl!"

The group seemed unimpressed, even when he excitedly explained that this owl was one of the planet's least-known bird species — it had not been seen alive in about thirty years. In all of history, in fact, the Golden Masked-Owl had been observed only three times by ornithologists: single sightings in 1967, 1985, and 1987. The island of New Britain, roughly the size of Taiwan, is virtually unexplored by birders, and those few who do visit tend to return to the same places over and over. Nobody knew where to look for a Golden Masked-Owl, so the bird had stayed off the world's radar.

The owl looks similar to a Barn Owl — flattened face, pale plumage, no "ear" tufts — with black speckles covering its golden yellow body. It is endemic to New Britain, in the Bismarck Archipelago northeast of New Guinea. Nobody knows where it nests, what it eats, what it sounds like, its population status, or even what habitat it prefers. It might have been thought extinct, except that in 2013 Joseph found a dead one on the grounds of the Walindi dive resort where he works. Since then he'd hoped to spot a live bird, and now one was staring straight at him with black, watery eyes.

"Does anyone have a camera?" he asked the tourists, but nobody did — they just wanted to see fireflies. After a minute, the owl flew away, and Joseph reluctantly continued his tour.

The next evening, he returned with a resort manager and located the bird again with a spotlight, this time capturing a short video — the first-ever footage of the species — which they posted to YouTube. Word of the discovery trickled out, and a couple weeks later a group of birdwatchers on a Rockjumper tour photographed the owl with Joseph's help. Each time, it was found in the same area, patrolling an oil palm plantation.

This was about the last place you'd expect to find a mega-rare bird: less than a mile from a popular resort, in a heavily degraded habitat. Oil palm plantations, widely regarded as one of the world's worst environmental scourges, have been blamed in recent years for wholesale destruction of tropical forests, especially in Africa and Asia. On New Britain, these plantations have replaced massive tracts of jungle: between 1990 and 2000 alone, a quarter of the island's lowland forest was cleared to make way for the lucrative crop, which is now one of Papua New Guinea's largest exports. If current trends continue, most of New Britain's forest will be gone by 2060.

Palm oil, squeezed from nuts produced on squat trees, is used in half of all supermarket products — including lipstick, soap, chocolate, instant noodles, bread, detergent, and ice cream — and labeled under a host of names, such as vegetable oil, vegetable fat, glyceryl, and *Elaeis guineensis* (the plant's scientific name). Just today, you've probably eaten palm oil, washed your clothes with it, and rubbed it on your scalp, skin, and teeth. The stuff is ubiquitous — it's even an ingredient in biofuels — but nearly invisible. Few people realize how much palm oil they consume, and even fewer know where it comes from. The global demand has doubled in the past decade and is expected to double again by 2050, "at the expense of tropical forest," according to the World Wildlife Fund.

It was surprising that this rare owl was staked out in, of all places, an oil palm plantation, which is about as environmentally friendly as a concrete parking lot. By the time I arrived in Papua New Guinea, I'd seen my share of these plantations elsewhere, especially in southeast Asia, and they seemed to offer little wildlife habitat. But I have looked for birds in some pretty strange places, so if finding a Golden Masked-Owl required entering an oil palm plantation, I didn't have a problem with that. I squeezed in a little extra time for the search.

But first I had other business to attend to. My visit to New Britain was an afterthought, added to a longer stay on the main island of New Guinea, which concluded an eventful month of island-hopping around the region. After leaving the Philippines, I spent a week in Thailand with a young bird addict named Panuwat "Par" Sasirat, who invited several friends for a whirlwind tour of his home country. Outside Bangkok we found the endangered Spoonbilled Sandpiper, a tiny shorebird with a spatulate-shaped bill, at a commercial saltwater evaporation facility — another super-rare bird in a manmade habitat. Then I made a quick visit to Sri Lanka, with its suite of endemics, before dropping into Peninsular Malaysia, where a friendly birder, Cheong Weng Chun, whisked me into the highlands for a few days. From there I bounced over to Borneo to spend a week looking at White-nest Swiftlets and orangutans in the deep jungle — and lucked out by snagging all three uncommon "Whiteheads" in one day: Whitehead's Broadbill, Whitehead's Trogon, and Whitehead's Spiderhunter. In Indonesia, on the island of Sulawesi, famed for its hundred species of endemic birds, a young man named Monal Capellone showed me the strange Maleo — a ground-dwelling, vaguely chickenlike bird that incubates its eggs in hot sand near volcanic vents. Finally, by way of a half-day layover in Bali with local birder Pak Yudi, I landed on the shores of Papua New Guinea.

When birders think of New Guinea, they usually imagine birds-of-paradise: about forty species of elaborately colorful and intricately decorated birds, confined to the remote jungles of New Guinea and surrounding islands. Sir David Attenborough, after filming his landmark *Attenborough in Paradise* documentary, grandly concluded that "birds-of-paradise are the most romantic and glamorous birds in the world." Alfred Russel Wallace, the nineteenth-century naturalist who copublished the theory of natural selection with Charles Darwin, called them "the most extraordinary and the most beautiful of the feathered inhabitants of the Earth." Birds-of-paradise were my priority here.

From Port Moresby, the country's rough and bustling capital, I took a prop plane to the settlement of Tari — a few buildings with a gravel airstrip — in the rugged, mountainous interior of New Guinea. I'd arranged to stay at Ambua Lodge, an eco-friendly accommodation in beautiful cloud forest at 7,000 feet, where birds-of-paradise can be found literally at the doorstep.

The first one I saw, a few minutes after stepping into my round, thatched-roof cabin, was phenomenal: a Superb Bird-of-paradise, which recently topped a BBC list of the world's "ten sexiest male birds," perched in a tree right outside. The display of this species is so bizarre that it doesn't even seem like a bird. When a female Superb Bird-of-paradise comes along, the male goes into a crouch, erects a shimmering green breast shield, raises a cape of black feathers from his back, and points his bill upward so that his body becomes an iridescent, abstract shape — more like a flying saucer than an animal. He rapidly bobs up and down, shuffles side to side, and snaps his tail, rotating his body each time the female moves so that she gets the full effect. If she likes him, they mate on the spot, and the female goes off to build a nest by herself.

My favorite bird-of-paradise, though, required a little more work. After hiking a couple of miles up a muddy track the next morning, I found a small bird with an elongated name: the King-of-Saxony Bird-of-paradise, which lives only in the mountains of central New Guinea. This one compensates for its diminutive size with a pair of slender, zebra-striped head plumes, attached above its eyes, that are almost twice the length of its body. The bird can move these plumes independently, like a pair of expressive antennae, and they look so weird that when the first specimens were shipped back to Europe, scientists thought they were fakes. I heard this one before I saw it: a rough, whirring buzz, increasing in volume over several seconds. Eventually I spied the bird, perched at the tip of a tall snag, waving its plumes around like a colorful insect, bobbing its body for extra effect.

These birds-of-paradise lived up to my expectations of New Guinea: wild and bizarre, lost in a pristine forest where uncontacted tribes still roam. The intrusions of outside civilization — the gravel airstrip at Tari, the lodge at Ambua, and a gravel road traversed by lumber and gas trucks — seemed slight against such rustic surroundings. I stayed in these mountains for several days, soaking up their birds and their ambience, before taking the prop plane back to Port Moresby. It was now a week into December, and my month of island-hopping was over; I had my sights set on Australia and the end of the year.

But before making the final leap Down Under, I wanted to chase the Golden Masked-Owl. When else would I have a chance to lock my eyes on such a rare bird? It was a tantalizingly short hop away — and so I took the connection over to New Britain.

The transfer from New Guinea's impenetrable highlands to the lowlands of New Britain looked like before-and-after photographs of a terrible catastrophe. As my plane descended over New Britain's shores, instead of jungle I saw miles of dark green, evenly gridded trees hugging the coastal plain: oil palm plantations. From the air, they resembled some of the banana farms I'd flown over in South and Central America earlier in the year, except on a more breathtaking scale. New Britain Palm Oil Limited, the main corporation on this island, has 227,000 acres under cultivation — more

than 350 square miles, an area nearly twice as large as Singapore —
which, at 150 plants per hectare, represents more than 13 million
oil palm trees. All of it was once rainforest.

Joseph, the owl guy, met me at the Walindi resort, a dense collection of cabins hemmed on three sides by oil palms and on the
remaining side by the ocean. I soon discovered that every other
guest here was seriously into scuba diving. The area between Indonesia and Papua New Guinea is part of the so-called Coral Tri-
angle, the world's most diverse reef system, which makes diving at
Walindi a little like birding in the Amazon. Coming for birds had
all the earmarks of searching for diamonds in a copper mine, but
I liked it that way. No wonder the Golden Masked-Owl had been
overlooked for so long — everyone on this island was preoccupied
with oil and coral.

The number of bird species on New Britain is relatively low,
especially in the cleared-out coastal areas, but a high percentage of
them are endemic. The island, which lies over the subduction zone
of the tiny Solomon Sea Plate, is one of the world's most active volcanic hotspots; one of its provincial capitals, Rabaul, was annihi-
lated as recently as 1994 when ten feet of ash buried the city. Because
New Britain has never been connected to the larger island of New
Guinea, its birds have had ample time and isolation to evolve into
new species such as the New Britain Kingfisher, New Britain Boo-
book, New Britain Rail, New Britain Thrush, New Britain Friar-
bird, and New Britain Sparrowhawk.

Joseph and I spent our daylight hours looking for some of these
endemics. He took me into the adjacent oil palm plantation, where
we drove slowly down the rows of trees, patrolling in one of the dive
resort's trucks. The plantation held more activity than I'd antici-
pated: Black Bitterns, White-browed Crakes, and Stephan's Doves
skulked in weedy spots, while enormous Blyth's Hornbills swept

between trees. Common Kingfishers perched on pipes beside irrigation ditches, and Eclectus Parrots squawked from unseen perches in the canopy. I had to admit that this place was lively.

As we waited for darkness, Joseph explained the basic operations of this plantation. Oil palms grow basketball-sized clumps of nuts, which crews of laborers cut off with twelve-meter-long saws. The oil is milled onsite, then shipped to special refineries. The trees are replanted on a twenty-year rotation — not because they've become too old, but because they have grown too tall to be harvested easily. We saw the whole process: the nuts were cut, thrown in large tractors, and taken to camps.

It was all very efficient, and efficiency is the main argument in favor of palm oil: compared to similar crops (such as soybeans and canola), palm trees can produce ten times as much oil per acre.

At dusk, we drove to the area where Joseph had first discovered the Golden Masked-Owl, about a mile from the resort. He'd seen it several times since, so I had high hopes. In darkness, we meandered slowly through the plantation, sweeping a powerful spotlight across the trees with their clumps of nuts hanging in silhouette.

The landscape wasn't exactly how I'd imagined Papua New Guinea. Everyone associates this country with wild, untamed wilderness — whether it's highland jungles, pristine offshore reefs, or vibrant indigenous cultures — without an oil palm in sight. Those people and places are all there, but exotic isolation is not the whole story.

"There!" exclaimed Joseph, pointing parallel to the beam of his spotlight. "Did you see it? The owl just flew up into the next tree."

We'd been searching for less than half an hour. On foot, we crept forward, holding our breath. I caught the eyeshine, and Joseph lit up the tree with his light.

"Yes," I said, quietly. "I've got it."

Until this year, nobody had seen a Golden Masked-Owl alive since before I was born. Now an owl gazed down at us, in full view, twisting its head with curiosity. It was my 5,605th bird of the year. Time, which had marched so fast lately, slowed down; it might have been ten seconds or ten minutes. I snapped a couple of photos. Then, as if remembering a prior errand, the owl turned, spread its wings, and silently flew down the next row of trees, disappearing like a ghost into the palms.

16

From End to End

CHRISTMAS ARRIVED in Paynes Find, in the dry interior of southwest Australia, with a predicted high temperature of ninety-five degrees Fahrenheit. The town, such as it was, consisted of a few outbuildings next to an old mine pit, a forlorn stand of windblown trees, and a faded highway sign that proclaimed, "Next services 275 kilometers." It was the least Christmassy place I could imagine.

For me, the holidays are about spending time with family, decorating a tree, putting up lights and stockings, opening presents, sipping hot chocolate, and curling up next to a fire on a snowy winter's day. None of those things would happen this year. In Australia, Christmas comes in midsummer, so the local traditions are a little different: many Aussies celebrate the day with seafood cookouts at the beach, swimming, and getting a tan. It's not unusual for Santa to arrive on a surfboard, or for people to do their shopping in shorts and flip-flops.

Not even those traditions applied to Paynes Find, which is a six-hour drive from the beach — or from anywhere, actually. I'd arrived here yesterday with Frank O'Connor, one of southwest Australia's top bird experts and the only Aussie I knew willing to spend the holiday with me. Frank showed up with a printed target list, including estimated probabilities of encountering each species, predicting that we'd find 30.6 new birds (well, make it 31) in the three days we had allotted. When I rolled out of bed at oh-dark-thirty, I found Frank already awake, sitting up with a genius-level Sudoku book propped in his lap, ready to go. He was just the guy I needed! The target list was my Christmas wish list, if only Santa were listening.

Frank had suggested we get up at 4 a.m. on Christmas to take advantage of the cool dawn hours at Paynes Find. By sunrise we were standing on an iron-red dirt road, surrounded by scrubby bush, as birds woke up all around us. I'd put in so many mornings this way, listening to birds while the sun gradually lightened the eastern horizon, that it felt comfortably familiar, even though nothing else about this Christmas was at all normal.

We spent a few hours prowling the back roads, turning up goodies like a jaunty Crimson Chat, a pretty little stocking stuffer, and several Mulga Parrots in the shade of a mulga tree.

"When you're birding, any tree could be a Christmas tree!" I said, and Frank smiled. The parrots, shiny green with bright red bellies, were aptly attired for the season.

The only real Christmas tree we saw was at the dusty roadhouse in Paynes Find, which had a handwritten "Closed for the holidays" sign propped in the window. Next to the lone gas pump out front, someone had stacked nine tractor tires in a rough pyramid with a traffic cone balanced on top, and painted the whole thing green. The tires were decorated with tinsel and hanging ornaments: Christmas, outback style.

Frank and I didn't encounter another human all morning, but we found a few special birds on my wish list, including a White-browed Treecreeper hitching up a gnarled snag. Once the heat set in, we began the 280-mile trip back to Perth, where Frank planned a late dinner of turkey pot roast at his house. On the Great Northern Highway, a flat ribbon of asphalt, the scenery came straight from a Mad Max movie.

Things had gone very well so far in Australia, in the weeks since I had left Papua New Guinea. For five days based out of Cairns, a proficient and laconic birder named Del Richards took me through mangroves, wet rainforest, and dry interior savanna. His strategy was to get all the honeyeaters, figuring the rest would show up along the way — and it worked perfectly. Del and I also tracked down the world's second- and third-largest birds: a wild Emu (properly pronounced eee-myew, not eee-moo) and a Southern Cassowary, a murderous-looking creature more dinosaur than bird. From Cairns, I hopped down to Brisbane for a thirty-six-hour blitz with a group of keen young birders, then continued straight to Melbourne, where I experienced my hottest temperature of the year — 110 degrees Fahrenheit — and visited the world's largest sewage treatment plant, a bird paradise. I made two fast out-and-back trips, one day in Tasmania followed by two days on the north island of New Zealand, to scoop up their impressive endemic birds before flying to Perth on Christmas Eve.

On my arrival in Australia I had lost all hope of reaching 6,000 species. When I passed my original goal of 5,000 in the Philippines, I toyed briefly with the thought that another 1,000 might be possible by year's end, but the pace slowed down in southeast Asia, and by the end of November I still needed 579 species to hit 6,000. It wasn't going to happen.

So I had decided to coast into the New Year without too much drama; I'd stay in Australia until time ran out, or maybe even fly back to the United States a day early to celebrate the end of my round-the-world trip at home. It would be disappointing to come close to such a big milestone without quite reaching it, but the year had already surpassed my wildest expectations, and I would be satisfied with any final number I hit.

As I made my way around Australia, though, the birds accumulated faster than I could have dreamed — mostly because the Aussies I met were some of the most fanatical, committed, hog-wild birders in the world.

"Don't worry, mate, you'll get your six thousand," Del said in a confident drawl when I landed in Cairns.

I laughed it off at the time, but two weeks later Del's prediction was no laughing matter, and I now found myself in a tricky situation. The last bird I added on Christmas Day, a White-backed Swallow flying around the mine pit at Paynes Find, was officially species number 5,966, which meant I was exactly 34 birds shy of 6,000 with six days remaining. Could I do it? Back in Perth, as Frank and I ate our turkey pot roast at 9 p.m. after an exhausting nineteen-hour day, we wrote out a comprehensive list of Australian birds I hadn't yet seen, and tried to figure out how I could get those 34 birds.

Our list included several dozen species, but they were spread all over the continent, and many were rare or difficult to find. For instance, the Plains-wanderer, an endangered species classified in its own family, required a nocturnal off-roading trip to the remote interior of New South Wales. I didn't have time to chase birds one by one, and Frank and I at last decided that the numbers didn't add up. I'd covered the birds in Australia so well that it wasn't likely I could find thirty-four more species by New Year's in six days anywhere in the country.

My heart beat faster. If not Australia, then where? I'd missed a few places during the year — Japan, Ethiopia, Namibia, Guyana, Cuba — any of which could add new sightings, but I'd get only one shot. Arranging a last-minute trip during the holidays would be difficult, and an extra ticket from southwest Australia, which isn't close to anything, would be expensive. Was it worth trying?

"Yes," I told Frank. "I have to go for it!"

Sleep could wait one more week. Late into the night on Christmas, I stayed up with my laptop, planning the next move. With thirty-four birds at stake, I had to get out of Australia. But where in the world should I go? So much for coasting into the New Year — this was going to be an all-out sprint to the finish.

✦ – ✦ – ✦

Near the end of the first round-the-world yacht race, held in 1968–1969, a French sailor named Bernard Moitessier found himself very close to winning: he'd sailed solo on an uninterrupted journey of nearly six months at sea, and all he had to do was round Cape Horn at the tip of South America, return to England, collect the trophy, and bask in fame and fortune. But that's not what he did. Instead, Moitessier kept going. He fired a message by slingshot onto the deck of a passing ship to announce his withdrawal from the race, explaining it was because "I am happy at sea and perhaps to save my soul." He sailed another two-thirds of the way around the world before finally putting in quietly at Tahiti.

Some claimed he went mad, but Moitessier wrote in his engrossing memoir that, after so many solitary months at sea, he just couldn't face the prospect of returning to Europe. He yearned to keep sailing, on his own terms.

Moitessier's decision had long fascinated me. I couldn't understand how, after such an intense effort, he could find it easier to keep going than to finish. But now, as I neared the end of my own round-the-world journey, I caught a glimpse into Moitessier's mind during that yacht race. The idea of stopping — and returning to regular life — was hard to contemplate. After a year of watching birds, I didn't want to do anything else.

Other birders have had the same feeling. After Sandy Komito set a North American Big Year record in 1987 with 722 species, he wasn't satisfied — so he did it again in 1998, upping his own tally to 748 birds (as portrayed by Owen Wilson in the movie *The Big Year*). The reigning Australian Big Year champion, John Weigel, made a supreme effort to see 745 Australian birds in 2012, then repeated the challenge in 2014 and finished with 770 species. Even then Weigel couldn't stop: in 2016, after my round-the-world trip wrapped up, he embarked on his third Big Year, this time in North America.

How glorious it would be to keep flying free. When all your energy is focused on a single purpose, nothing else seems to matter. That feeling can be incredibly seductive.

As the saying goes, though, nothing is as good as the first time. I knew from the beginning that I would give my all to this world Big Year, and then I would do something else. This year was a step toward the next stage of my life, whatever that might be. With my thirtieth birthday just a month away, I would go home and move on, and I wasn't interested in repeating the quest just to reach a higher number.

This had been a fantastic year. Visiting a lot of places, meeting a lot of birders, seeing half the birds in the world, and setting a world record, I had accomplished my goal and then some. My mission was not philanthropy — I didn't feel comfortable pressing people for money — nor was it meant to be a commentary on worldwide habitat destruction and conservation, though I witnessed plenty of both. It was, pure and simple, a celebration of birds, in all their fascinating detail, and how fun it is to watch them.

Unlike Moitessier, I longed for the green grass of home, and for the day when I didn't have to wake up before dawn or crawl through a muddy rainforest.

With six days left, only one piece of unfinished business remained — the 6,000th bird. That goal completely consumed my thoughts, and I didn't dwell too much on the aftermath. Next year could take care of itself. I was determined to live this one to the last minute.

+ - + - +

The website eBird.org, which I use to keep track of my sightings, introduced a neat feature in 2015: in any given area, it filters the birds you've seen against what others have reported. You can, for instance, make a list of all the species in Azerbaijan that would be lifers, and sort them in descending order of likelihood. It works for life lists, year lists, month lists, even day lists. That feature was fantastic for me because I could instantly see what I was missing in different parts of the world.

When I ran the numbers on Christmas, three countries stood out: Guyana, Ethiopia, and India. Each of them showed about a hundred species possible on a quick trip (plus some rarities) that would be new for my year. I briefly considered other options, like hopping across the Pacific to Hawaii, but it soon became clear that, to maximize new sightings, these three far-flung destinations were it. I was surprised that India made the list, as I'd already spent two weeks there earlier in the year.

This brought up an interesting question: when, exactly, should the year officially end? I'd kicked it off on the Antarctic Peninsula, which is in the same time zone as Argentina, and it stood to reason that a year should be measured from where and when it starts. But that was on the other side of the International Date Line. If I stayed in the Eastern Hemisphere, the 365 days wouldn't fully elapse until midday on January 1, local time — and yet it didn't feel right to continue birding past New Year's. By going west to east, my year would thus be cut to 364 and a half days. If I had traveled east to west instead, taking advantage of the date line, during a leap year, the year might have been extended to nearly 367 days.

Guyana, Ethiopia, and India each offered logistical difficulties. Reaching Guyana would require a very long flight from Australia, and getting to the remote forest wouldn't be easy on extremely short notice. Ethiopia was more accessible, but I couldn't find a single local birder who could help. That left India, a giant country with overwhelming diversity. In September I'd visited south and central India but had missed the relatively remote northeast corner, assuming I'd see most of those specialties elsewhere in Asia. Now, according to eBird, I could add dozens more species in the state of Assam, squeezed between Bhutan, China, and northern Myanmar. Skipping northeast India the first time had been a strategic mistake, but maybe now I could rectify it and catch my 6,000th species there.

Choices, choices . . . What to do? I checked my watch and saw that it had ticked past midnight. Christmas morning was just dawning in Oregon, sixteen hours behind the time in Perth. Realizing that I hadn't yet talked to my parents for the holiday, I picked up my cell phone and called home.

My mom came on the line.

"Merry Christmas!" she said. "It's so good to hear your voice! How are you doing?"

I told her about Paynes Find and the tractor-tire Christmas tree. My parents had followed my Big Year with laser intensity, quietly supporting the trip any way they could — which often meant listening at all hours to my enthusiastic reports of odd birds.

It was strange to think that I'd left home on Christmas exactly one year earlier, and now I was only a week away from returning to Oregon.

"Have you figured out where you'll be for New Year's?" she asked.

"Kind of," I said, hesitating. "Well, actually, I don't know. The practical thing would be to stay here in Australia and maybe stop in Hawaii on the way home, but I don't think I'd get enough birds that way to hit six thousand. It looks like I'd add the most species in northeast India — but that would be crazy! Flying to India, even if I could do it at the last minute, would probably zero out my account for the ticket."

There was a pause.

"So, you'd see the most birds by going back to India?" she asked.

"Yes," I said, "assuming I could get to the Assam province, in the northeast corner. I think I could manage it, but it'd be tight."

"Okay, hold on," she said, and seemed to confer with my dad away from the phone.

I wondered what was happening — was something wrong? Then she came back on the line.

"You're so far away that we can't give you a physical Christmas present this year," she said. "But we want you to follow your dream to the very end — so we're going to buy your plane ticket for this trip to India, and now you don't have any reason not to go!"

For a minute, words failed me. The thought of such a generous gift hadn't even crossed my mind, and it was so much more than any present under a tree. From the time I first became interested in birds as a ten-year-old, my parents had encouraged me every step of the way, and that support meant the world to me. Now, when I was talking myself out of splurging on this last-minute extension, they were right there cheering me on.

"Thanks, Mom," I said. "It'll be New Year's in India!"

"Merry Christmas!" she said, sounding delighted.

So many people had helped me in so many ways this year, I'd spend the rest of my life happily repaying favors. But this was, by about 4,300 miles (the distance from Perth to Dibrugarh), the best Christmas present I'd ever received.

Immediately, I emailed a bright twenty-four-year-old Indian birder named Ramit Singal, whom I'd met in Delhi in September. Within hours, Ramit had made arrangements for us to join a couple of others for a New Year's Eve birding bash.

And so, after celebrating Christmas in the heat of the Australian outback, Frank dropped me off at the Perth airport and I flew straight to central Asia in the dead of winter. The transition was fast and surreal. It took some fancy footwork with visas and flights and a brief layover in Singapore, but soon I was gazing across glaciated peaks of the Himalayas as I touched down in Dibrugarh, the so-called "Tea City of India."

When I walked off the plane on the afternoon of December 28, I abruptly realized that I'd just landed for the last time before the New Year. Since the beginning of January, I'd taken 112 flights, on 77 different days, totaling 100,514 miles — not including the additional miles by car, taxi, bus, motorbike, quad bike, jeepney, sleeper train, bullet train, ship, speedboat, ferry, Zodiac, outboard canoe, raft, bicycle, and on foot. It was bittersweet to think that the next time I took off, I would be done.

Ramit met me with two other birders, Binanda Hathibaruah and Bidyut Gogoi, and the three of us shot straight for the mountains above Dibrugarh. On the subfreezing morning of December 29, we woke up at 3:30 in a building without heat or electricity in the snow-covered Mishmi Hills, at 8,000 feet. Because all of India is on one time zone, this far east the sun would set just after 4:00 p.m., so we had to make the most of the precious midwinter daylight.

As the first rays lit up snowfields in a panorama of pink and gold, birds began to stir. Some were species I'd seen two months earlier in Myanmar and China, but many were new — the ones on my eBird target list. Shivering and stamping our feet to stay warm, Ramit, Binanda, Bidyut, and I picked out three new fulvettas, two yuhinas, and a sibia, followed by a teeny Rusty-throated Wren-Babbler, a Mishmi Hills specialty about the size and shape of a mouse. We worked our way down a single-lane dirt road, gradually descending into lusher forest at lower elevations, where mixed-species flocks flitted in the midcanopy.

At 11:15 a.m. Binanda spotted a weird bird called a Yellow-rumped Honeyguide in a rocky clearing. Small and finchlike with a gray body, lemon-yellow forehead, and namesake yellow rump, this species eats mostly beeswax gleaned from honeycombs of the Himalayan honeybee. Male honeyguides maintain territories around active hives and mate with multiple females, which lay their eggs in other birds' nests. They are tough birds to find, perhaps because their main habitat requirement — beehives — is so specific.

This was the one I'd been waiting for. I wanted to shout at the top of my lungs, jump up and down, and do the victory dance — but I was afraid that might scare the bird away. Instead, I turned slowly to Binanda and flashed a conspiratorial thumbs-up.

"Six thousand," I whispered. "That's the six-thousandth bird!"

Ramit and Bidyut, fully appreciating the significance of the moment, clustered around and exchanged serious handshakes.

"Congratulations," said Ramit.

"Yes," said Bidyut. "And what a great species!"

"Look, the honeyguide is showing his rump," said Binanda, and we all turned to train our binoculars on the bird, which perched with its back to us. For the next few minutes, it moved deliberately from branch to branch, patrolling its territory, while we watched in contented silence.

That the culmination of my yearlong world tour, into which I'd invested all my creativity and resources, was embodied in this obscure gray bird on a nameless hillside in a remote province of India seemed perfectly appropriate. Birding is about appreciating life's infinite details — and if subtlety is beauty, then a birder will never run short of wonder. That number 6,000 did not seem like a conquest — it felt like a fresh beginning.

Many things had come together near the end: the productive stretch in Australia, eBird, a generous Christmas present, and these three local birders glad to spend their New Year's season with me in India. To surpass my original goal by a thousand species less than two days before the clock ran out was pretty sweet. But the real prize, looking back, was the friendships I'd made — the hundreds of people who, at one point or another, had taken the time to share their sheer love of birds.

✦ — ✦ — ✦

If I had a bird for every time someone said, "You did a lifetime of birding in one year!" I could retire right now — my life list would be complete. Fortunately, I haven't quite reached that stage yet. Though it may have seemed like a lifetime, only one year passed, exactly the same year that everyone else had.

This distinction is worth noting: instead of compressing a whole existence into one year, I'd rather say I expanded one year to its maximum potential. It is worthwhile to do something intensely for a year, to really dig deep and get to the meat of it, and I came away from my Big Year with a clearer picture of the state of birds and birding in our world. Anyone could do the same; we all have opportunities to follow our interests. How we spend our days is an ongoing choice. Most of my own life still lies ahead, and I'm happy, at this point, to have pursued this dream when I had the chance.

The beauty of a year list is that at the end of December it resets to zero — unlike a life list, which expires when its author does. So when people comment about a "lifetime of birding," I gently point out that I am still very much alive and won't stop anytime soon. On New Year's Day, my list would start from scratch.

Officially, the last new bird of 2015 was a Silver-breasted Broadbill, seen just before sunset on December 31, which capped my list at 6,042 birds — 58.3 percent of the world's recognized species. Nobody had ever before recorded half the world's birds in one year, and to pass 6,000 exceeded my grandest expectations.

The number itself was ephemeral, though. Global bird taxonomy is in such flux that nobody agrees on how many species exist on Earth. The Clements Checklist counted 6,042 while the IOC World Bird List put my tally at 6,144. Both of those figures would become obsolete a few months later when new species splits were announced, and within a year a groundbreaking scientific paper would suggest that ornithologists have been far too conservative: using new techniques, a group of researchers estimated that there are actually 18,000 bird species worldwide, nearly doubling today's accepted totals. Sorting out all those cryptic splits will likely take decades of painstaking lab work, so the global bird list will keep inflating into the future, and the numbers will keep changing.

In the end, I visited forty-one countries on seven continents and spent about $60,000 on travel, lodging, food, guiding, gear, and carbon offsets during the year. With a strict budget, I spent just about what I earned writing a blog and a book. One of the biggest misconceptions about international travel is that it is prohibitively expensive. In truth, the cost of living in most of the world is much cheaper than in the United States if you're willing to act like a local. It's ultimately a matter of priorities: Would you rather drive a nice SUV or see the world? To me, $10 per bird seemed like a small price to pay.

On a personal level, the Big Year affirmed my lifelong dedication to birds. When I set out, I knew that I'd witness a heap of incredible species in exotic places, but I couldn't have foreseen how the quest would touch so many people, at home and abroad, who followed my progress. What began as a quiet adventure became a grassroots movement of environmental inspiration. My greatest lesson was that birding is a nearly universal interest, represented even in the farthest corners of the Earth. The future of birds on our planet is uncertain, but with so many people who care, I can't help but be optimistic. By working together across all kinds of borders, we can help make sure the next generation enjoys birds, too.

At the end of the year, I looked forward to returning home. I wanted to see friends and family again — and I was bowled over when fifty people surprised me at my local airport with welcome banners, balloons, and signs. On the first day home, I saw a Golden-crowned Sparrow in my backyard, which I hadn't seen during the Big Year. A month after the New Year, I celebrated my thirtieth birthday at a Mexican restaurant, eating plates of guacamole, the food I'd missed the most while traveling. I began other projects, including writing this book and beginning another book about birds, and returned to Antarctica, the place where my Big Year started. Life continued, and I kept watching birds.

Meanwhile, the minute I finished my world Big Year, the Dutchman, Arjan Dwarshuis, started his own Big Year in 2016, and began at a dizzying pace. I wished him luck, not just with the numbers, but with the adventure. Others will tackle the challenge in years to come, and will find ways to take it in new directions.

For anyone considering a round-the-world trip, here's some advice: pack light, go hard, and stay flexible. Don't be afraid to take detours, even if they are off the beaten path. Go solo when you can. Keep it personal, but don't make it about yourself. Tip well, smile often, and say thank you. If someone offers you a gift, take it graciously. Learn to say hello in the local language. Know that the world is much friendlier than it often seems, and don't be paranoid. Eat the street food — it's tasty, cheap, and healthy — and talk with the vendors. If a problem can be resolved for $20, spend it and move on. Hang out with locals as much as possible, respecting that their culture may be different from yours. Above all, don't let fear get in the way — everyone is afraid of something, but the worst that can happen is to never go at all.

+ - + - +

At 11 p.m. on New Year's Eve, in the dense forest outside the city of Tinsukia in India's Assam province, Ramit, Binanda, Bidyut, another birder named Pritam Baruah, and I heard something whistle tremulously in the dark. We stood still, listening. The five of us had spent the afternoon walking through the forest, and lingered after sundown to try for owls.

"Well, it's not a Spot-bellied Eagle-Owl," said Binanda, discerningly. The eagle-owl's call is a single descending cry, unlike this whistle, which repeated in a series of mournful notes. I didn't really hope to find an eagle-owl this evening — my only reasonable chance for a new species after the Silver-breasted Broadbill — but figured we might as well stay up until midnight.

"It does sound like some kind of owl, though," whispered Ramit. "I think it's an Oriental Bay-Owl!"

All of us had turned our flashlights off. We stood still, with hands cupped around our ears to amplify the noise. When the whistle sounded for a third time, there could be no doubt.

"Yes," Binanda said. "That's definitely a bay-owl."

I'd already seen an Oriental Bay-Owl months earlier in Malaysia, so this was nothing new for the Big Year, but it was unexpected in this spot. Bay-owls are rare in India, occurring only in this far

258 • *Birding Without Borders*

northeast corner of the country. Ramit probably had more experience with the species than any other Indian birder, and this was only his fourth encounter.

"Let's try to see it!" he said.

Pritam turned a spotlight on the trees. After a few seconds of careful scanning, he located the bird: a twelve-inch-tall, fluffy-bodied owl with a heart-shaped face and round, black eyes clung to an upright twig at eye level. Reflexively, I raised my camera to snap a photo. My heart skipped as I squeezed the shutter, the bird filling the frame.

"Wow," breathed Ramit. "As far as I know, that's the first-ever photograph of a wild bay-owl in India!"

We admired the view for a few more seconds before Pritam switched off the light, not wanting to disturb the owl. As the five of us resumed walking through the dark forest, I could hear the bay-owl's call behind us gradually fade into the distance. It was the last bird I'd see in 2015, but I didn't feel sad. All the same birds would still be around tomorrow, inviting more adventures.

Shortly after midnight we all turned in to bed, agreeing to set our alarms for 5 a.m. I'd flown halfway around the planet to reach this remote province and figured I might as well stay awhile with my new friends. In the morning, the New Year would bring a fresh dawn chorus to one of Earth's most diverse forests, and I would be out there, looking for birds.

ACKNOWLEDGMENTS

When I first teased my literary agent, Russell Galen, of the Scovil Galen Ghosh Literary Agency, with the loony scheme to dash around the world looking at birds for a year, he didn't flinch. Russ is a rare species — he knows words as well as birds — and the idea for this book was hatched with his vision and encouragement. I will always appreciate Russ for a dream come true.

I am especially grateful to Lisa White, my editor at Houghton Mifflin Harcourt, for her unflagging enthusiasm and follow-through at each step of the project. Without her commitment, the world Big Year might not have happened, and her skill and hard work helped this book fledge. I am also indebted to assistant editor Emily Snyder, jacket designer Martha Kennedy, production editor Beth Burleigh Fuller, publicist Taryn Roeder, marketing managers Katrina Kruse and Liz Anderson, copy editor Loma Huh, proofreader Diana Coe, legal consultant Loren Isenberg, designers Eugenie Delaney and Chloe Foster, compositor Margaret Rosewitz, and indexer Sheila Ryan for their excellent contributions to the book.

Susan Matthews, former senior web editor for the National Audubon Society, and former Audubon consulting editor Will Bourne built a beautiful page for the *Birding Without Borders* blog on Audubon's website. During the year, Susan carefully edited, posted, and promoted my daily dispatches — often received at weird hours — while photo editor Camilla Cerea sorted through the images. Thanks to the whole Audubon web team for relaying this story in real time. I am also grateful to Jennie Duberstein, coordinator of the Sonoran Joint Venture, for her help with Twitter updates.

Nothing is more important to a birder than optics, and my

Leicas held up to a rigorous field test. Jeff Bouton, marketing manager at Leica Sport Optics, generously supplied binoculars, a spotting scope, and a camera, giving me crystal-clear views and photographs of thousands of birds in the field.

You can go birding without borders, but not without plane tickets and visas! Thanks to everyone at AirTreks for finding the best way to get there from here: Adam Seper, Daniel Gamber, Kristina Ketelsen, Becky Kiner, Nai Piangjai, Valerie Depeyrot, Anthy Kapsalis, and Barbara Segria. And the people at VisaHQ have my respect for sorting out an impossible tangle of visa issues: Trevin Barker, Yulla-May Nicolas, Tom Schrandt, Keith Lamphier, Christopher Wizda, and Claire Malekian.

My mom and dad, Lisa Strycker and Bob Keefer, took some deep breaths when I told them about my plan to spend a year in some of the world's most far-flung corners — then they smiled and said, "Go for it!" From their sneaky care packages to their willingness to pick up the phone at 2 a.m. when I called in tears with a fever in Peru, I am one lucky son. Being a parent must be the most thankless job of all, and their eternal support and encouragement have helped me follow my dreams to the ends of the Earth and back.

✦ ─ ✦ ─ ✦

Of course, none of this would have been remotely possible without the hundreds of birders who hosted and accompanied me during my Big Year. The kindness of the international birding community just blew me away, and I am humbled at the generosity of the human spirit; I'll spend the rest of my life paying it forward. To list every person who supported this adventure — hospitality staff, drivers, friends, dinner companions, commenters, advice givers, blog and book readers — would be impossible. But here, in alphabetical order by country, is an account of the birders I met in the field. My heartfelt thank-you goes out to everyone, as well as my apologies to anyone whose name I missed.

Antarctica: One Ocean Expeditions, Steve Bailey. **Argentina:** Esteban Daniels, Rogelio "Roger" Espinosa, Freddy Burgos, Claudia Martin, Yoshitharo Kuroki, Fabricio "Fabri" Gorleri, José Segovia, Guy Cox, Patricio Ramírez Llorens, Marcelo Gavensky, Sergio Castedo, Martin Farina, Norbert Fratt, Kate Rooney, the farmers of Cerro Negro. **Australia:** Del Richards, John and Peta Nott, Mark Christiansen, Perry Marshall, Jeremy Ringma, Megan Barnes, Nick Leseberg, Richard Nowotny, Simon Starr, Sean Dooley, Dave Torr, Ian Denham, Mark Buckby, Michael Ramsey, Philip Peel, Frank O'Connor. **Australia — Tasmania:** Mona Loofs-Samorzewski, Els Wakefield, Nicole Sommer, Rob Hamilton. **Brazil:** Guto Carvalho, Marco and Patricia Antonio, Luis Avelino, René Santos, Jonas d'Abronzo, Giuliano Bernardon, Eloir Bernardon, Bianca Bernardon, Mario M. S. Timiraos, Fabiano Oliveira, Alex Lees, Nárgila Gomes De Moura, Leonardo Patrial. **Cameroon:** Benjamin "Benji" Jayin Jomi, Ntomnifor Richard Fru, Albert Aloebade, Sangale Guidjelie Merveille. **Chile:** Fred Homer, Fernando Díaz Segovia, Rodrigo Silva. **China:** Geraint "Sid" Francis. **Colombia:** Jim Danzenbaker, Bruce LaBar, Ryan Shaw, Luis Arturo Gómez, Leonor Pardo, Juan Ortíz, Juan Pablo López Ordóñez, Juan Diego Castillo Ramírez, Oswaldo Cortes, Giovanni Alberto Chaves Portilla, Lorenzo Bautista, Gabo Utria, José Luis Pushaina, Christopher Calonje, Juan José Arango, Anabel Vanin, José Luna, David Bancroft, Jeffrey Cooper, Albeiro Uribe, Diego Calderón-Franco, Gleison Fernando Guarin Largo. **Costa Rica:** Roy Orozco, Johan Fernández, Lisa Erb, Adrian Arroyo. **Ecuador:** Xavier Muñoz, Mercedes Rivadeneira, Manuel Sánchez, José Gallardo, Forrest Rowland, Edison Buenaño, Ángel Paz, Sergio Bastantes, Jarol Fernando Vaca, Renato Espinosa. **Ger-**

many: Peter and Kimberly Kaestner. **Ghana:** Kalu Afasi, Ziblim Illiasu, Jonathan Tsey, Robert Tindana, Cobby Kwabena Tawiah, Yaw Boateng. **Guatemala:** John Cahill, Rob Cahill, Tara Cahill, Carlos Aguilar, Pablo Chumil, Juan Chocoy, Max Noack. **Iceland:** Yann Kolbeinsson. **India:** Harsha Jayaramaiah, Junis F. S., Manoj Balraj, Sanu Sasi, Dhanesh Ayyappan, Eldhose K. V., Siddha Kuruvi, Ramit Singal, Dinesh Singal, Rakesh Ahlawat, Surat Singh Poonia, Abhishek Gulshan, Rohit Chakravarty, Sudhir Oswal, Pankaj Gupta, Taksh Sangwan, Hari Lama, Swati Sidhu, Hari Krishnan, Bishop H. G. Kuriakose Mor Eusebius, Bidyut Gogoi, Binanda Hathibaruah, Deborshee Gogoi, Pritam Baruah, Ranjan Kumar Das, Shashank Dalvi, Anish Aravind, Divya Mudappa, Kalyan Varma, Panchapakesan Jeganathan, Prashanth N. S., T. R. Shankar Raman, Tanya Seshadri, Raphy Kallettumkara, Sheeba Nanjan, Abhijith Surendran, Premchand Reghuvaran, Shah Jahan, Sumesh B., Arun Lal, Renjus Box, Vaisakh George, Birders Ezhupunna. **Indonesia–Bali:** Pak Yudi. **Indonesia–Sulawesi:** Mohamad Naliko (Monal Capellone), Adrianus Sampali, Yarsen Keba, Anes Pianaung. **Jamaica:** Elizabeth Ames, Barbara Heindl, Jay Wright, Tom Ryan. **Kenya:** Joseph Aengwo, Alan Grenon, David Ngala, Wilson Tiren, Justus Mwangi, Lazarus Kariuki, Eunice Thairu. **Madagascar:** Genot Andriamihaja, Jacky Ratiantsihoarana, Luc Rajarisoa. **Malaysia–Borneo:** Gary Albert, John Bakar, Cede Prudente, Robert Ong, Noredah Othman, Andrew Siani, Denis Degullacion, Kenneth Tizon, Ali Suffri, Ron Pudin, Winston Pudin, Jason Azahari Reyes, Andy Lee, Borneo Bird Club. **Malaysia–Peninsula:** Cheong Weng Chun, Azlina Mokhtar, Mohd Hazhman, Woei Ong. **Mexico:** Eric Antonio Martínez, Jilly Rodríguez Méndez, René Valdés, Phil Hansbro, Francisco García, Bryan Sharp, Viviana Sofia, Fernanda García-Triana, Durango Bird Club. **Myanmar:** Gideon Dun, Thiri Htin Hla. **New Zealand:** Harry Boorman, Chris Gaskin. **Norway:** Bjørn Olav Tveit.

Panama: Guido Berguido, Linda Harrison, Jerry Harrison, Panama Audubon Society, Rosabel Miró, Yenifer Díaz, Stephany Carty. **Papua New Guinea:** Leonard Vaieke, Walter North, Joseph Tano, Joseph Ando, Joseph Yenmoro, David Dau, Cheyne Benjamin. **Peru:** Gunnar Engblom, Alejandro Tello, Carlos Altamirano, Glenn Sibbald, Juan Julca, Francisco Vásquez, Noam Shany, José Luis Avendaño, Percy Avendaño, Silverio Duri, Julio Benites, Jeff Woodman. **Philippines:** Nicky Icarangal, Cristy Burlace, Emiliano "Blackie" Lumiston, Ramil Lumiston, Adrian Constantino. **Singapore:** Con Foley. **South Africa and Lesotho:** Wayne Jones, Adam Riley, Callan Cohen, Mike Buckham, Jean Buckham, Tommy Buckham, Adam Buckham, Jack Buckham, Emma Buckham, Ethan Kistler, Billi Krochuk, Klas Magnus Karlsson, Brian Rapoza, Alan Mitchnick, Martha Miller, Janine Gregory, Cliff Dorse, Greg de Klerk, Nelis Wolmarans. **Spain:** Gorka Gorospe, Farran López, Ricard Gutiérrez, Nacho Dies. **Sri Lanka:** Ashoka, Chandima Jayaweera. **Taiwan:** Wayne Hsu, Kuan-Chieh "Chuck" Hung, Tsai-Yu Wu, Da-Li Lin, Richard Foster, Jo-Szu "Ross" Tsai, Yukun Chen, Cynthia Su, Rodney Yang, Scott Lin. **Tanzania:** Anthony Raphael, Roger Msengi, Harv Schubothe, Kelle Herrick, David Heath. **Thailand:** Panuwat "Par" Sasirat, Kampol "Tui" Sukhumalind, Udorn "Nang" Jantboworn. **Turkey:** Emin Yoğurtçuoğlu, Ahmet Karataş, Mustafa Çulcuoğlu. **Uganda:** Livingstone Kalema, Rolf de By, Amos Monday. **United Arab Emirates:** Oscar Campbell, Mark Smiles. **United States:** Michael Retter, John Yerger, Scott Olmstead, Erin Olmstead, Jake Mohlmann, Dave Bell, Lance Benner, Frank Gilliland, Susan Gilliland, Dessi Sieburth, Luke Tiller, Anne Heyerly, Dan Heyerly, Peter Thiemann, Marshall Iliff, Tim Spahr, Tim Lenz, Tom Schulenberg, Bob Behrstock, Mary Gustafson, Tom Ford-Hutchinson.

GEAR FOR A BIG YEAR

40-liter REI Vagabond Tour 40 Travel Pack

Tumi luggage tag

Leica 10x42 Ultravid HD-Plus binoculars

Leica 65 mm Televid spotting scope with tripod

Leica V-Lux camera

GoPro Hero3 video camera with selfie stick

11" MacBook Air laptop

iPhone 6 (and iPhone 4) with an international phone plan

iPod nano and headphones

SureFire Fury LED flashlight with rechargeable batteries

Green laser pointer

Yalumi LED headlamp

Sea to Summit silk sleeping bag liner

Set of adapter plugs for the world

Two passports

Wallet

Two notebooks

Two Sharpie pens

Oakley sunglasses

Fossil watch

Asics GEL-Enduro 7 trail running shoes

Four Mountain Hardwear Wicked Lite short-sleeved T-shirts

Columbia Sportswear rain shell

Marmot down jacket

Two pairs of ExOfficio field pants

Three pairs of ExOfficio Give-N-Go boxer underwear

Two long-sleeved ExOfficio BugsAway insect-repelling shirts with sun protection

Two pairs of SmartWool socks

Two pairs of cotton Balega socks

Wildy Adventure anti-leech socks

Two bandanas

Plain black baseball cap

REI Campware spoon

Israeli water-purification tablets

Antimalarial pills

First-aid kit

Assorted toiletries (comb, lip balm, eye drops, toenail clippers, tweezers, toothbrush, toothpaste, floss, aspirin, Imodium, sunscreen)

BIG YEAR SNAPSHOT

Country	Days	Total	New	Unique	New per Day	Unique per Day	% New	% Unique
Antarctica/ Falklands	8	54	54	30	7	4	100%	56%
Argentina	12	435	374	101	31	8	86%	23%
Chile	4	137	107	43	27	11	78%	31%
Brazil	19	684	446	237	23	12	65%	35%
Peru	21	784	488	242	23	12	62%	31%
Ecuador	12	625	251	109	21	9	40%	17%
Colombia	27	749	260	173	10	6	35%	23%
Panama	3	299	69	33	23	11	23%	11%
Jamaica	3	121	61	43	20	14	50%	36%
Costa Rica	7	411	158	95	23	14	38%	23%
Guatemala	5	260	94	28	19	6	36%	11%
Mexico	17	483	173	100	10	6	36%	21%
United States	21	466	215	196	10	9	46%	42%
Iceland	1	54	36	14	36	14	67%	26%
Norway	4	142	102	31	26	8	72%	22%
Turkey	4	187	124	40	31	10	66%	21%
Spain	6	193	51	41	9	7	26%	21%
Germany	1	20	1	0	1	0	5%	0%
Ghana	8	318	295	89	37	11	93%	28%
Cameroon	9	201	97	40	11	4	48%	20%

Country	Days	Total	New	Unique	New per Day	Unique per Day	% New	% Unique
South Africa	18	442	304	167	17	9	69%	38%
Madagascar	8	98	77	74	10	9	79%	76%
Kenya	10	392	159	52	16	5	41%	13%
Tanzania	12	387	80	63	7	5	21%	16%
Uganda	14	517	128	126	9	9	25%	24%
UAE	1	118	39	19	39	19	33%	16%
India	22	572	373	201	17	9	65%	35%
Myanmar	8	272	136	55	17	7	50%	20%
China	7	215	121	93	17	13	56%	43%
Taiwan	3	118	45	35	15	12	38%	30%
Philippines	10	210	155	116	16	12	74%	55%
Thailand	6	266	84	41	14	7	32%	15%
Sri Lanka	3	86	31	31	10	10	36%	36%
Malaysia	14	366	173	161	12	12	47%	44%
Indonesia	9	198	110	99	12	11	56%	50%
Papua New Guinea	9	247	198	159	22	18	80%	64%
Australia	15	432	328	312	22	21	76%	72%
New Zealand	3	108	41	41	14	14	38%	38%
Singapore	1	30	4	3	4	3	13%	10%

Note. I visited France and Lesotho briefly and did not include them here.

BIG YEAR SPECIES LIST

#	Species	Date	Location	#	Species	Date	Location
1	Cape Petrel (9–10, 16)	1/1	Antarctica	48	Falkland Steamer-Duck	1/7	Falklands
2	Southern Fulmar	1/1	Antarctica	49	Flying Steamer-Duck	1/7	Falklands
3	Antarctic Tern	1/1	Antarctica	50	Ruddy-headed Goose	1/7	Falklands
4	Kelp Gull	1/1	Antarctica	51	Kelp Goose	1/7	Falklands
5	Brown Skua	1/1	Antarctica	52	Upland Goose	1/7	Falklands
6	Antarctic Shag	1/1	Antarctica	53	Black-necked Swan	1/7	Falklands
7	Wilson's Storm-Petrel	1/1	Antarctica	54	Chilean Skua	1/8	Argentina
8	Southern Giant-Petrel	1/1	Antarctica	55	House Sparrow	1/9	Argentina
9	Chinstrap Penguin (7, 17)	1/1	Antarctica	56	Black-chinned Siskin	1/9	Argentina
10	Gentoo Penguin (7)	1/1	Antarctica	57	Chimango Caracara	1/9	Argentina
11	South Polar Skua	1/1	Antarctica	58	Southern Caracara	1/9	Argentina
12	Snowy Sheathbill	1/1	Antarctica	59	White-throated Caracara	1/9	Argentina
13	Black-bellied Storm-Petrel	1/2	Antarctica	60	Southern Lapwing	1/9	Argentina
14	Adélie Penguin (17)	1/2	Antarctica	61	Black-chested Buzzard-Eagle	1/9	Argentina
15	Snow Petrel	1/2	Antarctica	62	Austral Blackbird	1/9	Argentina
16	Macaroni Penguin	1/4	Antarctica	63	Rufous-collared Sparrow	1/9	Argentina
17	White-chinned Petrel	1/5	Antarctica	64	Patagonian Sierra-Finch	1/9	Argentina
18	Antarctic Prion	1/5	Antarctica	65	Austral Thrush	1/9	Argentina
19	Blue Petrel	1/5	Antarctica	66	House Wren	1/9	Argentina
20	Light-mantled Albatross	1/5	Antarctica	67	Chilean Swallow	1/9	Argentina
21	Common Diving-Petrel	1/5	High Seas	68	White-crested Elaenia	1/9	Argentina
22	Black-browed Albatross	1/5	High Seas	69	Tufted Tit-Tyrant	1/9	Argentina
23	Gray-headed Albatross	1/5	High Seas	70	Thorn-tailed Rayadito	1/9	Argentina
24	Slender-billed Prion	1/5	High Seas	71	Dark-bellied Cinclodes	1/9	Argentina
25	Wandering Albatross	1/5	High Seas	72	White-throated Treerunner	1/9	Argentina
26	Gray-backed Storm-Petrel	1/6	Falklands	73	Magellanic Tapaculo	1/9	Argentina
27	Sooty Shearwater	1/6	Falklands	74	Austral Parakeet	1/9	Argentina
28	Great Shearwater	1/6	Falklands	75	Magellanic Woodpecker (18)	1/9	Argentina
29	Northern Giant-Petrel	1/6	Falklands	76	Austral Pygmy-Owl	1/9	Argentina
30	Royal Albatross	1/6	Falklands	77	Andean Condor (34)	1/9	Argentina
31	Long-tailed Meadowlark	1/7	Falklands	78	Black-faced Ibis	1/9	Argentina
32	White-bridled Finch	1/7	Falklands	79	Great Grebe	1/9	Argentina
33	Dark-faced Ground-Tyrant	1/7	Falklands	80	Yellow-billed Pintail	1/9	Argentina
34	Blackish Cinclodes	1/7	Falklands	81	Flightless Steamer-Duck	1/9	Argentina
35	Striated Caracara	1/7	Falklands	82	Ashy-headed Goose	1/9	Argentina
36	South American Tern	1/7	Falklands	83	Correndera Pipit	1/9	Argentina
37	Dolphin Gull	1/7	Falklands	84	Sedge Wren	1/9	Argentina
38	Rufous-chested Dotterel	1/7	Falklands	85	Austral Negrito	1/9	Argentina
39	Two-banded Plover	1/7	Falklands	86	South American Snipe	1/9	Argentina
40	Magellanic Oystercatcher	1/7	Falklands	87	Greater Yellowlegs	1/9	Argentina
41	Turkey Vulture (4)	1/7	Falklands	88	Blackish Oystercatcher	1/9	Argentina
42	Imperial Cormorant	1/7	Falklands	89	Neotropic Cormorant	1/9	Argentina
43	Magellanic Cormorant	1/7	Falklands	90	Yellow-billed Teal	1/9	Argentina
44	Southern Rockhopper Penguin (17)	1/7	Falklands	91	Red Shoveler	1/9	Argentina
45	Magellanic Penguin	1/7	Falklands	92	Gray-breasted Martin	1/9	Argentina
46	White-tufted Grebe	1/7	Falklands	93	Rock Pigeon	1/9	Argentina
47	Crested Duck	1/7	Falklands				

Note: Numbers in parentheses indicate pages on which species appear.

94	American Kestrel	1/10	Chile
95	Torrent Duck (28–29, 32)	1/10	Chile
96	Common Diuca-Finch	1/10	Chile
97	Gray-hooded Sierra-Finch	1/10	Chile
98	Chilean Mockingbird	1/10	Chile
99	Plain-mantled Tit-Spinetail	1/10	Chile
100	Crag Chilia	1/10	Chile
101	Moustached Turca	1/10	Chile
102	Chilean Flicker	1/10	Chile
103	Black-winged Ground-Dove	1/10	Chile
104	Blue-and-white Swallow	1/10	Chile
105	Rufous-naped Ground-Tyrant	1/10	Chile
106	Spot-billed Ground-Tyrant	1/10	Chile
107	Yellow-rumped Siskin	1/10	Chile
108	Greater Yellow-Finch	1/10	Chile
109	Plumbeous Sierra-Finch	1/10	Chile
110	Mourning Sierra-Finch	1/10	Chile
111	White-browed Ground-Tyrant	1/10	Chile
112	Sharp-billed Canastero	1/10	Chile
113	Scale-throated Earthcreeper	1/10	Chile
114	Mountain Parakeet	1/10	Chile
115	Black-fronted Ground-Tyrant	1/10	Chile
116	Buff-winged Cinclodes	1/10	Chile
117	Rufous-banded Miner	1/10	Chile
118	Gray-breasted Seedsnipe	1/10	Chile
119	Black-billed Shrike-Tyrant	1/10	Chile
120	Cordilleran Canastero	1/10	Chile
121	White-sided Hillstar	1/10	Chile
122	Gray-flanked Cinclodes	1/10	Chile
123	Diademed Sandpiper-Plover (12, 15–16, 19–21)	1/10	Chile
124	Creamy-rumped Miner	1/10	Chile
125	Variable Hawk	1/10	Chile
126	Ochre-naped Ground-Tyrant	1/10	Chile
127	Andean Goose	1/10	Chile
128	Andean Gull (18)	1/10	Chile
129	Shiny Cowbird	1/10	Chile
130	Eared Dove	1/10	Chile
131	Monk Parakeet	1/10	Chile
132	Rufous-tailed Plantcutter (21–22)	1/10	Chile
133	Giant Hummingbird	1/11	Chile
134	California Quail	1/11	Chile
135	Fire-eyed Diucon	1/11	Chile
136	White-throated Tapaculo	1/11	Chile
137	Dusky-tailed Canastero	1/11	Chile
138	Band-tailed Sierra-Finch	1/11	Chile
139	Dusky Tapaculo	1/11	Chile
140	Chilean Tinamou	1/11	Chile
141	Mountain Caracara	1/11	Chile
142	Cinereous Ground-Tyrant	1/11	Chile
143	Great Horned Owl	1/11	Chile
144	Great Shrike-Tyrant	1/11	Chile
145	Yellow-winged Blackbird	1/12	Chile
146	Picui Ground-Dove	1/12	Chile
147	Gray Gull	1/12	Chile
148	Sanderling	1/12	Chile
149	Whimbrel	1/12	Chile
150	American Oystercatcher	1/12	Chile
151	Red-gartered Coot	1/12	Chile
152	Spot-flanked Gallinule	1/12	Chile
153	Plumbeous Rail	1/12	Chile
154	Cocoi Heron	1/12	Chile
155	Stripe-backed Bittern	1/12	Chile
156	Peruvian Pelican	1/12	Chile
157	Pied-billed Grebe	1/12	Chile
158	Seaside Cinclodes	1/12	Chile
159	Striped Woodpecker	1/12	Chile
160	Ruddy Turnstone	1/12	Chile
161	Lesser Yellowlegs	1/12	Chile
162	Black Vulture	1/12	Chile
163	Snowy Egret	1/12	Chile
164	Guanay Cormorant	1/12	Chile
165	Red-legged Cormorant	1/12	Chile
166	Peruvian Booby	1/12	Chile
167	Pink-footed Shearwater	1/12	Chile
168	Salvin's Albatross	1/12	Chile
169	Humboldt Penguin	1/12	Chile
170	Franklin's Gull	1/12	Chile
171	Brown-hooded Gull	1/12	Chile
172	Black-necked Stilt	1/12	Chile
173	Red-fronted Coot	1/12	Chile
174	Black-crowned Night-Heron	1/12	Chile
175	Lake Duck (206)	1/12	Chile
176	Sandwich Tern	1/12	Chile
177	Common Tern	1/12	Chile
178	White-winged Coot	1/12	Chile
179	Silvery Grebe	1/12	Chile
180	Chiloe Wigeon	1/12	Chile
181	Coscoroba Swan	1/12	Chile
182	Spectacled Tyrant	1/12	Chile
183	Many-colored Rush Tyrant	1/12	Chile
184	Ticking Doradito	1/12	Chile
185	Wren-like Rushbird	1/12	Chile
186	Black Skimmer (60)	1/12	Chile
187	Elegant Tern	1/12	Chile
188	Baird's Sandpiper	1/12	Chile
189	Collared Plover	1/12	Chile
190	Black-bellied Plover	1/12	Chile
191	Great Egret	1/12	Chile
192	Peregrine Falcon (206)	1/12	Chile
193	Burrowing Owl	1/13	Chile
194	Harris's Hawk	1/13	Chile
195	Cinereous Harrier	1/13	Chile
196	White-faced Ibis	1/13	Chile
197	Cattle Egret	1/13	Chile
198	Black-headed Duck	1/13	Chile
199	Cinnamon Teal	1/13	Chile
200	Grassland Yellow-Finch	1/13	Chile
201	Chalk-browed Mockingbird	1/14	Argentina
202	Picazuro Pigeon	1/14	Argentina
203	Grayish Baywing	1/14	Argentina
204	Scarlet-headed Blackbird	1/14	Argentina
205	Great Kiskadee	1/14	Argentina
206	Limpkin	1/14	Argentina
207	Snail Kite	1/14	Argentina
208	Tropical Kingbird	1/14	Argentina
209	Whistling Heron	1/14	Argentina
210	Rufescent Tiger-Heron	1/14	Argentina
211	Maguari Stork (24)	1/14	Argentina
212	Fork-tailed Flycatcher	1/14	Argentina

213	Spot-winged Pigeon	1/14	Argentina	273	Black-and-rufous Warbling-Finch	1/14	Argentina
214	Roadside Hawk	1/14	Argentina	274	Long-tailed Reed Finch	1/14	Argentina
215	Hooded Siskin	1/14	Argentina	275	Barn Swallow	1/14	Argentina
216	Variable Oriole	1/14	Argentina	276	Sooty Tyrannulet	1/14	Argentina
217	Screaming Cowbird	1/14	Argentina	277	Yellow-chinned Spinetail	1/14	Argentina
218	Brown-and-yellow Marshbird	1/14	Argentina	278	Sulphur-throated Spinetail	1/14	Argentina
219	Chestnut-capped Blackbird	1/14	Argentina	279	Freckle-breasted Thornbird	1/14	Argentina
220	Ultramarine Grosbeak	1/14	Argentina	280	Curve-billed Reedhaunter	1/14	Argentina
221	Golden-billed Saltator	1/14	Argentina	281	Common Gallinule	1/14	Argentina
222	Double-collared Seedeater	1/14	Argentina	282	Spotted Rail	1/14	Argentina
223	Saffron Finch	1/14	Argentina	283	Rufous-sided Crake	1/14	Argentina
224	Black-capped Warbling-Finch	1/14	Argentina	284	Fulvous Whistling-Duck	1/14	Argentina
225	Sayaca Tanager	1/14	Argentina	285	Grassland Sparrow	1/14	Argentina
226	Yellow-billed Cardinal	1/14	Argentina	286	White Monjita	1/14	Argentina
227	Red-crested Cardinal	1/14	Argentina	287	Short-billed Canastero	1/14	Argentina
228	Masked Yellowthroat	1/14	Argentina	288	Nacunda Nighthawk	1/14	Argentina
229	Creamy-bellied Thrush	1/14	Argentina	289	Pectoral Sandpiper	1/14	Argentina
230	Masked Gnatcatcher	1/14	Argentina	290	Solitary Sandpiper	1/14	Argentina
231	Brown-chested Martin	1/14	Argentina	291	Black-bellied Whistling-Duck	1/14	Argentina
232	White-naped Xenopsaris	1/14	Argentina	292	White-faced Whistling-Duck	1/14	Argentina
233	White-tipped Plantcutter	1/14	Argentina	293	Grayish Saltator	1/14	Argentina
234	Crowned Slaty Flycatcher	1/14	Argentina	294	Hellmayr's Pipit	1/14	Argentina
235	Cattle Tyrant	1/14	Argentina	295	Yellowish Pipit	1/14	Argentina
236	Black-backed Water-Tyrant	1/14	Argentina	296	Bank Swallow	1/14	Argentina
237	Vermilion Flycatcher	1/14	Argentina	297	White-rumped Swallow	1/14	Argentina
238	Bran-colored Flycatcher	1/14	Argentina	298	Yellow-browed Tyrant	1/14	Argentina
239	White-crested Tyrannulet	1/14	Argentina	299	Warbling Doradito	1/14	Argentina
240	Small-billed Elaenia	1/14	Argentina	300	Greater Rhea (24)	1/14	Argentina
241	Suiriri Flycatcher	1/14	Argentina	301	White-browed Meadowlark	1/14	Argentina
242	Pale-breasted Spinetail	1/14	Argentina	302	Lark-like Brushrunner	1/14	Argentina
243	Sooty-fronted Spinetail	1/14	Argentina	303	Green Kingfisher	1/14	Argentina
244	Chotoy Spinetail	1/14	Argentina	304	Ringed Kingfisher	1/14	Argentina
245	Brown Cacholote	1/14	Argentina	305	Scissor-tailed Nightjar	1/14	Argentina
246	Stripe-crowned Spinetail	1/14	Argentina	306	Little Nightjar	1/14	Argentina
247	Little Thornbird	1/14	Argentina	307	American Golden-Plover	1/14	Argentina
248	Rufous Hornero	1/14	Argentina	308	Purple Gallinule	1/14	Argentina
249	Narrow-billed Woodcreeper	1/14	Argentina	309	Tawny-bellied Seedeater	1/15	Argentina
250	Scimitar-billed Woodcreeper	1/14	Argentina	310	Blue-black Grassquit	1/15	Argentina
251	Campo Flicker	1/14	Argentina	311	Rufous-browed Peppershrike	1/15	Argentina
252	Green-barred Woodpecker	1/14	Argentina	312	Streaked Flycatcher	1/15	Argentina
253	White-fronted Woodpecker	1/14	Argentina	313	Tawny-crowned Pygmy-Tyrant	1/15	Argentina
254	White Woodpecker	1/14	Argentina	314	Large Elaenia	1/15	Argentina
255	Gilded Hummingbird	1/14	Argentina	315	Firewood-gatherer	1/15	Argentina
256	Glittering-bellied Emerald	1/14	Argentina	316	White-barred Piculet	1/15	Argentina
257	Guira Cuckoo	1/14	Argentina	317	Striped Cuckoo	1/15	Argentina
258	Dark-billed Cuckoo	1/14	Argentina	318	Large-billed Tern	1/15	Argentina
259	White-tipped Dove	1/14	Argentina	319	Silver Teal	1/15	Argentina
260	Wattled Jacana	1/14	Argentina	320	Spotted Nothura	1/15	Argentina
261	Giant Wood-Rail	1/14	Argentina	321	Solitary Black Cacique	1/15	Argentina
262	Savanna Hawk	1/14	Argentina	322	Diademed Tanager	1/15	Argentina
263	Long-winged Harrier	1/14	Argentina	323	Tropical Parula	1/15	Argentina
264	Roseate Spoonbill (24)	1/14	Argentina	324	Rufous-bellied Thrush	1/15	Argentina
265	Bare-faced Ibis	1/14	Argentina	325	White-winged Becard	1/15	Argentina
266	Striated Heron	1/14	Argentina	326	Swainson's Flycatcher	1/15	Argentina
267	Wood Stork	1/14	Argentina	327	Euler's Flycatcher	1/15	Argentina
268	Rosy-billed Pochard	1/14	Argentina	328	Southern Beardless-Tyrannulet	1/15	Argentina
269	Brazilian Teal	1/14	Argentina	329	Variable Antshrike	1/15	Argentina
270	Ringed Teal	1/14	Argentina	330	Checkered Woodpecker	1/15	Argentina
271	Southern Screamer (24)	1/14	Argentina	331	Spix's Spinetail	1/15	Argentina
272	Great Pampa-Finch	1/14	Argentina	332	Straight-billed Reedhaunter	1/15	Argentina

333	Rufous-capped Antshrike	1/15	Argentina
334	Unicolored Blackbird	1/16	Argentina
335	European Starling (1)	1/16	Argentina
336	Nanday Parakeet	1/16	Argentina
337	Red-eyed Vireo	1/16	Argentina
338	Cliff Flycatcher (25, 26)	1/16	Argentina
339	Lined Seedeater	1/16	Argentina
340	Southern Martin	1/16	Argentina
341	Variegated Flycatcher	1/16	Argentina
342	Rothschild's Swift (27)	1/16	Argentina
343	Mitred Parakeet (27)	1/16	Argentina
344	White-browed Brushfinch	1/16	Argentina
345	Rusty-browed Warbling-Finch	1/16	Argentina
346	Blue-and-yellow Tanager	1/16	Argentina
347	Slaty Thrush	1/16	Argentina
348	Mountain Wren	1/16	Argentina
349	Streak-throated Bush-Tyrant	1/16	Argentina
350	Black Phoebe	1/16	Argentina
351	Smoke-colored Pewee	1/16	Argentina
352	White-throated Tyrannulet	1/16	Argentina
353	Buff-browed Foliage-gleaner	1/16	Argentina
354	White-bellied Hummingbird (95)	1/16	Argentina
355	Lyre-tailed Nightjar (109)	1/16	Argentina
356	Red-faced Guan	1/16	Argentina
357	Golden-winged Cacique	1/17	Argentina
358	Black-backed Grosbeak	1/17	Argentina
359	Common Chlorospingus	1/17	Argentina
360	Fawn-breasted Tanager	1/17	Argentina
361	Brown-capped Redstart	1/17	Argentina
362	Plush-crested Jay	1/17	Argentina
363	Crested Becard	1/17	Argentina
364	Dusky-capped Flycatcher	1/17	Argentina
365	Mottle-cheeked Tyrannulet	1/17	Argentina
366	Buff-banded Tyrannulet	1/17	Argentina
367	Azara's Spinetail	1/17	Argentina
368	Golden-olive Woodpecker	1/17	Argentina
369	Smoky-brown Woodpecker	1/17	Argentina
370	Slender-tailed Woodstar	1/17	Argentina
371	Fulvous-headed Brushfinch	1/17	Argentina
372	Rust-and-yellow Tanager	1/17	Argentina
373	Chiguanco Thrush	1/17	Argentina
374	Plumbeous Black-Tyrant	1/17	Argentina
375	Slaty Elaenia	1/17	Argentina
376	Spot-breasted Thornbird	1/17	Argentina
377	Zimmer's Tapaculo (35)	1/17	Argentina
378	Aplomado Falcon (34)	1/17	Argentina
379	Red-tailed Comet	1/17	Argentina
380	Sparkling Violetear	1/17	Argentina
381	Band-tailed Pigeon	1/17	Argentina
382	King Vulture (128)	1/17	Argentina
383	Andean Tinamou	1/17	Argentina
384	Huayco Tinamou	1/17	Argentina
385	Black Siskin	1/18	Argentina
386	Tucumán Mountain-Finch (35)	1/18	Argentina
387	Rufous-sided Warbling-Finch	1/18	Argentina
388	Short-tailed Finch	1/18	Argentina
389	Ash-breasted Sierra-Finch	1/18	Argentina
390	Rusty Flowerpiercer	1/18	Argentina
391	White-browed Chat-Tyrant	1/18	Argentina
392	Rufous-webbed Bush-Tyrant	1/18	Argentina
393	Maquis Canastero (35)	1/18	Argentina
394	Tawny Tit-Spinetail	1/18	Argentina
395	Brown-capped Tit-Spinetail	1/18	Argentina
396	Cream-winged Cinclodes	1/18	Argentina
397	Buff-breasted Earthcreeper	1/18	Argentina
398	Rock Earthcreeper	1/18	Argentina
399	Andean Flicker	1/18	Argentina
400	Andean Lapwing	1/18	Argentina
401	Buff-fronted Owl	1/18	Argentina
402	Montane Forest Screech-Owl	1/18	Argentina
403	Barn Owl (235)	1/18	Argentina
404	Subtropical Doradito	1/19	Argentina
405	Olive-crowned Crescentchest	1/19	Argentina
406	White-collared Swift	1/19	Argentina
407	Rufous-throated Dipper	1/20	Argentina
408	Piratic Flycatcher	1/20	Argentina
409	Sclater's Tyrannulet	1/20	Argentina
410	Red-rumped Cacique	1/21	Argentina
411	Bananaquit	1/21	Argentina
412	Chestnut-vented Conebill	1/21	Argentina
413	Yellow-bellied Elaenia	1/21	Argentina
414	Yellow-chevroned Parakeet	1/21	Argentina
415	Black-throated Mango	1/21	Argentina
416	Gray-rumped Swift	1/21	Argentina
417	Smooth-billed Ani	1/21	Argentina
418	Ruddy Ground-Dove	1/21	Argentina
419	Great Dusky Swift (50)	1/21	Argentina
420	Muscovy Duck	1/21	Argentina
421	Golden-crowned Warbler	1/21	Argentina
422	Swallow-tailed Manakin	1/21	Argentina
423	Greenish Elaenia	1/21	Argentina
424	Olivaceous Woodcreeper	1/21	Argentina
425	Blond-crested Woodpecker	1/21	Argentina
426	Yellow-fronted Woodpecker	1/21	Argentina
427	Toco Toucan	1/21	Argentina
428	Plumbeous Kite	1/21	Argentina
429	Squirrel Cuckoo	1/21	Argentina
430	Social Flycatcher	1/21	Argentina
431	Maroon-bellied Parakeet	1/21	Argentina
432	Amazon Kingfisher	1/21	Argentina
433	Greater Ani	1/21	Argentina
434	Gray-fronted Dove	1/21	Argentina
435	Black-tailed Tityra	1/21	Argentina
436	Swallow Tanager	1/21	Argentina
437	Southern Rough-winged Swallow	1/21	Argentina
438	Purple-throated Euphonia	1/21	Argentina
439	Green-winged Saltator	1/21	Argentina
440	Green-headed Tanager	1/21	Argentina
441	White-browed Warbler	1/21	Argentina
442	Boat-billed Flycatcher	1/21	Argentina
443	Short-crested Flycatcher	1/21	Argentina
444	Variegated Antpitta	1/21	Argentina
445	White-eyed Parakeet	1/21	Argentina
446	Scaly-headed Parrot	1/21	Argentina
447	Yellow-headed Caracara	1/21	Argentina
448	Sick's Swift	1/21	Argentina
449	Tropical Screech-Owl	1/21	Argentina
450	Pale-vented Pigeon	1/21	Argentina
451	Swallow-tailed Kite	1/21	Argentina
452	Blue-naped Chlorophonia	1/22	Argentina

453	Chestnut-bellied Euphonia	1/22	Argentina
454	Red-crowned Ant-Tanager	1/22	Argentina
455	Guira Tanager	1/22	Argentina
456	Blue Dacnis	1/22	Argentina
457	Ruby-crowned Tanager	1/22	Argentina
458	Black-goggled Tanager	1/22	Argentina
459	Magpie Tanager	1/22	Argentina
460	Creamy-bellied Gnatcatcher	1/22	Argentina
461	Chestnut-crowned Becard	1/22	Argentina
462	Greenish Schiffornis	1/22	Argentina
463	Wing-barred Piprites	1/22	Argentina
464	Sibilant Sirystes	1/22	Argentina
465	Long-tailed Tyrant	1/22	Argentina
466	Tropical Pewee	1/22	Argentina
467	White-throated Spadebill	1/22	Argentina
468	Yellow-olive Flycatcher	1/22	Argentina
469	Drab-breasted Pygmy-Tyrant	1/22	Argentina
470	Eared Pygmy-Tyrant	1/22	Argentina
471	Southern Antpipit	1/22	Argentina
472	Sepia-capped Flycatcher	1/22	Argentina
473	Gray Elaenia	1/22	Argentina
474	Gray-bellied Spinetail	1/22	Argentina
475	Rufous-capped Spinetail	1/22	Argentina
476	White-eyed Foliage-gleaner	1/22	Argentina
477	Ochre-breasted Foliage-gleaner	1/22	Argentina
478	Lesser Woodcreeper	1/22	Argentina
479	Rufous-breasted Leaftosser	1/22	Argentina
480	Short-tailed Antthrush	1/22	Argentina
481	Planalto Tapaculo	1/22	Argentina
482	Speckle-breasted Antpitta	1/22	Argentina
483	Rufous Gnateater	1/22	Argentina
484	White-shouldered Fire-eye	1/22	Argentina
485	Bertoni's Antbird	1/22	Argentina
486	Rufous-winged Antwren	1/22	Argentina
487	Plain Antvireo	1/22	Argentina
488	Tufted Antshrike	1/22	Argentina
489	Spot-backed Antshrike	1/22	Argentina
490	Collared Forest-Falcon	1/22	Argentina
491	Barred Forest-Falcon	1/22	Argentina
492	Robust Woodpecker	1/22	Argentina
493	Lineated Woodpecker	1/22	Argentina
494	White-spotted Woodpecker	1/22	Argentina
495	Ochre-collared Piculet	1/22	Argentina
496	Black-throated Trogon	1/22	Argentina
497	Short-tailed Nighthawk	1/22	Argentina
498	White-throated Hummingbird	1/22	Argentina
499	Violet-capped Woodnymph	1/22	Argentina
500	Surucua Trogon (51)	1/22	Argentina
501	Green Ibis	1/22	Argentina
502	Tataupa Tinamou	1/22	Argentina
503	Brown Tinamou	1/22	Argentina
504	Blackish-blue Seedeater	1/23	Argentina
505	Chestnut-headed Tanager	1/23	Argentina
506	Riverbank Warbler	1/23	Argentina
507	Pale-breasted Thrush	1/23	Argentina
508	Rufous-crowned Greenlet	1/23	Argentina
509	Ochre-faced Tody-Flycatcher	1/23	Argentina
510	Planalto Tyrannulet	1/23	Argentina
511	Yellow Tyrannulet	1/23	Argentina
512	White-browed Foliage-gleaner	1/23	Argentina
513	Sharp-tailed Streamcreeper	1/23	Argentina
514	Scalloped Woodcreeper	1/23	Argentina
515	Red-breasted Toucan	1/23	Argentina
516	Ruddy Quail-Dove	1/23	Argentina
517	Slaty-breasted Wood-Rail	1/23	Argentina
518	Gray-headed Kite	1/23	Argentina
519	Black-fronted Piping-Guan	1/23	Argentina
520	Red-crested Finch	1/23	Argentina
521	Sharp-shinned Hawk	1/23	Argentina
522	Araucaria Tit-Spinetail	1/23	Argentina
523	Vinaceous-breasted Parrot	1/23	Argentina
524	White-necked Thrush	1/24	Argentina
525	Black-crowned Tityra	1/24	Argentina
526	Southern Bristle-Tyrant	1/24	Argentina
527	Buff-fronted Foliage-gleaner	1/24	Argentina
528	Streaked Xenops	1/24	Argentina
529	White-bearded Antshrike	1/24	Argentina
530	Rufous-capped Motmot	1/24	Argentina
531	Violaceous Euphonia	1/24	Argentina
532	Versicolored Emerald	1/24	Argentina
533	Swallow-tailed Hummingbird	1/24	Argentina
534	Planalto Hermit	1/24	Argentina
535	Black Jacobin	1/24	Argentina
536	Half-collared Sparrow	1/25	Brazil
537	Black-throated Grosbeak	1/25	Brazil
538	Palm Tanager	1/25	Brazil
539	Golden-chevroned Tanager	1/25	Brazil
540	Azure-shouldered Tanager	1/25	Brazil
541	Olive-green Tanager	1/25	Brazil
542	Yellow-legged Thrush	1/25	Brazil
543	Pin-tailed Manakin	1/25	Brazil
544	Hooded Berryeater	1/25	Brazil
545	Gray-hooded Attila	1/25	Brazil
546	Rufous-tailed Attila	1/25	Brazil
547	Whiskered Flycatcher	1/25	Brazil
548	Gray-hooded Flycatcher	1/25	Brazil
549	Black-capped Foliage-gleaner	1/25	Brazil
550	Pale-browed Treehunter	1/25	Brazil
551	White-collared Foliage-gleaner	1/25	Brazil
552	Plain Xenops	1/25	Brazil
553	White-throated Woodcreeper	1/25	Brazil
554	Such's Antthrush	1/25	Brazil
555	Mouse-colored Tapaculo	1/25	Brazil
556	White-breasted Tapaculo	1/25	Brazil
557	Squamate Antbird	1/25	Brazil
558	Star-throated Antwren	1/25	Brazil
559	Plain Parakeet	1/25	Brazil
560	White-browed Woodpecker	1/25	Brazil
561	Crescent-chested Puffbird	1/25	Brazil
562	Sombre Hummingbird	1/25	Brazil
563	Brazilian Ruby	1/25	Brazil
564	Scale-throated Hermit	1/25	Brazil
565	Plumbeous Pigeon	1/25	Brazil
566	Mantled Hawk	1/25	Brazil
567	Bicolored Hawk	1/25	Brazil
568	Solitary Tinamou	1/25	Brazil
569	Rufous-headed Tanager	1/26	Brazil
570	Red-necked Tanager	1/26	Brazil
571	Long-billed Gnatwren	1/26	Brazil
572	Bare-throated Bellbird	1/26	Brazil

573	Red-ruffed Fruitcrow	1/26	Brazil	633	Great Antshrike	1/30	Brazil
574	Large-headed Flatbill	1/26	Brazil	634	Dusky-headed Parakeet	1/30	Brazil
575	Hangnest Tody-Tyrant	1/26	Brazil	635	Peach-fronted Parakeet	1/30	Brazil
576	Gray-capped Tyrannulet	1/26	Brazil	636	Blue-headed Parrot (58)	1/30	Brazil
577	Bay-ringed Tyrannulet	1/26	Brazil	637	Bat Falcon (58)	1/30	Brazil
578	Oustalet's Tyrannulet	1/26	Brazil	638	Red-necked Woodpecker (60)	1/30	Brazil
579	Pallid Spinetail	1/26	Brazil	639	Cream-colored Woodpecker	1/30	Brazil
580	Plain-winged Woodcreeper	1/26	Brazil	640	Little Woodpecker	1/30	Brazil
581	Streak-capped Antwren	1/26	Brazil	641	Yellow-tufted Woodpecker (58)	1/30	Brazil
582	Dusky-tailed Antbird	1/26	Brazil	642	Chestnut-eared Aracari	1/30	Brazil
583	Ferruginous Antbird	1/26	Brazil	643	Lettered Aracari (58)	1/30	Brazil
584	Giant Antshrike	1/26	Brazil	644	Rufous-tailed Jacamar	1/30	Brazil
585	Spot-billed Toucanet	1/26	Brazil	645	Brown Jacamar	1/30	Brazil
586	Rusty-breasted Nunlet	1/26	Brazil	646	Swallow-winged Puffbird	1/30	Brazil
587	Green-backed Trogon	1/26	Brazil	647	Black-fronted Nunbird	1/30	Brazil
588	Amethyst Woodstar	1/26	Brazil	648	Blue-crowned Trogon	1/30	Brazil
589	Festive Coquette	1/26	Brazil	649	Black-tailed Trogon	1/30	Brazil
590	Red-and-white Crake	1/26	Brazil	650	Fork-tailed Woodnymph	1/30	Brazil
591	Magnificent Frigatebird	1/27	Brazil	651	Ferruginous Pygmy-Owl (58)	1/30	Brazil
592	Masked Water-Tyrant	1/27	Brazil	652	Scaled Dove	1/30	Brazil
593	Brazilian Tanager	1/27	Brazil	653	Scaled Pigeon (60)	1/30	Brazil
594	Long-billed Wren	1/27	Brazil	654	Gray-lined Hawk	1/30	Brazil
595	Blue-winged Parrotlet	1/27	Brazil	655	Double-toothed Kite	1/30	Brazil
596	Mealy Parrot	1/27	Brazil	656	Black-and-white Hawk-Eagle (60–61)	1/30	Brazil
597	Greenish Tyrannulet	1/28	Brazil	657	Harpy Eagle (55–56, 133, 225)	1/30	Brazil
598	Rufous-capped Antthrush	1/28	Brazil	658	Greater Yellow-headed Vulture	1/30	Brazil
599	Black-cheeked Gnateater	1/28	Brazil	659	Buff-necked Ibis	1/30	Brazil
600	Saw-billed Hermit	1/28	Brazil	660	Capped Heron	1/30	Brazil
601	Little Blue Heron	1/28	Brazil	661	Least Grebe	1/30	Brazil
602	Common Waxbill	1/28	Brazil	662	Undulated Tinamou	1/30	Brazil
603	Gray-headed Tody-Flycatcher	1/28	Brazil	663	Little Tinamou	1/30	Brazil
604	Orange-eyed Thornbird	1/28	Brazil	664	Crested Oropendola	1/30	Brazil
605	Scaled Antbird	1/28	Brazil	665	Giant Cowbird	1/30	Brazil
606	Common Pauraque	1/28	Brazil	666	Rusty-collared Seedeater	1/30	Brazil
607	Black-capped Becard	1/29	Brazil	667	Black-capped Donacobius	1/30	Brazil
608	White-bearded Manakin	1/29	Brazil	668	White-throated Kingbird	1/30	Brazil
609	Eye-ringed Tody-Tyrant	1/29	Brazil	669	White-rumped Monjita	1/30	Brazil
610	Spot-breasted Antvireo (53)	1/29	Brazil	670	White-lored Spinetail	1/30	Brazil
611	Laughing Falcon	1/29	Brazil	671	Rufous Cacholote	1/30	Brazil
612	White-chinned Sapphire	1/29	Brazil	672	Yellow-collared Macaw	1/30	Brazil
613	Glittering-throated Emerald	1/29	Brazil	673	Hyacinth Macaw	1/30	Brazil
614	Reddish Hermit	1/29	Brazil	674	Orange-winged Parrot	1/30	Brazil
615	White-bellied Seedeater	1/29	Brazil	675	Turquoise-fronted Parrot	1/30	Brazil
616	Red-shouldered Macaw	1/29	Brazil	676	Great Potoo	1/30	Brazil
617	Fork-tailed Palm-Swift	1/29	Brazil	677	Band-tailed Nighthawk	1/30	Brazil
618	Orange-backed Troupial	1/30	Brazil	678	Long-tailed Ground-Dove	1/30	Brazil
619	Epaulet Oriole (60)	1/30	Brazil	679	Gray-breasted Crake	1/30	Brazil
620	Chopi Blackbird	1/30	Brazil	680	Black-collared Hawk	1/30	Brazil
621	Black-throated Saltator (60)	1/30	Brazil	681	Plumbeous Ibis	1/30	Brazil
622	White-lined Tanager	1/30	Brazil	682	Least Bittern	1/30	Brazil
623	Moustached Wren	1/30	Brazil	683	Jabiru	1/30	Brazil
624	Thrush-like Wren (58)	1/30	Brazil	684	Red-throated Piping-Guan	1/30	Brazil
625	Purplish Jay	1/30	Brazil	685	Chestnut-bellied Guan	1/30	Brazil
626	Masked Tityra	1/30	Brazil	686	Chaco Chachalaca	1/30	Brazil
627	Rusty-fronted Tody-Flycatcher	1/30	Brazil	687	Saffron-billed Sparrow	1/31	Brazil
628	Straight-billed Woodcreeper	1/30	Brazil	688	Silver-beaked Tanager	1/31	Brazil
629	Buff-throated Woodcreeper	1/30	Brazil	689	Gray-headed Tanager	1/31	Brazil
630	Black-throated Antbird	1/30	Brazil	690	Flavescent Warbler	1/31	Brazil
631	Rondonia Warbling-Antbird	1/30	Brazil	691	Ashy-headed Greenlet	1/31	Brazil
632	Barred Antshrike	1/30	Brazil	692	Helmeted Manakin	1/31	Brazil

693	Lesser Kiskadee	1/31	Brazil
694	Rufous Casiornis	1/31	Brazil
695	Dull-capped Attila	1/31	Brazil
696	Fuscous Flycatcher	1/31	Brazil
697	Pearly-vented Tody-Tyrant	1/31	Brazil
698	Forest Elaenia	1/31	Brazil
699	Red-billed Scythebill	1/31	Brazil
700	Great Rufous Woodcreeper	1/31	Brazil
701	Band-tailed Antbird	1/31	Brazil
702	Mato Grosso Antbird	1/31	Brazil
703	Black-bellied Antwren	1/31	Brazil
704	Planalto Slaty-Antshrike	1/31	Brazil
705	Crimson-crested Woodpecker	1/31	Brazil
706	Pale-crested Woodpecker	1/31	Brazil
707	White-wedged Piculet	1/31	Brazil
708	American Pygmy Kingfisher	1/31	Brazil
709	Green-and-rufous Kingfisher	1/31	Brazil
710	Cinnamon-throated Hermit	1/31	Brazil
711	Russet-crowned Crake	1/31	Brazil
712	Boat-billed Heron	1/31	Brazil
713	Zigzag Heron	1/31	Brazil
714	Bare-faced Curassow	1/31	Brazil
715	Rusty-margined Flycatcher	1/31	Brazil
716	Rusty-backed Spinetail	1/31	Brazil
717	White-tailed Goldenthroat	1/31	Brazil
718	Great Black Hawk	1/31	Brazil
719	Chestnut-bellied Seed-Finch	2/1	Brazil
720	Mouse-colored Tyrannulet	2/1	Brazil
721	Greater Thornbird	2/1	Brazil
722	Pale-legged Hornero	2/1	Brazil
723	Large-billed Antwren	2/1	Brazil
724	Gray-necked Wood-Rail	2/1	Brazil
725	Sunbittern (127, 129)	2/1	Brazil
726	Lesser Yellow-headed Vulture	2/1	Brazil
727	Wedge-tailed Grass-Finch	2/1	Brazil
728	White-winged Swallow	2/1	Brazil
729	White-headed Marsh Tyrant	2/1	Brazil
730	Anhinga	2/1	Brazil
731	Amazonian Motmot	2/1	Brazil
732	Plumbeous Seedeater	2/1	Brazil
733	Curl-crested Jay	2/1	Brazil
734	Gray Monjita	2/1	Brazil
735	Red-legged Seriema	2/1	Brazil
736	Red-winged Tinamou	2/1	Brazil
737	Small-billed Tinamou	2/1	Brazil
738	Stripe-tailed Yellow-Finch	2/1	Brazil
739	White-banded Tanager	2/1	Brazil
740	Red-and-green Macaw	2/1	Brazil
741	Red-bellied Macaw	2/1	Brazil
742	Horned Sungem	2/1	Brazil
743	Biscutate Swift	2/1	Brazil
744	Least Nighthawk	2/1	Brazil
745	Coal-crested Finch	2/2	Brazil
746	Burnished-buff Tanager	2/2	Brazil
747	White-rumped Tanager	2/2	Brazil
748	Black-faced Tanager	2/2	Brazil
749	Plain-crested Elaenia	2/2	Brazil
750	Rusty-backed Antwren	2/2	Brazil
751	Rufous-winged Antshrike	2/2	Brazil
752	White-eared Puffbird	2/2	Brazil
753	Pheasant Cuckoo	2/2	Brazil
754	Thick-billed Euphonia	2/2	Brazil
755	Pectoral Sparrow	2/2	Brazil
756	Buff-breasted Wren	2/2	Brazil
757	Band-tailed Manakin	2/2	Brazil
758	White-backed Fire-eye	2/2	Brazil
759	Channel-billed Toucan	2/2	Brazil
760	Fiery-capped Manakin	2/2	Brazil
761	Stripe-necked Tody-Tyrant	2/2	Brazil
762	Blue Finch	2/2	Brazil
763	Crested Black-Tyrant	2/2	Brazil
764	Collared Crescentchest	2/3	Brazil
765	Blue-winged Macaw	2/3	Brazil
766	White-vented Violetear	2/3	Brazil
767	Rufous-sided Pygmy-Tyrant	2/3	Brazil
768	Chapada Flycatcher	2/3	Brazil
769	Golden-sided Euphonia	2/4	Brazil
770	Olive Oropendola	2/4	Brazil
771	Green Oropendola	2/4	Brazil
772	Yellow-rumped Cacique	2/4	Brazil
773	Blue-black Grosbeak	2/4	Brazil
774	Purple Honeycreeper	2/4	Brazil
775	Gray-chested Greenlet	2/4	Brazil
776	Red-headed Manakin	2/4	Brazil
777	Purple-throated Fruitcrow	2/4	Brazil
778	Sulphury Flycatcher	2/4	Brazil
779	Bright-rumped Attila (126)	2/4	Brazil
780	Cinnamon Attila	2/4	Brazil
781	Yellow-breasted Flycatcher	2/4	Brazil
782	Gray-crowned Flycatcher	2/4	Brazil
783	Olivaceous Flatbill	2/4	Brazil
784	Yellow-browed Tody-Flycatcher	2/4	Brazil
785	Spotted Tody-Flycatcher	2/4	Brazil
786	Helmeted Pygmy-Tyrant	2/4	Brazil
787	Short-tailed Pygmy-Tyrant	2/4	Brazil
788	Yellow-crowned Tyrannulet	2/4	Brazil
789	Plain-crowned Spinetail	2/4	Brazil
790	Spix's Woodcreeper	2/4	Brazil
791	Amazonian Barred-Woodcreeper	2/4	Brazil
792	Wedge-billed Woodcreeper (101)	2/4	Brazil
793	Plain-brown Woodcreeper	2/4	Brazil
794	Xingu Scale-backed Antbird	2/4	Brazil
795	Silvered Antbird	2/4	Brazil
796	White-fringed Antwren	2/4	Brazil
797	White-shouldered Antshrike	2/4	Brazil
798	Golden-winged Parakeet	2/4	Brazil
799	White-winged Parakeet	2/4	Brazil
800	Red-throated Caracara	2/4	Brazil
801	Chestnut Woodpecker	2/4	Brazil
802	Waved Woodpecker	2/4	Brazil
803	White-throated Toucan	2/4	Brazil
804	Red-necked Aracari	2/4	Brazil
805	Black-necked Aracari	2/4	Brazil
806	Paradise Jacamar	2/4	Brazil
807	Blue-cheeked Jacamar	2/4	Brazil
808	Collared Puffbird	2/4	Brazil
809	Rufous-breasted Hermit	2/4	Brazil
810	Short-tailed Swift	2/4	Brazil
811	Little Cuckoo	2/4	Brazil
812	Buff-throated Saltator	2/4	Brazil

813	Guianan Tyrannulet	2/4	Brazil	873	Cinereous Antshrike	2/6	Brazil
814	Amazonian Antshrike	2/4	Brazil	874	Dusky Parrot	2/6	Brazil
815	Chestnut-backed Antshrike	2/4	Brazil	875	Red-stained Woodpecker	2/6	Brazil
816	Band-rumped Swift	2/4	Brazil	876	Gould's Toucanet	2/6	Brazil
817	Amazonian Pygmy-Owl	2/4	Brazil	877	Pied Puffbird	2/6	Brazil
818	Wing-barred Seedeater	2/4	Brazil	878	Rufous-throated Sapphire	2/6	Brazil
819	Blue-gray Tanager	2/4	Brazil	879	Gray-breasted Sabrewing	2/6	Brazil
820	Blue-chinned Sapphire	2/4	Brazil	880	Lesser Swallow-tailed Swift	2/6	Brazil
821	Red-breasted Meadowlark	2/4	Brazil	881	Common Potoo	2/6	Brazil
822	Tropical Gnatcatcher	2/4	Brazil	882	Blackish Nightjar	2/6	Brazil
823	Common Tody-Flycatcher	2/4	Brazil	883	Black Hawk-Eagle	2/6	Brazil
824	Point-tailed Palmcreeper	2/4	Brazil	884	Variegated Tinamou	2/6	Brazil
825	Common Ground-Dove	2/4	Brazil	885	White-throated Tinamou	2/6	Brazil
826	Yellow-billed Tern	2/4	Brazil	886	Yellow-bellied Seedeater	2/6	Brazil
827	Least Sandpiper	2/4	Brazil	887	Opal-rumped Tanager	2/6	Brazil
828	Cinereous Becard	2/4	Brazil	888	Ruddy-breasted Seedeater	2/6	Brazil
829	Bicolored Conebill	2/5	Brazil	889	Turquoise Tanager	2/7	Brazil
830	Brown-crested Flycatcher	2/5	Brazil	890	Slate-headed Tody-Flycatcher	2/7	Brazil
831	White-bellied Piculet	2/5	Brazil	891	Amazonian Streaked-Antwren	2/7	Brazil
832	Plain-bellied Emerald	2/5	Brazil	892	Crane Hawk	2/7	Brazil
833	Mangrove Cuckoo	2/5	Brazil	893	Cinereous Tinamou	2/7	Brazil
834	Semipalmated Plover	2/5	Brazil	894	Cocoa Thrush	2/7	Brazil
835	White-tailed Hawk	2/5	Brazil	895	Pink-throated Becard	2/7	Brazil
836	Rufous Crab Hawk	2/5	Brazil	896	Brown-winged Schiffornis	2/7	Brazil
837	White-tailed Kite	2/5	Brazil	897	Blue-backed Manakin	2/7	Brazil
838	Scarlet Ibis	2/5	Brazil	898	Black-chested Tyrant	2/7	Brazil
839	Yellow-crowned Night-Heron	2/5	Brazil	899	Ochre-bellied Flycatcher	2/7	Brazil
840	Tricolored Heron	2/5	Brazil	900	Striped Woodcreeper	2/7	Brazil
841	White-cheeked Pintail	2/5	Brazil	901	Black-faced Antthrush	2/7	Brazil
842	Tropical Mockingbird	2/5	Brazil	902	Spot-winged Antshrike	2/7	Brazil
843	Royal Tern	2/5	Brazil	903	Sapphire-rumped Parrotlet	2/7	Brazil
844	Gull-billed Tern	2/5	Brazil	904	Yellow-throated Woodpecker	2/7	Brazil
845	Laughing Gull	2/5	Brazil	905	White-fronted Nunbird	2/7	Brazil
846	Parasitic Jaeger	2/5	Brazil	906	Amazonian Trogon	2/7	Brazil
847	Short-billed Dowitcher	2/5	Brazil	907	Long-tailed Hermit	2/7	Brazil
848	Semipalmated Sandpiper	2/5	Brazil	908	Pale-tailed Barbthroat	2/7	Brazil
849	Spotted Sandpiper	2/5	Brazil	909	McConnell's Flycatcher	2/7	Brazil
850	Wilson's Plover	2/5	Brazil	910	White-bellied Parrot	2/7	Brazil
851	Mangrove Rail	2/5	Brazil	911	Vulturine Parrot	2/7	Brazil
852	Willet	2/5	Brazil	912	Caatinga Cacholote	2/8	Brazil
853	Short-tailed Hawk	2/5	Brazil	913	Campo Troupial	2/8	Brazil
854	Pinnated Bittern	2/5	Brazil	914	Red-cowled Cardinal	2/8	Brazil
855	Yellow-green Grosbeak	2/6	Brazil	915	Ash-throated Crake	2/8	Brazil
856	Slate-colored Grosbeak	2/6	Brazil	916	Dubois's Seedeater	2/8	Brazil
857	Fulvous-crested Tanager	2/6	Brazil	917	Scarlet-throated Tanager	2/8	Brazil
858	Flame-crested Tanager	2/6	Brazil	918	Pale Baywing	2/8	Brazil
859	Red-billed Pied Tanager	2/6	Brazil	919	Wing-banded Hornero	2/8	Brazil
860	Opal-crowned Manakin	2/6	Brazil	920	Slender Antbird	2/8	Brazil
861	Dwarf Tyrant-Manakin	2/6	Brazil	921	Stripe-backed Antbird	2/8	Brazil
862	Screaming Piha (14)	2/6	Brazil	922	Cactus Parakeet	2/8	Brazil
863	Spangled Cotinga	2/6	Brazil	923	Sapphire-spangled Emerald	2/8	Brazil
864	Yellow-margined Flycatcher	2/6	Brazil	924	Ruby-topaz Hummingbird	2/8	Brazil
865	Para Foliage-gleaner	2/6	Brazil	925	Pygmy Nightjar	2/8	Brazil
866	Layard's Woodcreeper	2/6	Brazil	926	Mottled Owl	2/8	Brazil
867	Gray Antbird	2/6	Brazil	927	Tawny-browed Owl	2/8	Brazil
868	Willis's Antbird	2/6	Brazil	928	Silvery-cheeked Antshrike	2/9	Brazil
869	Gray Antwren	2/6	Brazil	929	East Brazilian Chachalaca	2/9	Brazil
870	Long-winged Antwren	2/6	Brazil	930	Pileated Finch	2/9	Brazil
871	White-flanked Antwren	2/6	Brazil	931	Gray-eyed Greenlet	2/9	Brazil
872	Plain-throated Antwren	2/6	Brazil	932	Ochre-cheeked Spinetail	2/9	Brazil

933	Gray-headed Spinetail	2/9	Brazil
934	Rufous-fronted Thornbird	2/9	Brazil
935	Narrow-billed Antwren	2/9	Brazil
936	Caatinga Antwren	2/9	Brazil
937	Spotted Piculet	2/9	Brazil
938	Blue Ground-Dove	2/9	Brazil
939	Plain-breasted Ground-Dove	2/9	Brazil
940	White-throated Seedeater	2/9	Brazil
941	Green-backed Becard	2/9	Brazil
942	Spot-backed Puffbird	2/9	Brazil
943	Black-billed Scythebill	2/9	Brazil
944	Gilt-edged Tanager	2/9	Brazil
945	Cinnamon-vented Piha	2/9	Brazil
946	Sharpbill	2/9	Brazil
947	Fork-tailed Pygmy-Tyrant	2/9	Brazil
948	Bahia Spinetail	2/9	Brazil
949	Striated Softtail	2/9	Brazil
950	White-bibbed Antbird	2/9	Brazil
951	Rio de Janeiro Antbird	2/9	Brazil
952	Ochre-rumped Antbird	2/9	Brazil
953	Giant Snipe	2/9	Brazil
954	Buffy-fronted Seedeater	2/10	Brazil
955	Green Honeycreeper	2/10	Brazil
956	Buff-throated Purpletuft	2/10	Brazil
957	Black-headed Berryeater	2/10	Brazil
958	Grayish Mourner	2/10	Brazil
959	Bahia Tyrannulet	2/10	Brazil
960	Pink-legged Graveteiro	2/10	Brazil
961	Golden-capped Parakeet	2/10	Brazil
962	Golden-spangled Piculet	2/10	Brazil
963	Least Pygmy-Owl	2/10	Brazil
964	White-crowned Manakin	2/10	Brazil
965	Striped Manakin	2/10	Brazil
966	Bahia Tapaculo	2/10	Brazil
967	Uniform Crake	2/10	Brazil
968	Hooded Tanager	2/10	Brazil
969	Smoky-fronted Tody-Flycatcher	2/10	Brazil
970	Cinereous-breasted Spinetail	2/10	Brazil
971	Orange-bellied Euphonia	2/11	Brazil
972	Red-legged Honeycreeper	2/11	Brazil
973	White-winged Cotinga	2/11	Brazil
974	Bahia Antwren	2/11	Brazil
975	Band-tailed Antwren	2/11	Brazil
976	Sooretama Slaty-Antshrike	2/11	Brazil
977	Golden-tailed Parrotlet	2/11	Brazil
978	Ringed Woodpecker	2/11	Brazil
979	Yellow-backed Tanager	2/11	Brazil
980	Black-eared Fairy	2/11	Brazil
981	Great-billed Hermit	2/12	Brazil
982	West Peruvian Dove	2/13	Peru
983	Wilson's Phalarope	2/13	Peru
984	Killdeer	2/13	Peru
985	Peruvian Thick-knee	2/13	Peru
986	Croaking Ground-Dove	2/13	Peru
987	Raimondi's Yellow-Finch	2/13	Peru
988	Cactus Canastero	2/13	Peru
989	Grayish Miner	2/13	Peru
990	Thick-billed Miner	2/13	Peru
991	Peruvian Meadowlark	2/13	Peru
992	Coastal Miner	2/13	Peru
993	Least Seedsnipe	2/13	Peru
994	Belcher's Gull	2/13	Peru
995	Scrub Blackbird	2/14	Peru
996	Golden Grosbeak	2/14	Peru
997	Bright-rumped Yellow-Finch	2/14	Peru
998	Great Inca-Finch	2/14	Peru
999	Long-tailed Mockingbird	2/14	Peru
1000	Pied-crested Tit-Tyrant (67)	2/14	Peru
1001	Black-necked Woodpecker	2/14	Peru
1002	Purple-collared Woodstar	2/14	Peru
1003	White-winged Cinclodes	2/14	Peru
1004	Bronze-tailed Comet	2/14	Peru
1005	Rusty-bellied Brushfinch	2/14	Peru
1006	Black Metaltail	2/14	Peru
1007	Peruvian Sierra-Finch	2/14	Peru
1008	Brown-bellied Swallow	2/14	Peru
1009	White-cheeked Cotinga	2/14	Peru
1010	d'Orbigny's Chat-Tyrant	2/14	Peru
1011	Canyon Canastero	2/14	Peru
1012	Rusty-crowned Tit-Spinetail	2/14	Peru
1013	Striated Earthcreeper	2/14	Peru
1014	Shining Sunbeam (174)	2/14	Peru
1015	Black-breasted Hillstar	2/14	Peru
1016	Junin Canastero	2/14	Peru
1017	White-bellied Cinclodes	2/14	Peru
1018	Giant Coot	2/14	Peru
1019	Puna Ibis	2/14	Peru
1020	Ruddy Duck	2/14	Peru
1021	White-winged Diuca-Finch	2/14	Peru
1022	White-fronted Ground-Tyrant	2/14	Peru
1023	Puna Ground-Tyrant	2/14	Peru
1024	Streak-throated Canastero	2/14	Peru
1025	Dark-winged Miner	2/14	Peru
1026	Rufous-bellied Seedsnipe	2/14	Peru
1027	Black-spectacled Brushfinch (72–75)	2/15	Peru
1028	Plain-colored Seedeater	2/15	Peru
1029	Black-throated Flowerpiercer	2/15	Peru
1030	Scarlet-bellied Mountain-Tanager (75)	2/15	Peru
1031	Spectacled Redstart	2/15	Peru
1032	Citrine Warbler (81)	2/15	Peru
1033	Great Thrush	2/15	Peru
1034	White-capped Dipper (75)	2/15	Peru
1035	Red-crested Cotinga (84)	2/15	Peru
1036	Creamy-crested Spinetail	2/15	Peru
1037	Rufous Antpitta	2/15	Peru
1038	Mountain Velvetbreast	2/15	Peru
1039	Violet-throated Starfrontlet	2/15	Peru
1040	Tyrian Metaltail	2/15	Peru
1041	Amethyst-throated Sunangel	2/15	Peru
1042	Many-striped Canastero (84)	2/15	Peru
1043	Slaty Brushfinch	2/15	Peru
1044	Golden-collared Tanager	2/15	Peru
1045	Lacrimose Mountain-Tanager	2/15	Peru
1046	Gray-hooded Bush Tanager	2/15	Peru
1047	Superciliaried Hemispingus	2/15	Peru
1048	Rufous-breasted Chat-Tyrant	2/15	Peru
1049	White-banded Tyrannulet	2/15	Peru
1050	Tricolored Brushfinch	2/15	Peru

1051	Masked Flowerpiercer	2/15	Peru
1052	Capped Conebill	2/15	Peru
1053	Flame-faced Tanager	2/15	Peru
1054	Blue-and-black Tanager	2/15	Peru
1055	Blue-capped Tanager	2/15	Peru
1056	Yellow-scarfed Tanager (81)	2/15	Peru
1057	Grass-green Tanager	2/15	Peru
1058	Hooded Mountain-Tanager	2/15	Peru
1059	Glossy-black Thrush	2/15	Peru
1060	Gray-breasted Wood-Wren	2/15	Peru
1061	Cinnamon Flycatcher	2/15	Peru
1062	Montane Woodcreeper	2/15	Peru
1063	Crimson-mantled Woodpecker	2/15	Peru
1064	Gray-breasted Mountain-Toucan	2/15	Peru
1065	Blue-banded Toucanet	2/15	Peru
1066	Collared Inca	2/15	Peru
1067	Andean Guan	2/15	Peru
1068	Junin Tapaculo	2/15	Peru
1069	Paradise Tanager	2/15	Peru
1070	Blue-necked Tanager	2/15	Peru
1071	Green Jay	2/15	Peru
1072	Amazonian Umbrellabird	2/15	Peru
1073	Golden-crowned Flycatcher	2/15	Peru
1074	Slaty-capped Flycatcher	2/15	Peru
1075	Dusky-green Oropendola	2/16	Peru
1076	Yellow-throated Tanager	2/16	Peru
1077	Russet-crowned Warbler	2/16	Peru
1078	Pale-legged Warbler	2/16	Peru
1079	White-eared Solitaire	2/16	Peru
1080	Slaty-backed Nightingale-Thrush	2/16	Peru
1081	Andean Solitaire	2/16	Peru
1082	Masked Fruiteater	2/16	Peru
1083	Rufous-tailed Tyrant	2/16	Peru
1084	Scale-crested Pygmy-Tyrant	2/16	Peru
1085	Streaked Tuftedcheek	2/16	Peru
1086	Rufous-vented Tapaculo	2/16	Peru
1087	Bay Antpitta	2/16	Peru
1088	Speckle-faced Parrot	2/16	Peru
1089	Andean Motmot	2/16	Peru
1090	White-bellied Woodstar	2/16	Peru
1091	Bronzy Inca (95)	2/16	Peru
1092	Swallow-tailed Nightjar	2/16	Peru
1093	Rufous-banded Owl	2/16	Peru
1094	Sickle-winged Guan	2/16	Peru
1095	Speckled Chachalaca	2/16	Peru
1096	Saffron-crowned Tanager	2/16	Peru
1097	Green-and-white Hummingbird	2/16	Peru
1098	Coraya Wren	2/16	Peru
1099	Yellow-browed Sparrow	2/16	Peru
1100	Bluish-fronted Jacamar	2/16	Peru
1101	Broad-winged Hawk	2/16	Peru
1102	Violaceous Jay	2/16	Peru
1103	Torrent Tyrannulet	2/16	Peru
1104	Fasciated Tiger-Heron	2/16	Peru
1105	Ornate Tinamou	2/16	Peru
1106	Andean Negrito	2/16	Peru
1107	Common Miner	2/16	Peru
1108	Slate-colored Coot	2/16	Peru
1109	Chilean Flamingo	2/16	Peru
1110	Junin Grebe	2/16	Peru
1111	Puna Teal	2/16	Peru
1112	Golden-backed Mountain-Tanager (77, 80–82, 94)	2/17	Peru
1113	Pardusco (82)	2/17	Peru
1114	Paramo Pipit	2/17	Peru
1115	Barred Fruiteater (81)	2/17	Peru
1116	Brown-backed Chat-Tyrant (81)	2/17	Peru
1117	Ochraceous-breasted Flycatcher	2/17	Peru
1118	Baron's Spinetail	2/17	Peru
1119	White-chinned Thistletail	2/17	Peru
1120	Pearled Treerunner (81)	2/17	Peru
1121	Tschudi's Tapaculo	2/17	Peru
1122	Neblina Tapaculo	2/17	Peru
1123	Undulated Antpitta	2/17	Peru
1124	Coppery Metaltail	2/17	Peru
1125	Blue-mantled Thornbill (81)	2/17	Peru
1126	Puna Snipe	2/17	Peru
1127	Band-tailed Seedeater	2/17	Peru
1128	Sierran Elaenia	2/17	Peru
1129	Plushcap	2/18	Peru
1130	Moustached Flowerpiercer	2/18	Peru
1131	Blue-backed Conebill	2/18	Peru
1132	Rufous-chested Tanager	2/18	Peru
1133	Black-capped Hemispingus	2/18	Peru
1134	Peruvian Wren	2/18	Peru
1135	White-collared Jay	2/18	Peru
1136	Smoky Bush-Tyrant	2/18	Peru
1137	Rufous-headed Pygmy-Tyrant	2/18	Peru
1138	White-tailed Tyrannulet	2/18	Peru
1139	Rufous Spinetail	2/18	Peru
1140	Chestnut Antpitta	2/18	Peru
1141	Streak-headed Antbird	2/18	Peru
1142	Golden-plumed Parakeet	2/18	Peru
1143	Bar-bellied Woodpecker	2/18	Peru
1144	Black-and-white Seedeater	2/18	Peru
1145	Cinereous Conebill	2/18	Peru
1146	Black-crested Tit-Tyrant	2/18	Peru
1147	Cinereous Finch	2/19	Peru
1148	Superciliated Wren	2/19	Peru
1149	Fasciated Wren	2/19	Peru
1150	Chestnut-collared Swallow	2/19	Peru
1151	Peruvian Plantcutter	2/19	Peru
1152	Rufous Flycatcher	2/19	Peru
1153	Gray-and-white Tyrannulet	2/19	Peru
1154	Collared Antshrike	2/19	Peru
1155	Pacific Parrotlet	2/19	Peru
1156	Scarlet-backed Woodpecker	2/19	Peru
1157	Amazilia Hummingbird	2/19	Peru
1158	Lesser Nighthawk	2/19	Peru
1159	Streaked Saltator	2/19	Peru
1160	Variable Seedeater	2/19	Peru
1161	Parrot-billed Seedeater	2/19	Peru
1162	Short-tailed Field Tyrant	2/19	Peru
1163	Short-tailed Woodstar	2/19	Peru
1164	Groove-billed Ani	2/19	Peru
1165	Gray-hooded Gull	2/19	Peru
1166	Snowy Plover	2/19	Peru
1167	Tumbes Sparrow (88)	2/19	Peru

1168	Sulphur-throated Finch	2/19	Peru
1169	Baird's Flycatcher	2/19	Peru
1170	White-edged Oriole	2/19	Peru
1171	White-headed Brushfinch	2/19	Peru
1172	Collared Warbling-Finch	2/19	Peru
1173	White-tailed Jay	2/19	Peru
1174	Snowy-throated Kingbird	2/19	Peru
1175	Sooty-crowned Flycatcher	2/19	Peru
1176	Tumbes Tyrant (88)	2/19	Peru
1177	Necklaced Spinetail	2/19	Peru
1178	Streak-headed Woodcreeper	2/19	Peru
1179	Elegant Crescentchest (88)	2/19	Peru
1180	Red-masked Parakeet	2/19	Peru
1181	Scrub Nightjar (88)	2/19	Peru
1182	Peruvian Screech-Owl (88)	2/19	Peru
1183	White-winged Guan	2/19	Peru
1184	Osprey	2/19	Peru
1185	Tumbes Swallow	2/20	Peru
1186	Peruvian Pygmy-Owl	2/20	Peru
1187	Black-cowled Saltator	2/20	Peru
1188	Piura Chat-Tyrant (88)	2/20	Peru
1189	Chestnut-crowned Antpitta (109)	2/20	Peru
1190	Chapman's Antshrike	2/20	Peru
1191	Hook-billed Kite	2/21	Peru
1192	Northern Slaty-Antshrike	2/21	Peru
1193	Hepatic Tanager	2/21	Peru
1194	Black-capped Sparrow	2/21	Peru
1195	Speckle-breasted Wren	2/21	Peru
1196	Peruvian Pigeon	2/21	Peru
1197	Buff-bellied Tanager	2/21	Peru
1198	Marañon Thrush	2/21	Peru
1199	Koepcke's Screech-Owl	2/21	Peru
1200	Chestnut-breasted Coronet	2/21	Peru
1201	Rainbow Starfrontlet	2/21	Peru
1202	Speckled Hummingbird	2/21	Peru
1203	Purple-throated Sunangel	2/21	Peru
1204	Green Violetear	2/21	Peru
1205	Mountain Cacique	2/21	Peru
1206	Red-hooded Tanager	2/21	Peru
1207	Rufous-backed Treehunter	2/21	Peru
1208	Chestnut-collared Swift	2/21	Peru
1209	Gray-winged Inca-Finch	2/22	Peru
1210	Lesser Goldfinch	2/22	Peru
1211	Yellow-tailed Oriole	2/22	Peru
1212	Chestnut-backed Thornbird	2/22	Peru
1213	Buff-bridled Inca-Finch	2/22	Peru
1214	Scarlet-fronted Parakeet	2/22	Peru
1215	Spot-throated Hummingbird	2/22	Peru
1216	Russet-mantled Softtail	2/22	Peru
1217	Sapphire-vented Puffleg	2/22	Peru
1218	Drab Hemispingus	2/22	Peru
1219	Blackish Tapaculo	2/22	Peru
1220	Dull-colored Grassquit	2/22	Peru
1221	Silvery Tanager	2/22	Peru
1222	White-tipped Swift	2/22	Peru
1223	Yellow-billed Cacique	2/23	Peru
1224	Yellow-breasted Brushfinch	2/23	Peru
1225	White-sided Flowerpiercer	2/23	Peru
1226	Plain-tailed Wren	2/23	Peru
1227	Trilling Tapaculo	2/23	Peru
1228	Rusty-tinged Antpitta	2/23	Peru
1229	Pale-billed Antpitta	2/23	Peru
1230	Powerful Woodpecker	2/23	Peru
1231	Highland Elaenia	2/23	Peru
1232	Speckle-chested Piculet	2/23	Peru
1233	Andean Emerald	2/23	Peru
1234	Violet-fronted Brilliant	2/23	Peru
1235	Marvelous Spatuletail (68, 87, 93–96)	2/23	Peru
1236	Long-tailed Sylph (95)	2/23	Peru
1237	Green-tailed Trainbearer	2/23	Peru
1238	Black-tailed Trainbearer	2/23	Peru
1239	Bluish Flowerpiercer	2/23	Peru
1240	Beryl-spangled Tanager	2/23	Peru
1241	Chestnut-breasted Wren	2/23	Peru
1242	Barred Becard	2/23	Peru
1243	Green-and-black Fruiteater	2/23	Peru
1244	Black-throated Tody-Tyrant	2/23	Peru
1245	Peruvian Tyrannulet	2/23	Peru
1246	Emerald Toucanet	2/23	Peru
1247	Fawn-breasted Brilliant	2/23	Peru
1248	Sword-billed Hummingbird (102)	2/23	Peru
1249	Emerald-bellied Puffleg	2/23	Peru
1250	Russet-backed Oropendola	2/23	Peru
1251	Black-bellied Tanager	2/23	Peru
1252	Black-billed Thrush	2/23	Peru
1253	Western Wood-Pewee	2/23	Peru
1254	Dark-breasted Spinetail	2/23	Peru
1255	Lined Antshrike	2/23	Peru
1256	Long-billed Starthroat	2/23	Peru
1257	Blue-fronted Lancebill	2/23	Peru
1258	Green-fronted Lancebill	2/23	Peru
1259	Long-whiskered Owlet	2/23	Peru
1260	White-throated Screech-Owl	2/24	Peru
1261	Cinnamon Screech-Owl	2/24	Peru
1262	Black-eared Hemispingus	2/24	Peru
1263	Chestnut-crested Cotinga	2/24	Peru
1264	Strong-billed Woodcreeper	2/24	Peru
1265	Brown-capped Vireo	2/24	Peru
1266	Black-capped Tyrannulet	2/24	Peru
1267	Olivaceous Siskin	2/24	Peru
1268	Ashy-throated Chlorospingus	2/24	Peru
1269	Pale-edged Flycatcher	2/24	Peru
1270	Johnson's Tody-Flycatcher	2/24	Peru
1271	Rufous-crested Tanager	2/24	Peru
1272	Booted Racket-tail	2/24	Peru
1273	Bar-winged Wood-Wren	2/24	Peru
1274	Streak-necked Flycatcher	2/24	Peru
1275	Greenish Puffleg	2/24	Peru
1276	Red-billed Parrot	2/24	Peru
1277	Slate-throated Redstart	2/24	Peru
1278	Orange-breasted Falcon	2/24	Peru
1279	Green Hermit	2/24	Peru
1280	Golden-naped Tanager	2/24	Peru
1281	Olivaceous Greenlet	2/24	Peru
1282	Andean Cock-of-the-rock (104, 106–107)	2/24	Peru
1283	Ornate Flycatcher	2/24	Peru
1284	White-crowned Tapaculo	2/24	Peru
1285	Blackish Antbird	2/24	Peru
1286	Yellow-breasted Antwren	2/24	Peru

1287	Gilded Barbet	2/24	Peru
1288	Cobalt-winged Parakeet	2/24	Peru
1289	Spot-breasted Woodpecker	2/24	Peru
1290	Black Caracara	2/24	Peru
1291	Pale-eyed Blackbird	2/24	Peru
1292	Black-billed Seed-Finch	2/24	Peru
1293	Masked Duck	2/24	Peru
1294	Varzea Thrush	2/24	Peru
1295	Scaly-breasted Wren (125)	2/24	Peru
1296	Gray-capped Flycatcher	2/24	Peru
1297	Golden-tailed Sapphire	2/24	Peru
1298	Rufous-crested Coquette	2/24	Peru
1299	Black-throated Hermit	2/24	Peru
1300	Band-bellied Owl	2/24	Peru
1301	Oilbird	2/24	Peru
1302	Swainson's Thrush	2/25	Peru
1303	Golden-headed Manakin	2/25	Peru
1304	Blue-crowned Manakin	2/25	Peru
1305	Thrush-like Antpitta	2/25	Peru
1306	Black-faced Antbird	2/25	Peru
1307	Pygmy Antwren	2/25	Peru
1308	Golden-collared Toucanet	2/25	Peru
1309	Gould's Jewelfront	2/25	Peru
1310	Koepcke's Hermit	2/25	Peru
1311	White-necked Jacobin (127)	2/25	Peru
1312	Spix's Guan	2/25	Peru
1313	White-banded Swallow	2/25	Peru
1314	Carmiol's Tanager	2/25	Peru
1315	Summer Tanager	2/25	Peru
1316	Yellow-bellied Tanager	2/25	Peru
1317	Dotted Tanager	2/25	Peru
1318	Buff-throated Foliage-gleaner	2/25	Peru
1319	Oriole Blackbird	2/25	Peru
1320	Red-capped Cardinal	2/25	Peru
1321	Buckley's Forest-Falcon	2/25	Peru
1322	Sand-colored Nighthawk	2/25	Peru
1323	White-browed Purpletuft	2/26	Peru
1324	Citron-bellied Attila	2/26	Peru
1325	Rufous-tailed Flatbill	2/26	Peru
1326	Mishana Tyrannulet	2/26	Peru
1327	Ruddy Spinetail	2/26	Peru
1328	Zimmer's Antbird	2/26	Peru
1329	Yellow-browed Antbird	2/26	Peru
1330	Ancient Antwren	2/26	Peru
1331	Pearly Antshrike	2/26	Peru
1332	Mouse-colored Antshrike	2/26	Peru
1333	Black-headed Parrot	2/26	Peru
1334	Scale-breasted Woodpecker	2/26	Peru
1335	Ivory-billed Aracari	2/26	Peru
1336	Yellow-billed Nunbird	2/26	Peru
1337	Broad-billed Motmot	2/26	Peru
1338	Rufous Motmot	2/26	Peru
1339	Gray-legged Tinamou	2/26	Peru
1340	Chestnut-bellied Seedeater	2/26	Peru
1341	Orange-headed Tanager	2/26	Peru
1342	Yellow Warbler	2/26	Peru
1343	Stilt Sandpiper	2/26	Peru
1344	Hudsonian Godwit	2/26	Peru
1345	Inca Tern	2/26	Peru
1346	Surfbird	2/26	Peru
1347	Surf Cinclodes	2/26	Peru
1348	Peruvian Sheartail	2/26	Peru
1349	Chestnut-breasted Mountain-Finch	2/27	Peru
1350	Yellow-billed Tit-Tyrant	2/27	Peru
1351	Rusty-fronted Canastero	2/27	Peru
1352	Bearded Mountaineer	2/27	Peru
1353	Black-naped Brushfinch	2/27	Peru
1354	Black-billed Treehunter	2/27	Peru
1355	Deep-blue Flowerpiercer	2/27	Peru
1356	Blackburnian Warbler	2/27	Peru
1357	Slaty-backed Chat-Tyrant	2/27	Peru
1358	Inca Flycatcher	2/27	Peru
1359	Golden-headed Quetzal	2/27	Peru
1360	Rufous-breasted Wood-Quail	2/27	Peru
1361	Scaly-naped Parrot	2/27	Peru
1362	Andean Potoo	2/27	Peru
1363	Golden-bellied Warbler	2/28	Peru
1364	Two-banded Warbler	2/28	Peru
1365	Plum-throated Cotinga	2/28	Peru
1366	Dusky-cheeked Foliage-gleaner	2/28	Peru
1367	Black-spotted Bare-eye	2/28	Peru
1368	Spot-backed Antbird	2/28	Peru
1369	Goeldi's Antbird	2/28	Peru
1370	Chestnut-tailed Antbird	2/28	Peru
1371	White-lined Antbird	2/28	Peru
1372	White-browed Antbird	2/28	Peru
1373	Manu Antbird	2/28	Peru
1374	Yellow-breasted Warbling-Antbird	2/28	Peru
1375	Dot-winged Antwren	2/28	Peru
1376	Bluish-slate Antshrike	2/28	Peru
1377	Plain-winged Antshrike	2/28	Peru
1378	Bamboo Antshrike	2/28	Peru
1379	Chestnut-fronted Macaw	2/28	Peru
1380	Blue-and-yellow Macaw	2/28	Peru
1381	Blue-headed Macaw	2/28	Peru
1382	Chestnut-capped Puffbird	2/28	Peru
1383	Hoatzin	2/28	Peru
1384	Black-capped Tinamou	2/28	Peru
1385	Black-backed Tody-Flycatcher	2/28	Peru
1386	Cabanis's Spinetail	2/28	Peru
1387	Foothill Antwren	2/28	Peru
1388	Yellow-throated Chlorospingus	2/28	Peru
1389	Yungas Manakin	2/28	Peru
1390	Solitary Eagle	2/28	Peru
1391	Drab Water Tyrant	3/1	Peru
1392	Pied Lapwing	3/1	Peru
1393	Hauxwell's Thrush	3/1	Peru
1394	Dusky-capped Greenlet	3/1	Peru
1395	Cinnamon-throated Woodcreeper	3/1	Peru
1396	Rusty-belted Tapaculo	3/1	Peru
1397	Plumbeous Antbird	3/1	Peru
1398	White-eyed Antwren	3/1	Peru
1399	Dusky-throated Antshrike	3/1	Peru
1400	Fasciated Antshrike	3/1	Peru
1401	Ocellated Poorwill	3/1	Peru
1402	Tawny-bellied Screech-Owl	3/1	Peru
1403	Starred Wood-Quail	3/1	Peru
1404	Bartlett's Tinamou	3/1	Peru
1405	Great Tinamou	3/1	Peru
1406	Black-faced Dacnis	3/2	Peru

1407	Green-and-gold Tanager	3/2	Peru
1408	Masked Tanager	3/2	Peru
1409	Lawrence's Thrush	3/2	Peru
1410	Slaty-capped Shrike-Vireo	3/2	Peru
1411	Yellow-green Vireo	3/2	Peru
1412	Sulphur-bellied Flycatcher	3/2	Peru
1413	Long-crested Pygmy-Tyrant	3/2	Peru
1414	Striped Woodhaunter	3/2	Peru
1415	Chestnut-crowned Foliage-gleaner	3/2	Peru
1416	Cinnamon-rumped Foliage-gleaner	3/2	Peru
1417	Peruvian Warbling-Antbird	3/2	Peru
1418	Sclater's Antwren	3/2	Peru
1419	Stipple-throated Antwren	3/2	Peru
1420	Great Jacamar	3/2	Peru
1421	Collared Trogon	3/2	Peru
1422	Ladder-tailed Nightjar	3/2	Peru
1423	Black-banded Owl	3/2	Peru
1424	Ruddy Pigeon	3/2	Peru
1425	Pale-winged Trumpeter	3/2	Peru
1426	Slender-billed Kite	3/2	Peru
1427	Blue-throated Piping-Guan	3/2	Peru
1428	White-shouldered Tanager	3/3	Peru
1429	Musician Wren	3/3	Peru
1430	Round-tailed Manakin	3/3	Peru
1431	Golden-crowned Spadebill	3/3	Peru
1432	White-bellied Tody-Tyrant	3/3	Peru
1433	Flammulated Pygmy-Tyrant	3/3	Peru
1434	Peruvian Recurvebill	3/3	Peru
1435	Black-tailed Leaftosser	3/3	Peru
1436	Rufous-fronted Antthrush	3/3	Peru
1437	Black Antbird	3/3	Peru
1438	Striated Antbird	3/3	Peru
1439	Banded Antbird	3/3	Peru
1440	White-browed Hawk	3/3	Peru
1441	White-throated Jacamar	3/3	Peru
1442	Purus Jacamar	3/3	Peru
1443	Black-banded Crake	3/3	Peru
1444	Rufous-bellied Euphonia	3/4	Peru
1445	Eastern Kingbird	3/4	Peru
1446	Eastern Wood-Pewee	3/4	Peru
1447	White-throated Antbird	3/4	Peru
1448	Rufous-headed Woodpecker	3/4	Peru
1449	Rufous-capped Nunlet	3/4	Peru
1450	Ruddy-tailed Flycatcher	3/4	Peru
1451	Olive-backed Foliage-gleaner	3/4	Peru
1452	Scarlet Macaw (128)	3/4	Peru
1453	Western Puffbird	3/4	Peru
1454	Crested Owl	3/4	Peru
1455	Dusky-tailed Flatbill	3/5	Peru
1456	Elegant Woodcreeper	3/5	Peru
1457	Ornate Antwren	3/5	Peru
1458	Black-capped Parakeet	3/5	Peru
1459	Dusky-billed Parrotlet	3/5	Peru
1460	Yellow-crowned Parrot	3/5	Peru
1461	Orange-cheeked Parrot	3/5	Peru
1462	Golden-green Woodpecker	3/5	Peru
1463	Curl-crested Aracari	3/5	Peru
1464	Lemon-throated Barbet	3/5	Peru
1465	White-bearded Hermit	3/5	Peru
1466	Pale-rumped Swift	3/5	Peru
1467	Slate-colored Hawk	3/5	Peru
1468	Horned Screamer	3/5	Peru
1469	Amazonian Antpitta	3/5	Peru
1470	Black Flowerpiercer	3/6	Ecuador
1471	Glossy Flowerpiercer	3/6	Ecuador
1472	Crowned Chat-Tyrant	3/6	Ecuador
1473	Rufous-crowned Tody-Flycatcher	3/6	Ecuador
1474	Ocellated Tapaculo	3/6	Ecuador
1475	Tawny Antpitta	3/6	Ecuador
1476	Great Sapphirewing	3/6	Ecuador
1477	Buff-winged Starfrontlet	3/6	Ecuador
1478	Golden-breasted Puffleg (102)	3/6	Ecuador
1479	Rainbow-bearded Thornbill (102)	3/6	Ecuador
1480	Andean Pygmy-Owl (102)	3/6	Ecuador
1481	Black-crested Warbler	3/6	Ecuador
1482	Golden Tanager	3/6	Ecuador
1483	Blue-winged Mountain-Tanager	3/6	Ecuador
1484	Three-striped Warbler	3/6	Ecuador
1485	Turquoise Jay	3/6	Ecuador
1486	Red-faced Spinetail	3/6	Ecuador
1487	Spillmann's Tapaculo	3/6	Ecuador
1488	Moustached Antpitta (109)	3/6	Ecuador
1489	Plate-billed Mountain-Toucan	3/6	Ecuador
1490	Black-chinned Mountain-Tanager	3/6	Ecuador
1491	Masked Trogon	3/6	Ecuador
1492	Purple-throated Woodstar	3/6	Ecuador
1493	Purple-bibbed Whitetip	3/6	Ecuador
1494	Buff-tailed Coronet	3/6	Ecuador
1495	Violet-tailed Sylph	3/6	Ecuador
1496	Gorgeted Sunangel	3/6	Ecuador
1497	Black-winged Saltator	3/6	Ecuador
1498	Black-capped Tanager	3/6	Ecuador
1499	Red-headed Barbet	3/6	Ecuador
1500	Rufous-tailed Hummingbird (127)	3/6	Ecuador
1501	White-tailed Hillstar	3/6	Ecuador
1502	Brown Inca	3/6	Ecuador
1503	Brown Violetear	3/6	Ecuador
1504	Flame-rumped Tanager	3/6	Ecuador
1505	Crowned Woodnymph (131)	3/6	Ecuador
1506	Empress Brilliant	3/6	Ecuador
1507	Green-crowned Brilliant	3/6	Ecuador
1508	Velvet-purple Coronet	3/6	Ecuador
1509	White-eared Jacamar	3/7	Ecuador
1510	Scarlet-crowned Barbet	3/7	Ecuador
1511	Many-banded Aracari	3/7	Ecuador
1512	Riparian Antbird	3/7	Ecuador
1513	Bare-necked Fruitcrow	3/8	Ecuador
1514	Double-banded Pygmy-Tyrant	3/8	Ecuador
1515	White-lored Tyrannulet	3/8	Ecuador
1516	Chestnut-winged Hookbill	3/8	Ecuador
1517	Black-banded Woodcreeper	3/8	Ecuador
1518	Common Scale-backed Antbird	3/8	Ecuador
1519	Dot-backed Antbird	3/8	Ecuador
1520	White-shouldered Antbird	3/8	Ecuador
1521	Moustached Antwren	3/8	Ecuador
1522	Brown-backed Antwren	3/8	Ecuador
1523	Maroon-tailed Parakeet	3/8	Ecuador
1524	Purplish Jacamar	3/8	Ecuador
1525	White-necked Puffbird	3/8	Ecuador
1526	Rufous Potoo	3/8	Ecuador

1527	Black-bellied Cuckoo	3/8	Ecuador	1587	Bronze-winged Parrot	3/12	Ecuador
1528	Golden-bellied Euphonia	3/9	Ecuador	1588	Choco Toucan	3/12	Ecuador
1529	Lesson's Seedeater	3/9	Ecuador	1589	Yellow-throated Toucan	3/12	Ecuador
1530	Yellow-bellied Dacnis	3/9	Ecuador	1590	Collared Aracari	3/12	Ecuador
1531	Masked Crimson Tanager	3/9	Ecuador	1591	Green Thorntail	3/12	Ecuador
1532	Buff-rumped Warbler	3/9	Ecuador	1592	White-whiskered Hermit	3/12	Ecuador
1533	Blackpoll Warbler	3/9	Ecuador	1593	Chestnut-capped Brushfinch	3/12	Ecuador
1534	White-breasted Wood-Wren (126)	3/9	Ecuador	1594	Wedge-billed Hummingbird	3/12	Ecuador
1535	Tawny-crowned Greenlet	3/9	Ecuador	1595	Rufous-bellied Nighthawk (109)	3/12	Ecuador
1536	Lemon-chested Greenlet	3/9	Ecuador	1596	Colombian Screech-Owl	3/12	Ecuador
1537	Cinereous Mourner	3/9	Ecuador	1597	Dusky Chlorospingus	3/13	Ecuador
1538	Black-necked Red-Cotinga	3/9	Ecuador	1598	Sharpe's Wren	3/13	Ecuador
1539	White-eyed Tody-Tyrant	3/9	Ecuador	1599	Cinnamon Becard	3/13	Ecuador
1540	Ocellated Woodcreeper	3/9	Ecuador	1600	Olivaceous Piha (109)	3/13	Ecuador
1541	Yellow-billed Jacamar	3/9	Ecuador	1601	Scaled Fruiteater	3/13	Ecuador
1542	Spotted Puffbird	3/9	Ecuador	1602	Streak-capped Treehunter	3/13	Ecuador
1543	Black-throated Brilliant	3/9	Ecuador	1603	Rufous-breasted Antthrush (109)	3/13	Ecuador
1544	Fiery Topaz	3/9	Ecuador	1604	Nariño Tapaculo	3/13	Ecuador
1545	Tiny Hawk	3/9	Ecuador	1605	Ochre-breasted Antpitta (109, 110)	3/13	Ecuador
1546	Casqued Cacique	3/10	Ecuador	1606	Scaled Antpitta (109)	3/13	Ecuador
1547	Opal-crowned Tanager	3/10	Ecuador	1607	Giant Antpitta (103–105, 108)	3/13	Ecuador
1548	Wire-tailed Manakin	3/10	Ecuador	1608	Dark-backed Wood-Quail (107)	3/13	Ecuador
1549	Ringed Antpipit	3/10	Ecuador	1609	Golden-winged Manakin	3/13	Ecuador
1550	Orange-fronted Plushcrown	3/10	Ecuador	1610	Marble-faced Bristle-Tyrant	3/13	Ecuador
1551	Lunulated Antbird	3/10	Ecuador	1611	Rusty-winged Barbtail	3/13	Ecuador
1552	Spot-winged Antbird	3/10	Ecuador	1612	Thick-billed Seed-Finch	3/13	Ecuador
1553	Rufous-tailed Antwren	3/10	Ecuador	1613	Bay-headed Tanager	3/13	Ecuador
1554	Marbled Wood-Quail	3/10	Ecuador	1614	Bay Wren	3/13	Ecuador
1555	Nocturnal Curassow	3/10	Ecuador	1615	White-thighed Swallow	3/13	Ecuador
1556	Short-billed Leaftosser	3/11	Ecuador	1616	Scarlet-browed Tanager	3/13	Ecuador
1557	Sooty Antbird	3/11	Ecuador	1617	Gray-and-gold Tanager	3/13	Ecuador
1558	Straight-billed Hermit	3/11	Ecuador	1618	Slate-throated Gnatcatcher	3/13	Ecuador
1559	Long-billed Woodcreeper	3/11	Ecuador	1619	Lesser Greenlet	3/13	Ecuador
1560	Herring Gull	3/11	Ecuador	1620	Choco Tyrannulet	3/13	Ecuador
1561	Blue-winged Teal	3/11	Ecuador	1621	Sooty-headed Tyrannulet	3/13	Ecuador
1562	White-winged Brushfinch	3/12	Ecuador	1622	White-tailed Trogon	3/13	Ecuador
1563	Gray-browed Brushfinch	3/12	Ecuador	1623	Blue-tailed Trogon	3/13	Ecuador
1564	Yellow-bellied Chat-Tyrant	3/12	Ecuador	1624	Purple-chested Hummingbird	3/13	Ecuador
1565	Band-winged Nightjar	3/12	Ecuador	1625	Olive-crowned Yellowthroat	3/14	Ecuador
1566	White-throated Quail-Dove	3/12	Ecuador	1626	Slaty Spinetail	3/14	Ecuador
1567	Metallic-green Tanager	3/12	Ecuador	1627	Black-striped Woodcreeper	3/14	Ecuador
1568	Canada Warbler (126)	3/12	Ecuador	1628	Chestnut-backed Antbird	3/14	Ecuador
1569	Black-and-white Becard	3/12	Ecuador	1629	Pacific Antwren	3/14	Ecuador
1570	Ashy-headed Tyrannulet	3/12	Ecuador	1630	Black-crowned Antshrike	3/14	Ecuador
1571	Tawny-bellied Hermit	3/12	Ecuador	1631	Red-rumped Woodpecker	3/14	Ecuador
1572	Lineated Foliage-gleaner	3/12	Ecuador	1632	Black-cheeked Woodpecker	3/14	Ecuador
1573	Crimson-rumped Toucanet	3/12	Ecuador	1633	Purple-crowned Fairy	3/14	Ecuador
1574	Toucan Barbet	3/12	Ecuador	1634	Pallid Dove	3/14	Ecuador
1575	Tanager Finch	3/12	Ecuador	1635	Brown Wood-Rail	3/14	Ecuador
1576	Beautiful Jay	3/12	Ecuador	1636	Orange-crowned Euphonia	3/14	Ecuador
1577	Yellow-breasted Antpitta (109)	3/12	Ecuador	1637	Scarlet-rumped Cacique	3/14	Ecuador
1578	Ochre-breasted Tanager	3/12	Ecuador	1638	Scarlet-thighed Dacnis	3/14	Ecuador
1579	Silver-throated Tanager	3/12	Ecuador	1639	Rufous-winged Tanager	3/14	Ecuador
1580	Ecuadorian Thrush	3/12	Ecuador	1640	Brown-capped Tyrannulet	3/14	Ecuador
1581	Club-winged Manakin	3/12	Ecuador	1641	Guayaquil Woodpecker	3/14	Ecuador
1582	Sulphur-rumped Flycatcher	3/12	Ecuador	1642	Cinnamon Woodpecker	3/14	Ecuador
1583	Scaly-throated Foliage-gleaner	3/12	Ecuador	1643	Orange-fronted Barbet	3/14	Ecuador
1584	Spotted Woodcreeper	3/12	Ecuador	1644	Blue-chested Hummingbird	3/14	Ecuador
1585	Zeledon's Antbird	3/12	Ecuador	1645	Dusky Pigeon	3/14	Ecuador
1586	Slaty Antwren	3/12	Ecuador	1646	Plumbeous Hawk	3/14	Ecuador

1647	Yellow-collared Chlorophonia	3/14	Ecuador
1648	Rufous-throated Tanager	3/14	Ecuador
1649	Yellow-faced Grassquit	3/14	Ecuador
1650	Indigo Flowerpiercer	3/15	Ecuador
1651	Golden-collared Honeycreeper	3/15	Ecuador
1652	Glistening-green Tanager	3/15	Ecuador
1653	Moss-backed Tanager	3/15	Ecuador
1654	Black Solitaire	3/15	Ecuador
1655	Black-billed Peppershrike	3/15	Ecuador
1656	Choco Vireo	3/15	Ecuador
1657	Orange-breasted Fruiteater	3/15	Ecuador
1658	Bronze-olive Pygmy-Tyrant	3/15	Ecuador
1659	Olive-striped Flycatcher	3/15	Ecuador
1660	Spotted Barbtail	3/15	Ecuador
1661	Plain-backed Antpitta	3/15	Ecuador
1662	Esmeraldas Antbird	3/15	Ecuador
1663	Barred Hawk	3/15	Ecuador
1664	Chestnut-winged Cinclodes	3/15	Ecuador
1665	Carunculated Caracara	3/15	Ecuador
1666	Viridian Metaltail	3/15	Ecuador
1667	Giant Conebill	3/15	Ecuador
1668	Plain-capped Ground-Tyrant	3/15	Ecuador
1669	Andean Tit-Spinetail	3/15	Ecuador
1670	Stout-billed Cinclodes	3/15	Ecuador
1671	Ecuadorian Hillstar	3/15	Ecuador
1672	Andean Teal	3/15	Ecuador
1673	Pale-naped Brushfinch	3/16	Ecuador
1674	Black-backed Bush Tanager	3/16	Ecuador
1675	Golden-crowned Tanager	3/16	Ecuador
1676	Buff-breasted Mountain-Tanager	3/16	Ecuador
1677	Black-chested Mountain-Tanager	3/16	Ecuador
1678	Masked Mountain-Tanager	3/16	Ecuador
1679	Agile Tit-Tyrant	3/16	Ecuador
1680	Paramo Tapaculo	3/16	Ecuador
1681	Tourmaline Sunangel	3/16	Ecuador
1682	Golden-rumped Euphonia	3/16	Ecuador
1683	Oleaginous Hemispingus (174)	3/16	Ecuador
1684	Lemon-browed Flycatcher	3/16	Ecuador
1685	Handsome Flycatcher	3/16	Ecuador
1686	Rufous-breasted Flycatcher	3/16	Ecuador
1687	Sulphur-bellied Tyrannulet	3/16	Ecuador
1688	Long-tailed Tapaculo	3/16	Ecuador
1689	White-bellied Antpitta	3/16	Ecuador
1690	Gorgeted Woodstar	3/16	Ecuador
1691	White-rumped Hawk	3/16	Ecuador
1692	Olive-backed Woodcreeper	3/17	Ecuador
1693	Slate-crowned Antpitta	3/17	Ecuador
1694	Wattled Guan	3/17	Ecuador
1695	Golden-faced Tyrannulet	3/17	Ecuador
1696	Variegated Bristle-Tyrant	3/17	Ecuador
1697	Military Macaw (137)	3/17	Ecuador
1698	Bronze-green Euphonia	3/17	Ecuador
1699	Wing-banded Wren	3/17	Ecuador
1700	Spotted Tanager	3/17	Ecuador
1701	Gray-mantled Wren	3/17	Ecuador
1702	Rufous-naped Greenlet	3/17	Ecuador
1703	Montane Foliage-gleaner	3/17	Ecuador
1704	Stripe-chested Antwren	3/17	Ecuador
1705	Chestnut-tipped Toucanet	3/17	Ecuador
1706	Cerulean Warbler	3/17	Ecuador
1707	Spotted Nightingale-Thrush	3/17	Ecuador
1708	Olive-chested Flycatcher	3/17	Ecuador
1709	Fulvous-breasted Flatbill	3/17	Ecuador
1710	Dusky Spinetail	3/17	Ecuador
1711	Chestnut-crowned Gnateater	3/17	Ecuador
1712	White-streaked Antvireo	3/17	Ecuador
1713	Black-streaked Puffbird	3/17	Ecuador
1714	Many-spotted Hummingbird	3/17	Ecuador
1715	Napo Sabrewing	3/17	Ecuador
1716	Violet-headed Hummingbird	3/17	Ecuador
1717	Rufous-vented Whitetip	3/17	Ecuador
1718	Ecuadorian Piedtail	3/17	Ecuador
1719	Wire-crested Thorntail	3/17	Ecuador
1720	Gray-chinned Hermit	3/17	Ecuador
1721	Plain-colored Tanager	3/18	Colombia
1722	Spectacled Parrotlet	3/18	Colombia
1723	Crimson-backed Tanager	3/18	Colombia
1724	Yellow-bellied Siskin	3/19	Colombia
1725	Orange-crowned Oriole	3/19	Colombia
1726	Rose-breasted Grosbeak	3/19	Colombia
1727	Gray Seedeater	3/19	Colombia
1728	White-eared Conebill	3/19	Colombia
1729	Speckled Tanager	3/19	Colombia
1730	Scrub Tanager	3/19	Colombia
1731	Rufous-capped Warbler	3/19	Colombia
1732	Bay-breasted Warbler	3/19	Colombia
1733	American Redstart	3/19	Colombia
1734	Mourning Warbler	3/19	Colombia
1735	Tennessee Warbler	3/19	Colombia
1736	Black-and-white Warbler	3/19	Colombia
1737	Golden-winged Warbler	3/19	Colombia
1738	Northern Waterthrush	3/19	Colombia
1739	Spectacled Thrush	3/19	Colombia
1740	Bicolored Wren	3/19	Colombia
1741	Black-chested Jay	3/19	Colombia
1742	White-bibbed Manakin	3/19	Colombia
1743	Rufous Mourner	3/19	Colombia
1744	Acadian Flycatcher	3/19	Colombia
1745	Southern Bentbill	3/19	Colombia
1746	Mountain Elaenia	3/19	Colombia
1747	Double-banded Graytail	3/19	Colombia
1748	Orange-chinned Parakeet	3/19	Colombia
1749	Red-crowned Woodpecker	3/19	Colombia
1750	Indigo-capped Hummingbird	3/19	Colombia
1751	Chestnut-bellied Hummingbird	3/19	Colombia
1752	White-vented Plumeleteer	3/19	Colombia
1753	Colombian Chachalaca	3/19	Colombia
1754	Sooty Ant-Tanager	3/20	Colombia
1755	Orange-billed Sparrow (130)	3/20	Colombia
1756	Gray-cheeked Thrush	3/20	Colombia
1757	Tawny-faced Gnatwren	3/20	Colombia
1758	Song Wren	3/20	Colombia
1759	Yellow-browed Shrike-Vireo	3/20	Colombia
1760	Olive-sided Flycatcher	3/20	Colombia
1761	Cocoa Woodcreeper	3/20	Colombia
1762	Magdalena Antbird	3/20	Colombia
1763	Saffron-headed Parrot	3/20	Colombia
1764	Beautiful Woodpecker	3/20	Colombia
1765	Barred Puffbird	3/20	Colombia
1766	Bar-crested Antshrike	3/20	Colombia

1767	Red-billed Emerald	3/20	Colombia
1768	Yellow-backed Oriole	3/21	Colombia
1769	Carib Grackle	3/21	Colombia
1770	Eastern Meadowlark (138)	3/21	Colombia
1771	Whiskered Wren	3/21	Colombia
1772	Flavescent Flycatcher	3/21	Colombia
1773	Magdalena Tapaculo	3/21	Colombia
1774	Parker's Antbird	3/21	Colombia
1775	Black Inca	3/21	Colombia
1776	Lined Quail-Dove	3/21	Colombia
1777	Highland Tinamou	3/21	Colombia
1778	Brown-billed Scythebill	3/22	Colombia
1779	Uniform Antshrike	3/22	Colombia
1780	White-mantled Barbet	3/22	Colombia
1781	Turquoise Dacnis	3/23	Colombia
1782	Nicéforo's Wren	3/23	Colombia
1783	White-vented Euphonia	3/23	Colombia
1784	Gray-throated Warbler	3/24	Colombia
1785	Black-bellied Wren	3/24	Colombia
1786	Blue-lored Antbird	3/24	Colombia
1787	White-bellied Antbird	3/24	Colombia
1788	Olivaceous Piculet	3/24	Colombia
1789	American Coot	3/24	Colombia
1790	Silvery-throated Spinetail	3/24	Colombia
1791	Ochre-breasted Brushfinch	3/25	Colombia
1792	Golden-fronted Redstart	3/25	Colombia
1793	Black-collared Jay	3/25	Colombia
1794	Cundinamarca Antpitta (160)	3/25	Colombia
1795	Brown-breasted Parakeet	3/25	Colombia
1796	Rufous Wren	3/25	Colombia
1797	Tawny-rumped Tyrannulet	3/25	Colombia
1798	White-browed Spinetail	3/25	Colombia
1799	Pale-bellied Tapaculo	3/25	Colombia
1800	Blue-throated Starfrontlet	3/25	Colombia
1801	Scarlet Tanager	3/25	Colombia
1802	Brown-throated Parakeet	3/25	Colombia
1803	Green-bellied Hummingbird	3/25	Colombia
1804	Andean Siskin	3/26	Colombia
1805	Chestnut-breasted Chlorophonia	3/26	Colombia
1806	Tyrannine Woodcreeper	3/26	Colombia
1807	Black-billed Mountain-Toucan	3/26	Colombia
1808	Rufous-browed Conebill	3/26	Colombia
1809	Glowing Puffleg	3/26	Colombia
1810	Bogotá Rail	3/26	Colombia
1811	Apolinar's Wren	3/27	Colombia
1812	Green-bearded Helmetcrest	3/27	Colombia
1813	Bronze-tailed Thornbill	3/27	Colombia
1814	Noble Snipe	3/27	Colombia
1815	Moustached Brushfinch	3/27	Colombia
1816	Ash-browed Spinetail	3/27	Colombia
1817	Golden-bellied Starfrontlet	3/27	Colombia
1818	Velvet-fronted Euphonia	3/28	Colombia
1819	Black-faced Grassquit	3/28	Colombia
1820	Scrub Greenlet	3/28	Colombia
1821	Lance-tailed Manakin	3/28	Colombia
1822	Apical Flycatcher	3/28	Colombia
1823	Pale-eyed Pygmy-Tyrant	3/28	Colombia
1824	Jet Antbird	3/28	Colombia
1825	Crested Caracara	3/28	Colombia
1826	Whooping Motmot	3/28	Colombia
1827	Great-tailed Grackle	3/29	Colombia
1828	Black-backed Antshrike	3/29	Colombia
1829	Zone-tailed Hawk (137)	3/29	Colombia
1830	Baltimore Oriole	3/29	Colombia
1831	Golden-winged Sparrow	3/29	Colombia
1832	Rufous-breasted Wren	3/29	Colombia
1833	Keel-billed Toucan (125)	3/29	Colombia
1834	Steely-vented Hummingbird	3/29	Colombia
1835	Pale-bellied Hermit	3/29	Colombia
1836	Rufous Nightjar	3/29	Colombia
1837	Kentucky Warbler	3/29	Colombia
1838	Rufous-and-white Wren	3/29	Colombia
1839	Panama Flycatcher	3/30	Colombia
1840	Santa Marta Brushfinch	3/30	Colombia
1841	Sierra Nevada Brushfinch	3/30	Colombia
1842	White-lored Warbler	3/30	Colombia
1843	Santa Marta Tapaculo	3/30	Colombia
1844	Stripe-throated Hermit	3/30	Colombia
1845	Black-headed Tanager	3/30	Colombia
1846	Orange-billed Nightingale-Thrush	3/30	Colombia
1847	Streak-capped Spinetail	3/30	Colombia
1848	Santa Marta Foliage-gleaner	3/30	Colombia
1849	Rusty-breasted Antpitta	3/30	Colombia
1850	Santa Marta Antbird	3/30	Colombia
1851	Gartered Trogon	3/30	Colombia
1852	Band-tailed Guan	3/30	Colombia
1853	Rosy Thrush-Tanager	3/30	Colombia
1854	Groove-billed Toucanet	3/30	Colombia
1855	Yellow-crowned Redstart	3/30	Colombia
1856	Black-hooded Thrush	3/30	Colombia
1857	Golden-breasted Fruiteater	3/30	Colombia
1858	Santa Marta Antpitta	3/30	Colombia
1859	White-tipped Quetzal	3/30	Colombia
1860	Lazuline Sabrewing	3/30	Colombia
1861	White-tailed Starfrontlet	3/30	Colombia
1862	Black-cheeked Mountain-Tanager	3/30	Colombia
1863	Rusty-headed Spinetail	3/30	Colombia
1864	Brown-rumped Tapaculo	3/30	Colombia
1865	Stygian Owl (13)	3/31	Colombia
1866	Santa Marta Warbler	3/31	Colombia
1867	Santa Marta Bush-Tyrant	3/31	Colombia
1868	Flammulated Treehunter	3/31	Colombia
1869	Santa Marta Parakeet	3/31	Colombia
1870	Gray-throated Leaftosser	3/31	Colombia
1871	Black-fronted Wood-Quail	3/31	Colombia
1872	Moustached Puffbird	3/31	Colombia
1873	Santa Marta Woodstar	3/31	Colombia
1874	Santa Marta Blossomcrown	3/31	Colombia
1875	Scaled Piculet	4/1	Colombia
1876	Common Black Hawk	4/1	Colombia
1877	Black-striped Sparrow	4/1	Colombia
1878	Lesser Elaenia	4/1	Colombia
1879	Golden-fronted Greenlet	4/1	Colombia
1880	Brown Pelican (153–155)	4/1	Colombia
1881	Trinidad Euphonia	4/1	Colombia
1882	Green-rumped Parrotlet	4/1	Colombia
1883	Yellow-billed Cuckoo	4/1	Colombia
1884	Pale-tipped Tyrannulet	4/1	Colombia
1885	Black-crested Antshrike	4/1	Colombia
1886	Russet-throated Puffbird	4/1	Colombia

1887	Bare-eyed Pigeon	4/1	Colombia
1888	Rufous-vented Chachalaca	4/1	Colombia
1889	Northern Scrub-Flycatcher	4/1	Colombia
1890	White-whiskered Spinetail	4/1	Colombia
1891	Blue-crowned Parakeet	4/1	Colombia
1892	Merlin	4/1	Colombia
1893	Chestnut Piculet	4/1	Colombia
1894	Crested Bobwhite	4/1	Colombia
1895	Double-striped Thick-knee	4/1	Colombia
1896	Dickcissel	4/2	Colombia
1897	Orinocan Saltator	4/2	Colombia
1898	Glaucous Tanager	4/2	Colombia
1899	Black-whiskered Vireo	4/2	Colombia
1900	Slender-billed Tyrannulet	4/2	Colombia
1901	Shining-green Hummingbird	4/2	Colombia
1902	Buffy Hummingbird	4/2	Colombia
1903	Yellow Oriole	4/2	Colombia
1904	Vermilion Cardinal	4/2	Colombia
1905	Tocuyo Sparrow	4/2	Colombia
1906	Pearl Kite	4/2	Colombia
1907	White Ibis	4/2	Colombia
1908	Reddish Egret	4/2	Colombia
1909	American Flamingo	4/2	Colombia
1910	Chestnut-winged Chachalaca	4/3	Colombia
1911	Belted Kingfisher	4/3	Colombia
1912	Western Sandpiper	4/3	Colombia
1913	Bronzed Cowbird	4/3	Colombia
1914	Pied Water-Tyrant	4/3	Colombia
1915	Sapphire-bellied Hummingbird	4/3	Colombia
1916	Yellow-hooded Blackbird	4/3	Colombia
1917	Glossy Ibis	4/3	Colombia
1918	Northern Shoveler	4/3	Colombia
1919	White-naped Brushfinch	4/4	Colombia
1920	Chestnut Wood-Quail	4/4	Colombia
1921	Multicolored Tanager	4/4	Colombia
1922	Tawny-throated Leaftosser	4/4	Colombia
1923	Crested Quetzal	4/4	Colombia
1924	Blue-headed Sapphire	4/4	Colombia
1925	Ornate Hawk-Eagle	4/4	Colombia
1926	Golden-collared Manakin	4/4	Colombia
1927	Western Emerald	4/4	Colombia
1928	Dwarf Cuckoo	4/5	Colombia
1929	Grayish Piculet	4/5	Colombia
1930	Common Nighthawk	4/5	Colombia
1931	Dusky-faced Tanager	4/5	Colombia
1932	Blue-whiskered Tanager	4/5	Colombia
1933	Tawny-crested Tanager	4/5	Colombia
1934	Black-tipped Cotinga	4/5	Colombia
1935	Black-capped Pygmy-Tyrant	4/5	Colombia
1936	Thicket Antpitta	4/5	Colombia
1937	Streak-chested Antpitta	4/5	Colombia
1938	Stub-tailed Antbird	4/5	Colombia
1939	Lanceolated Monklet	4/5	Colombia
1940	Black-breasted Puffbird	4/5	Colombia
1941	Bronzy Hermit	4/5	Colombia
1942	Chestnut-headed Oropendola	4/6	Colombia
1943	Pacific Flatbill	4/6	Colombia
1944	Dusky Antbird	4/6	Colombia
1945	Five-colored Barbet	4/6	Colombia
1946	Band-tailed Barbthroat	4/6	Colombia
1947	Choco Poorwill	4/6	Colombia
1948	Golden-hooded Tanager	4/6	Colombia
1949	Ruddy Foliage-gleaner	4/7	Colombia
1950	Chestnut-bellied Flowerpiercer	4/8	Colombia
1951	Purplish-mantled Tanager	4/8	Colombia
1952	Gold-ringed Tanager	4/8	Colombia
1953	Munchique Wood-Wren	4/8	Colombia
1954	Pale-eyed Thrush	4/8	Colombia
1955	Bicolored Antvireo	4/8	Colombia
1956	Crested Ant-Tanager	4/9	Colombia
1957	Olive Finch	4/9	Colombia
1958	Black-and-gold Tanager	4/9	Colombia
1959	Sooty-headed Wren	4/9	Colombia
1960	Uniform Treehunter	4/9	Colombia
1961	Choco Tapaculo	4/9	Colombia
1962	Yellow-vented Woodpecker	4/9	Colombia
1963	Semicollared Hawk	4/9	Colombia
1964	Blackish Rail	4/9	Colombia
1965	Chapman's Swift	4/10	Colombia
1966	Ash-colored Tapaculo	4/10	Colombia
1967	Brown-banded Antpitta	4/10	Colombia
1968	Dusky Piha	4/11	Colombia
1969	Chestnut-naped Antpitta	4/11	Colombia
1970	Bicolored Antpitta	4/11	Colombia
1971	Buffy Helmetcrest	4/12	Colombia
1972	Paramo Seedeater	4/12	Colombia
1973	Rufous-fronted Parakeet	4/12	Colombia
1974	Black-thighed Puffleg	4/12	Colombia
1975	Acorn Woodpecker (138)	4/12	Colombia
1976	Clay-colored Thrush	4/13	Colombia
1977	Antioquia Wren	4/13	Colombia
1978	Red-bellied Grackle	4/13	Colombia
1979	Yellow-headed Manakin	4/13	Colombia
1980	Stiles's Tapaculo	4/13	Colombia
1981	Fulvous-vented Euphonia	4/14	Panama
1982	Yellow-crowned Euphonia	4/14	Panama
1983	Bicolored Antbird	4/14	Panama
1984	White-headed Wren	4/14	Panama
1985	Green Shrike-Vireo	4/14	Panama
1986	Speckled Mourner	4/14	Panama
1987	Russet-winged Schiffornis	4/14	Panama
1988	Red-capped Manakin	4/14	Panama
1989	Rufous Piha	4/14	Panama
1990	Blue Cotinga	4/14	Panama
1991	White-ringed Flycatcher	4/14	Panama
1992	Great Crested Flycatcher	4/14	Panama
1993	Royal Flycatcher	4/14	Panama
1994	Black-headed Tody-Flycatcher	4/14	Panama
1995	Paltry Tyrannulet	4/14	Panama
1996	Yellow-green Tyrannulet	4/14	Panama
1997	Black-crowned Antpitta	4/14	Panama
1998	Ocellated Antbird	4/14	Panama
1999	Spotted Antbird	4/14	Panama
2000	Shining Honeycreeper (113)	4/14	Panama
2001	Bare-crowned Antbird	4/14	Panama
2002	Checker-throated Antwren	4/14	Panama
2003	Black Antshrike	4/14	Panama
2004	Red-lored Parrot	4/14	Panama
2005	White-whiskered Puffbird	4/14	Panama
2006	Slaty-tailed Trogon	4/14	Panama

2007	Blue-throated Goldentail	4/14	Panama
2008	Snowy-bellied Hummingbird	4/14	Panama
2009	Scaly-breasted Hummingbird	4/14	Panama
2010	Long-billed Hermit	4/14	Panama
2011	Gray-chested Dove	4/14	Panama
2012	Short-billed Pigeon	4/14	Panama
2013	White Hawk	4/14	Panama
2014	Gray-headed Chachalaca	4/14	Panama
2015	Sapphire-throated Hummingbird	4/14	Panama
2016	One-colored Becard	4/14	Panama
2017	Green Heron	4/14	Panama
2018	Great Blue Heron	4/14	Panama
2019	Tawny-capped Euphonia	4/15	Panama
2020	Black-and-yellow Tanager	4/15	Panama
2021	Sulphur-rumped Tanager	4/15	Panama
2022	Stripe-throated Wren	4/15	Panama
2023	Dull-mantled Antbird	4/15	Panama
2024	Spiny-faced Antshrike	4/15	Panama
2025	Spot-crowned Antvireo	4/15	Panama
2026	Sapayoa	4/15	Panama
2027	Brown-hooded Parrot	4/15	Panama
2028	Bronze-tailed Plumeleteer	4/15	Panama
2029	White-throated Crake	4/15	Panama
2030	Violet-capped Hummingbird	4/15	Panama
2031	Stripe-cheeked Woodpecker	4/15	Panama
2032	Black-eared Wood-Quail	4/15	Panama
2033	Northern Barred-Woodcreeper	4/16	Panama
2034	Blue-fronted Parrotlet	4/16	Panama
2035	Yellow-eared Toucanet	4/16	Panama
2036	White-tipped Sicklebill	4/16	Panama
2037	White-ruffed Manakin	4/16	Panama
2038	Rufous-vented Ground-Cuckoo	4/16	Panama
2039	Mississippi Kite (31)	4/16	Panama
2040	Plain Wren	4/16	Panama
2041	Red Knot	4/16	Panama
2042	Marbled Godwit	4/16	Panama
2043	Mangrove Swallow	4/16	Panama
2044	Red-throated Ant-Tanager (125–126)	4/16	Panama
2045	Violet-bellied Hummingbird	4/16	Panama
2046	Black-and-white Owl	4/16	Panama
2047	Vermiculated Screech-Owl	4/16	Panama
2048	Garden Emerald	4/17	Panama
2049	Blue-footed Booby	4/17	Panama
2050	Loggerhead Kingbird	4/17	Jamaica
2051	Greater Antillean Grackle	4/17	Jamaica
2052	Northern Mockingbird	4/17	Jamaica
2053	Antillean Palm-Swift	4/17	Jamaica
2054	Cave Swallow	4/17	Jamaica
2055	White-winged Dove	4/17	Jamaica
2056	Red-tailed Hawk	4/17	Jamaica
2057	Gray Kingbird	4/17	Jamaica
2058	Zenaida Dove	4/17	Jamaica
2059	Jamaican Crow	4/17	Jamaica
2060	White-crowned Pigeon	4/17	Jamaica
2061	Jamaican Euphonia	4/17	Jamaica
2062	Jamaican Oriole	4/17	Jamaica
2063	Jamaican Spindalis	4/17	Jamaica
2064	Black-throated Blue Warbler	4/17	Jamaica
2065	Magnolia Warbler	4/17	Jamaica
2066	White-chinned Thrush	4/17	Jamaica
2067	Olive-throated Parakeet	4/17	Jamaica
2068	Jamaican Woodpecker	4/17	Jamaica
2069	Jamaican Tody	4/17	Jamaica
2070	Streamertail	4/17	Jamaica
2071	Jamaican Owl	4/17	Jamaica
2072	Antillean Nighthawk	4/18	Jamaica
2073	Yellow-shouldered Grassquit	4/18	Jamaica
2074	Greater Antillean Bullfinch	4/18	Jamaica
2075	Orangequit	4/18	Jamaica
2076	Chestnut-sided Warbler	4/18	Jamaica
2077	Northern Parula	4/18	Jamaica
2078	Arrowhead Warbler	4/18	Jamaica
2079	Common Yellowthroat	4/18	Jamaica
2080	Worm-eating Warbler	4/18	Jamaica
2081	White-eyed Thrush	4/18	Jamaica
2082	Rufous-throated Solitaire	4/18	Jamaica
2083	Jamaican Vireo	4/18	Jamaica
2084	Jamaican Becard	4/18	Jamaica
2085	Rufous-tailed Flycatcher	4/18	Jamaica
2086	Sad Flycatcher	4/18	Jamaica
2087	Jamaican Pewee	4/18	Jamaica
2088	Jamaican Elaenia	4/18	Jamaica
2089	Yellow-billed Parrot	4/18	Jamaica
2090	Black-billed Parrot	4/18	Jamaica
2091	Vervain Hummingbird	4/18	Jamaica
2092	Jamaican Mango	4/18	Jamaica
2093	Chestnut-bellied Cuckoo	4/18	Jamaica
2094	Caribbean Dove	4/18	Jamaica
2095	Crested Quail-Dove	4/18	Jamaica
2096	Ring-tailed Pigeon	4/18	Jamaica
2097	Plain Pigeon	4/18	Jamaica
2098	White-tailed Tropicbird	4/18	Jamaica
2099	Jamaican Blackbird	4/18	Jamaica
2100	Blue Mountain Vireo	4/18	Jamaica
2101	Greater Antillean Elaenia	4/18	Jamaica
2102	Jamaican Lizard-Cuckoo	4/18	Jamaica
2103	Northern Potoo	4/18	Jamaica
2104	Scaly-breasted Munia	4/18	Jamaica
2105	Northern Rough-winged Swallow	4/19	Jamaica
2106	Stolid Flycatcher	4/19	Jamaica
2107	Northern Jacana	4/19	Jamaica
2108	Sora	4/19	Jamaica
2109	Least Tern	4/19	Jamaica
2110	West Indian Whistling-Duck	4/19	Jamaica
2111	Montezuma Oropendola	4/20	Costa Rica
2112	Crimson-fronted Parakeet	4/20	Costa Rica
2113	Hoffmann's Woodpecker	4/20	Costa Rica
2114	Red-billed Pigeon	4/20	Costa Rica
2115	Elegant Euphonia	4/20	Costa Rica
2116	Inca Dove	4/20	Costa Rica
2117	Mountain Thrush	4/20	Costa Rica
2118	Brown Jay (126)	4/20	Costa Rica
2119	Silvery-fronted Tapaculo	4/20	Costa Rica
2120	Scintillant Hummingbird	4/20	Costa Rica
2121	Purple-throated Mountain-gem	4/20	Costa Rica
2122	Golden-browed Chlorophonia	4/20	Costa Rica
2123	Melodious Blackbird	4/20	Costa Rica
2124	Spangle-cheeked Tanager	4/20	Costa Rica
2125	Wilson's Warbler	4/20	Costa Rica
2126	Black-cheeked Warbler	4/20	Costa Rica

2127	Flame-throated Warbler	4/20	Costa Rica
2128	Long-tailed Silky-flycatcher	4/20	Costa Rica
2129	American Dipper	4/20	Costa Rica
2130	Dark Pewee	4/20	Costa Rica
2131	Tufted Flycatcher	4/20	Costa Rica
2132	Spot-crowned Woodcreeper	4/20	Costa Rica
2133	White-crowned Parrot	4/20	Costa Rica
2134	Hairy Woodpecker (147)	4/20	Costa Rica
2135	Prong-billed Barbet	4/20	Costa Rica
2136	Black-bellied Hummingbird	4/20	Costa Rica
2137	Violet Sabrewing	4/20	Costa Rica
2138	Magenta-throated Woodstar	4/20	Costa Rica
2139	Magnificent Hummingbird	4/20	Costa Rica
2140	Black-headed Nightingale-Thrush	4/20	Costa Rica
2141	Coppery-headed Emerald	4/20	Costa Rica
2142	White-bellied Mountain-gem	4/20	Costa Rica
2143	Red-winged Blackbird	4/20	Costa Rica
2144	Passerini's Tanager	4/20	Costa Rica
2145	Black-faced Solitaire	4/20	Costa Rica
2146	Black-headed Saltator	4/20	Costa Rica
2147	Olive-backed Euphonia	4/20	Costa Rica
2148	Black-cowled Oriole	4/20	Costa Rica
2149	Black-faced Grosbeak	4/20	Costa Rica
2150	Stripe-breasted Wren	4/20	Costa Rica
2151	Black-throated Wren	4/20	Costa Rica
2152	Band-backed Wren	4/20	Costa Rica
2153	White-collared Manakin	4/20	Costa Rica
2154	Rufous-winged Woodpecker	4/20	Costa Rica
2155	Great Curassow	4/20	Costa Rica
2156	Crested Guan	4/20	Costa Rica
2157	White-collared Seedeater	4/20	Costa Rica
2158	Great Green Macaw	4/20	Costa Rica
2159	Bare-throated Tiger-Heron	4/20	Costa Rica
2160	Snowy Cotinga	4/21	Costa Rica
2161	Pale-billed Woodpecker	4/21	Costa Rica
2162	Chestnut-colored Woodpecker	4/21	Costa Rica
2163	Olive-backed Quail-Dove	4/21	Costa Rica
2164	Slaty-breasted Tinamou	4/21	Costa Rica
2165	Nicaraguan Seed-Finch	4/21	Costa Rica
2166	Gray Hawk	4/21	Costa Rica
2167	Lattice-tailed Trogon	4/21	Costa Rica
2168	Snowcap	4/21	Costa Rica
2169	Black-crested Coquette	4/21	Costa Rica
2170	White-throated Flycatcher	4/21	Costa Rica
2171	Dusky Nightjar	4/21	Costa Rica
2172	Bare-shanked Screech-Owl (124)	4/21	Costa Rica
2173	Yellow-bellied Flycatcher (126)	4/22	Costa Rica
2174	Tawny-chested Flycatcher (127)	4/22	Costa Rica
2175	Green-breasted Mango (127)	4/22	Costa Rica
2176	Paint-billed Crake	4/22	Costa Rica
2177	Crimson-collared Tanager	4/22	Costa Rica
2178	Blue-crowned Motmot	4/22	Costa Rica
2179	Sooty-capped Chlorospingus (117)	4/22	Costa Rica
2180	Yellow-thighed Finch (116)	4/22	Costa Rica
2181	Slaty Flowerpiercer	4/22	Costa Rica
2182	Black-and-yellow Silky-flycatcher (116)	4/22	Costa Rica
2183	Sooty Thrush	4/22	Costa Rica
2184	Black-billed Nightingale-Thrush	4/22	Costa Rica
2185	Timberline Wren (116, 117)	4/22	Costa Rica
2186	Ruddy Treerunner	4/22	Costa Rica
2187	Barred Parakeet	4/22	Costa Rica
2188	Resplendent Quetzal (115, 117–119, 121, 132)	4/22	Costa Rica
2189	Volcano Hummingbird (116)	4/22	Costa Rica
2190	Fiery-throated Hummingbird (115)	4/22	Costa Rica
2191	Large-footed Finch	4/22	Costa Rica
2192	Collared Redstart	4/22	Costa Rica
2193	Black-capped Flycatcher	4/22	Costa Rica
2194	Wrenthrush	4/23	Costa Rica
2195	Black Guan	4/23	Costa Rica
2196	Flame-colored Tanager	4/23	Costa Rica
2197	Black-throated Green Warbler	4/23	Costa Rica
2198	Yellow-winged Vireo	4/23	Costa Rica
2199	Spotted Wood-Quail	4/23	Costa Rica
2200	Buffy-crowned Wood-Partridge	4/23	Costa Rica
2201	Black-thighed Grosbeak	4/23	Costa Rica
2202	Ruddy-capped Nightingale-Thrush	4/23	Costa Rica
2203	Ochraceous Wren (117)	4/23	Costa Rica
2204	Yellowish Flycatcher	4/23	Costa Rica
2205	Buffy Tuftedcheek	4/23	Costa Rica
2206	Sulphur-winged Parakeet	4/23	Costa Rica
2207	Stripe-tailed Hummingbird	4/23	Costa Rica
2208	White-throated Mountain-gem	4/23	Costa Rica
2209	Buff-fronted Quail-Dove	4/23	Costa Rica
2210	Volcano Junco (115)	4/23	Costa Rica
2211	Indigo Bunting	4/23	Costa Rica
2212	Cherrie's Tanager	4/23	Costa Rica
2213	Philadelphia Vireo	4/23	Costa Rica
2214	Turquoise Cotinga	4/23	Costa Rica
2215	Spot-crowned Euphonia	4/23	Costa Rica
2216	Riverside Wren	4/23	Costa Rica
2217	Orange-collared Manakin	4/23	Costa Rica
2218	Black-tailed Flycatcher	4/23	Costa Rica
2219	Tawny-winged Woodcreeper	4/23	Costa Rica
2220	Russet Antshrike	4/23	Costa Rica
2221	Black-hooded Antshrike	4/23	Costa Rica
2222	Baird's Trogon	4/23	Costa Rica
2223	Charming Hummingbird	4/23	Costa Rica
2224	Fiery-billed Aracari	4/23	Costa Rica
2225	Costa Rican Swift	4/23	Costa Rica
2226	Striped Owl	4/23	Costa Rica
2227	Golden-naped Woodpecker	4/24	Costa Rica
2228	Brown Booby	4/24	Costa Rica
2229	Scrub Euphonia	4/24	Costa Rica
2230	Rufous-naped Wren	4/24	Costa Rica
2231	Northern Bentbill	4/24	Costa Rica
2232	Turquoise-browed Motmot	4/24	Costa Rica
2233	Black-headed Trogon	4/24	Costa Rica
2234	Plain-capped Starthroat	4/24	Costa Rica
2235	Yellow-throated Euphonia	4/24	Costa Rica
2236	Rose-throated Becard	4/24	Costa Rica
2237	Eye-ringed Flatbill	4/24	Costa Rica
2238	Mangrove Vireo	4/24	Costa Rica
2239	Stripe-headed Sparrow	4/24	Costa Rica
2240	Nutting's Flycatcher	4/24	Costa Rica
2241	Orange-fronted Parakeet	4/24	Costa Rica
2242	Cinnamon Hummingbird	4/24	Costa Rica
2243	Yellow-naped Parrot	4/24	Costa Rica
2244	Mangrove Hummingbird	4/24	Costa Rica

2245	Olive Sparrow	4/24	Costa Rica
2246	White-throated Magpie-Jay	4/24	Costa Rica
2247	Lesser Ground-Cuckoo	4/24	Costa Rica
2248	Banded Wren	4/24	Costa Rica
2249	Spectacled Owl	4/24	Costa Rica
2250	White-eared Ground-Sparrow	4/25	Costa Rica
2251	White-fronted Parrot	4/25	Costa Rica
2252	Orange-bellied Trogon	4/25	Costa Rica
2253	Black-breasted Wood-Quail	4/25	Costa Rica
2254	White-throated Thrush	4/25	Costa Rica
2255	Golden-bellied Flycatcher	4/25	Costa Rica
2256	Ovenbird	4/25	Costa Rica
2257	Long-tailed Manakin	4/25	Costa Rica
2258	Three-wattled Bellbird	4/25	Costa Rica
2259	Vaux's Swift	4/25	Costa Rica
2260	Chiriqui Quail-Dove	4/25	Costa Rica
2261	Blue Grosbeak	4/25	Costa Rica
2262	Gray-crowned Yellowthroat	4/25	Costa Rica
2263	Emerald Tanager	4/26	Costa Rica
2264	Nightingale Wren	4/26	Costa Rica
2265	Streak-crowned Antvireo	4/26	Costa Rica
2266	Keel-billed Motmot	4/26	Costa Rica
2267	Blue-and-gold Tanager	4/26	Costa Rica
2268	Northern Schiffornis	4/26	Costa Rica
2269	Prevost's Ground-Sparrow	4/27	Guatemala
2270	Yellow-winged Tanager	4/27	Guatemala
2271	Bushtit	4/27	Guatemala
2272	White-eared Hummingbird	4/27	Guatemala
2273	Azure-crowned Hummingbird	4/27	Guatemala
2274	Black-vented Oriole	4/27	Guatemala
2275	Western Tanager	4/27	Guatemala
2276	Rusty Sparrow	4/27	Guatemala
2277	MacGillivray's Warbler	4/27	Guatemala
2278	Nashville Warbler	4/27	Guatemala
2279	Gray Silky-flycatcher	4/27	Guatemala
2280	Blue-and-white Mockingbird	4/27	Guatemala
2281	Brown-backed Solitaire	4/27	Guatemala
2282	Eastern Bluebird	4/27	Guatemala
2283	Bushy-crested Jay	4/27	Guatemala
2284	Chestnut-sided Shrike-Vireo	4/27	Guatemala
2285	Buff-breasted Flycatcher	4/27	Guatemala
2286	Least Flycatcher	4/27	Guatemala
2287	Greater Pewee	4/27	Guatemala
2288	Pacific Parakeet	4/27	Guatemala
2289	Northern Flicker	4/27	Guatemala
2290	Golden-fronted Woodpecker	4/27	Guatemala
2291	Blue-throated Motmot	4/27	Guatemala
2292	Rufous Sabrewing	4/27	Guatemala
2293	White-throated Swift	4/27	Guatemala
2294	Warbling Vireo	4/27	Guatemala
2295	Black-capped Swallow	4/27	Guatemala
2296	Black-capped Siskin	4/27	Guatemala
2297	Pine Siskin	4/27	Guatemala
2298	Yellow-eyed Junco	4/27	Guatemala
2299	Cinnamon-bellied Flowerpiercer	4/27	Guatemala
2300	Pink-headed Warbler	4/27	Guatemala
2301	Crescent-chested Warbler	4/27	Guatemala
2302	Olive Warbler	4/27	Guatemala
2303	Rufous-collared Robin	4/27	Guatemala
2304	Black Thrush	4/27	Guatemala
2305	Rufous-browed Wren	4/27	Guatemala
2306	Steller's Jay	4/27	Guatemala
2307	Amethyst-throated Hummingbird	4/27	Guatemala
2308	Mexican Whip-poor-will	4/27	Guatemala
2309	Mourning Dove	4/27	Guatemala
2310	Golden-browed Warbler	4/28	Guatemala
2311	Townsend's Warbler	4/28	Guatemala
2312	Unicolored Jay	4/28	Guatemala
2313	Black-throated Jay	4/28	Guatemala
2314	Hutton's Vireo	4/28	Guatemala
2315	Mountain Trogon	4/28	Guatemala
2316	Garnet-throated Hummingbird	4/28	Guatemala
2317	Green-throated Mountain-gem	4/28	Guatemala
2318	Fulvous Owl	4/28	Guatemala
2319	Maroon-chested Ground-Dove	4/28	Guatemala
2320	Highland Guan	4/28	Guatemala
2321	Blue-crowned Chlorophonia	4/28	Guatemala
2322	Azure-rumped Tanager	4/28	Guatemala
2323	Buff-collared Nightjar (139–140)	4/28	Guatemala
2324	Altamira Oriole	4/29	Guatemala
2325	Spot-breasted Oriole	4/29	Guatemala
2326	Streak-backed Oriole	4/29	Guatemala
2327	Varied Bunting	4/29	Guatemala
2328	Yellow Grosbeak	4/29	Guatemala
2329	White-lored Gnatcatcher	4/29	Guatemala
2330	Northern Beardless-Tyrannulet	4/29	Guatemala
2331	Russet-crowned Motmot	4/29	Guatemala
2332	Elegant Trogon	4/29	Guatemala
2333	Canivet's Emerald	4/29	Guatemala
2334	Lesser Roadrunner	4/29	Guatemala
2335	Plain Chachalaca	4/29	Guatemala
2336	Grace's Warbler	4/29	Guatemala
2337	Slate-colored Solitaire	4/29	Guatemala
2338	White-winged Tanager	4/29	Guatemala
2339	Gray Catbird	4/29	Guatemala
2340	Hammond's Flycatcher	4/29	Guatemala
2341	Belted Flycatcher	4/29	Guatemala
2342	Slender Sheartail	4/29	Guatemala
2343	Northern Pygmy-Owl	4/29	Guatemala
2344	Ruddy Crake	4/29	Guatemala
2345	Black-headed Siskin	4/30	Guatemala
2346	Green-backed Sparrow	4/30	Guatemala
2347	Spot-breasted Wren	4/30	Guatemala
2348	Blue-headed Vireo	4/30	Guatemala
2349	Couch's Kingbird	4/30	Guatemala
2350	Alder Flycatcher	4/30	Guatemala
2351	Rufous-breasted Spinetail	4/30	Guatemala
2352	Hooded Grosbeak	4/30	Guatemala
2353	Lincoln's Sparrow	5/1	Guatemala
2354	Gray-collared Becard	5/1	Guatemala
2355	Ocellated Quail	5/1	Guatemala
2356	Cliff Swallow	5/1	Guatemala
2357	Scissor-tailed Flycatcher	5/1	Guatemala
2358	Painted Redstart	5/1	Guatemala
2359	Plumbeous Vireo	5/1	Guatemala
2360	Chipping Sparrow	5/1	Guatemala
2361	Carolina Wren (146)	5/1	Guatemala
2362	Botteri's Sparrow	5/1	Guatemala
2363	Orange-breasted Bunting	5/2	Mexico
2364	Northern Cardinal	5/2	Mexico

2365	Rufous-backed Robin	5/2	Mexico	2425	Ladder-backed Woodpecker	5/6	Mexico
2366	Golden-cheeked Woodpecker	5/2	Mexico	2426	Blue-gray Gnatcatcher	5/6	Mexico
2367	Citreoline Trogon	5/2	Mexico	2427	Western Scrub-Jay	5/6	Mexico
2368	Colima Pygmy-Owl	5/2	Mexico	2428	Cooper's Hawk	5/6	Mexico
2369	West Mexican Chachalaca	5/2	Mexico	2429	Bridled Titmouse	5/6	Mexico
2370	Yellow-winged Cacique	5/3	Mexico	2430	Cordilleran Flycatcher	5/6	Mexico
2371	Happy Wren (137)	5/3	Mexico	2431	White-striped Woodcreeper	5/6	Mexico
2372	Audubon's Oriole	5/3	Mexico	2432	Rufous-capped Brushfinch	5/6	Mexico
2373	Golden Vireo	5/3	Mexico	2433	American Robin	5/6	Mexico
2374	Ivory-billed Woodcreeper	5/3	Mexico	2434	White-breasted Nuthatch	5/6	Mexico
2375	Blue Bunting	5/3	Mexico	2435	Collared Towhee	5/6	Mexico
2376	Red-headed Tanager	5/3	Mexico	2436	Russet Nightingale-Thrush	5/6	Mexico
2377	Blue Mockingbird	5/3	Mexico	2437	Gray-barred Wren	5/6	Mexico
2378	Gray-crowned Woodpecker	5/3	Mexico	2438	Red Crossbill	5/6	Mexico
2379	Berylline Hummingbird	5/3	Mexico	2439	Red Warbler	5/6	Mexico
2380	Blue-capped Hummingbird	5/3	Mexico	2440	Mexican Chickadee	5/6	Mexico
2381	White-faced Quail-Dove	5/3	Mexico	2441	Blue-throated Hummingbird	5/6	Mexico
2382	Long-tailed Wood-Partridge	5/3	Mexico	2442	Aztec Thrush	5/6	Mexico
2383	Golden-crowned Emerald	5/3	Mexico	2443	Slaty Vireo (135)	5/6	Mexico
2384	Black Tern	5/3	Mexico	2444	Black Swift	5/6	Mexico
2385	Pomarine Jaeger	5/3	Mexico	2445	Golden-crowned Kinglet	5/7	Mexico
2386	Red-necked Phalarope	5/3	Mexico	2446	Brown Creeper	5/7	Mexico
2387	Black Storm-Petrel	5/3	Mexico	2447	Dwarf Jay	5/7	Mexico
2388	Leach's Storm-Petrel	5/3	Mexico	2448	Violet-crowned Hummingbird	5/7	Mexico
2389	Galapagos Shearwater	5/3	Mexico	2449	Azure-hooded Jay	5/7	Mexico
2390	Wedge-tailed Shearwater	5/3	Mexico	2450	Central American Pygmy-Owl	5/7	Mexico
2391	Red-breasted Chat	5/4	Mexico	2451	White-bellied Emerald	5/7	Mexico
2392	Flammulated Flycatcher	5/4	Mexico	2452	White-bellied Wren	5/8	Mexico
2393	Broad-billed Hummingbird	5/4	Mexico	2453	Sumichrast's Wren	5/8	Mexico
2394	Eurasian Collared-Dove	5/4	Mexico	2454	Ash-throated Flycatcher	5/8	Mexico
2395	American White Pelican	5/4	Mexico	2455	Stub-tailed Spadebill	5/8	Mexico
2396	Western Kingbird	5/4	Mexico	2456	Wedge-tailed Sabrewing	5/8	Mexico
2397	Northern Bobwhite	5/4	Mexico	2457	Gray-headed Dove	5/8	Mexico
2398	Yellow-rumped Warbler	5/5	Mexico	2458	Thicket Tinamou	5/8	Mexico
2399	Green Parakeet	5/5	Mexico	2459	Yellow-bellied Tyrannulet	5/8	Mexico
2400	Rose-bellied Bunting	5/5	Mexico	2460	Long-tailed Sabrewing	5/8	Mexico
2401	Cinnamon-tailed Sparrow	5/5	Mexico	2461	Bumblebee Hummingbird (3)	5/8	Mexico
2402	Beautiful Hummingbird	5/5	Mexico	2462	Tody Motmot	5/8	Mexico
2403	Bridled Sparrow	5/5	Mexico	2463	Buff-bellied Hummingbird	5/9	Mexico
2404	Green-fronted Hummingbird	5/5	Mexico	2464	Loggerhead Shrike	5/9	Mexico
2405	Dusky Hummingbird	5/5	Mexico	2465	Dusky Flycatcher	5/9	Mexico
2406	House Finch	5/5	Mexico	2466	Rufous-crowned Sparrow	5/10	Mexico
2407	Vesper Sparrow	5/5	Mexico	2467	Brown-headed Cowbird	5/11	Mexico
2408	Clay-colored Sparrow	5/5	Mexico	2468	Yellow-breasted Chat	5/11	Mexico
2409	White-throated Towhee	5/5	Mexico	2469	Sinaloa Wren	5/11	Mexico
2410	Curve-billed Thrasher	5/5	Mexico	2470	Sinaloa Crow	5/11	Mexico
2411	Boucard's Wren	5/5	Mexico	2471	Purplish-backed Jay	5/11	Mexico
2412	Cassin's Kingbird	5/5	Mexico	2472	Black-throated Magpie-Jay	5/11	Mexico
2413	Gray-breasted Woodpecker	5/5	Mexico	2473	Gila Woodpecker	5/11	Mexico
2414	Canyon Wren	5/5	Mexico	2474	Elegant Quail	5/11	Mexico
2415	Rock Wren (135)	5/6	Mexico	2475	Rufous-bellied Chachalaca	5/11	Mexico
2416	Black-headed Grosbeak	5/6	Mexico	2476	Black-capped Gnatcatcher	5/11	Mexico
2417	Oaxaca Sparrow	5/6	Mexico	2477	Forster's Tern	5/11	Mexico
2418	Spotted Towhee	5/6	Mexico	2478	American Avocet	5/11	Mexico
2419	Ocellated Thrasher	5/6	Mexico	2479	Heermann's Gull	5/11	Mexico
2420	Bewick's Wren	5/6	Mexico	2480	Wandering Tattler (174)	5/11	Mexico
2421	Common Raven	5/6	Mexico	2481	Ring-billed Gull	5/11	Mexico
2422	Dwarf Vireo	5/6	Mexico	2482	Red-billed Tropicbird	5/11	Mexico
2423	Thick-billed Kingbird	5/6	Mexico	2483	Ridgway's Rail	5/12	Mexico
2424	Pileated Flycatcher	5/6	Mexico	2484	Rusty-crowned Ground-Sparrow	5/12	Mexico

2485	White-naped Swift	5/12	Mexico
2486	Whiskered Screech-Owl	5/12	Mexico
2487	Green-striped Brushfinch	5/13	Mexico
2488	Tufted Jay	5/13	Mexico
2489	Arizona Woodpecker	5/13	Mexico
2490	Northern Saw-whet Owl	5/13	Mexico
2491	Sinaloa Martin	5/13	Mexico
2492	Spotted Wren	5/13	Mexico
2493	San Blas Jay	5/14	Mexico
2494	Mexican Woodnymph	5/14	Mexico
2495	Savannah Sparrow	5/15	Mexico
2496	Long-billed Curlew	5/15	Mexico
2497	Hooded Oriole	5/15	Mexico
2498	Fan-tailed Warbler	5/16	Mexico
2499	Striped Sparrow (138)	5/16	Mexico
2500	Common Poorwill (139–141)	5/16	Mexico
2501	Western Bluebird (138)	5/16	Mexico
2502	Say's Phoebe	5/16	Mexico
2503	Mallard	5/16	Mexico
2504	Canyon Towhee	5/16	Mexico
2505	Red-faced Warbler	5/17	Mexico
2506	Townsend's Solitaire	5/17	Mexico
2507	Pygmy Nuthatch	5/17	Mexico
2508	Violet-green Swallow	5/17	Mexico
2509	Mexican Jay	5/17	Mexico
2510	Pine Flycatcher	5/17	Mexico
2511	Eared Quetzal	5/17	Mexico
2512	Montezuma Quail	5/17	Mexico
2513	Black-backed Oriole	5/17	Mexico
2514	Orchard Oriole	5/17	Mexico
2515	Yellow-headed Blackbird	5/17	Mexico
2516	White-crowned Sparrow	5/17	Mexico
2517	Green-winged Teal	5/17	Mexico
2518	Gadwall	5/17	Mexico
2519	Chihuahuan Raven	5/17	Mexico
2520	Crimson-collared Grosbeak	5/17	Mexico
2521	Long-billed Thrasher	5/17	Mexico
2522	Western Meadowlark	5/18	Mexico
2523	Worthen's Sparrow (145)	5/18	Mexico
2524	Cassin's Sparrow	5/18	Mexico
2525	Horned Lark	5/18	Mexico
2526	Greater Roadrunner	5/18	Mexico
2527	Scaled Quail	5/18	Mexico
2528	Black-throated Sparrow	5/18	Mexico
2529	Black-chinned Sparrow	5/18	Mexico
2530	Black-tailed Gnatcatcher	5/18	Mexico
2531	Hooded Yellowthroat	5/18	Mexico
2532	Colima Warbler	5/18	Mexico
2533	Maroon-fronted Parrot	5/18	Mexico
2534	Broad-tailed Hummingbird	5/18	Mexico
2535	Black-crested Titmouse	5/18	Mexico
2536	Pine Warbler	5/18	USA-Texas
2537	Carolina Chickadee	5/18	USA-Texas
2538	Blue Jay (146)	5/18	USA-Texas
2539	White-eyed Vireo	5/18	USA-Texas
2540	Pileated Woodpecker	5/18	USA-Texas
2541	Red-cockaded Woodpecker (145, 146–147)	5/18	USA-Texas
2542	Bachman's Sparrow	5/19	USA-Texas
2543	Brown-headed Nuthatch	5/19	USA-Texas
2544	American Crow	5/19	USA-Texas
2545	Red-bellied Woodpecker	5/19	USA-Texas
2546	Chimney Swift	5/19	USA-Texas
2547	Chuck-will's-widow	5/19	USA-Texas
2548	Cedar Waxwing	5/19	USA-Texas
2549	Tufted Titmouse (146)	5/19	USA-Texas
2550	Purple Martin	5/19	USA-Texas
2551	Yellow-throated Vireo	5/19	USA-Texas
2552	Red-headed Woodpecker	5/19	USA-Texas
2553	Ruby-throated Hummingbird	5/19	USA-Texas
2554	Wood Duck	5/19	USA-Texas
2555	Prairie Warbler	5/19	USA-Texas
2556	Red-shouldered Hawk	5/19	USA-Texas
2557	Common Grackle	5/19	USA-Texas
2558	Yellow-throated Warbler	5/19	USA-Texas
2559	Prothonotary Warbler	5/19	USA-Texas
2560	Hooded Warbler	5/19	USA-Texas
2561	Swainson's Warbler	5/19	USA-Texas
2562	White-rumped Sandpiper	5/19	USA-Texas
2563	Double-crested Cormorant	5/19	USA-Texas
2564	Painted Bunting	5/19	USA-Texas
2565	Fish Crow	5/19	USA-Texas
2566	Northern Harrier	5/19	USA-Texas
2567	Mottled Duck	5/19	USA-Texas
2568	Boat-tailed Grackle	5/19	USA-Texas
2569	Seaside Sparrow	5/19	USA-Texas
2570	Marsh Wren	5/19	USA-Texas
2571	King Rail	5/19	USA-Texas
2572	Swainson's Hawk	5/19	USA-Texas
2573	Clapper Rail	5/19	USA-Texas
2574	Caspian Tern	5/19	USA-Texas
2575	Dunlin	5/19	USA-Texas
2576	Piping Plover	5/19	USA-Texas
2577	Lark Sparrow	5/20	USA-Texas
2578	Field Sparrow	5/20	USA-Texas
2579	Scott's Oriole	5/20	USA-Texas
2580	Golden-cheeked Warbler (145)	5/20	USA-Texas
2581	Louisiana Waterthrush	5/20	USA-Texas
2582	Black-capped Vireo (145)	5/20	USA-Texas
2583	Eastern Phoebe	5/20	USA-Texas
2584	Black-chinned Hummingbird	5/20	USA-Texas
2585	Verdin	5/20	USA-Texas
2586	Bell's Vireo	5/20	USA-Texas
2587	Wild Turkey (206)	5/20	USA-Texas
2588	Pyrrhuloxia	5/20	USA-Texas
2589	Bullock's Oriole	5/20	USA-Texas
2590	Red-crowned Parrot	5/20	USA-Texas
2591	Eastern Screech-Owl	5/20	USA-Texas
2592	Black Rail	5/21	USA-Texas
2593	Redhead	5/21	USA-Texas
2594	Bald Eagle	5/21	USA-Texas
2595	Brown Thrasher	5/21	USA-Texas
2596	Downy Woodpecker (147)	5/21	USA-Texas
2597	Tree Swallow	5/21	USA-Texas
2598	Pacific Loon	5/21	USA-Texas
2599	Anna's Hummingbird	5/22	USA-Arizona
2600	Abert's Towhee	5/22	USA-Arizona
2601	Gambel's Quail	5/22	USA-Arizona
2602	Le Conte's Thrasher	5/22	USA-Arizona
2603	Bendire's Thrasher	5/22	USA-Arizona

2604	Cactus Wren	5/22	USA-Arizona
2605	Song Sparrow	5/22	USA-Arizona
2606	California Gull	5/22	USA-Arizona
2607	Northern Pintail	5/22	USA-Arizona
2608	American Wigeon	5/22	USA-Arizona
2609	Rosy-faced Lovebird	5/22	USA-Arizona
2610	Canada Goose	5/22	USA-Arizona
2611	Lucy's Warbler	5/22	USA-Arizona
2612	Gray Vireo	5/22	USA-Arizona
2613	Phainopepla	5/22	USA-Arizona
2614	Crissal Thrasher	5/22	USA-Arizona
2615	Juniper Titmouse	5/22	USA-Arizona
2616	Gilded Flicker	5/22	USA-Arizona
2617	Virginia's Warbler	5/23	USA-Arizona
2618	Hermit Thrush	5/23	USA-Arizona
2619	Lucifer Hummingbird	5/23	USA-Arizona
2620	Golden Eagle	5/23	USA-Arizona
2621	Grasshopper Sparrow	5/23	USA-Arizona
2622	Elf Owl	5/23	USA-Arizona
2623	Costa's Hummingbird	5/24	USA-Arizona
2624	Rufous-winged Sparrow	5/24	USA-Arizona
2625	Five-striped Sparrow (149)	5/24	USA-Arizona
2626	Spotted Owl	5/24	USA-California
2627	Western Screech-Owl	5/24	USA-California
2628	Flammulated Owl	5/24	USA-California
2629	California Towhee	5/25	USA-California
2630	Orange-crowned Warbler	5/25	USA-California
2631	Wrentit	5/25	USA-California
2632	Oak Titmouse	5/25	USA-California
2633	Pacific-slope Flycatcher	5/25	USA-California
2634	Lawrence's Goldfinch	5/25	USA-California
2635	Brewer's Blackbird	5/25	USA-California
2636	Bell's Sparrow	5/25	USA-California
2637	Willow Flycatcher	5/25	USA-California
2638	Ross's Goose	5/25	USA-California
2639	Snow Goose	5/25	USA-California
2640	Greater White-fronted Goose	5/25	USA-California
2641	Clark's Grebe	5/25	USA-California
2642	Eared Grebe	5/25	USA-California
2643	Lesser Scaup	5/25	USA-California
2644	American Goldfinch	5/25	USA-California
2645	Tricolored Blackbird	5/25	USA-California
2646	Western Gull	5/25	USA-California
2647	Common Loon	5/25	USA-California
2648	Surf Scoter	5/25	USA-California
2649	Brandt's Cormorant	5/25	USA-California
2650	Red-throated Loon	5/25	USA-California
2651	Bonaparte's Gull	5/25	USA-California
2652	Cassin's Auklet	5/25	USA-California
2653	Pigeon Guillemot	5/25	USA-California
2654	Common Murre	5/25	USA-California
2655	Pelagic Cormorant	5/25	USA-California
2656	Black Oystercatcher	5/25	USA-California
2657	California Thrasher	5/26	USA-California
2658	Nuttall's Woodpecker	5/26	USA-California
2659	Allen's Hummingbird	5/26	USA-California
2660	Black-vented Shearwater	5/26	USA-California
2661	California Gnatcatcher	5/26	USA-California
2662	Cackling Goose	5/26	USA-California
2663	Western Grebe	5/26	USA-California
2664	California Condor	5/26	USA-California
2665	Calliope Hummingbird	5/26	USA-California
2666	Mountain Quail	5/26	USA-California
2667	Cassin's Finch	5/26	USA-California
2668	Purple Finch	5/26	USA-California
2669	Black-throated Gray Warbler	5/26	USA-California
2670	Fox Sparrow	5/26	USA-California
2671	Green-tailed Towhee	5/26	USA-California
2672	Mountain Chickadee	5/26	USA-California
2673	Dark-eyed Junco	5/26	USA-California
2674	White-headed Woodpecker	5/26	USA-California
2675	Red-breasted Sapsucker	5/26	USA-California
2676	Yellow-billed Magpie	5/27	USA-California
2677	Glaucous-winged Gull	5/27	USA-California
2678	Brant	5/27	USA-California
2679	Long-billed Dowitcher	5/27	USA-California
2680	Black Turnstone	5/27	USA-California
2681	Evening Grosbeak	5/28	USA-Oregon
2682	Hermit Warbler	5/28	USA-Oregon
2683	Pacific Wren	5/28	USA-Oregon
2684	Red-breasted Nuthatch	5/28	USA-Oregon
2685	Chestnut-backed Chickadee	5/28	USA-Oregon
2686	Black-capped Chickadee (1)	5/28	USA-Oregon
2687	Rufous Hummingbird	5/28	USA-Oregon
2688	Lazuli Bunting	5/28	USA-Oregon
2689	Gray Jay	5/28	USA-Oregon
2690	Hooded Merganser	5/28	USA-Oregon
2691	Virginia Rail	5/29	USA-Oregon
2692	American Bittern	5/29	USA-Oregon
2693	Cassin's Vireo	5/29	USA-Oregon
2694	Ring-necked Pheasant	5/29	USA-Oregon
2695	Varied Thrush	5/30	USA-Oregon
2696	Sooty Grouse	5/30	USA-Oregon
2697	Greater Scaup (149)	5/30	USA-Oregon
2698	Common Merganser	5/30	USA-Oregon
2699	Harlequin Duck	5/30	USA-Oregon
2700	Marbled Murrelet	5/30	USA-Oregon
2701	Tufted Puffin (149, 150–151, 157)	5/30	USA-Oregon
2702	Black Scoter	5/30	USA-Oregon
2703	Rhinoceros Auklet	5/31	USA-Oregon
2704	White-winged Scoter	5/31	USA-Oregon
2705	Wilson's Snipe	6/1	USA-Oregon
2706	Mountain Bluebird	6/1	USA-Oregon
2707	Clark's Nutcracker	6/1	USA-Oregon
2708	Black-backed Woodpecker	6/1	USA-Oregon
2709	Pinyon Jay	6/1	USA-Oregon
2710	Gray Flycatcher	6/1	USA-Oregon
2711	Lewis's Woodpecker	6/1	USA-Oregon
2712	Great Gray Owl	6/1	USA-Oregon
2713	Sandhill Crane	6/1	USA-Oregon
2714	Yellow Rail	6/1	USA-Oregon
2715	Ferruginous Hawk	6/1	USA-Oregon
2716	Ring-necked Duck	6/1	USA-Oregon
2717	Sagebrush Sparrow	6/2	USA-Oregon
2718	Brewer's Sparrow	6/2	USA-Oregon
2719	Sage Thrasher	6/2	USA-Oregon
2720	Prairie Falcon	6/2	USA-Oregon
2721	Black-billed Magpie	6/2	USA-Oregon
2722	Long-eared Owl	6/2	USA-Oregon
2723	Chukar	6/2	USA-Oregon

2724	Red-naped Sapsucker	6/2	USA-Oregon
2725	Short-eared Owl	6/2	USA-Oregon
2726	Bufflehead	6/2	USA-Oregon
2727	Canvasback	6/2	USA-Oregon
2728	Trumpeter Swan	6/2	USA-Oregon
2729	Williamson's Sapsucker	6/3	USA-Oregon
2730	Barrow's Goldeneye	6/3	USA-Oregon
2731	Ruby-crowned Kinglet	6/3	USA-Oregon
2732	Ruffed Grouse	6/4	USA-Oregon
2733	Great Black-backed Gull	6/5	USA-New York
2734	Wood Thrush	6/5	USA-New York
2735	Veery	6/5	USA-New York
2736	Barred Owl	6/5	USA-New York
2737	Red-breasted Merganser	6/6	USA-New York
2738	Eastern Towhee	6/6	USA-New York
2739	Blue-winged Warbler	6/6	USA-New York
2740	Bobolink	6/6	USA-New York
2741	Upland Sandpiper (153)	6/6	USA-New York
2742	Swamp Sparrow	6/6	USA-New York
2743	White-throated Sparrow	6/6	USA-New York
2744	Winter Wren	6/6	USA-New York
2745	Yellow-bellied Sapsucker	6/6	USA-New York
2746	Black-billed Cuckoo	6/6	USA-New York
2747	American Black Duck (153, 155)	6/6	USA-New York
2748	American Woodcock	6/6	USA-New York
2749	Henslow's Sparrow	6/7	USA-New York
2750	Eastern Whip-poor-will	6/7	USA-New York
2751	Northern Wheatear	6/9	Iceland
2752	Arctic Tern (157)	6/9	Iceland
2753	Lesser Black-backed Gull	6/9	Iceland
2754	Iceland Gull (157)	6/9	Iceland
2755	Black-headed Gull	6/9	Iceland
2756	Black-legged Kittiwake	6/9	Iceland
2757	Common Redshank	6/9	Iceland
2758	Common Ringed Plover	6/9	Iceland
2759	Eurasian Oystercatcher	6/9	Iceland
2760	Great Cormorant	6/9	Iceland
2761	Common Eider (157)	6/9	Iceland
2762	Tufted Duck	6/9	Iceland
2763	Graylag Goose	6/9	Iceland
2764	Whooper Swan	6/9	Iceland
2765	Glaucous Gull	6/9	Iceland
2766	Purple Sandpiper	6/9	Iceland
2767	Northern Gannet	6/9	Iceland
2768	Northern Fulmar	6/9	Iceland
2769	Meadow Pipit	6/9	Iceland
2770	Atlantic Puffin (157)	6/9	Iceland
2771	Razorbill	6/9	Iceland
2772	Thick-billed Murre (157)	6/9	Iceland
2773	European Golden-Plover	6/9	Iceland
2774	Redwing	6/9	Iceland
2775	Rock Ptarmigan	6/9	Iceland
2776	Common Snipe	6/9	Iceland
2777	Black-tailed Godwit	6/9	Iceland
2778	Horned Grebe	6/9	Iceland
2779	Long-tailed Duck	6/9	Iceland
2780	Eurasian Wigeon (157)	6/9	Iceland
2781	Common Redpoll	6/9	Iceland
2782	Eurasian Blackbird	6/9	Iceland
2783	European Shag	6/9	Iceland
2784	Common Shelduck	6/9	Iceland
2785	White Wagtail	6/9	Iceland
2786	Manx Shearwater	6/9	Iceland
2787	Fieldfare	6/10	Norway
2788	Hooded Crow	6/10	Norway
2789	Eurasian Jackdaw	6/10	Norway
2790	Eurasian Magpie	6/10	Norway
2791	Eurasian Siskin	6/10	Norway
2792	Common Chaffinch	6/10	Norway
2793	Yellowhammer	6/10	Norway
2794	Garden Warbler	6/10	Norway
2795	Willow Warbler	6/10	Norway
2796	Goldcrest	6/10	Norway
2797	Eurasian Kestrel	6/10	Norway
2798	Common Swift	6/10	Norway
2799	Common Buzzard	6/10	Norway
2800	European Goldfinch	6/10	Norway
2801	European Greenfinch	6/10	Norway
2802	Tree Pipit	6/10	Norway
2803	Dunnock	6/10	Norway
2804	Whinchat	6/10	Norway
2805	Greater Whitethroat	6/10	Norway
2806	Eurasian Blackcap	6/10	Norway
2807	Common Chiffchaff	6/10	Norway
2808	Eurasian Wren	6/10	Norway
2809	Eurasian Blue Tit	6/10	Norway
2810	Great Tit	6/10	Norway
2811	Common House-Martin	6/10	Norway
2812	Common Wood-Pigeon	6/10	Norway
2813	Stock Dove	6/10	Norway
2814	Mew Gull	6/10	Norway
2815	Eurasian Bullfinch	6/10	Norway
2816	Mistle Thrush	6/10	Norway
2817	Song Thrush	6/10	Norway
2818	Spotted Flycatcher	6/10	Norway
2819	Green Sandpiper	6/10	Norway
2820	Eurasian Tree Sparrow	6/10	Norway
2821	Sky Lark	6/10	Norway
2822	Common Crane	6/10	Norway
2823	Reed Bunting	6/10	Norway
2824	Marsh Warbler	6/10	Norway
2825	Great Spotted Woodpecker	6/10	Norway
2826	Eurasian Curlew	6/10	Norway
2827	Northern Lapwing	6/10	Norway
2828	Common Cuckoo	6/10	Norway
2829	Eurasian Woodcock	6/10	Norway
2830	Common Redstart	6/11	Norway
2831	Wood Lark	6/11	Norway
2832	Ortolan Bunting	6/11	Norway
2833	European Robin	6/11	Norway
2834	Lesser Whitethroat	6/11	Norway
2835	Common Goldeneye	6/11	Norway
2836	Icterine Warbler	6/11	Norway
2837	Great Crested Grebe	6/11	Norway
2838	Arctic Loon	6/11	Norway
2839	Mute Swan	6/11	Norway
2840	Red-backed Shrike	6/11	Norway
2841	Crested Tit	6/11	Norway
2842	Eurasian Jay	6/11	Norway
2843	Black Woodpecker	6/11	Norway

2844	European Pied Flycatcher	6/11	Norway
2845	Willow Tit	6/11	Norway
2846	Brambling	6/11	Norway
2847	Bohemian Waxwing	6/11	Norway
2848	Gray Wagtail	6/11	Norway
2849	Western Yellow Wagtail	6/11	Norway
2850	Northern Shrike	6/11	Norway
2851	Common Greenshank	6/11	Norway
2852	Broad-billed Sandpiper	6/11	Norway
2853	Little Ringed Plover	6/11	Norway
2854	Rook	6/11	Norway
2855	Black Grouse	6/12	Norway
2856	Common Rosefinch	6/12	Norway
2857	Wood Sandpiper	6/12	Norway
2858	Common Sandpiper	6/12	Norway
2859	Eurasian Sparrowhawk	6/12	Norway
2860	Ring Ouzel	6/12	Norway
2861	Bluethroat	6/12	Norway
2862	Lapland Longspur	6/12	Norway
2863	Temminck's Stint	6/12	Norway
2864	Siberian Jay	6/12	Norway
2865	White-throated Dipper	6/12	Norway
2866	Gray Heron	6/12	Norway
2867	Hazel Grouse	6/12	Norway
2868	Eurasian Capercaillie	6/12	Norway
2869	Tawny Owl	6/12	Norway
2870	Coal Tit	6/13	Norway
2871	Blyth's Reed-Warbler	6/13	Norway
2872	Eurasian Nuthatch	6/13	Norway
2873	Corn Crake	6/13	Norway
2874	Eurasian Reed-Warbler	6/13	Norway
2875	Lesser Redpoll	6/13	Norway
2876	Thrush Nightingale	6/13	Norway
2877	Eurasian Treecreeper	6/13	Norway
2878	Marsh Tit	6/13	Norway
2879	Eurasian Green Woodpecker	6/13	Norway
2880	Eurasian Coot	6/13	Norway
2881	Northern Goshawk	6/13	Norway
2882	Eurasian Marsh-Harrier	6/13	Norway
2883	Garganey	6/13	Norway
2884	Hawfinch	6/13	Norway
2885	Wood Warbler	6/13	Norway
2886	Eurasian Linnet	6/13	Norway
2887	Eurasian Wryneck	6/13	Norway
2888	Barnacle Goose	6/13	Norway
2889	Blue Rock-Thrush	6/14	Turkey
2890	Rüppell's Warbler	6/14	Turkey
2891	Short-toed Treecreeper	6/14	Turkey
2892	Rock Nuthatch	6/14	Turkey
2893	Krüper's Nuthatch	6/14	Turkey
2894	Red-rumped Swallow	6/14	Turkey
2895	Middle Spotted Woodpecker	6/14	Turkey
2896	Lesser Spotted Woodpecker	6/14	Turkey
2897	Eurasian Hoopoe	6/14	Turkey
2898	Alpine Swift	6/14	Turkey
2899	European Turtle-Dove	6/14	Turkey
2900	Brown Fish-Owl	6/14	Turkey
2901	Black-eared Wheatear	6/14	Turkey
2902	Eastern Orphean Warbler	6/14	Turkey
2903	White-spectacled Bulbul	6/14	Turkey
2904	Masked Shrike	6/14	Turkey
2905	Syrian Woodpecker	6/14	Turkey
2906	Corn Bunting	6/14	Turkey
2907	Black-headed Bunting	6/14	Turkey
2908	Olive-tree Warbler	6/14	Turkey
2909	Sombre Tit	6/14	Turkey
2910	Crested Lark	6/14	Turkey
2911	Cretzschmar's Bunting	6/14	Turkey
2912	Long-tailed Tit	6/14	Turkey
2913	European Serin	6/14	Turkey
2914	Rosy Starling	6/14	Turkey
2915	Isabelline Wheatear	6/14	Turkey
2916	Great Reed-Warbler	6/14	Turkey
2917	Eastern Olivaceous Warbler	6/14	Turkey
2918	Cetti's Warbler	6/14	Turkey
2919	Lesser Short-toed Lark	6/14	Turkey
2920	Long-legged Buzzard	6/14	Turkey
2921	Rock Petronia	6/14	Turkey
2922	Lesser Gray Shrike	6/14	Turkey
2923	Eurasian Hobby	6/14	Turkey
2924	Common Nightingale	6/14	Turkey
2925	Eurasian Penduline-Tit	6/14	Turkey
2926	Eurasian Golden Oriole	6/14	Turkey
2927	Whiskered Tern	6/14	Turkey
2928	Spur-winged Lapwing	6/14	Turkey
2929	Black-winged Stilt	6/14	Turkey
2930	Little Egret (222)	6/14	Turkey
2931	White Stork	6/14	Turkey
2932	Greater Flamingo	6/14	Turkey
2933	Squacco Heron	6/14	Turkey
2934	Purple Heron	6/14	Turkey
2935	Little Bittern	6/14	Turkey
2936	Ferruginous Duck	6/14	Turkey
2937	Red-crested Pochard	6/14	Turkey
2938	Ruddy Shelduck	6/14	Turkey
2939	Fire-fronted Serin	6/14	Turkey
2940	Eurasian Crag-Martin	6/14	Turkey
2941	Red-billed Chough	6/14	Turkey
2942	European Scops-Owl	6/14	Turkey
2943	White-winged Snowfinch	6/14	Turkey
2944	Rock Bunting	6/14	Turkey
2945	White-throated Robin	6/14	Turkey
2946	Finsch's Wheatear	6/15	Turkey
2947	Crimson-winged Finch	6/15	Turkey
2948	Water Pipit	6/15	Turkey
2949	Radde's Accentor	6/15	Turkey
2950	Alpine Accentor	6/15	Turkey
2951	Rufous-tailed Rock-Thrush	6/15	Turkey
2952	Black Redstart	6/15	Turkey
2953	Wallcreeper	6/15	Turkey
2954	Yellow-billed Chough	6/15	Turkey
2955	Caspian Snowcock	6/15	Turkey
2956	European Bee-eater	6/15	Turkey
2957	Booted Eagle	6/15	Turkey
2958	Lesser Spotted Eagle	6/15	Turkey
2959	Short-toed Snake-Eagle	6/15	Turkey
2960	Bonelli's Eagle	6/15	Turkey
2961	Little Owl	6/15	Turkey
2962	Laughing Dove	6/15	Turkey
2963	Graceful Prinia	6/15	Turkey

2964	Pied Kingfisher	6/15	Turkey	3024	Curlew Sandpiper	6/19	Spain
2965	White-throated Kingfisher	6/15	Turkey	3025	Marbled Teal	6/19	Spain
2966	Little Tern	6/15	Turkey	3026	Black Wheatear	6/19	Spain
2967	Eurasian Moorhen (180)	6/15	Turkey	3027	Western Olivaceous Warbler	6/19	Spain
2968	Pygmy Cormorant	6/15	Turkey	3028	Bearded Reedling	6/19	Spain
2969	Calandra Lark	6/15	Turkey	3029	Water Rail	6/19	Spain
2970	Yellow-legged Gull	6/15	Turkey	3030	White-headed Duck	6/19	Spain
2971	Mediterranean Gull	6/15	Turkey	3031	Trumpeter Finch	6/19	Spain
2972	Slender-billed Gull	6/15	Turkey	3032	Western Orphean Warbler	6/19	Spain
2973	Bar-tailed Godwit (112)	6/15	Turkey	3033	Thekla Lark	6/19	Spain
2974	Kentish Plover	6/15	Turkey	3034	Carrion Crow	6/20	Spain
2975	Pied Avocet	6/15	Turkey	3035	Great Bustard	6/20	Spain
2976	Eurasian Thick-knee	6/15	Turkey	3036	Black Kite	6/20	Spain
2977	Eurasian Spoonbill	6/15	Turkey	3037	Red Kite	6/20	Spain
2978	Great White Pelican	6/15	Turkey	3038	Iberian Magpie	6/20	Spain
2979	Lesser Kestrel	6/16	Turkey	3039	Eurasian Nightjar	6/20	Spain
2980	Dead Sea Sparrow	6/16	Turkey	3040	Cinereous Vulture	6/20	Spain
2981	Iraq Babbler	6/16	Turkey	3041	Red-legged Partridge	6/20	Spain
2982	Menetries's Warbler	6/16	Turkey	3042	White-rumped Swift	6/20	Spain
2983	European Roller	6/16	Turkey	3043	Red-necked Nightjar	6/20	Spain
2984	Black Francolin	6/16	Turkey	3044	European Stonechat	6/21	Spain
2985	Chestnut-shouldered Petronia	6/16	Turkey	3045	Cirl Bunting	6/21	Spain
2986	Little Swift	6/16	Turkey	3046	Dartford Warbler	6/21	Spain
2987	Pallid Swift	6/16	Turkey	3047	Iberian Chiffchaff	6/21	Spain
2988	Pallid Scops-Owl	6/16	Turkey	3048	Spanish Eagle	6/21	Spain
2989	Rufous-tailed Scrub-Robin	6/16	Turkey	3049	Egyptian Vulture	6/21	Spain
2990	Little Grebe	6/16	Turkey	3050	Melodious Warbler	6/21	Spain
2991	Spanish Sparrow	6/16	Turkey	3051	Little Bustard	6/21	Spain
2992	Desert Finch	6/16	Turkey	3052	Dupont's Lark	6/22	Spain
2993	Black-bellied Sandgrouse	6/16	Turkey	3053	Pin-tailed Sandgrouse	6/22	Spain
2994	Upcher's Warbler	6/16	Turkey	3054	Southern Gray Shrike	6/22	Spain
2995	Persian Nuthatch	6/16	Turkey	3055	Subalpine Warbler	6/22	Spain
2996	Eurasian Eagle-Owl	6/16	Turkey	3056	Western Bonelli's Warbler	6/22	Spain
2997	See-see Partridge	6/16	Turkey	3057	Firecrest	6/22	Spain
2998	Pale Rockfinch	6/17	Turkey	3058	Lammergeier	6/22	Spain
2999	Cinereous Bunting	6/17	Turkey	3059	Citril Finch	6/22	France
3000	Tawny Pipit (159)	6/17	Turkey	3060	White-backed Woodpecker	6/23	Spain
3001	Red-tailed Wheatear	6/17	Turkey	3061	Smew	6/23	Spain
3002	Woodchat Shrike	6/17	Turkey	3062	European Honey-buzzard	6/23	Spain
3003	Armenian Gull	6/17	Turkey	3063	Common Grasshopper-Warbler	6/23	Spain
3004	Eurasian Griffon	6/17	Turkey	3064	Egyptian Goose (161)	6/24	Germany
3005	Black Stork	6/17	Turkey	3065	Bronze Mannikin (167)	6/25	Ghana
3006	Spectacled Warbler	6/17	Turkey	3066	Copper Sunbird	6/25	Ghana
3007	Greater Short-toed Lark	6/17	Turkey	3067	African Thrush	6/25	Ghana
3008	Bimaculated Lark	6/17	Turkey	3068	Pied Crow (167)	6/25	Ghana
3009	Montagu's Harrier	6/17	Turkey	3069	Hooded Vulture	6/25	Ghana
3010	Black-shouldered Kite	6/17	Turkey	3070	Pin-tailed Whydah	6/25	Ghana
3011	Common Quail	6/17	Turkey	3071	Bar-breasted Firefinch	6/25	Ghana
3012	Blue-cheeked Bee-eater	6/17	Turkey	3072	Black-rumped Waxbill	6/25	Ghana
3013	Spotless Starling	6/18	Spain	3073	Orange-cheeked Waxbill	6/25	Ghana
3014	Zitting Cisticola (180)	6/18	Spain	3074	Yellow-shouldered Widowbird	6/25	Ghana
3015	Audouin's Gull	6/18	Spain	3075	Black-winged Bishop	6/25	Ghana
3016	Western Swamphen	6/18	Spain	3076	Northern Red Bishop	6/25	Ghana
3017	Cory's Shearwater	6/18	Spain	3077	Village Weaver	6/25	Ghana
3018	Common Pochard	6/18	Spain	3078	Northern Gray-headed Sparrow	6/25	Ghana
3019	Sardinian Warbler	6/18	Spain	3079	Splendid Starling	6/25	Ghana
3020	Savi's Warbler	6/19	Spain	3080	Snowy-crowned Robin-Chat	6/25	Ghana
3021	Moustached Warbler	6/19	Spain	3081	Tawny-flanked Prinia	6/25	Ghana
3022	Common Kingfisher (241)	6/19	Spain	3082	Siffling Cisticola (180)	6/25	Ghana
3023	Collared Pratincole	6/19	Spain	3083	Croaking Cisticola (180)	6/25	Ghana

3084	Singing Cisticola (180)	6/25	Ghana
3085	Red-faced Cisticola	6/25	Ghana
3086	Green-backed Camaroptera	6/25	Ghana
3087	Moustached Grass-Warbler	6/25	Ghana
3088	Common Bulbul	6/25	Ghana
3089	Yellow-crowned Gonolek	6/25	Ghana
3090	Black-crowned Tchagra	6/25	Ghana
3091	Double-toothed Barbet	6/25	Ghana
3092	African Gray Hornbill	6/25	Ghana
3093	Senegal Coucal	6/25	Ghana
3094	Pied Cuckoo	6/25	Ghana
3095	Western Plantain-eater	6/25	Ghana
3096	Guinea Turaco (167)	6/25	Ghana
3097	Blue-spotted Wood-Dove	6/25	Ghana
3098	Black-billed Wood-Dove	6/25	Ghana
3099	Red-eyed Dove	6/25	Ghana
3100	African Jacana	6/25	Ghana
3101	Black-bellied Bustard (167)	6/25	Ghana
3102	Shikra	6/25	Ghana
3103	Yellow-crowned Bishop	6/25	Ghana
3104	Black-necked Weaver	6/25	Ghana
3105	Green-headed Sunbird	6/25	Ghana
3106	Malachite Kingfisher	6/25	Ghana
3107	Allen's Gallinule	6/25	Ghana
3108	African Swamphen	6/25	Ghana
3109	Black Crake	6/25	Ghana
3110	African Harrier-Hawk	6/25	Ghana
3111	Western Reef-Heron	6/25	Ghana
3112	Intermediate Egret	6/25	Ghana
3113	Long-tailed Cormorant	6/25	Ghana
3114	Vieillot's Weaver	6/25	Ghana
3115	Western Olive Sunbird	6/25	Ghana
3116	Fanti Sawwing	6/25	Ghana
3117	Black-and-white Shrike-flycatcher	6/25	Ghana
3118	Yellow-rumped Tinkerbird	6/25	Ghana
3119	African Pied Hornbill	6/25	Ghana
3120	African Pygmy-Kingfisher	6/25	Ghana
3121	African Palm-Swift (179)	6/25	Ghana
3122	African Pygmy-Goose	6/25	Ghana
3123	White-breasted Nigrita	6/26	Ghana
3124	Chestnut-breasted Nigrita	6/26	Ghana
3125	Gray-headed Nigrita	6/26	Ghana
3126	Maxwell's Black Weaver	6/26	Ghana
3127	Yellow-mantled Weaver	6/26	Ghana
3128	Red-headed Malimbe	6/26	Ghana
3129	Buff-throated Sunbird	6/26	Ghana
3130	Blue-throated Brown Sunbird	6/26	Ghana
3131	Collared Sunbird	6/26	Ghana
3132	Green Sunbird	6/26	Ghana
3133	Fraser's Sunbird	6/26	Ghana
3134	Chestnut-winged Starling	6/26	Ghana
3135	Finsch's Flycatcher-Thrush	6/26	Ghana
3136	African Forest-Flycatcher	6/26	Ghana
3137	Violet-backed Hyliota	6/26	Ghana
3138	Rufous-crowned Eremomela	6/26	Ghana
3139	Yellow-browed Camaroptera	6/26	Ghana
3140	Sharpe's Apalis	6/26	Ghana
3141	Chestnut-capped Flycatcher	6/26	Ghana
3142	Tit-hylia (173)	6/26	Ghana
3143	Green Hylia	6/26	Ghana
3144	Gray Longbill	6/26	Ghana
3145	Little Greenbul	6/26	Ghana
3146	Yellow-whiskered Greenbul	6/26	Ghana
3147	Gray Greenbul	6/26	Ghana
3148	Western Bearded-Greenbul	6/26	Ghana
3149	Spotted Greenbul	6/26	Ghana
3150	Honeyguide Greenbul	6/26	Ghana
3151	Slender-billed Greenbul	6/26	Ghana
3152	Black-headed Paradise-Flycatcher	6/26	Ghana
3153	Velvet-mantled Drongo	6/26	Ghana
3154	Fire-bellied Woodpecker	6/26	Ghana
3155	Melancholy Woodpecker (174)	6/26	Ghana
3156	Hairy-breasted Barbet	6/26	Ghana
3157	Yellow-throated Tinkerbird (173)	6/26	Ghana
3158	Red-rumped Tinkerbird	6/26	Ghana
3159	Speckled Tinkerbird	6/26	Ghana
3160	Naked-faced Barbet	6/26	Ghana
3161	Black-casqued Hornbill (173)	6/26	Ghana
3162	Blue-throated Roller	6/26	Ghana
3163	Sabine's Spinetail	6/26	Ghana
3164	Yellowbill	6/26	Ghana
3165	Klaas's Cuckoo (173)	6/26	Ghana
3166	Yellow-billed Turaco	6/26	Ghana
3167	African Green-Pigeon	6/26	Ghana
3168	Tambourine Dove (173)	6/26	Ghana
3169	Palm-nut Vulture	6/26	Ghana
3170	Orange Weaver	6/26	Ghana
3171	Red-chested Goshawk	6/26	Ghana
3172	Woodland Kingfisher	6/26	Ghana
3173	Wilson's Indigobird	6/26	Ghana
3174	Western Bluebill	6/26	Ghana
3175	Red-headed Quelea	6/26	Ghana
3176	Splendid Sunbird	6/26	Ghana
3177	Olive-bellied Sunbird	6/26	Ghana
3178	Red-winged Prinia	6/26	Ghana
3179	Oriole Warbler (179)	6/26	Ghana
3180	Simple Greenbul	6/26	Ghana
3181	Gray-headed Bristlebill	6/26	Ghana
3182	Mosque Swallow	6/26	Ghana
3183	Ethiopian Swallow	6/26	Ghana
3184	Northern Fiscal	6/26	Ghana
3185	Sulphur-breasted Bushshrike (191)	6/26	Ghana
3186	Tropical Boubou	6/26	Ghana
3187	Brown-crowned Tchagra	6/26	Ghana
3188	Marsh Tchagra	6/26	Ghana
3189	Brown-throated Wattle-eye	6/26	Ghana
3190	Buff-spotted Woodpecker	6/26	Ghana
3191	Piping Hornbill	6/26	Ghana
3192	Little Bee-eater	6/26	Ghana
3193	Long-tailed Nightjar	6/26	Ghana
3194	Great Spotted Cuckoo	6/26	Ghana
3195	Wattled Lapwing	6/26	Ghana
3196	Senegal Thick-knee	6/26	Ghana
3197	Double-spurred Francolin	6/26	Ghana
3198	Black-and-white Mannikin	6/27	Ghana
3199	Blue-billed Malimbe	6/27	Ghana
3200	African Pied Wagtail	6/27	Ghana
3201	Forest Robin	6/27	Ghana
3202	Fire-crested Alethe	6/27	Ghana
3203	Dusky-blue Flycatcher	6/27	Ghana

3204	Puvel's Illadopsis	6/27	Ghana
3205	Whistling Cisticola (180)	6/27	Ghana
3206	Olive-green Camaroptera	6/27	Ghana
3207	Icterine Greenbul	6/27	Ghana
3208	Swamp Greenbul	6/27	Ghana
3209	Lesser Striped-Swallow	6/27	Ghana
3210	Western Nicator	6/27	Ghana
3211	Lowland Sooty Boubou	6/27	Ghana
3212	Red-cheeked Wattle-eye	6/27	Ghana
3213	Gray Kestrel	6/27	Ghana
3214	White-spotted Flufftail	6/27	Ghana
3215	Black-bellied Seedcracker	6/27	Ghana
3216	Narrow-tailed Starling	6/27	Ghana
3217	Copper-tailed Starling (185)	6/27	Ghana
3218	Blackcap Illadopsis	6/27	Ghana
3219	Green Crombec	6/27	Ghana
3220	Plain Greenbul	6/27	Ghana
3221	Red-billed Dwarf Hornbill	6/27	Ghana
3222	Forest Woodhoopoe	6/27	Ghana
3223	Dideric Cuckoo	6/27	Ghana
3224	Preuss's Swallow	6/27	Ghana
3225	White-throated Blue Swallow	6/27	Ghana
3226	Rock Pratincole	6/27	Ghana
3227	White-necked Rockfowl	6/27	Ghana
3228	Western Black-headed Oriole	6/27	Ghana
3229	Rufous-sided Broadbill	6/27	Ghana
3230	Red-fronted Parrot	6/27	Ghana
3231	Rock Martin	6/28	Ghana
3232	Kemp's Longbill	6/28	Ghana
3233	Red-tailed Greenbul	6/28	Ghana
3234	Blue-headed Crested-Flycatcher	6/28	Ghana
3235	Black-winged Oriole	6/28	Ghana
3236	Fiery-breasted Bushshrike	6/28	Ghana
3237	Sabine's Puffback	6/28	Ghana
3238	Northern Puffback	6/28	Ghana
3239	White-crested Hornbill	6/28	Ghana
3240	Cassin's Spinetail	6/28	Ghana
3241	Blue-headed Wood-Dove	6/28	Ghana
3242	Bronze-naped Pigeon	6/28	Ghana
3243	African Cuckoo-Hawk	6/28	Ghana
3244	Blue-bellied Roller	6/28	Ghana
3245	Lizard Buzzard	6/28	Ghana
3246	Dark Chanting-Goshawk	6/28	Ghana
3247	Wire-tailed Swallow	6/28	Ghana
3248	Fork-tailed Drongo	6/28	Ghana
3249	Bearded Barbet	6/28	Ghana
3250	Vinaceous Dove	6/28	Ghana
3251	Grasshopper Buzzard	6/28	Ghana
3252	Gabar Goshawk	6/28	Ghana
3253	Purple Starling	6/28	Ghana
3254	Rufous-crowned Roller	6/28	Ghana
3255	Speckled Pigeon	6/28	Ghana
3256	Zebra Waxbill	6/28	Ghana
3257	Red-chested Swallow	6/28	Ghana
3258	Piapiac	6/28	Ghana
3259	Egyptian Plover	6/28	Ghana
3260	Red-necked Buzzard	6/28	Ghana
3261	Bateleur	6/28	Ghana
3262	Black-headed Heron	6/28	Ghana
3263	Senegal Parrot	6/28	Ghana
3264	Green Woodhoopoe	6/28	Ghana
3265	Abyssinian Roller	6/28	Ghana
3266	Brown Babbler	6/28	Ghana
3267	Standard-winged Nightjar	6/28	Ghana
3268	White-throated Francolin	6/28	Ghana
3269	Red-cheeked Cordonbleu (180)	6/29	Ghana
3270	Little Weaver	6/29	Ghana
3271	Chestnut-crowned Sparrow-Weaver	6/29	Ghana
3272	Yellow-fronted Canary	6/29	Ghana
3273	Violet-backed Starling	6/29	Ghana
3274	White-crowned Robin-Chat	6/29	Ghana
3275	Northern Black-Flycatcher	6/29	Ghana
3276	African Yellow White-eye	6/29	Ghana
3277	Senegal Eremomela	6/29	Ghana
3278	White-shouldered Black-Tit	6/29	Ghana
3279	Red-shouldered Cuckooshrike	6/29	Ghana
3280	Senegal Batis	6/29	Ghana
3281	Red-chested Cuckoo	6/29	Ghana
3282	Bruce's Green-Pigeon	6/29	Ghana
3283	Saddle-billed Stork	6/29	Ghana
3284	Stone Partridge	6/29	Ghana
3285	Red-billed Firefinch	6/29	Ghana
3286	Lavender Waxbill	6/29	Ghana
3287	Beautiful Sunbird	6/29	Ghana
3288	Scarlet-chested Sunbird	6/29	Ghana
3289	Long-tailed Glossy Starling	6/29	Ghana
3290	Bronze-tailed Starling (185)	6/29	Ghana
3291	Swamp Flycatcher	6/29	Ghana
3292	Blackcap Babbler	6/29	Ghana
3293	Yellow-breasted Apalis	6/29	Ghana
3294	African Blue-Flycatcher	6/29	Ghana
3295	African Paradise-Flycatcher	6/29	Ghana
3296	Rose-ringed Parakeet (179)	6/29	Ghana
3297	Black Scimitarbill	6/29	Ghana
3298	Broad-billed Roller	6/29	Ghana
3299	Red-throated Bee-eater	6/29	Ghana
3300	Blue-breasted Kingfisher	6/29	Ghana
3301	Gray-headed Kingfisher	6/29	Ghana
3302	Lesser Moorhen (179–180)	6/29	Ghana
3303	White-backed Vulture (190)	6/29	Ghana
3304	Hadada Ibis	6/29	Ghana
3305	Hamerkop	6/29	Ghana
3306	Woolly-necked Stork	6/29	Ghana
3307	Helmeted Guineafowl	6/29	Ghana
3308	Western Violet-backed Sunbird	6/29	Ghana
3309	Gray Tit-Flycatcher	6/29	Ghana
3310	Brubru	6/29	Ghana
3311	African Gray Woodpecker	6/29	Ghana
3312	African Scops-Owl	6/29	Ghana
3313	Bush Petronia	6/29	Ghana
3314	Rufous Cisticola	6/29	Ghana
3315	Yellow-billed Shrike	6/29	Ghana
3316	Gray-headed Bushshrike	6/29	Ghana
3317	Fine-spotted Woodpecker	6/29	Ghana
3318	Brown-rumped Bunting	6/29	Ghana
3319	Sun Lark	6/29	Ghana
3320	Flappet Lark	6/29	Ghana
3321	Vieillot's Barbet	6/29	Ghana
3322	Yellow-fronted Tinkerbird	6/29	Ghana
3323	Forbes's Plover	6/29	Ghana

3324	Gambaga Flycatcher	6/29	Ghana
3325	Grayish Eagle-Owl	6/29	Ghana
3326	Familiar Chat	6/30	Ghana
3327	Violet Turaco	6/30	Ghana
3328	Pearl-spotted Owlet	6/30	Ghana
3329	Red-headed Lovebird	6/30	Ghana
3330	Square-tailed Drongo	6/30	Ghana
3331	Cabanis's Bunting	6/30	Ghana
3332	Pale Flycatcher	6/30	Ghana
3333	Winding Cisticola (180)	6/30	Ghana
3334	Black-backed Cisticola	6/30	Ghana
3335	Magpie Mannikin	7/1	Ghana
3336	Tiny Sunbird	7/1	Ghana
3337	Gray-throated Tit-Flycatcher	7/1	Ghana
3338	Little Flycatcher	7/1	Ghana
3339	Ussher's Flycatcher	7/1	Ghana
3340	Black-capped Apalis	7/1	Ghana
3341	Lemon-bellied Crombec	7/1	Ghana
3342	Red-tailed Bristlebill	7/1	Ghana
3343	Square-tailed Sawwing	7/1	Ghana
3344	Shining Drongo	7/1	Ghana
3345	Red-billed Helmetshrike	7/1	Ghana
3346	West African Wattle-eye	7/1	Ghana
3347	Yellow-spotted Barbet	7/1	Ghana
3348	Brown-cheeked Hornbill	7/1	Ghana
3349	Chocolate-backed Kingfisher	7/1	Ghana
3350	Fraser's Eagle-Owl	7/1	Ghana
3351	Black-throated Coucal	7/1	Ghana
3352	African Emerald Cuckoo	7/1	Ghana
3353	Ayres's Hawk-Eagle	7/1	Ghana
3354	Yellow-throated Longclaw	7/2	Ghana
3355	Plain-backed Pipit	7/2	Ghana
3356	Northern Crombec	7/2	Ghana
3357	Yellow-throated Greenbul	7/2	Ghana
3358	White-throated Bee-eater	7/2	Ghana
3359	Black Heron	7/2	Ghana
3360	Gray Parrot	7/3	Cameroon
3361	African Darter	7/3	Cameroon
3362	Yellow-billed Duck	7/3	Cameroon
3363	Hartlaub's Duck	7/3	Cameroon
3364	Gray-necked Rockfowl (187)	7/3	Cameroon
3365	Great Blue Turaco	7/3	Cameroon
3366	Crested Malimbe	7/4	Cameroon
3367	Black-throated Malimbe	7/4	Cameroon
3368	Sooty Flycatcher	7/4	Cameroon
3369	Eastern Bearded-Greenbul	7/4	Cameroon
3370	Yellow-billed Barbet	7/4	Cameroon
3371	Black-and-white-casqued Hornbill	7/4	Cameroon
3372	Mottled Spinetail	7/4	Cameroon
3373	Black-crowned Waxbill	7/5	Cameroon
3374	Black-billed Weaver	7/5	Cameroon
3375	Northern Double-collared Sunbird	7/5	Cameroon
3376	Mountain Robin-Chat	7/5	Cameroon
3377	Dusky-brown Flycatcher	7/5	Cameroon
3378	African Hill Babbler	7/5	Cameroon
3379	Banded Prinia	7/5	Cameroon
3380	Chubb's Cisticola	7/5	Cameroon
3381	Chattering Cisticola (180)	7/5	Cameroon
3382	Green Longtail	7/5	Cameroon
3383	White-chinned Prinia	7/5	Cameroon
3384	Gray Apalis	7/5	Cameroon
3385	Evergreen-forest Warbler	7/5	Cameroon
3386	Greater Swamp-Warbler	7/5	Cameroon
3387	Western Mountain-Greenbul	7/5	Cameroon
3388	Mountain Sawwing	7/5	Cameroon
3389	Mackinnon's Shrike	7/5	Cameroon
3390	Yellow-breasted Boubou	7/5	Cameroon
3391	Green-backed Woodpecker	7/5	Cameroon
3392	Western Tinkerbird	7/5	Cameroon
3393	Speckled Mousebird	7/5	Cameroon
3394	Buff-spotted Flufftail	7/5	Cameroon
3395	Red-faced Crimson-wing	7/5	Cameroon
3396	Shelley's Oliveback	7/5	Cameroon
3397	Yellow Bishop	7/5	Cameroon
3398	Brown-capped Weaver	7/5	Cameroon
3399	Forest Weaver	7/5	Cameroon
3400	Oriole Finch	7/5	Cameroon
3401	Cameroon Sunbird	7/5	Cameroon
3402	Waller's Starling	7/5	Cameroon
3403	White-bellied Crested-Flycatcher	7/5	Cameroon
3404	Mountain Sooty Boubou	7/5	Cameroon
3405	Thick-billed Seedeater	7/5	Cameroon
3406	African Stonechat	7/5	Cameroon
3407	Cameroon Speirops	7/5	Cameroon
3408	Cameroon Mountain Greenbul	7/5	Cameroon
3409	Cameroon Francolin	7/5	Cameroon
3410	Pale-fronted Nigrita	7/6	Cameroon
3411	Orange-tufted Sunbird	7/6	Cameroon
3412	Cardinal Woodpecker	7/6	Cameroon
3413	Scaly Francolin	7/6	Cameroon
3414	African Firefinch	7/7	Cameroon
3415	Dybowski's Twinspot	7/7	Cameroon
3416	Gray-headed Oliveback	7/7	Cameroon
3417	Baglafecht Weaver	7/7	Cameroon
3418	Streaky-headed Seedeater	7/7	Cameroon
3419	Variable Sunbird	7/7	Cameroon
3420	Superb Sunbird	7/7	Cameroon
3421	Bamenda Apalis	7/7	Cameroon
3422	Black Sawwing	7/7	Cameroon
3423	Rufous-vented Paradise-Flycatcher	7/7	Cameroon
3424	Gray-green Bushshrike	7/7	Cameroon
3425	Luehder's Bushshrike	7/7	Cameroon
3426	Red-eyed Puffback	7/7	Cameroon
3427	Black Goshawk	7/7	Cameroon
3428	Mountain Wagtail	7/7	Cameroon
3429	Pectoral-patch Cisticola	7/7	Cameroon
3430	Black-collared Apalis	7/7	Cameroon
3431	Bangwa Warbler	7/7	Cameroon
3432	Bannerman's Turaco	7/7	Cameroon
3433	Bannerman's Weaver	7/8	Cameroon
3434	Marsh Widowbird	7/8	Cameroon
3435	Black-faced Rufous-Warbler	7/9	Cameroon
3436	Bates's Paradise-Flycatcher	7/9	Cameroon
3437	Bates's Swift	7/9	Cameroon
3438	Blue-headed Coucal	7/9	Cameroon
3439	Black Coucal	7/9	Cameroon
3440	Preuss's Weaver	7/9	Cameroon
3441	Crossley's Ground-Thrush	7/9	Cameroon
3442	Rufous Flycatcher-Thrush	7/9	Cameroon
3443	White-bellied Robin-Chat	7/9	Cameroon

3444	Yellow-footed Flycatcher	7/9	Cameroon
3445	Many-colored Bushshrike	7/9	Cameroon
3446	Black-necked Wattle-eye	7/9	Cameroon
3447	Gabon Woodpecker	7/9	Cameroon
3448	Brown-chested Alethe	7/9	Cameroon
3449	White-tailed Warbler	7/9	Cameroon
3450	Gray-headed Greenbul	7/9	Cameroon
3451	Mt. Kupe Bushshrike	7/9	Cameroon
3452	Elliot's Woodpecker	7/10	Cameroon
3453	Long-crested Eagle	7/10	Cameroon
3454	Reichenbach's Sunbird	7/11	Cameroon
3455	Cassin's Flycatcher	7/11	Cameroon
3456	Giant Kingfisher	7/11	Cameroon
3457	Red-headed Finch	7/12	South Africa
3458	Southern Masked-Weaver	7/12	South Africa
3459	Cape Sparrow	7/12	South Africa
3460	Karoo Thrush	7/12	South Africa
3461	Sacred Ibis	7/12	South Africa
3462	Southern Red Bishop	7/12	South Africa
3463	Cape Wagtail	7/12	South Africa
3464	Common Myna	7/12	South Africa
3465	Levaillant's Cisticola	7/12	South Africa
3466	Crowned Lapwing	7/12	South Africa
3467	Blacksmith Lapwing	7/12	South Africa
3468	Red-knobbed Coot	7/12	South Africa
3469	Southern Pochard	7/12	South Africa
3470	Long-tailed Widowbird	7/12	South Africa
3471	Capped Wheatear	7/12	South Africa
3472	African Marsh-Harrier	7/12	South Africa
3473	Orange-throated Longclaw	7/12	South Africa
3474	Secretary-bird	7/12	South Africa
3475	Jackal Buzzard	7/12	South Africa
3476	Cape Canary	7/12	South Africa
3477	Long-billed Pipit	7/12	South Africa
3478	African Pied Starling	7/12	South Africa
3479	Southern Fiscal	7/12	South Africa
3480	Bokmakierie	7/12	South Africa
3481	Spur-winged Goose	7/12	South Africa
3482	Buffy Pipit	7/12	South Africa
3483	Mountain Wheatear	7/12	South Africa
3484	Buff-streaked Bushchat	7/12	South Africa
3485	Sentinel Rock-Thrush	7/12	South Africa
3486	Eastern Long-billed Lark	7/12	South Africa
3487	Cape Crow	7/12	South Africa
3488	Rock Kestrel	7/12	South Africa
3489	Gurney's Sugarbird	7/12	South Africa
3490	Cape White-eye	7/12	South Africa
3491	Chinspot Batis (191)	7/12	South Africa
3492	White-fronted Bee-eater	7/12	South Africa
3493	Red-winged Starling	7/12	South Africa
3494	Sombre Greenbul	7/12	South Africa
3495	Verreaux's Eagle	7/12	South Africa
3496	Cape Griffon	7/12	South Africa
3497	Southern Yellow-billed Hornbill	7/12	South Africa
3498	Southern Black-Flycatcher	7/12	South Africa
3499	Gray-rumped Swallow	7/12	South Africa
3500	Gray Go-away-bird (191–192)	7/12	South Africa
3501	Lilac-breasted Roller	7/12	South Africa
3502	Magpie Shrike	7/12	South Africa
3503	Red-billed Oxpecker	7/13	South Africa
3504	African Black Duck	7/13	South Africa
3505	Burchell's Starling	7/13	South Africa
3506	Cape Crombec (191)	7/13	South Africa
3507	Southern Red-billed Hornbill	7/13	South Africa
3508	Ring-necked Dove	7/13	South Africa
3509	Swainson's Francolin	7/13	South Africa
3510	Natal Francolin	7/13	South Africa
3511	Crested Francolin	7/13	South Africa
3512	Red-billed Buffalo-Weaver	7/13	South Africa
3513	African Pipit	7/13	South Africa
3514	Sabota Lark	7/13	South Africa
3515	Bearded Woodpecker	7/13	South Africa
3516	Double-banded Sandgrouse	7/13	South Africa
3517	Tawny Eagle	7/13	South Africa
3518	Green-winged Pytilia (190–191)	7/13	South Africa
3519	Yellow-throated Petronia	7/13	South Africa
3520	Golden-breasted Bunting	7/13	South Africa
3521	White-breasted Sunbird	7/13	South Africa
3522	Cape Starling	7/13	South Africa
3523	Arrow-marked Babbler	7/13	South Africa
3524	Miombo Wren-Warbler (191)	7/13	South Africa
3525	African Black-headed Oriole	7/13	South Africa
3526	Black-backed Puffback	7/13	South Africa
3527	Southern Ground-Hornbill (190)	7/13	South Africa
3528	Common Scimitarbill	7/13	South Africa
3529	Mourning Collared-Dove	7/13	South Africa
3530	Three-banded Plover	7/13	South Africa
3531	African Fish-Eagle	7/13	South Africa
3532	Southern Gray-headed Sparrow	7/13	South Africa
3533	Mariqua Sunbird	7/13	South Africa
3534	Greater Blue-eared Starling	7/13	South Africa
3535	Groundscraper Thrush	7/13	South Africa
3536	Southern Black-Tit	7/13	South Africa
3537	White-crowned Shrike	7/13	South Africa
3538	Brown-headed Parrot	7/13	South Africa
3539	Golden-tailed Woodpecker	7/13	South Africa
3540	Crested Barbet	7/13	South Africa
3541	Southern Cordonbleu	7/13	South Africa
3542	White-winged Widowbird	7/13	South Africa
3543	Yellow-billed Oxpecker	7/13	South Africa
3544	Chestnut-backed Sparrow-Lark	7/13	South Africa
3545	Lanner Falcon	7/13	South Africa
3546	Namaqua Dove	7/13	South Africa
3547	Brown Snake-Eagle	7/13	South Africa
3548	African Swift	7/13	South Africa
3549	Kori Bustard (190)	7/13	South Africa
3550	Martial Eagle	7/13	South Africa
3551	Plain Martin	7/13	South Africa
3552	White-fronted Plover	7/13	South Africa
3553	Goliath Heron	7/13	South Africa
3554	Red-crested Bustard	7/13	South Africa
3555	White-headed Vulture	7/13	South Africa
3556	White-browed Coucal	7/13	South Africa
3557	Bronze-winged Courser	7/13	South Africa
3558	White-throated Robin-Chat	7/13	South Africa
3559	Yellow-bellied Greenbul	7/13	South Africa
3560	Yellow-bellied Eremomela	7/14	South Africa
3561	Jameson's Firefinch	7/14	South Africa
3562	Kurrichane Thrush	7/14	South Africa
3563	Rattling Cisticola (180)	7/14	South Africa

3564	White Helmetshrike	7/14	South Africa	3624	White-bellied Bustard	7/18	South Africa
3565	Bennett's Woodpecker	7/14	South Africa	3625	Red-winged Francolin	7/18	South Africa
3566	Emerald-spotted Wood-Dove	7/14	South Africa	3626	Crowned Hornbill	7/18	South Africa
3567	Red-backed Scrub-Robin	7/14	South Africa	3627	Fiscal Flycatcher	7/18	South Africa
3568	Lappet-faced Vulture	7/14	South Africa	3628	Bearded Scrub-Robin	7/18	South Africa
3569	Spectacled Weaver	7/14	South Africa	3629	Pink-throated Twinspot	7/19	South Africa
3570	White-browed Robin-Chat	7/14	South Africa	3630	Purple-banded Sunbird	7/19	South Africa
3571	Terrestrial Brownbul	7/14	South Africa	3631	Rudd's Apalis	7/19	South Africa
3572	Black-collared Barbet	7/14	South Africa	3632	African Penduline-Tit	7/19	South Africa
3573	Brown-hooded Kingfisher	7/14	South Africa	3633	Four-colored Bushshrike	7/19	South Africa
3574	Red-capped Robin-Chat	7/14	South Africa	3634	Purple-crested Turaco	7/19	South Africa
3575	Ashy Flycatcher	7/14	South Africa	3635	Pied Barbet	7/19	South Africa
3576	African Goshawk	7/14	South Africa	3636	Burnt-neck Eremomela	7/19	South Africa
3577	Southern Boubou	7/15	South Africa	3637	Neergaard's Sunbird	7/19	South Africa
3578	Violet-eared Waxbill	7/15	South Africa	3638	Trumpeter Hornbill	7/19	South Africa
3579	Little Sparrowhawk	7/15	South Africa	3639	Pink-backed Pelican	7/19	South Africa
3580	Greater Kestrel	7/15	South Africa	3640	African Openbill	7/19	South Africa
3581	Senegal Lapwing	7/15	South Africa	3641	Crowned Eagle	7/19	South Africa
3582	White-headed Lapwing	7/15	South Africa	3642	African Yellow-Warbler	7/19	South Africa
3583	African Spoonbill	7/15	South Africa	3643	African Crested-Flycatcher	7/20	South Africa
3584	Yellow-billed Stork	7/15	South Africa	3644	Wattled Starling	7/20	South Africa
3585	Marabou Stork	7/15	South Africa	3645	Fasciated Snake-Eagle	7/20	South Africa
3586	Mocking Cliff-Chat	7/15	South Africa	3646	Mouse-colored Sunbird	7/20	South Africa
3587	Fiery-necked Nightjar	7/15	South Africa	3647	Red-fronted Tinkerbird	7/20	South Africa
3588	Water Thick-knee	7/16	South Africa	3648	Grosbeak Weaver	7/20	South Africa
3589	Crested Guineafowl	7/16	South Africa	3649	Lesser Masked-Weaver	7/20	South Africa
3590	Striped Kingfisher	7/16	South Africa	3650	Brimstone Canary	7/20	South Africa
3591	Rock-loving Cisticola (180)	7/16	South Africa	3651	Black-bellied Starling	7/20	South Africa
3592	Holub's Golden-Weaver	7/16	South Africa	3652	Banded Martin	7/20	South Africa
3593	Greater Double-collared Sunbird	7/16	South Africa	3653	Eastern Nicator	7/20	South Africa
3594	Red-faced Mousebird	7/16	South Africa	3654	White-eared Barbet	7/20	South Africa
3595	African Snipe	7/16	South Africa	3655	Southern Brown-throated Weaver	7/20	South Africa
3596	Kittlitz's Plover	7/16	South Africa	3656	Woodward's Batis	7/20	South Africa
3597	Cape Teal	7/16	South Africa	3657	Livingstone's Turaco	7/20	South Africa
3598	Hottentot Teal	7/16	South Africa	3658	African Wood-Owl	7/20	South Africa
3599	Red-billed Duck	7/16	South Africa	3659	Green-backed Twinspot	7/21	South Africa
3600	Cape Shoveler	7/16	South Africa	3660	Eastern Olive Sunbird	7/21	South Africa
3601	Southern Anteater-Chat	7/16	South Africa	3661	Spotted Ground-Thrush	7/21	South Africa
3602	Red-capped Lark	7/17	South Africa	3662	Chorister Robin-Chat	7/21	South Africa
3603	Ground Woodpecker	7/17	South Africa	3663	Bar-throated Apalis	7/21	South Africa
3604	Blue Bustard	7/17	South Africa	3664	Gray Cuckooshrike	7/21	South Africa
3605	Fan-tailed Widowbird	7/17	South Africa	3665	Scaly-throated Honeyguide	7/21	South Africa
3606	Wing-snapping Cisticola (180)	7/17	South Africa	3666	Lemon Dove	7/21	South Africa
3607	Lesser Swamp-Warbler	7/17	South Africa	3667	Delegorgue's Pigeon	7/21	South Africa
3608	African Rail	7/17	South Africa	3668	Rameron Pigeon	7/21	South Africa
3609	Gray-winged Francolin	7/17	South Africa	3669	African Golden-Weaver	7/21	South Africa
3610	Spike-heeled Lark	7/17	South Africa	3670	Black-breasted Snake-Eagle	7/21	South Africa
3611	Rudd's Lark	7/17	South Africa	3671	Red-collared Widowbird	7/22	South Africa
3612	South African Shelduck	7/17	South Africa	3672	Gray Crowned-Crane	7/22	South Africa
3613	Blue Crane	7/17	South Africa	3673	Forest Canary	7/22	South Africa
3614	Black Harrier	7/17	South Africa	3674	Southern Double-collared Sunbird	7/22	South Africa
3615	Southern Bald Ibis	7/17	South Africa	3675	Amethyst Sunbird	7/22	South Africa
3616	Cape Weaver	7/18	South Africa	3676	Bush Blackcap	7/22	South Africa
3617	Olive Thrush	7/18	South Africa	3677	Orange Ground-Thrush	7/22	South Africa
3618	Cape Robin-Chat	7/18	South Africa	3678	Cape Batis	7/22	South Africa
3619	Cape Grassbird	7/18	South Africa	3679	Knysna Turaco	7/22	South Africa
3620	Rufous-necked Wryneck	7/18	South Africa	3680	Wattled Crane	7/22	South Africa
3621	Red-billed Quelea	7/18	South Africa	3681	Forest Buzzard	7/22	South Africa
3622	Rufous-naped Lark	7/18	South Africa	3682	Piping Cisticola (180)	7/22	South Africa
3623	Black-winged Lapwing	7/18	South Africa	3683	Drakensberg Prinia	7/23	South Africa

3684	Yellow-throated Woodland-Warbler	7/23	South Africa	3744	Pririt Batis	7/28	South Africa
3685	Olive Woodpecker	7/23	South Africa	3745	Rufous-vented Warbler	7/28	South Africa
3686	African Quailfinch	7/23	South Africa	3746	Yellow-rumped Eremomela	7/28	South Africa
3687	White-necked Raven	7/23	South Africa	3747	Rufous-eared Warbler	7/28	South Africa
3688	Denham's Bustard	7/23	South Africa	3748	Pale Chanting-Goshawk	7/28	South Africa
3689	Sicklewing Chat	7/23	South Africa	3749	Tractrac Chat	7/28	South Africa
3690	Wailing Cisticola (180)	7/23	South Africa	3750	Karoo Lark	7/28	South Africa
3691	Cape Rock-Thrush	7/23	South Africa	3751	Burchell's Courser	7/28	South Africa
3692	Drakensberg Siskin	7/23	Lesotho	3752	Ludwig's Bustard	7/28	South Africa
3693	Drakensberg Rockjumper	7/23	Lesotho	3753	Cape Lark	7/29	South Africa
3694	Cape Bunting	7/23	Lesotho	3754	Layard's Warbler	7/29	South Africa
3695	Large-billed Lark	7/23	Lesotho	3755	Southern Penduline-Tit	7/29	South Africa
3696	African Grass-Owl	7/23	South Africa	3756	Gray Tit	7/29	South Africa
3697	Swee Waxbill	7/24	South Africa	3757	Lesser Honeyguide	7/29	South Africa
3698	White-starred Robin	7/24	South Africa	3758	White-backed Mousebird	7/29	South Africa
3699	Barratt's Warbler	7/24	South Africa	3759	Lesser Flamingo	7/29	South Africa
3700	Olive Bushshrike	7/24	South Africa	3760	Chestnut-banded Plover	7/29	South Africa
3701	Southern Tchagra	7/24	South Africa	3761	Madagascar Munia	7/30	Madagascar
3702	Shelley's Francolin	7/24	South Africa	3762	Madagascar Cisticola	7/31	Madagascar
3703	Red-chested Flufftail	7/24	South Africa	3763	Red Fody	7/31	Madagascar
3704	Little Rush-Warbler	7/24	South Africa	3764	Souimanga Sunbird	7/31	Madagascar
3705	Wahlberg's Honeyguide	7/24	South Africa	3765	Madagascar Magpie-Robin	7/31	Madagascar
3706	White-backed Duck	7/24	South Africa	3766	Common Jery	7/31	Madagascar
3707	Common Ostrich (3)	7/24	South Africa	3767	Long-billed Bernieria	7/31	Madagascar
3708	Hartlaub's Gull	7/24	South Africa	3768	Madagascar Bulbul	7/31	Madagascar
3709	Cape Siskin	7/25	South Africa	3769	Madagascar Paradise-Flycatcher	7/31	Madagascar
3710	Malachite Sunbird	7/25	South Africa	3770	Crested Drongo	7/31	Madagascar
3711	Cape Bulbul	7/25	South Africa	3771	Ashy Cuckooshrike	7/31	Madagascar
3712	Cape Sugarbird	7/25	South Africa	3772	Van Dam's Vanga	7/31	Madagascar
3713	Karoo Prinia	7/25	South Africa	3773	Rufous Vanga	7/31	Madagascar
3714	Orange-breasted Sunbird	7/25	South Africa	3774	Blue Vanga	7/31	Madagascar
3715	Victorin's Warbler	7/25	South Africa	3775	Chabert Vanga	7/31	Madagascar
3716	Cape Rockjumper	7/25	South Africa	3776	Common Newtonia	7/31	Madagascar
3717	Red-headed Cisticola	7/25	South Africa	3777	Gray-headed Lovebird	7/31	Madagascar
3718	African Oystercatcher	7/25	South Africa	3778	Lesser Vasa-Parrot	7/31	Madagascar
3719	Bank Cormorant	7/25	South Africa	3779	Madagascar Kestrel	7/31	Madagascar
3720	Cape Cormorant	7/25	South Africa	3780	Madagascar Hoopoe	7/31	Madagascar
3721	Cape Gannet	7/25	South Africa	3781	Madagascar Bee-eater	7/31	Madagascar
3722	Jackass Penguin (174)	7/25	South Africa	3782	Malagasy Kingfisher	7/31	Madagascar
3723	Cape Francolin	7/25	South Africa	3783	Madagascar Nightjar	7/31	Madagascar
3724	Great Crested Tern	7/25	South Africa	3784	Madagascar Coucal	7/31	Madagascar
3725	Spotted Thick-knee	7/25	South Africa	3785	Crested Coua	7/31	Madagascar
3726	Maccoa Duck	7/25	South Africa	3786	Red-capped Coua	7/31	Madagascar
3727	White-capped Albatross	7/26	South Africa	3787	Coquerel's Coua	7/31	Madagascar
3728	Yellow-nosed Albatross	7/26	South Africa	3788	Madagascar Turtle-Dove	7/31	Madagascar
3729	Crowned Cormorant	7/26	South Africa	3789	Madagascar Buttonquail	7/31	Madagascar
3730	Spotted Eagle-Owl	7/27	South Africa	3790	Madagascar Buzzard	7/31	Madagascar
3731	Yellow Canary	7/27	South Africa	3791	Madagascar Fish-Eagle	7/31	Madagascar
3732	Agulhas Lark	7/27	South Africa	3792	Frances's Goshawk	7/31	Madagascar
3733	Karoo Scrub-Robin	7/27	South Africa	3793	Madagascar Pond-Heron	7/31	Madagascar
3734	Knysna Woodpecker	7/27	South Africa	3794	Madagascar Jacana	7/31	Madagascar
3735	White-throated Canary	7/27	South Africa	3795	Madagascar Sunbird	7/31	Madagascar
3736	Cloud Cisticola	7/27	South Africa	3796	White-headed Vanga	8/1	Madagascar
3737	Black Bustard	7/27	South Africa	3797	Sickle-billed Vanga	8/1	Madagascar
3738	Karoo Bustard	7/27	South Africa	3798	Hook-billed Vanga	8/1	Madagascar
3739	Protea Canary	7/27	South Africa	3799	Schlegel's Asity	8/1	Madagascar
3740	Namaqua Prinia	7/27	South Africa	3800	Cuckoo-Roller	8/1	Madagascar
3741	Karoo Chat	7/28	South Africa	3801	Torotoroka Scops-Owl	8/1	Madagascar
3742	Kopje Warbler	7/28	South Africa	3802	Madagascar Green-Pigeon	8/1	Madagascar
3743	Fairy Flycatcher	7/28	South Africa	3803	White-throated Rail	8/1	Madagascar

3804	White-breasted Mesite	8/1	Madagascar	3864	Black-faced Sandgrouse	8/7	Kenya
3805	Madagascar Wagtail	8/2	Madagascar	3865	Eastern Chanting-Goshawk	8/7	Kenya
3806	Madagascar Lark	8/2	Madagascar	3868	Kenya Violet-backed Sunbird	8/8	Kenya
3807	Nelicourvi Weaver	8/3	Madagascar	3867	Slate-colored Boubou	8/8	Kenya
3808	Madagascar White-eye	8/3	Madagascar	3868	Nubian Woodpecker	8/8	Kenya
3809	White-throated Oxylabes	8/3	Madagascar	3869	Spot-flanked Barbet	8/8	Kenya
3810	Madagascar Brush-Warbler	8/3	Madagascar	3870	Somali Bunting	8/8	Kenya
3811	Ward's Flycatcher	8/3	Madagascar	3871	Hunter's Sunbird	8/8	Kenya
3812	Crossley's Vanga	8/3	Madagascar	3872	Pink-breasted Lark	8/8	Kenya
3813	Nuthatch-Vanga	8/3	Madagascar	3873	Red-winged Lark	8/8	Kenya
3814	Red-tailed Vanga	8/3	Madagascar	3874	Taita Fiscal	8/8	Kenya
3815	Tylas Vanga	8/3	Madagascar	3875	Pygmy Falcon	8/8	Kenya
3816	Dark Newtonia	8/3	Madagascar	3876	Blue-naped Mousebird	8/8	Kenya
3817	Sunbird Asity	8/3	Madagascar	3877	Black-headed Lapwing	8/8	Kenya
3818	Velvet Asity	8/3	Madagascar	3878	Buff-crested Bustard	8/8	Kenya
3819	Madagascar Swift	8/3	Madagascar	3879	Somali Ostrich	8/8	Kenya
3820	Collared Nightjar	8/3	Madagascar	3880	Tsavo Sunbird	8/8	Kenya
3821	Madagascar Long-eared Owl	8/3	Madagascar	3881	Chestnut-headed Sparrow-Lark	8/8	Kenya
3822	Malagasy Scops-Owl	8/3	Madagascar	3882	Rosy-patched Bushshrike	8/8	Kenya
3823	Blue Coua	8/3	Madagascar	3883	Somali Courser	8/8	Kenya
3824	Red-fronted Coua	8/3	Madagascar	3884	Pangani Longclaw	8/8	Kenya
3825	Madagascar Blue-Pigeon	8/3	Madagascar	3885	Pygmy Batis	8/8	Kenya
3826	Madagascar Flufftail	8/3	Madagascar	3886	Somali Bee-eater	8/8	Kenya
3827	Madagascar Wood-Rail	8/3	Madagascar	3887	Rüppell's Griffon	8/8	Kenya
3828	Madagascar Ibis	8/3	Madagascar	3888	Yellow-necked Francolin	8/8	Kenya
3829	Greater Vasa-Parrot	8/4	Madagascar	3889	Northern Brownbul	8/9	Kenya
3830	Forest Fody	8/4	Madagascar	3890	House Crow	8/9	Kenya
3831	Spectacled Tetraka	8/4	Madagascar	3891	Yellow-bellied Waxbill	8/9	Kenya
3832	Scaly Ground-Roller	8/4	Madagascar	3892	Reichenow's Seedeater	8/9	Kenya
3833	Malagasy Spinetail	8/4	Madagascar	3893	Striped Pipit	8/9	Kenya
3834	Madagascar Grebe	8/4	Madagascar	3894	Taita Thrush	8/9	Kenya
3835	Meller's Duck	8/4	Madagascar	3895	Broad-ringed White-eye	8/9	Kenya
3836	Gray-crowned Tetraka	8/5	Madagascar	3896	Black-headed Apalis	8/9	Kenya
3837	Comb Duck	8/6	Madagascar	3897	Stripe-cheeked Greenbul	8/9	Kenya
3838	Superb Starling	8/7	Kenya	3898	Hartlaub's Turaco	8/9	Kenya
3839	Long-tailed Fiscal	8/7	Kenya	3899	Augur Buzzard	8/9	Kenya
3840	White-bellied Go-away-bird	8/7	Kenya	3900	Red-headed Weaver	8/9	Kenya
3841	Crimson-rumped Waxbill	8/7	Kenya	3901	White-bellied Tit	8/9	Kenya
3842	White-breasted White-eye	8/7	Kenya	3902	Sokoke Pipit	8/10	Kenya
3843	White-browed Sparrow-Weaver	8/7	Kenya	3903	Malindi Pipit	8/10	Kenya
3844	Fischer's Starling	8/7	Kenya	3904	Amani Sunbird	8/10	Kenya
3845	Blue-capped Cordonbleu	8/7	Kenya	3905	Plain-backed Sunbird	8/10	Kenya
3846	White-headed Buffalo-Weaver	8/7	Kenya	3906	East Coast Akalat	8/10	Kenya
3847	Yellow-spotted Petronia	8/7	Kenya	3907	Yellow Flycatcher	8/10	Kenya
3848	Parrot-billed Sparrow	8/7	Kenya	3908	Tiny Greenbul	8/10	Kenya
3849	Golden-breasted Starling	8/7	Kenya	3909	Fischer's Greenbul	8/10	Kenya
3850	African Bare-eyed Thrush	8/7	Kenya	3910	Black Cuckooshrike	8/10	Kenya
3851	Grayish Flycatcher	8/7	Kenya	3911	Zanzibar Boubou	8/10	Kenya
3852	Gray Wren-Warbler	8/7	Kenya	3912	Chestnut-fronted Helmetshrike	8/10	Kenya
3853	Red-fronted Warbler	8/7	Kenya	3913	Retz's Helmetshrike	8/10	Kenya
3854	White-rumped Shrike	8/7	Kenya	3914	Pale Batis	8/10	Kenya
3855	Three-streaked Tchagra	8/7	Kenya	3915	Short-tailed Batis	8/10	Kenya
3856	Red-bellied Parrot	8/7	Kenya	3916	Mombasa Woodpecker	8/10	Kenya
3857	Black-throated Barbet	8/7	Kenya	3917	Green Tinkerbird	8/10	Kenya
3858	D'Arnaud's Barbet	8/7	Kenya	3918	Green Barbet	8/10	Kenya
3859	Red-and-yellow Barbet	8/7	Kenya	3919	Mangrove Kingfisher	8/10	Kenya
3860	Von der Decken's Hornbill	8/7	Kenya	3920	Narina Trogon	8/10	Kenya
3861	Eastern Yellow-billed Hornbill	8/7	Kenya	3921	African Barred Owlet	8/10	Kenya
3862	Northern Red-billed Hornbill	8/7	Kenya	3922	Sokoke Scops-Owl	8/10	Kenya
3863	Abyssinian Scimitarbill	8/7	Kenya	3923	Fischer's Turaco	8/10	Kenya

3924	Golden Palm Weaver	8/10	Kenya
3925	Clarke's Weaver	8/11	Kenya
3926	Scaly Babbler	8/11	Kenya
3927	African Golden Oriole	8/11	Kenya
3928	Levaillant's Cuckoo	8/11	Kenya
3929	Crab Plover	8/11	Kenya
3930	Little Stint	8/11	Kenya
3931	Wahlberg's Eagle	8/11	Kenya
3932	Bronze Sunbird	8/12	Kenya
3933	Abyssinian Thrush	8/12	Kenya
3934	Northern Pied-Babbler	8/12	Kenya
3935	African Citril	8/12	Kenya
3936	Purple Grenadier	8/12	Kenya
3937	Spotted Morning-Thrush	8/12	Kenya
3938	Pallid Honeyguide	8/12	Kenya
3939	White-headed Barbet	8/12	Kenya
3940	Cinnamon-chested Bee-eater	8/12	Kenya
3941	Long-toed Lapwing	8/12	Kenya
3942	Village Indigobird	8/12	Kenya
3943	Streaky Seedeater	8/12	Kenya
3944	Eastern Double-collared Sunbird	8/12	Kenya
3945	Tacazze Sunbird	8/12	Kenya
3946	White-eyed Slaty-Flycatcher	8/12	Kenya
3947	Hunter's Cisticola	8/12	Kenya
3948	Chestnut-throated Apalis	8/12	Kenya
3949	Brown Woodland-Warbler	8/12	Kenya
3950	Cabanis's Greenbul	8/12	Kenya
3951	Eastern Mountain-Greenbul	8/12	Kenya
3952	White-tailed Crested-Flycatcher	8/12	Kenya
3953	Black-tailed Oriole	8/12	Kenya
3954	Tullberg's Woodpecker	8/12	Kenya
3955	Moustached Tinkerbird	8/12	Kenya
3956	Silvery-cheeked Hornbill	8/12	Kenya
3957	Kandt's Waxbill	8/13	Kenya
3958	Black-throated Apalis	8/13	Kenya
3959	Cinnamon Bracken-Warbler	8/13	Kenya
3960	Doherty's Bushshrike	8/13	Kenya
3961	Abyssinian Nightjar	8/13	Kenya
3962	Mountain Buzzard	8/13	Kenya
3963	Kenya Rufous Sparrow	8/13	Kenya
3964	Speke's Weaver	8/13	Kenya
3965	Cape Eagle-Owl	8/13	Kenya
3966	Jackson's Widowbird	8/13	Kenya
3967	Golden-winged Sunbird	8/14	Kenya
3968	Gray-capped Warbler	8/14	Kenya
3969	Dusky Turtle-Dove	8/14	Kenya
3970	Northern Anteater-Chat	8/14	Kenya
3971	Golden-backed Weaver	8/14	Kenya
3972	Rueppell's Starling	8/14	Kenya
3973	Buff-bellied Warbler	8/14	Kenya
3974	Mottled Swift	8/14	Kenya
3975	Northern Masked-Weaver	8/14	Kenya
3976	Bristle-crowned Starling	8/14	Kenya
3977	Jackson's Hornbill	8/14	Kenya
3978	Vitelline Masked-Weaver	8/14	Kenya
3979	White-billed Buffalo-Weaver	8/14	Kenya
3980	Brown-tailed Chat	8/14	Kenya
3981	Rufous Chatterer	8/14	Kenya
3982	Pale Prinia	8/14	Kenya
3983	Fan-tailed Raven	8/14	Kenya
3984	Slender-tailed Nightjar	8/14	Kenya
3985	Northern White-faced Owl	8/14	Kenya
3986	Three-banded Courser	8/14	Kenya
3987	Verreaux's Eagle-Owl	8/15	Kenya
3988	Red-fronted Barbet	8/15	Kenya
3989	Hemprich's Hornbill	8/15	Kenya
3990	White-bellied Canary	8/15	Kenya
3991	Red-faced Crombec	8/15	Kenya
3992	Somali Tit	8/15	Kenya
3993	Chestnut Weaver	8/16	Kenya
3994	Gray-backed Fiscal	8/16	Kenya
3995	Silverbird	8/16	Kenya
3996	Sharpe's Longclaw	8/16	Kenya
3997	Hildebrandt's Starling	8/17	Tanzania
3998	Abyssinian Wheatear	8/17	Tanzania
3999	Beesley's Lark	8/17	Tanzania
4000	Mountain Gray Woodpecker (194)	8/17	Tanzania
4001	Black Bishop	8/17	Tanzania
4002	Speckle-fronted Weaver	8/17	Tanzania
4003	Ashy Starling	8/17	Tanzania
4004	Banded Warbler	8/17	Tanzania
4005	Yellow-collared Lovebird	8/17	Tanzania
4006	Red-necked Francolin	8/17	Tanzania
4007	Rufous-tailed Weaver	8/17	Tanzania
4008	Swahili Sparrow	8/18	Tanzania
4009	Foxy Lark	8/18	Tanzania
4010	Greater Honeyguide	8/18	Tanzania
4011	Yellow-throated Sandgrouse	8/18	Tanzania
4012	Coqui Francolin	8/18	Tanzania
4013	Bare-faced Go-away-bird	8/18	Tanzania
4014	Chestnut-bellied Sandgrouse	8/18	Tanzania
4015	Double-banded Courser	8/18	Tanzania
4016	Meyer's Parrot	8/18	Tanzania
4017	Greater Painted-Snipe	8/18	Tanzania
4018	Fischer's Sparrow-Lark	8/18	Tanzania
4019	Brown-headed Apalis	8/19	Tanzania
4020	Black-lored Babbler	8/19	Tanzania
4021	Gray-breasted Francolin	8/19	Tanzania
4022	Ruff	8/19	Tanzania
4023	Stout Cisticola	8/20	Tanzania
4024	Fischer's Lovebird (195)	8/20	Tanzania
4025	Temminck's Courser (195)	8/20	Tanzania
4026	Red-throated Tit (195)	8/20	Tanzania
4027	Gray-headed Social-Weaver (195)	8/20	Tanzania
4028	Karamoja Apalis (194–197)	8/20	Tanzania
4029	Tanzanian Red-billed Hornbill	8/20	Tanzania
4030	Desert Cisticola	8/21	Tanzania
4031	Schalow's Turaco	8/22	Tanzania
4032	Southern Citril	8/22	Tanzania
4033	Rueppell's Robin-Chat	8/22	Tanzania
4034	White-tailed Blue-Flycatcher	8/22	Tanzania
4035	Green-backed Honeyguide	8/22	Tanzania
4036	Taveta Golden-Weaver	8/23	Tanzania
4037	African Reed-Warbler	8/23	Tanzania
4038	Zanzibar Red Bishop	8/23	Tanzania
4039	Southern Grosbeak-Canary	8/23	Tanzania
4040	White-winged Tern	8/23	Tanzania
4041	Marsh Sandpiper	8/23	Tanzania
4042	Gray-headed Silverbill	8/23	Tanzania
4043	Cut-throat	8/23	Tanzania

4044	Scaly Chatterer	8/23	Tanzania
4045	Tiny Cisticola	8/23	Tanzania
4046	Mouse-colored Penduline-Tit	8/23	Tanzania
4047	Pringle's Puffback	8/23	Tanzania
4048	White-headed Mousebird	8/23	Tanzania
4049	Eastern Paradise-Whydah	8/24	Tanzania
4050	Cinnamon-breasted Bunting	8/24	Tanzania
4051	Black-bellied Sunbird	8/24	Tanzania
4052	Black-headed Batis	8/24	Tanzania
4053	Hildebrandt's Francolin	8/24	Tanzania
4054	Nyanza Swift	8/24	Tanzania
4055	Usambara Greenbul	8/25	Tanzania
4056	Brown-breasted Barbet	8/25	Tanzania
4057	Kenrick's Starling	8/25	Tanzania
4058	Usambara Thrush	8/25	Tanzania
4059	White-chested Alethe	8/25	Tanzania
4060	Spot-throat	8/25	Tanzania
4061	African Tailorbird	8/25	Tanzania
4062	Shelley's Greenbul	8/25	Tanzania
4063	Black-fronted Bushshrike	8/25	Tanzania
4064	Fuelleborn's Boubou	8/25	Tanzania
4065	Usambara Weaver	8/25	Tanzania
4066	Yellow-streaked Greenbul	8/25	Tanzania
4067	Uluguru Violet-backed Sunbird	8/26	Tanzania
4068	Red-tailed Ant-Thrush	8/26	Tanzania
4069	Green-headed Oriole	8/26	Tanzania
4070	Banded Sunbird	8/27	Tanzania
4071	Long-billed Tailorbird	8/27	Tanzania
4072	African Broadbill	8/27	Tanzania
4073	Half-collared Kingfisher	8/27	Tanzania
4074	Scarce Swift	8/27	Tanzania
4075	Usambara Eagle-Owl	8/27	Tanzania
4076	Usambara Hyliota	8/28	Tanzania
4077	Eastern Plantain-eater	8/29	Uganda
4078	Sooty Chat	8/29	Uganda
4079	White-headed Sawwing	8/29	Uganda
4080	Angola Swallow	8/29	Uganda
4081	Black-headed Weaver	8/29	Uganda
4082	Northern Brown-throated Weaver	8/29	Uganda
4083	Slender-billed Weaver	8/29	Uganda
4084	Red-chested Sunbird	8/29	Uganda
4085	Blue-breasted Bee-eater	8/29	Uganda
4086	Lesser Jacana	8/29	Uganda
4087	Shoebill	8/29	Uganda
4088	White-winged Swamp-Warbler	8/29	Uganda
4089	African Hobby	8/29	Uganda
4090	Ross's Turaco	8/30	Uganda
4091	Black-headed Gonolek	8/30	Uganda
4092	Banded Snake-Eagle	8/30	Uganda
4093	Lesser Blue-eared Starling	8/30	Uganda
4094	African Cuckoo	8/30	Uganda
4095	White-crested Turaco	8/30	Uganda
4096	Brown Twinspot	8/31	Uganda
4097	Purple-headed Starling	8/31	Uganda
4098	Yellow Longbill	8/31	Uganda
4099	White-throated Greenbul	8/31	Uganda
4100	Chestnut Wattle-eye	8/31	Uganda
4101	Golden-crowned Woodpecker	8/31	Uganda
4102	Thick-billed Honeyguide	8/31	Uganda
4103	White-thighed Hornbill	8/31	Uganda
4104	Dusky Long-tailed Cuckoo	8/31	Uganda
4105	Black-billed Turaco	8/31	Uganda
4106	Afep Pigeon	8/31	Uganda
4107	Abyssinian Ground-Hornbill	8/31	Uganda
4108	Fawn-breasted Waxbill	8/31	Uganda
4109	Red-winged Gray Warbler	8/31	Uganda
4110	Bat Hawk	8/31	Uganda
4111	Black-chinned Quailfinch	9/1	Uganda
4112	Shelley's Rufous Sparrow	9/1	Uganda
4113	Green-backed Eremomela	9/1	Uganda
4114	Foxy Cisticola	9/1	Uganda
4115	Papyrus Gonolek	9/1	Uganda
4116	Red-necked Falcon	9/1	Uganda
4117	Black-billed Barbet	9/1	Uganda
4118	Northern Carmine Bee-eater	9/1	Uganda
4119	Swallow-tailed Bee-eater	9/1	Uganda
4120	Heuglin's Francolin	9/1	Uganda
4121	Pennant-winged Nightjar	9/1	Uganda
4122	Dusky Babbler	9/2	Uganda
4123	White-rumped Seedeater	9/2	Uganda
4124	Red-headed Bluebill	9/2	Uganda
4125	Stuhlmann's Starling	9/2	Uganda
4126	Blue-shouldered Robin-Chat	9/2	Uganda
4127	Masked Apalis	9/2	Uganda
4128	Dusky Tit	9/2	Uganda
4129	Petit's Cuckooshrike	9/2	Uganda
4130	Gray-throated Barbet	9/2	Uganda
4131	Carruthers's Cisticola	9/2	Uganda
4132	Seimund's Sunbird	9/3	Uganda
4133	White-tailed Ant-Thrush	9/3	Uganda
4134	Scaly-breasted Illadopsis	9/3	Uganda
4135	Brown Illadopsis	9/3	Uganda
4136	Buff-throated Apalis	9/3	Uganda
4137	African Shrike-flycatcher	9/3	Uganda
4138	Green-breasted Pitta (200)	9/3	Uganda
4139	Black Bee-eater	9/3	Uganda
4140	Red-chested Owlet	9/3	Uganda
4141	Brown-backed Scrub-Robin	9/3	Uganda
4142	Compact Weaver	9/4	Uganda
4143	Shining-blue Kingfisher	9/4	Uganda
4144	Joyful Greenbul	9/4	Uganda
4145	Trilling Cisticola (180)	9/4	Uganda
4146	Square-tailed Nightjar	9/4	Uganda
4147	African Crake	9/4	Uganda
4148	African Skimmer	9/4	Uganda
4149	Fan-tailed Grassbird	9/5	Uganda
4150	Rufous-chested Swallow	9/5	Uganda
4151	Small Buttonquail	9/5	Uganda
4152	Gray-headed Sunbird	9/5	Uganda
4153	Pink-footed Puffback	9/5	Uganda
4154	Green-throated Sunbird	9/6	Uganda
4155	Gray-winged Robin-Chat	9/6	Uganda
4156	Blue-headed Sunbird	9/6	Uganda
4157	Oberlaender's Ground-Thrush	9/6	Uganda
4158	Equatorial Akalat	9/6	Uganda
4159	Red-throated Alethe	9/6	Uganda
4160	Chapin's Flycatcher	9/6	Uganda
4161	Mountain Illadopsis	9/6	Uganda
4162	Black-faced Apalis	9/6	Uganda
4163	Red-faced Woodland-Warbler	9/6	Uganda

4164	Neumann's Warbler	9/6	Uganda
4165	Grauer's Warbler	9/6	Uganda
4166	White-browed Crombec	9/6	Uganda
4167	Ansorge's Greenbul	9/6	Uganda
4168	Willard's Sooty Boubou	9/6	Uganda
4169	Willcocks's Honeyguide	9/6	Uganda
4170	White-headed Woodhoopoe	9/6	Uganda
4171	Bar-tailed Trogon	9/6	Uganda
4172	Olive Long-tailed Cuckoo	9/6	Uganda
4173	Western Citril	9/7	Uganda
4174	Dusky Twinspot	9/7	Uganda
4175	Yellow-crowned Canary	9/7	Uganda
4176	Ruwenzori Apalis	9/7	Uganda
4177	Stripe-breasted Tit	9/7	Uganda
4178	Ruwenzori Batis	9/7	Uganda
4179	Strange Weaver	9/7	Uganda
4180	Archer's Robin-Chat	9/7	Uganda
4181	Mountain Yellow-Warbler	9/7	Uganda
4182	Montane Nightjar	9/7	Uganda
4183	Handsome Francolin	9/7	Uganda
4184	Regal Sunbird	9/7	Uganda
4185	Grauer's Broadbill	9/7	Uganda
4186	Dusky Crimson-wing	9/8	Uganda
4187	Slender-billed Starling	9/8	Uganda
4188	Yellow-eyed Black-Flycatcher	9/8	Uganda
4189	Grauer's Swamp-Warbler	9/8	Uganda
4190	Dwarf Honeyguide	9/8	Uganda
4191	Barred Long-tailed Cuckoo	9/8	Uganda
4192	Papyrus Canary	9/9	Uganda
4193	Red-faced Barbet	9/9	Uganda
4194	Brown-chested Lapwing	9/9	Uganda
4195	White-winged Black-Tit	9/9	Uganda
4196	Swamp Nightjar	9/9	Uganda
4197	Black-shouldered Nightjar	9/9	Uganda
4198	African Finfoot	9/9	Uganda
4199	Greencap Eremomela	9/10	Uganda
4200	Tabora Cisticola	9/10	Uganda
4201	Freckled Nightjar	9/10	Uganda
4202	White-backed Night-Heron	9/10	Uganda
4203	Rufous-bellied Heron	9/10	Uganda
4204	Weyns's Weaver	9/11	Uganda
4205	Black-crowned Sparrow-Lark	9/12	UAE
4206	Brown-necked Raven	9/12	UAE
4207	Cream-colored Courser	9/12	UAE
4208	Gray Francolin	9/12	UAE
4209	Indian Silverbill	9/12	UAE
4210	Citrine Wagtail	9/12	UAE
4211	Purple Sunbird	9/12	UAE
4212	Arabian Babbler	9/12	UAE
4213	Clamorous Reed-Warbler	9/12	UAE
4214	White-eared Bulbul	9/12	UAE
4215	Lesser Sand-Plover	9/12	UAE
4216	Red-wattled Lapwing	9/12	UAE
4217	Green Warbler (201)	9/12	UAE
4218	Green Bee-eater	9/12	UAE
4219	White-tailed Lapwing	9/12	UAE
4220	Desert Wheatear	9/12	UAE
4221	Asian Desert Warbler	9/12	UAE
4222	Great Knot	9/12	UAE
4223	Terek Sandpiper	9/12	UAE
4224	Greater Sand-Plover	9/12	UAE
4225	Indian Roller	9/12	UAE
4226	Caspian Plover	9/12	UAE
4227	Pacific Golden-Plover	9/12	UAE
4228	Lesser Crested Tern	9/12	UAE
4229	White-cheeked Tern	9/12	UAE
4230	Saunders's Tern	9/12	UAE
4231	Bridled Tern	9/12	UAE
4232	Socotra Cormorant	9/12	UAE
4233	Striolated Bunting	9/12	UAE
4234	Hume's Wheatear	9/12	UAE
4235	Scrub Warbler	9/12	UAE
4236	Desert Lark	9/12	UAE
4237	Lichtenstein's Sandgrouse	9/12	UAE
4238	Sand Partridge	9/12	UAE
4239	Bank Myna	9/12	UAE
4240	Variable Wheatear	9/12	UAE
4241	Oriental Skylark	9/12	UAE
4242	Red-tailed Shrike	9/12	UAE
4243	Pin-tailed Snipe	9/12	UAE
4244	Long-billed Sunbird	9/13	India
4245	Purple-rumped Sunbird	9/13	India
4246	Pale-billed Flowerpecker	9/13	India
4247	Black Drongo	9/13	India
4248	Indian Pond-Heron	9/13	India
4249	Lesser Whistling-Duck	9/13	India
4250	Yellow-browed Bulbul	9/13	India
4251	Vernal Hanging-Parrot	9/13	India
4252	Southern Hill Myna	9/13	India
4253	Jungle Babbler	9/13	India
4254	Red-whiskered Bulbul	9/13	India
4255	Rufous Treepie	9/13	India
4256	Greater Racket-tailed Drongo	9/13	India
4257	Malabar Parakeet	9/13	India
4258	Greater Flameback	9/13	India
4259	White-cheeked Barbet (212)	9/13	India
4260	Stork-billed Kingfisher	9/13	India
4261	Greater Coucal	9/13	India
4262	Common Hawk-Cuckoo	9/13	India
4263	Rufous Babbler	9/13	India
4264	Indian Swiftlet	9/13	India
4265	Dusky Crag-Martin	9/13	India
4266	Jungle Owlet	9/13	India
4267	Golden-fronted Leafbird	9/14	India
4268	Malabar Whistling-Thrush	9/14	India
4269	Oriental Magpie-Robin	9/14	India
4270	Indian Scimitar-Babbler	9/14	India
4271	Common Tailorbird	9/14	India
4272	Square-tailed Bulbul	9/14	India
4273	Nilgiri Flowerpecker	9/14	India
4274	Long-tailed Shrike	9/14	India
4275	Plum-headed Parakeet	9/14	India
4276	Black-rumped Flameback	9/14	India
4277	Streak-throated Woodpecker	9/14	India
4278	Spotted Dove	9/14	India
4279	Pied Bushchat	9/14	India
4280	Hill Swallow	9/14	India
4281	Large-billed Crow	9/14	India
4282	White-browed Wagtail	9/14	India
4283	Crimson-backed Sunbird	9/14	India

4284	Nilgiri Flycatcher	9/14	India	4344	Crested Serpent-Eagle	9/17	India
4285	Oriental White-eye	9/14	India	4345	Brown Boobook	9/17	India
4286	Gray-breasted Prinia	9/14	India	4346	Asian Brown Flycatcher	9/17	India
4287	Indian Tit	9/14	India	4347	Large Cuckooshrike	9/17	India
4288	Gray-headed Canary-Flycatcher	9/14	India	4348	Jerdon's Nightjar	9/17	India
4289	Orange Minivet	9/14	India	4349	Oriental Scops-Owl	9/17	India
4290	Speckled Piculet	9/14	India	4350	Indian Scops-Owl	9/17	India
4291	Nilgiri Pipit	9/14	India	4351	Mottled Wood-Owl	9/17	India
4292	Indian Blackbird	9/14	India	4352	Malabar Woodshrike	9/17	India
4293	White-bellied Shortwing	9/14	India	4353	Legge's Hawk-Eagle	9/17	India
4294	Kerala Laughingthrush	9/14	India	4354	Crested Hawk-Eagle	9/17	India
4295	Plain Prinia	9/14	India	4355	Dollarbird	9/17	India
4296	Black Eagle	9/14	India	4356	Little Spiderhunter	9/17	India
4297	Black-and-rufous Flycatcher	9/14	India	4357	Banded Bay Cuckoo	9/17	India
4298	Velvet-fronted Nuthatch	9/14	India	4358	Tickell's Blue-Flycatcher	9/17	India
4299	Bar-winged Flycatcher-shrike	9/14	India	4359	Rufous Woodpecker	9/17	India
4300	Jungle Myna	9/14	India	4360	Crested Treeswift	9/17	India
4301	Ashy Prinia	9/14	India	4361	Oriental Honey-buzzard	9/17	India
4302	Little Cormorant	9/14	India	4362	Yellow-billed Babbler	9/18	India
4303	Emerald Dove	9/15	India	4363	Red-vented Bulbul	9/18	India
4304	Nilgiri Wood-Pigeon	9/15	India	4364	Asian Fairy-bluebird	9/18	India
4305	Gray Junglefowl	9/15	India	4365	Orange-headed Thrush	9/18	India
4306	Broad-tailed Grassbird (203)	9/15	India	4366	Great Hornbill	9/18	India
4307	Greenish Warbler	9/15	India	4367	Mountain Imperial-Pigeon	9/18	India
4308	Brahminy Kite	9/15	India	4368	Indian Peafowl	9/19	India
4309	Crested Goshawk	9/15	India	4369	Jerdon's Leafbird	9/19	India
4310	Brown-cheeked Fulvetta	9/15	India	4370	White-browed Bulbul	9/19	India
4311	Puff-throated Babbler	9/15	India	4371	Yellow-throated Bulbul	9/19	India
4312	Malabar Barbet	9/15	India	4372	Brown-headed Barbet	9/19	India
4313	Painted Bush-Quail	9/15	India	4373	Besra	9/19	India
4314	Black-throated Munia	9/16	India	4374	Indian Robin	9/19	India
4315	Lesser Fish-Eagle	9/16	India	4375	Jerdon's Bushlark	9/19	India
4316	Malabar Gray Hornbill (212)	9/16	India	4376	White-bellied Drongo	9/19	India
4317	Asian Palm-Swift	9/16	India	4377	Common Woodshrike	9/19	India
4318	Ashy Woodswallow	9/16	India	4378	Coppersmith Barbet	9/19	India
4319	Oriental Darter	9/16	India	4379	Blue-faced Malkoha	9/19	India
4320	Black-hooded Oriole	9/16	India	4380	Indian Thick-knee	9/19	India
4321	Red Spurfowl	9/16	India	4381	Large Gray Babbler	9/19	India
4322	Green Imperial-Pigeon	9/16	India	4382	Asian Koel	9/19	India
4323	Malabar Starling	9/16	India	4383	White-eyed Buzzard	9/19	India
4324	White-bellied Blue-Flycatcher	9/16	India	4384	Rock Bush-Quail	9/19	India
4325	Dark-fronted Babbler (208)	9/16	India	4385	Brahminy Starling	9/19	India
4326	Flame-throated Bulbul (208)	9/16	India	4386	Ashy-crowned Sparrow-Lark	9/19	India
4327	Cinereous Tit	9/16	India	4387	Rock Eagle-Owl	9/19	India
4328	White-bellied Treepie (208)	9/16	India	4388	Sykes's Warbler	9/19	India
4329	Black-naped Monarch	9/16	India	4389	Singing Bushlark	9/19	India
4330	Bronzed Drongo	9/16	India	4390	Bay-backed Shrike	9/19	India
4331	Small Minivet	9/16	India	4391	Indian Nightjar	9/19	India
4332	Heart-spotted Woodpecker (208)	9/16	India	4392	Spotted Owlet	9/19	India
4333	Lesser Yellownape	9/16	India	4393	Barred Buttonquail	9/19	India
4334	Brown-capped Woodpecker	9/16	India	4394	Indian Cormorant	9/19	India
4335	Malabar Trogon (208)	9/16	India	4395	Indian Spot-billed Duck	9/19	India
4336	Brown-backed Needletail	9/16	India	4396	Black-chinned Laughingthrush	9/20	India
4337	White-rumped Needletail (209)	9/16	India	4397	White-rumped Shama	9/20	India
4338	White-rumped Munia (209)	9/16	India	4398	Gray-headed Bulbul	9/20	India
4339	White-breasted Waterhen (209)	9/16	India	4399	Brown Wood-Owl	9/20	India
4340	Gray-fronted Green-Pigeon (209)	9/16	India	4400	Tawny-bellied Babbler	9/20	India
4341	Common Iora (209)	9/16	India	4401	Yellow-eyed Babbler	9/20	India
4342	Sri Lanka Frogmouth (211–212)	9/16	India	4402	Indian Nuthatch	9/20	India
4343	Chestnut-headed Bee-eater	9/17	India	4403	Malabar Lark	9/20	India

4404	White-bellied Minivet	9/20	India		4464	Indian Vulture	9/25	India
4405	White-rumped Vulture	9/20	India		4465	Small Pratincole	9/25	India
4406	Jungle Bush-Quail	9/20	India		4466	Tricolored Munia	9/26	India
4407	White-browed Fantail	9/20	India		4467	Pallas's Gull	9/26	India
4408	Jungle Nightjar	9/20	India		4468	River Lapwing	9/26	India
4409	White-bellied Woodpecker	9/21	India		4469	Streaked Weaver	9/26	India
4410	Spot-breasted Fantail	9/21	India		4470	Bengal Bushlark	9/26	India
4411	White-naped Woodpecker	9/21	India		4471	Alexandrine Parakeet	9/26	India
4412	Yellow-crowned Woodpecker	9/21	India		4472	Jungle Prinia	9/26	India
4413	Red-headed Vulture	9/21	India		4473	Striated Prinia	9/27	India
4414	Blue-tailed Bee-eater	9/21	India		4474	Crimson Sunbird	9/27	India
4415	Indian Gray Hornbill	9/21	India		4475	Rufous Sibia	9/27	India
4416	Yellow-footed Pigeon	9/21	India		4476	Himalayan Bulbul	9/27	India
4417	Red-naped Ibis	9/21	India		4477	Gray Treepie	9/27	India
4418	Black-headed Ibis	9/21	India		4478	Mountain Scops-Owl	9/27	India
4419	Asian Openbill	9/21	India		4479	Black-throated Sunbird	9/27	India
4420	Spot-billed Pelican	9/21	India		4480	Tickell's Thrush	9/27	India
4421	Painted Stork	9/21	India		4481	Blue-capped Rock-Thrush	9/27	India
4422	Bronze-winged Jacana	9/21	India		4482	Ultramarine Flycatcher	9/27	India
4423	Gray-headed Swamphen	9/21	India		4483	Blue Whistling-Thrush	9/27	India
4424	Yellow-wattled Lapwing	9/22	India		4484	Verditer Flycatcher	9/27	India
4425	Asian Pied Starling	9/22	India		4485	Blue-winged Minla	9/27	India
4426	Gray-throated Martin	9/22	India		4486	Red-billed Leiothrix	9/27	India
4427	Isabelline Shrike	9/22	India		4487	Streaked Laughingthrush	9/27	India
4428	Pheasant-tailed Jacana	9/22	India		4488	Gray-hooded Warbler	9/27	India
4429	Bengal Weaver	9/22	India		4489	Mountain Bulbul	9/27	India
4430	Baya Weaver	9/22	India		4490	Ashy Bulbul	9/27	India
4431	Striated Babbler	9/22	India		4491	Black Bulbul	9/27	India
4432	Yellow-bellied Prinia	9/22	India		4492	Bar-tailed Treecreeper	9/27	India
4433	Sarus Crane	9/22	India		4493	Chestnut-bellied Nuthatch	9/27	India
4434	Red Avadavat	9/23	India		4494	Black-throated Tit	9/27	India
4435	Sind Sparrow	9/23	India		4495	Black-lored Tit	9/27	India
4436	Paddyfield Pipit	9/23	India		4496	Green-backed Tit	9/27	India
4437	Indian Chat	9/23	India		4497	Red-billed Blue-Magpie	9/27	India
4438	Siberian Stonechat	9/23	India		4498	White-throated Fantail	9/27	India
4439	Common Babbler	9/23	India		4499	Ashy Drongo	9/27	India
4440	Hume's Warbler	9/23	India		4500	Maroon Oriole	9/27	India
4441	Streak-throated Swallow	9/23	India		4501	Himalayan Shrike-Babbler	9/27	India
4442	Dusky Eagle-Owl	9/23	India		4502	Slaty-headed Parakeet	9/27	India
4443	White-browed Bushchat	9/23	India		4503	Gray-headed Woodpecker	9/27	India
4444	Rufous-fronted Prinia	9/23	India		4504	Brown-fronted Woodpecker	9/27	India
4445	Rufous-tailed Lark	9/23	India		4505	Blue-throated Barbet	9/27	India
4446	Indian Bushlark	9/23	India		4506	Great Barbet	9/27	India
4447	Laggar Falcon	9/23	India		4507	Rufous-throated Partridge	9/27	India
4448	Yellow-legged Buttonquail	9/23	India		4508	White-throated Laughingthrush	9/27	India
4449	Pallid Harrier	9/23	India		4509	Rufous-chinned Laughingthrush	9/27	India
4450	Steppe Eagle	9/23	India		4510	Rusty-cheeked Scimitar-Babbler	9/27	India
4451	Hume's Whitethroat	9/24	India		4511	Kalij Pheasant	9/27	India
4452	Indian Golden Oriole	9/24	India		4512	Plumbeous Redstart	9/27	India
4453	Red Collared-Dove	9/24	India		4513	Spotted Forktail	9/27	India
4454	Indian Spotted Eagle	9/24	India		4514	Striated Laughingthrush	9/27	India
4455	Rain Quail	9/24	India		4515	Crested Kingfisher	9/27	India
4456	River Tern	9/24	India		4516	Yellow-breasted Greenfinch	9/27	India
4457	Chestnut-breasted Bunting	9/24	India		4517	Gray Bushchat	9/27	India
4458	Gray-hooded Bunting	9/24	India		4518	Brown Dipper	9/27	India
4459	Painted Sandgrouse	9/24	India		4519	Oriental Turtle-Dove	9/27	India
4460	Large-billed Leaf Warbler	9/24	India		4520	Russet Sparrow	9/27	India
4461	Indian Paradise-Flycatcher	9/25	India		4521	Black-headed Jay	9/27	India
4462	Black Bittern (240)	9/25	India		4422	Whiskered Yuhina	9/28	India
4463	Cotton Pygmy-Goose	9/25	India		4523	Black-chinned Babbler	9/28	India

4524	Long-tailed Minivet	9/28	India	4584	Black-naped Oriole	10/3	Myanmar
4525	Asian Barred Owlet	9/28	India	4585	Himalayan Swiftlet	10/3	Myanmar
4526	Fire-breasted Flowerpecker	9/28	India	4586	Olive-backed Pipit	10/3	Myanmar
4527	Gray-winged Blackbird	9/28	India	4587	Little Pied Flycatcher	10/3	Myanmar
4528	Plain-backed Thrush	9/28	India	4588	Slaty-backed Flycatcher	10/3	Myanmar
4529	Chestnut-crowned Laughingthrush	9/28	India	4589	Pale Blue-Flycatcher	10/3	Myanmar
4530	White-tailed Nuthatch	9/28	India	4590	Spot-breasted Scimitar-Babbler	10/3	Myanmar
4531	Hill Partridge	9/28	India	4591	Chin Hills Wren-Babbler	10/3	Myanmar
4532	Rufous-bellied Woodpecker	9/28	India	4592	Yellow-browed Warbler	10/3	Myanmar
4533	Chestnut-bellied Rock-Thrush	9/28	India	4593	Pygmy Cupwing	10/3	Myanmar
4534	Western Crowned Leaf Warbler	9/28	India	4594	Flavescent Bulbul	10/3	Myanmar
4535	Black-faced Warbler	9/28	India	4595	Crested Finchbill	10/3	Myanmar
4536	Yellow-browed Tit	9/28	India	4596	Hume's Treecreeper	10/3	Myanmar
4537	Himalayan Woodpecker	9/28	India	4597	Chestnut-vented Nuthatch	10/3	Myanmar
4538	Himalayan Owl	9/28	India	4598	Yellow-bellied Fairy-Fantail	10/3	Myanmar
4539	Collared Owlet	9/28	India	4599	Short-billed Minivet	10/3	Myanmar
4540	Upland Pipit	9/28	India	4600	Streak-breasted Woodpecker	10/3	Myanmar
4541	Rufous-bellied Niltava	9/28	India	4601	Crimson-breasted Woodpecker	10/3	Myanmar
4542	Koklass Pheasant	9/28	India	4602	Hodgson's Frogmouth	10/4	Myanmar
4543	Cheer Pheasant	9/29	India	4603	Brown Bullfinch	10/4	Myanmar
4544	Black-crested Bulbul	9/29	India	4604	Fire-tailed Sunbird	10/4	Myanmar
4545	Scarlet Minivet	9/29	India	4605	Rufous-gorgeted Flycatcher	10/4	Myanmar
4546	Blue-throated Flycatcher	9/29	India	4606	Slaty-blue Flycatcher	10/4	Myanmar
4547	White-crested Laughingthrush	9/29	India	4607	Chestnut-tailed Minla	10/4	Myanmar
4548	Himalayan Flameback	9/29	India	4608	Streak-throated Barwing	10/4	Myanmar
4549	Lineated Barbet	9/29	India	4609	Red-tailed Minla	10/4	Myanmar
4550	Dark-sided Flycatcher	9/30	India	4610	Gray Sibia	10/4	Myanmar
4551	Blyth's Leaf Warbler	9/30	India	4611	Assam Laughingthrush	10/4	Myanmar
4552	Pale-rumped Warbler	9/30	India	4612	Brown-capped Laughingthrush	10/4	Myanmar
4553	Common Green-Magpie	9/30	India	4613	Chinese Babax	10/4	Myanmar
4554	Hair-crested Drongo	9/30	India	4614	Himalayan Cutia	10/4	Myanmar
4555	Black-winged Cuckooshrike	9/30	India	4615	Rufous-winged Fulvetta	10/4	Myanmar
4556	Rosy Minivet	9/30	India	4616	Streak-breasted Scimitar-Babbler	10/4	Myanmar
4557	Collared Falconet	9/30	India	4617	Stripe-throated Yuhina	10/4	Myanmar
4558	Fulvous-breasted Woodpecker	9/30	India	4618	Black-throated Parrotbill	10/4	Myanmar
4559	Gray-capped Woodpecker	9/30	India	4619	White-browed Fulvetta	10/4	Myanmar
4560	Square-tailed Drongo-Cuckoo	9/30	India	4620	Gray-crowned Warbler	10/4	Myanmar
4561	Red Junglefowl (11)	9/30	India	4621	Ashy-throated Warbler	10/4	Myanmar
4562	Pallas's Fish-Eagle	9/30	India	4622	Buff-barred Warbler	10/4	Myanmar
4563	Changeable Hawk-Eagle	9/30	India	4623	Aberrant Bush-Warbler	10/4	Myanmar
4564	Plain-backed Sparrow	10/2	Myanmar	4624	Chestnut-headed Tesia	10/4	Myanmar
4565	Richard's Pipit	10/2	Myanmar	4625	Striated Bulbul	10/4	Myanmar
4566	Vinous-breasted Starling	10/2	Myanmar	4626	White-browed Nuthatch	10/4	Myanmar
4567	White-throated Babbler	10/2	Myanmar	4627	Black-browed Tit	10/4	Myanmar
4568	Brown Prinia	10/2	Myanmar	4628	Black-bibbed Tit	10/4	Myanmar
4569	Oriental Reed-Warbler	10/2	Myanmar	4629	Yellow-billed Blue-Magpie	10/4	Myanmar
4570	Streak-eared Bulbul	10/2	Myanmar	4630	Green Shrike-Babbler	10/4	Myanmar
4571	Burmese Bushlark	10/2	Myanmar	4631	Blyth's Shrike-Babbler	10/4	Myanmar
4572	Burmese Shrike	10/2	Myanmar	4632	Black-headed Shrike-Babbler	10/4	Myanmar
4573	Chinese Francolin	10/2	Myanmar	4633	Bay Woodpecker	10/4	Myanmar
4574	House Swift	10/2	Myanmar	4634	Darjeeling Woodpecker	10/4	Myanmar
4575	Plaintive Cuckoo	10/2	Myanmar	4635	Golden-throated Barbet	10/4	Myanmar
4576	Lesser Cuckoo	10/2	Myanmar	4636	Cook's Swift	10/4	Myanmar
4577	Chinese Pond-Heron	10/2	Myanmar	4637	Ashy Wood-Pigeon	10/4	Myanmar
4578	Taiga Flycatcher	10/2	Myanmar	4638	Green-tailed Sunbird	10/4	Myanmar
4579	Dusky Warbler	10/2	Myanmar	4639	Black-backed Forktail	10/4	Myanmar
4580	Hooded Treepie	10/2	Myanmar	4640	Rusty-fronted Barwing	10/4	Myanmar
4581	Amur Falcon	10/2	Myanmar	4641	Rusty-capped Fulvetta	10/4	Myanmar
4582	Chinese Sparrowhawk	10/2	Myanmar	4642	Spotted Elachura	10/4	Myanmar
4583	Scarlet-backed Flowerpecker	10/3	Myanmar	4643	Gray-bellied Tesia	10/4	Myanmar

No.	Species	Date	Country	No.	Species	Date	Country
4644	Large Niltava	10/5	Myanmar	4704	Rosy Pipit	10/9	China
4645	Red-faced Liocichla	10/5	Myanmar	4705	Rufous-breasted Accentor	10/9	China
4646	Silver-eared Mesia	10/5	Myanmar	4706	White-capped Redstart	10/9	China
4647	Striped Laughingthrush	10/5	Myanmar	4707	Blue-fronted Redstart	10/9	China
4648	Chestnut-crowned Warbler	10/5	Myanmar	4708	Golden Bush-Robin (218)	10/9	China
4649	Two-barred Warbler	10/5	Myanmar	4709	Himalayan Bluetail	10/9	China
4650	Mountain Tailorbird	10/5	Myanmar	4710	Grandala	10/9	China
4651	Greater Necklaced Laughingthrush	10/5	Myanmar	4711	Elliot's Laughingthrush	10/9	China
4652	Lesser Racket-tailed Drongo	10/5	Myanmar	4712	Giant Laughingthrush (218)	10/9	China
4653	Mountain Hawk-Eagle	10/5	Myanmar	4713	Chinese Fulvetta	10/9	China
4654	Oriental Cuckoo	10/5	Myanmar	4714	Sichuan Leaf Warbler	10/9	China
4655	Brown Shrike	10/6	Myanmar	4715	Alpine Leaf Warbler	10/9	China
4656	Chestnut-tailed Starling	10/6	Myanmar	4716	Yellowish-bellied Bush-Warbler	10/9	China
4657	White-browed Scimitar-Babbler	10/6	Myanmar	4717	White-browed Tit-Warbler	10/9	China
4658	Japanese Tit	10/6	Myanmar	4718	Sichuan Tit	10/9	China
4659	Black-headed Greenfinch	10/6	Myanmar	4719	Himalayan Griffon	10/9	China
4660	Black-collared Starling	10/6	Myanmar	4720	White Eared-Pheasant	10/9	China
4661	Black-breasted Thrush	10/6	Myanmar	4721	Tibetan Snowcock	10/9	China
4662	Spectacled Barwing	10/6	Myanmar	4722	Daurian Redstart	10/9	China
4663	Black-backed Sibia	10/6	Myanmar	4723	Chinese Leaf Warbler	10/9	China
4664	White-browed Laughingthrush	10/6	Myanmar	4724	Yellow-streaked Warbler	10/9	China
4665	Rufous-fronted Babbler	10/6	Myanmar	4725	Gray-crested Tit	10/9	China
4666	Golden Babbler	10/6	Myanmar	4726	Rufous-vented Tit	10/9	China
4667	Spot-breasted Parrotbill	10/6	Myanmar	4727	White-winged Grosbeak	10/9	China
4668	Hill Prinia	10/6	Myanmar	4728	Collared Grosbeak	10/9	China
4669	Striated Grassbird	10/6	Myanmar	4729	Vinaceous Rosefinch	10/9	China
4670	Davison's Leaf Warbler	10/6	Myanmar	4730	Gray-headed Bullfinch	10/9	China
4671	White-bellied Erpornis	10/6	Myanmar	4731	Blyth's Pipit	10/9	China
4672	Gray-headed Parakeet	10/6	Myanmar	4732	Chestnut Thrush	10/9	China
4673	Blue-bearded Bee-eater	10/6	Myanmar	4733	Barred Laughingthrush	10/9	China
4674	Black-tailed Crake	10/6	Myanmar	4734	Great Parrotbill	10/9	China
4677	Yellow-vented Flowerpecker	10/7	Myanmar	4735	Buff-throated Warbler	10/9	China
4676	Orange-bellied Leafbird	10/7	Myanmar	4736	Eastern Buzzard	10/9	China
4677	Hill Blue-Flycatcher	10/7	Myanmar	4737	Gray-faced Buzzard	10/9	China
4678	White-gorgeted Flycatcher	10/7	Myanmar	4738	Blood Pheasant	10/9	China
4679	Scarlet-faced Liocichla	10/7	Myanmar	4739	Three-banded Rosefinch	10/10	China
4680	Silver-eared Laughingthrush	10/7	Myanmar	4740	Crimson-browed Finch	10/10	China
4681	Burmese Yuhina	10/7	Myanmar	4741	White-backed Thrush	10/10	China
4682	Slaty-bellied Tesia	10/7	Myanmar	4742	White-throated Redstart	10/10	China
4683	Yellow-cheeked Tit	10/7	Myanmar	4743	Crested Tit-Warbler	10/10	China
4684	Slender-billed Oriole	10/7	Myanmar	4744	Himalayan Buzzard	10/10	China
4685	Gray-backed Shrike	10/7	Myanmar	4745	Little Bunting	10/10	China
4686	Gray-chinned Minivet	10/7	Myanmar	4746	Pere David's Laughingthrush	10/10	China
4687	Common Flameback	10/7	Myanmar	4747	White-browed Tit	10/10	China
4688	Red-headed Trogon	10/7	Myanmar	4748	Ground Tit	10/10	China
4689	Green-billed Malkoha	10/7	Myanmar	4749	Chinese Gray Shrike	10/10	China
4690	Pin-tailed Pigeon	10/7	Myanmar	4750	Black-necked Crane	10/10	China
4693	Forest Wagtail	10/8	Myanmar	4751	Upland Buzzard	10/10	China
4694	Olive-backed Sunbird	10/8	Myanmar	4752	White-tailed Eagle	10/10	China
4693	Ruby-cheeked Sunbird	10/8	Myanmar	4753	Azure-winged Magpie	10/10	China
4694	Lesser Necklaced Laughingthrush	10/8	Myanmar	4754	Brown-headed Gull	10/10	China
4695	Ferruginous Babbler	10/8	Myanmar	4755	Rufous-necked Snowfinch	10/10	China
4696	Dark-necked Tailorbird	10/8	Myanmar	4756	White-rumped Snowfinch	10/10	China
4697	Stripe-throated Bulbul	10/8	Myanmar	4757	Twite	10/10	China
4698	Racket-tailed Treepie	10/8	Myanmar	4758	White-cheeked Starling	10/10	China
4699	Green Peafowl	10/8	Myanmar	4759	Saker Falcon	10/10	China
4700	Streaked Rosefinch	10/9	China	4760	Godlewski's Bunting	10/11	China
4701	Chinese White-browed Rosefinch	10/9	China	4761	Blue Eared-Pheasant	10/11	China
4702	Pink-rumped Rosefinch	10/9	China	4762	Robin Accentor	10/11	China
4703	Plain Mountain-Finch	10/9	China	4763	Hodgson's Redstart	10/11	China

4764	Sukatschev's Laughingthrush	10/11	China
4765	Hodgson's Treecreeper	10/11	China
4766	Przevalski's Nuthatch	10/11	China
4767	Daurian Jackdaw	10/11	China
4768	Asian House-Martin	10/11	China
4769	Black-streaked Scimitar-Babbler	10/11	China
4770	Kloss's Leaf Warbler	10/11	China
4771	Sooty Tit	10/11	China
4772	Slaty Bunting	10/12	China
4773	White-browed Shortwing	10/12	China
4774	Spotted Laughingthrush	10/12	China
4775	Moustached Laughingthrush	10/12	China
4776	Chinese Hwamei	10/12	China
4777	David's Fulvetta	10/12	China
4778	Rufous-capped Babbler	10/12	China
4779	Vinous-throated Parrotbill	10/12	China
4780	Spectacled Fulvetta	10/12	China
4781	Claudia's Leaf Warbler	10/12	China
4782	Brownish-flanked Bush-Warbler	10/12	China
4783	Rufous-faced Warbler	10/12	China
4784	Brown-breasted Bulbul	10/12	China
4785	Collared Finchbill	10/12	China
4786	Yellow-bellied Tit	10/12	China
4787	Eurasian Nutcracker	10/12	China
4788	Golden Pheasant	10/12	China
4789	Collared Crow	10/12	China
4790	Light-vented Bulbul	10/12	China
4791	Chinese Blackbird	10/12	China
4792	Eastern Spot-billed Duck	10/12	China
4793	Oriental Greenfinch	10/12	China
4794	Red-billed Starling	10/12	China
4795	Yellow-billed Grosbeak	10/12	China
4796	Gray-faced Liocichla	10/13	China
4797	Red-winged Laughingthrush	10/13	China
4798	White-collared Yuhina	10/13	China
4799	Gray-hooded Fulvetta	10/13	China
4800	Japanese White-eye	10/13	China
4801	Golden-breasted Fulvetta	10/13	China
4802	Speckled Wood-Pigeon	10/13	China
4803	Slaty-backed Forktail	10/13	China
4804	Little Forktail	10/13	China
4805	Ashy-throated Parrotbill	10/13	China
4806	Fork-tailed Sunbird	10/13	China
4807	Black-headed Sibia	10/13	China
4808	Chinese Bamboo-Partridge	10/13	China
4809	Crested Myna	10/13	China
4810	White-crowned Forktail	10/13	China
4811	White-browed Bush-Robin	10/14	China
4812	Black-faced Laughingthrush	10/14	China
4813	Gray-hooded Parrotbill	10/14	China
4814	Chestnut-crowned Bush-Warbler	10/14	China
4815	Fire-capped Tit	10/14	China
4816	Long-billed Plover	10/14	China
4817	Northern Boobook	10/14	China
4818	Collared Scops-Owl	10/14	China
4819	Dusky Fulvetta	10/15	China
4820	Chinese Cupwing	10/15	China
4821	Savanna Nightjar	10/15	Taiwan
4822	White-tailed Robin	10/16	Taiwan
4823	Taiwan Whistling-Thrush	10/16	Taiwan

4824	Vivid Niltava	10/16	Taiwan
4825	Steere's Liocichla	10/16	Taiwan
4826	White-eared Sibia	10/16	Taiwan
4827	Black-necklaced Scimitar-Babbler	10/16	Taiwan
4828	Taiwan Cupwing	10/16	Taiwan
4829	Yellow Tit	10/16	Taiwan
4830	Swinhoe's Pheasant (217)	10/16	Taiwan
4831	Taiwan Partridge	10/16	Taiwan
4832	Taiwan Yuhina	10/16	Taiwan
4833	Collared Bush-Robin	10/16	Taiwan
4834	White-whiskered Laughingthrush	10/16	Taiwan
4835	Rusty Laughingthrush	10/16	Taiwan
4836	Morrison's Fulvetta	10/16	Taiwan
4837	Taiwan Fulvetta	10/16	Taiwan
4838	Flamecrest	10/16	Taiwan
4839	Taiwan Rosefinch	10/16	Taiwan
4840	Taiwan Bush-Warbler	10/16	Taiwan
4841	Striated Swallow	10/16	Taiwan
4842	Mikado Pheasant (217)	10/16	Taiwan
4843	Silver-backed Needletail	10/16	Taiwan
4844	Taiwan Barwing	10/17	Taiwan
4845	Snowy-browed Flycatcher	10/17	Taiwan
4846	Taiwan Hwamei	10/17	Taiwan
4847	Varied Tit	10/17	Taiwan
4848	Pacific Swallow	10/17	Taiwan
4849	Taiwan Barbet	10/17	Taiwan
4850	Taiwan Scimitar-Babbler	10/17	Taiwan
4851	Blue-and-white Flycatcher	10/17	Taiwan
4852	Taiwan Blue-Magpie (217)	10/17	Taiwan
4853	Malayan Night-Heron	10/17	Taiwan
4854	Taiwan Bamboo-Partridge	10/17	Taiwan
4855	Arctic/Kamchatka Leaf/ Japanese Leaf Warbler	10/18	Taiwan
4856	Black-faced Spoonbill	10/18	Taiwan
4857	Javan Myna	10/18	Taiwan
4858	Red-necked Stint	10/18	Taiwan
4859	Japanese Sparrowhawk	10/18	Taiwan
4860	Eastern Yellow Wagtail	10/18	Taiwan
4861	Oriental Pratincole	10/18	Taiwan
4862	Eastern Marsh-Harrier	10/18	Taiwan
4863	Siberian Crane (221–223)	10/18	Taiwan
4864	Rufous-tailed Robin	10/18	Taiwan
4865	Pacific Reef-Heron	10/18	Taiwan
4866	Collared Kingfisher	10/19	Philippines
4867	Gray-tailed Tattler	10/19	Philippines
4868	Philippine Pied-Fantail	10/19	Philippines
4869	Pale Spiderhunter	10/19	Philippines
4870	Lovely Sunbird	10/19	Philippines
4871	Palawan Flowerpecker	10/19	Philippines
4872	Common Hill Myna	10/19	Philippines
4873	White-vented Shama	10/19	Philippines
4874	Gray-streaked Flycatcher	10/19	Philippines
4875	Pin-striped Tit-Babbler	10/19	Philippines
4876	Rufous-tailed Tailorbird	10/19	Philippines
4877	Sulphur-bellied Bulbul	10/19	Philippines
4878	Gray-throated Bulbul	10/19	Philippines
4879	Palawan Tit	10/19	Philippines
4880	Fiery Minivet	10/19	Philippines
4881	Blue-naped Parrot	10/19	Philippines
4882	Ameline Swiftlet	10/19	Philippines

4883	Glossy Swiftlet	10/19	Philippines
4884	Chestnut-breasted Malkoha	10/19	Philippines
4885	Violet Cuckoo	10/19	Philippines
4886	White-bellied Sea-Eagle	10/19	Philippines
4887	Philippine Cockatoo	10/19	Philippines
4888	Great Slaty Woodpecker	10/19	Philippines
4889	Palawan Hornbill	10/19	Philippines
4890	Pygmy Swiftlet	10/19	Philippines
4891	Lesser Coucal	10/19	Philippines
4892	Zebra Dove	10/19	Philippines
4893	Hooded Pitta	10/19	Philippines
4894	Palawan Frogmouth	10/19	Philippines
4895	Ruddy Kingfisher	10/20	Philippines
4896	Spotted Wood-Owl	10/20	Philippines
4897	White-bellied Munia	10/20	Philippines
4898	Asian Glossy Starling	10/20	Philippines
4899	Palawan Blue-Flycatcher	10/20	Philippines
4900	Ashy-headed Babbler	10/20	Philippines
4901	Slender-billed Crow	10/20	Philippines
4902	Blue Paradise-Flycatcher	10/20	Philippines
4903	Dark-throated Oriole	10/20	Philippines
4904	Mangrove Whistler	10/20	Philippines
4905	Blue-headed Racquet-tail	10/20	Philippines
4906	Red-headed Flameback	10/20	Philippines
4907	Germain's Swiftlet	10/20	Philippines
4908	Palawan Peacock-Pheasant	10/20	Philippines
4909	Tabon Scrubfowl	10/20	Philippines
4910	Pied Triller	10/20	Philippines
4911	Luzon Boobook	10/21	Philippines
4912	Chocolate Boobook	10/21	Philippines
4913	Philippine Scops-Owl	10/21	Philippines
4914	Spotted Kingfisher	10/21	Philippines
4915	Brown-breasted Kingfisher	10/21	Philippines
4916	Coleto	10/21	Philippines
4917	Stripe-sided Rhabdornis	10/21	Philippines
4918	Philippine Bulbul	10/21	Philippines
4919	Yellow-vented Bulbul	10/21	Philippines
4920	Balicassiao	10/21	Philippines
4921	Blackish Cuckooshrike	10/21	Philippines
4922	Bar-bellied Cuckooshrike	10/21	Philippines
4923	Guaiabero	10/21	Philippines
4924	Green Racquet-tail	10/21	Philippines
4925	Luzon Flameback	10/21	Philippines
4926	Whiskered Treeswift	10/21	Philippines
4927	Philippine Coucal	10/21	Philippines
4928	Red-crested Malkoha	10/21	Philippines
4929	White-eared Brown-Dove	10/21	Philippines
4930	Plain Bush-hen	10/21	Philippines
4931	Philippine Hawk-Eagle	10/21	Philippines
4932	White-browed Shama	10/21	Philippines
4933	Green-backed Tailorbird	10/21	Philippines
4934	White-breasted Woodswallow	10/21	Philippines
4935	Northern Sooty-Woodpecker	10/21	Philippines
4936	Rufous-crowned Bee-eater	10/21	Philippines
4937	Luzon Hornbill	10/21	Philippines
4938	Rufous Coucal	10/21	Philippines
4939	Philippine Serpent-Eagle	10/21	Philippines
4940	Philippine Hanging-Parrot	10/21	Philippines
4941	Pechora Pipit	10/22	Philippines
4942	Pygmy Flowerpecker	10/22	Philippines
4943	White-bellied Flowerpecker	10/22	Philippines
4944	Ferruginous Flycatcher	10/22	Philippines
4945	Philippine Fairy-bluebird	10/22	Philippines
4946	Yellowish White-eye	10/22	Philippines
4947	Gray-backed Tailorbird	10/22	Philippines
4948	Elegant Tit	10/22	Philippines
4949	Rufous Paradise-Flycatcher	10/22	Philippines
4950	Blue-headed Fantail	10/22	Philippines
4951	Yellow-bellied Whistler	10/22	Philippines
4952	Philippine Trogon	10/22	Philippines
4953	Scale-feathered Malkoha	10/22	Philippines
4954	Amethyst Brown-Dove	10/22	Philippines
4955	Luzon Bleeding-heart	10/22	Philippines
4956	Philippine Cuckoo-Dove	10/22	Philippines
4957	Lowland White-eye	10/22	Philippines
4958	Philippine Woodpecker	10/22	Philippines
4959	Flaming Sunbird	10/22	Philippines
4960	Red-striped Flowerpecker	10/22	Philippines
4961	Ashy Minivet	10/22	Philippines
4962	Indigo-banded Kingfisher	10/22	Philippines
4963	Spotted Buttonquail	10/22	Philippines
4964	Philippine Leaf Warbler	10/23	Philippines
4965	Everett's Scops-Owl	10/23	Philippines
4966	Northern Silvery-Kingfisher	10/23	Philippines
4967	Purple-throated Sunbird	10/23	Philippines
4968	Striated Wren-Babbler	10/23	Philippines
4969	Yellow-breasted Tailorbird	10/23	Philippines
4970	Rufous-fronted Tailorbird	10/23	Philippines
4971	Samar Hornbill	10/23	Philippines
4972	Great Eared-Nightjar	10/23	Philippines
4973	Philippine Frogmouth	10/23	Philippines
4974	Black-faced Coucal	10/23	Philippines
4975	Philippine Drongo-Cuckoo	10/23	Philippines
4976	Barred Rail	10/23	Philippines
4977	Bohol Sunbird	10/24	Philippines
4978	Chestnut-tailed Jungle-Flycatcher	10/24	Philippines
4979	Brown Tit-Babbler	10/24	Philippines
4980	Black-crowned Babbler	10/24	Philippines
4981	Yellow-wattled Bulbul	10/24	Philippines
4982	Visayan Blue-Fantail	10/24	Philippines
4983	Philippine Oriole	10/24	Philippines
4984	Azure-breasted Pitta	10/24	Philippines
4985	Rufous-lored Kingfisher	10/24	Philippines
4986	Yellow-breasted Fruit-Dove	10/24	Philippines
4987	Chestnut Munia	10/24	Philippines
4988	Javan Pond-Heron	10/24	Philippines
4989	Mindanao Scops-Owl	10/25	Philippines
4990	Giant Scops-Owl	10/25	Philippines
4991	Cinnamon Ibon (231)	10/26	Philippines
4992	Gray-hooded Sunbird	10/26	Philippines
4993	Bicolored Flowerpecker	10/26	Philippines
4994	Olive-capped Flowerpecker	10/26	Philippines
4995	Stripe-breasted Rhabdornis (230)	10/26	Philippines
4996	Island Flycatcher (231)	10/26	Philippines
4997	Mountain White-eye (231)	10/26	Philippines
4998	Tawny Grassbird (231)	10/26	Philippines
4999	Mountain Warbler (231)	10/26	Philippines
5000	Flame-crowned Flowerpecker (231)	10/26	Philippines
5001	Rufous-headed Tailorbird	10/26	Philippines
5002	Sulphur-billed Nuthatch	10/26	Philippines

5003	Black-and-cinnamon Fantail (227)	10/26	Philippines
5004	McGregor's Cuckooshrike	10/26	Philippines
5005	Mindanao Racquet-tail	10/26	Philippines
5006	Philippine Falconet	10/26	Philippines
5007	Buff-spotted Flameback	10/26	Philippines
5008	Blue-capped Kingfisher	10/26	Philippines
5009	Mindanao Hornbill	10/26	Philippines
5010	Philippine Swiftlet	10/26	Philippines
5011	Brush Cuckoo	10/26	Philippines
5012	Pinsker's Hawk-Eagle	10/26	Philippines
5013	Bundok Flycatcher	10/27	Philippines
5014	Long-tailed Bush-Warbler	10/27	Philippines
5015	Ashy Thrush	10/28	Philippines
5016	Mangrove Blue-Flycatcher	10/28	Philippines
5017	Philippine Magpie-Robin	10/28	Philippines
5018	Golden-bellied Gerygone	10/28	Philippines
5019	Philippine Nightjar	10/28	Philippines
5020	White-browed Crake (43)	10/28	Philippines
5021	Van Hassell's Sunbird	10/29	Thailand
5022	Blue-winged Leafbird	10/29	Thailand
5023	Hainan Blue-Flycatcher	10/29	Thailand
5024	Abbott's Babbler	10/29	Thailand
5025	Pale-legged Leaf Warbler	10/29	Thailand
5026	Puff-throated Bulbul	10/29	Thailand
5027	Great Iora	10/29	Thailand
5028	Banded Broadbill	10/29	Thailand
5029	Banded Kingfisher	10/29	Thailand
5030	Oriental Pied-Hornbill	10/29	Thailand
5031	Thick-billed Pigeon	10/29	Thailand
5032	Scaly-breasted Partridge	10/29	Thailand
5033	Golden-headed Cisticola	10/29	Thailand
5034	Sulphur-breasted Warbler	10/29	Thailand
5035	Gray-eyed Bulbul	10/29	Thailand
5036	Moustached Barbet	10/29	Thailand
5037	Green-eared Barbet	10/29	Thailand
5038	Blue-eared Barbet	10/29	Thailand
5039	Plain Flowerpecker	10/29	Thailand
5040	Siberian Blue Robin	10/29	Thailand
5041	Great Myna	10/29	Thailand
5042	Red-breasted Parakeet	10/29	Thailand
5043	Laced Woodpecker	10/30	Thailand
5044	Black-throated Laughingthrush	10/30	Thailand
5045	Large Scimitar-Babbler	10/30	Thailand
5046	Orange-breasted Trogon	10/30	Thailand
5047	Coral-billed Ground-Cuckoo	10/30	Thailand
5048	Limestone Wren-Babbler	10/30	Thailand
5049	Malaysian Pied-Fantail	10/30	Thailand
5050	Sooty-headed Bulbul	10/30	Thailand
5051	Java Sparrow	10/30	Thailand
5052	Black-capped Kingfisher	10/31	Thailand
5053	Asian Dowitcher	10/31	Thailand
5054	Plain-throated Sunbird	10/31	Thailand
5055	Long-toed Stint	10/31	Thailand
5056	Gray-headed Lapwing	10/31	Thailand
5057	Malaysian Plover	10/31	Thailand
5058	Chinese Egret	10/31	Thailand
5059	Nordmann's Greenshank	10/31	Thailand
5060	Milky Stork	10/31	Thailand
5061	Yellow Bittern	10/31	Thailand
5062	Black-browed Reed-Warbler	11/1	Thailand
5063	Asian Golden Weaver	11/1	Thailand
5064	Eared Pitta	11/1	Thailand
5065	Black-headed Bulbul	11/1	Thailand
5066	Red-legged Crake	11/1	Thailand
5067	Chestnut-capped Babbler	11/1	Thailand
5068	Large-tailed Nightjar	11/1	Thailand
5069	Yellow-eared Spiderhunter	11/2	Thailand
5070	Thick-billed Flowerpecker	11/2	Thailand
5071	Sultan Tit	11/2	Thailand
5072	Greater Yellownape	11/2	Thailand
5073	White-fronted Scops-Owl	11/2	Thailand
5074	Fork-tailed Drongo-Cuckoo	11/2	Thailand
5075	Rufous-bellied Eagle	11/2	Thailand
5076	Collared Babbler	11/2	Thailand
5077	Ratchet-tailed Treepie	11/2	Thailand
5078	Streaked Spiderhunter	11/2	Thailand
5079	Plain Sunbird	11/2	Thailand
5080	Orange-bellied Flowerpecker	11/2	Thailand
5081	Greater Green Leafbird	11/2	Thailand
5082	Rufous-browed Flycatcher	11/2	Thailand
5083	Spot-necked Babbler	11/2	Thailand
5084	Everett's White-eye	11/2	Thailand
5085	Plain-tailed Warbler	11/2	Thailand
5086	Yellow-bellied Warbler	11/2	Thailand
5087	Ochraceous Bulbul	11/2	Thailand
5088	Amur Paradise-Flycatcher	11/2	Thailand
5089	Brown-rumped Minivet	11/2	Thailand
5090	Maroon-breasted Philentoma	11/2	Thailand
5091	Black-and-yellow Broadbill	11/2	Thailand
5092	Long-tailed Broadbill	11/2	Thailand
5093	Black-and-buff Woodpecker	11/2	Thailand
5094	White-browed Piculet	11/2	Thailand
5095	Red-bearded Bee-eater	11/2	Thailand
5096	Chestnut-bellied Malkoha	11/2	Thailand
5097	Jerdon's Baza	11/2	Thailand
5098	Gray Peacock-Pheasant	11/2	Thailand
5099	Bar-backed Partridge	11/2	Thailand
5100	Black-and-red Broadbill	11/3	Thailand
5101	Black-thighed Falconet	11/3	Thailand
5102	Gray-rumped Treeswift	11/3	Thailand
5103	Spoon-billed Sandpiper (237)	11/3	Thailand
5104	Indochinese Bushlark	11/3	Thailand
5105	Spot-winged Thrush	11/4	Sri Lanka
5106	Brown-breasted Flycatcher	11/4	Sri Lanka
5107	Orange-billed Babbler	11/4	Sri Lanka
5108	Sri Lanka White-eye	11/4	Sri Lanka
5109	Black-capped Bulbul	11/4	Sri Lanka
5110	Sri Lanka Swallow	11/4	Sri Lanka
5111	Sri Lanka Drongo	11/4	Sri Lanka
5112	Indian Pitta	11/4	Sri Lanka
5113	Sri Lanka Hanging-Parrot	11/4	Sri Lanka
5114	Layard's Parakeet	11/4	Sri Lanka
5115	Crimson-backed Flameback	11/4	Sri Lanka
5116	Yellow-fronted Barbet	11/4	Sri Lanka
5117	Black-backed Dwarf-Kingfisher	11/4	Sri Lanka
5118	Sri Lanka Gray Hornbill	11/4	Sri Lanka
5119	Chestnut-backed Owlet	11/4	Sri Lanka
5120	Serendib Scops-Owl	11/4	Sri Lanka
5121	Green-billed Coucal	11/4	Sri Lanka
5122	Sri Lanka Green-Pigeon	11/4	Sri Lanka

5123	Sri Lanka Junglefowl	11/4	Sri Lanka	5183	Rufous-collared Kingfisher	11/9	Malaysia
5124	White-throated Flowerpecker	11/5	Sri Lanka	5184	Scarlet-rumped Trogon	11/9	Malaysia
5125	Indian Blue Robin	11/5	Sri Lanka	5185	Red-billed Malkoha	11/9	Malaysia
5126	Ashy-headed Laughingthrush	11/5	Sri Lanka	5186	Gray-headed Fish-Eagle	11/9	Malaysia
5127	Brown-capped Babbler	11/5	Sri Lanka	5187	Rufous-bellied Swallow	11/10	Malaysia
5128	Sri Lanka Scimitar-Babbler	11/5	Sri Lanka	5188	Blue-crowned Hanging-Parrot	11/10	Malaysia
5129	Sri Lanka Blue-Magpie	11/5	Sri Lanka	5189	Bushy-crested Hornbill	11/10	Malaysia
5130	White-faced Starling	11/6	Sri Lanka	5190	Silver-rumped Needletail	11/10	Malaysia
5131	Sri Lanka Myna	11/6	Sri Lanka	5191	Malaysian Nightjar	11/10	Malaysia
5132	Sri Lanka Thrush	11/6	Sri Lanka	5192	Little Cuckoo-Dove	11/10	Malaysia
5133	Black-headed Cuckooshrike	11/6	Sri Lanka	5193	Large Hawk-Cuckoo	11/10	Malaysia
5134	Red-faced Malkoha	11/6	Sri Lanka	5194	Pygmy Blue-Flycatcher	11/10	Malaysia
5135	Sri Lanka Spurfowl	11/6	Sri Lanka	5195	Lesser Shortwing	11/10	Malaysia
5136	Malayan Laughingthrush	11/7	Malaysia	5196	Black-and-crimson Oriole	11/10	Malaysia
5137	Chestnut-capped Laughingthrush	11/7	Malaysia	5197	Black-eared Shrike-Babbler	11/10	Malaysia
5138	Streaked Wren-Babbler	11/7	Malaysia	5198	Fire-tufted Barbet	11/10	Malaysia
5139	Long-tailed Sibia	11/7	Malaysia	5199	Buff-breasted Babbler	11/10	Malaysia
5140	Mountain Fulvetta	11/7	Malaysia	5200	Rufescent Prinia	11/10	Malaysia
5141	Gray-throated Babbler	11/7	Malaysia	5201	Indian Cuckoo	11/10	Malaysia
5142	Sooty Barbet	11/7	Malaysia	5202	Black Laughingthrush	11/11	Malaysia
5143	Red-eyed Bulbul	11/7	Malaysia	5203	Gray-breasted Partridge	11/11	Malaysia
5144	Scaly-breasted Bulbul	11/7	Malaysia	5204	Lesser Adjutant	11/11	Malaysia
5145	Blyth's Hawk-Eagle	11/7	Malaysia	5205	Ashy Tailorbird	11/11	Malaysia
5146	Pink-necked Pigeon	11/7	Malaysia	5206	Sunda Woodpecker	11/11	Malaysia
5147	Wrinkled Hornbill	11/8	Malaysia	5207	Korean Flycatcher	11/11	Malaysia
5148	Tiger Shrike	11/8	Malaysia	5208	Black Baza	11/11	Malaysia
5149	Black-browed Barbet	11/8	Malaysia	5209	White-headed Munia	11/11	Malaysia
5150	Gold-whiskered Barbet	11/8	Malaysia	5210	Pied Harrier	11/11	Malaysia
5151	Rhinoceros Hornbill	11/8	Malaysia	5211	Cinnamon Bittern	11/11	Malaysia
5152	Ferruginous Partridge	11/8	Malaysia	5212	Copper-throated Sunbird	11/12	Malaysia
5153	Purple-naped Spiderhunter	11/8	Malaysia	5213	Daurian Starling	11/12	Malaysia
5154	Long-billed Spiderhunter	11/8	Malaysia	5214	Pin-tailed Parrotfinch	11/13	Malaysia
5155	Red-throated Sunbird	11/8	Malaysia	5215	Yellow-breasted Flowerpecker	11/13	Malaysia
5156	Chestnut-rumped Babbler	11/8	Malaysia	5216	Rufous-chested Flycatcher	11/13	Malaysia
5157	Spectacled Bulbul	11/8	Malaysia	5217	Brown-chested Jungle-Flycatcher	11/13	Malaysia
5158	Cream-vented Bulbul	11/8	Malaysia	5218	Rufous-backed Dwarf-Kingfisher	11/13	Malaysia
5159	Malayan Banded-Pitta	11/8	Malaysia	5219	Blue-banded Kingfisher	11/13	Malaysia
5160	Buff-necked Woodpecker	11/8	Malaysia	5220	Red-naped Trogon	11/13	Malaysia
5161	Black Hornbill	11/8	Malaysia	5221	Blue-eared Kingfisher	11/14	Malaysia
5162	Raffles's Malkoha	11/8	Malaysia	5222	Gray-cheeked Bulbul	11/14	Malaysia
5163	Jambu Fruit-Dove	11/8	Malaysia	5223	White-fronted Falconet	11/14	Malaysia
5164	Spectacled Spiderhunter	11/9	Malaysia	5224	Black-bellied Malkoha	11/14	Malaysia
5165	Crimson-breasted Flowerpecker	11/9	Malaysia	5225	Wallace's Hawk-Eagle	11/14	Malaysia
5166	Black-capped Babbler	11/9	Malaysia	5226	Dusky Munia	11/15	Malaysia
5167	Sooty-capped Babbler	11/9	Malaysia	5227	Lesser Green Leafbird	11/15	Malaysia
5168	Chestnut-winged Babbler	11/9	Malaysia	5228	Brown Fulvetta	11/15	Malaysia
5169	Buff-vented Bulbul	11/9	Malaysia	5229	Black-throated Babbler	11/15	Malaysia
5170	Hairy-backed Bulbul	11/9	Malaysia	5230	Fluffy-backed Tit-Babbler	11/15	Malaysia
5171	Olive-winged Bulbul	11/9	Malaysia	5231	Streaked Bulbul	11/15	Malaysia
5172	Blyth's Paradise-Flycatcher	11/9	Malaysia	5232	Yellow-bellied Bulbul	11/15	Malaysia
5173	Rufous-winged Philentoma	11/9	Malaysia	5233	Green Iora	11/15	Malaysia
5174	Black-winged Flycatcher-shrike	11/9	Malaysia	5234	Black-crowned Pitta	11/15	Malaysia
5175	Garnet Pitta	11/9	Malaysia	5235	Gray-and-buff Woodpecker	11/15	Malaysia
5176	Dusky Broadbill	11/9	Malaysia	5236	Banded Woodpecker	11/15	Malaysia
5177	Orange-backed Woodpecker	11/9	Malaysia	5237	Rufous Piculet	11/15	Malaysia
5178	Buff-rumped Woodpecker	11/9	Malaysia	5238	Puff-backed Bulbul	11/15	Malaysia
5179	Checker-throated Woodpecker	11/9	Malaysia	5239	White-crowned Hornbill	11/15	Malaysia
5180	Crimson-winged Woodpecker	11/9	Malaysia	5240	Chestnut-winged Cuckoo	11/15	Malaysia
5181	Red-crowned Barbet	11/9	Malaysia	5241	Buffy Fish-Owl	11/15	Malaysia
5182	Blue-throated Bee-eater	11/9	Malaysia	5242	Barred Eagle-Owl	11/15	Malaysia

5243	Oriental Bay-Owl (257–258)	11/15	Malaysia
5244	Yellow-rumped Flowerpecker	11/16	Malaysia
5245	Malaysian Blue-Flycatcher	11/16	Malaysia
5246	Striped Wren-Babbler	11/16	Malaysia
5247	White-chested Babbler	11/16	Malaysia
5248	Bold-striped Tit-Babbler	11/16	Malaysia
5249	Black Magpie	11/16	Malaysia
5250	Brown Barbet	11/16	Malaysia
5251	Moustached Hawk-Cuckoo	11/16	Malaysia
5252	Storm's Stork	11/16	Malaysia
5253	Chestnut-necklaced Partridge	11/16	Malaysia
5254	Scaly-crowned Babbler	11/16	Malaysia
5255	White-nest Swiftlet (237)	11/16	Malaysia
5256	Black-nest Swiftlet	11/16	Malaysia
5257	Mossy-nest Swiftlet	11/16	Malaysia
5258	Long-tailed Parakeet	11/17	Malaysia
5259	Little Green-Pigeon	11/17	Malaysia
5260	Bornean Spiderhunter	11/17	Malaysia
5261	White-tailed Flycatcher	11/17	Malaysia
5262	Gray-headed Babbler	11/17	Malaysia
5263	Gold-faced Barbet	11/17	Malaysia
5264	Yellow-crowned Barbet	11/17	Malaysia
5265	Red-throated Barbet	11/17	Malaysia
5266	Malaysian Hawk-Cuckoo	11/17	Malaysia
5267	Whitehead's Spiderhunter (237)	11/18	Malaysia
5268	Temminck's Sunbird	11/18	Malaysia
5269	Black-sided Flowerpecker	11/18	Malaysia
5270	Mugimaki Flycatcher	11/18	Malaysia
5271	Bornean Whistling-Thrush	11/18	Malaysia
5271	Eyebrowed Jungle-Flycatcher	11/18	Malaysia
5273	Indigo Flycatcher	11/18	Malaysia
5274	Chestnut-hooded Laughingthrush	11/18	Malaysia
5275	Sunda Laughingthrush	11/18	Malaysia
5276	Mountain Wren-Babbler	11/18	Malaysia
5277	Temminck's Babbler	11/18	Malaysia
5278	Black-capped White-eye	11/18	Malaysia
5279	Mountain Black-eye	11/18	Malaysia
5280	Chestnut-crested Yuhina	11/18	Malaysia
5281	Yellow-breasted Warbler	11/18	Malaysia
5282	Sunda Bush-Warbler	11/18	Malaysia
5283	Bornean Stubtail	11/18	Malaysia
5284	Bornean Treepie	11/18	Malaysia
5285	Bornean Green-Magpie	11/18	Malaysia
5286	Bornean Whistler	11/18	Malaysia
5287	Sunda Cuckooshrike	11/18	Malaysia
5288	Whitehead's Broadbill (237)	11/18	Malaysia
5289	Golden-naped Barbet	11/18	Malaysia
5290	Wreathed Hornbill	11/18	Malaysia
5291	Whitehead's Trogon (237)	11/18	Malaysia
5292	Bornean Swiftlet	11/18	Malaysia
5293	Crimson-headed Partridge	11/18	Malaysia
5294	Red-breasted Partridge	11/18	Malaysia
5295	Bornean Leafbird	11/19	Malaysia
5296	Fruit-hunter	11/19	Malaysia
5297	Pygmy White-eye	11/19	Malaysia
5298	Bornean Bulbul	11/19	Malaysia
5299	Mountain Barbet	11/19	Malaysia
5300	Bornean Barbet	11/19	Malaysia
5301	Fulvous-chested Jungle-Flycatcher	11/19	Malaysia
5302	Buff-banded Rail	11/19	Malaysia
5303	Watercock	11/20	Malaysia
5304	Wandering Whistling-Duck	11/20	Malaysia
5305	Short-tailed Babbler	11/20	Malaysia
5306	Maroon Woodpecker	11/20	Malaysia
5307	Diard's Trogon	11/20	Malaysia
5308	Rufous Night-Heron (235)	11/20	Malaysia
5309	Lemon-bellied White-eye	11/21	Indonesia
5310	White-shouldered Triller	11/21	Indonesia
5311	Uniform Swiftlet	11/21	Indonesia
5312	Gray-sided Flowerpecker	11/21	Indonesia
5313	Sulawesi Babbler	11/21	Indonesia
5314	Black-ringed White-eye	11/21	Indonesia
5315	Pale-blue Monarch	11/21	Indonesia
5316	Pale-headed Munia	11/21	Indonesia
5317	Red-backed Buttonquail	11/21	Indonesia
5318	Hylocitrea	11/22	Indonesia
5319	Yellow-sided Flowerpecker	11/22	Indonesia
5320	Finch-billed Myna	11/22	Indonesia
5321	Fiery-browed Myna	11/22	Indonesia
5322	Sulawesi Thrush	11/22	Indonesia
5323	Sulawesi Blue-Flycatcher	11/22	Indonesia
5324	Blue-fronted Flycatcher	11/22	Indonesia
5325	Sulawesi Streaked Flycatcher	11/22	Indonesia
5326	Black-crowned White-eye	11/22	Indonesia
5327	Sulawesi White-eye	11/22	Indonesia
5328	Streak-headed White-eye	11/22	Indonesia
5329	Chestnut-backed Bush-Warbler	11/22	Indonesia
5330	Malia	11/22	Indonesia
5331	Sulawesi Leaf Warbler	11/22	Indonesia
5332	Citrine Canary-Flycatcher	11/22	Indonesia
5333	Rusty-bellied Fantail	11/22	Indonesia
5334	Sulawesi Drongo	11/22	Indonesia
5335	Sulphur-bellied Whistler	11/22	Indonesia
5336	Maroon-backed Whistler	11/22	Indonesia
5337	Pygmy Cuckooshrike	11/22	Indonesia
5338	Ivory-backed Woodswallow	11/22	Indonesia
5339	Sulawesi Myzomela	11/22	Indonesia
5340	Dark-eared Myza	11/22	Indonesia
5341	Yellow-and-green Lorikeet	11/22	Indonesia
5342	Golden-mantled Racquet-tail	11/22	Indonesia
5343	Spotted Kestrel	11/22	Indonesia
5344	Ashy Woodpecker	11/22	Indonesia
5345	Sulawesi Woodpecker	11/22	Indonesia
5346	Purple Needletail	11/22	Indonesia
5347	Yellow-billed Malkoha	11/22	Indonesia
5348	Red-eared Fruit-Dove	11/22	Indonesia
5349	Slender-billed Cuckoo-Dove	11/22	Indonesia
5350	Sulawesi Goshawk	11/22	Indonesia
5351	Sulawesi Hawk-Eagle	11/22	Indonesia
5352	Sunda Teal	11/22	Indonesia
5353	Pacific Black Duck	11/22	Indonesia
5354	Sulawesi Cicadabird	11/23	Indonesia
5355	Cerulean Cuckooshrike	11/23	Indonesia
5356	Sulawesi Hanging-Parrot	11/23	Indonesia
5357	Knobbed Hornbill	11/23	Indonesia
5358	Sulawesi Serpent-Eagle	11/23	Indonesia
5359	Black Sunbird	11/23	Indonesia
5360	Black-faced Munia	11/23	Indonesia
5361	Azure-rumped Parrot	11/24	Indonesia
5362	Sulawesi Hornbill	11/24	Indonesia

5363	Black-billed Koel	11/24	Indonesia
5364	Black-naped Fruit-Dove	11/24	Indonesia
5365	Maleo (237)	11/24	Indonesia
5366	Ornate Lorikeet	11/25	Indonesia
5367	Yellow-breasted Racquet-tail	11/25	Indonesia
5368	Lilac-cheeked Kingfisher	11/25	Indonesia
5369	Sulawesi Swiftlet	11/25	Indonesia
5370	Speckled Boobook	11/25	Indonesia
5371	Bay Coucal	11/25	Indonesia
5372	Maroon-chinned Fruit-Dove	11/25	Indonesia
5373	Isabelline Bush-hen	11/25	Indonesia
5374	Sulawesi Scops-Owl	11/25	Indonesia
5375	Sulawesi Myna	11/26	Indonesia
5376	Purple-winged Roller	11/26	Indonesia
5377	Silver-tipped Imperial-Pigeon	11/26	Indonesia
5378	White-bellied Imperial-Pigeon	11/26	Indonesia
5379	Gray-cheeked Pigeon	11/26	Indonesia
5380	White-necked Myna	11/26	Indonesia
5381	Rusty-backed Thrush	11/26	Indonesia
5382	Elegant Pitta	11/26	Indonesia
5383	Green-backed Kingfisher	11/26	Indonesia
5384	Sulawesi Nightjar	11/26	Indonesia
5385	Stephan's Dove (240)	11/26	Indonesia
5386	Lesser Frigatebird	11/26	Indonesia
5387	White-rumped Cuckooshrike	11/26	Indonesia
5388	Great-billed Kingfisher	11/26	Indonesia
5389	White-rumped Triller	11/27	Indonesia
5390	Sulawesi Dwarf-Kingfisher	11/27	Indonesia
5391	Superb Fruit-Dove	11/27	Indonesia
5392	Spot-tailed Goshawk	11/27	Indonesia
5393	White-faced Cuckoo-Dove	11/27	Indonesia
5394	Scaly-breasted Kingfisher	11/27	Indonesia
5395	Dusky Moorhen	11/28	Indonesia
5396	Black-backed Swamphen	11/28	Indonesia
5397	Blood-breasted Flowerpecker	11/29	Indonesia
5398	Javan Whistling-Thrush	11/29	Indonesia
5399	Olive-backed Tailorbird	11/29	Indonesia
5400	Javan Cuckooshrike	11/29	Indonesia
5401	Yellow-throated Hanging-Parrot	11/29	Indonesia
5402	Freckle-breasted Woodpecker	11/29	Indonesia
5403	Flame-fronted Barbet	11/29	Indonesia
5404	Short-tailed Starling	11/29	Indonesia
5405	Crescent-chested Babbler	11/29	Indonesia
5406	Javan Gray-throated White-eye	11/29	Indonesia
5407	Bar-winged Prinia	11/29	Indonesia
5408	Cave Swiftlet	11/29	Indonesia
5409	Javan Owlet	11/29	Indonesia
5410	Javan Munia	11/29	Indonesia
5411	Javan Kingfisher	11/29	Indonesia
5412	Scarlet-headed Flowerpecker	11/29	Indonesia
5413	Small Blue Kingfisher	11/29	Indonesia
5414	Javan Plover	11/29	Indonesia
5415	Beach Thick-knee	11/29	Indonesia
5416	Little Pied Cormorant	11/29	Indonesia
5417	Island Collared-Dove	11/29	Indonesia
5418	Little Black Cormorant	11/29	Indonesia
5419	Welcome Swallow	11/30	Australia
5420	Australian Ibis	11/30	Australia
5421	Red-capped Flowerpecker	12/1	Papua New Guinea
5422	Black-fronted White-eye	12/1	Papua New Guinea
5423	Papuan Scrub-Robin	12/1	Papua New Guinea
5424	White-faced Robin	12/1	Papua New Guinea
5425	Lemon-bellied Flycatcher	12/1	Papua New Guinea
5426	Raggiana Bird-of-Paradise	12/1	Papua New Guinea
5427	Magnificent Riflebird	12/1	Papua New Guinea
5428	Glossy-mantled Manucode	12/1	Papua New Guinea
5429	Torresian Crow	12/1	Papua New Guinea
5430	Leaden Flycatcher	12/1	Papua New Guinea
5431	Frilled Monarch	12/1	Papua New Guinea
5432	Black-faced Monarch	12/1	Papua New Guinea
5433	Chestnut-bellied Fantail	12/1	Papua New Guinea
5434	Spangled Drongo	12/1	Papua New Guinea
5435	Brown Oriole	12/1	Papua New Guinea
5436	Variable Pitohui	12/1	Papua New Guinea
5437	Hooded Pitohui	12/1	Papua New Guinea
5438	Little Shrikethrush	12/1	Papua New Guinea
5439	Rusty Pitohui	12/1	Papua New Guinea
5440	Black Cicadabird	12/1	Papua New Guinea
5441	White-bellied Cuckooshrike	12/1	Papua New Guinea
5442	Black-faced Cuckooshrike	12/1	Papua New Guinea
5443	Boyer's Cuckooshrike	12/1	Papua New Guinea
5444	Barred Cuckooshrike	12/1	Papua New Guinea
5445	Stout-billed Cuckooshrike	12/1	Papua New Guinea
5446	Black Butcherbird	12/1	Papua New Guinea
5447	Hooded Butcherbird	12/1	Papua New Guinea
5448	Pygmy Longbill	12/1	Papua New Guinea
5449	Black Berrypecker	12/1	Papua New Guinea
5450	Green-backed Gerygone	12/1	Papua New Guinea
5451	Pale-billed Scrubwren	12/1	Papua New Guinea
5452	Rusty Mouse-Warbler	12/1	Papua New Guinea
5453	Helmeted Friarbird	12/1	Papua New Guinea
5454	White-throated Honeyeater	12/1	Papua New Guinea
5455	White-shouldered Fairywren	12/1	Papua New Guinea
5456	Rainbow Lorikeet	12/1	Papua New Guinea
5457	Black-capped Lory	12/1	Papua New Guinea
5458	Red-cheeked Parrot	12/1	Papua New Guinea
5459	Eclectus Parrot (241)	12/1	Papua New Guinea
5460	Papuan King-Parrot	12/1	Papua New Guinea
5461	Buff-breasted Paradise-Kingfisher	12/1	Papua New Guinea
5462	Brown-headed Paradise-Kingfisher	12/1	Papua New Guinea
5463	Yellow-billed Kingfisher	12/1	Papua New Guinea
5464	Rufous-bellied Kookaburra	12/1	Papua New Guinea
5465	Azure Kingfisher	12/1	Papua New Guinea
5466	Barred Owlet-nightjar	12/1	Papua New Guinea
5467	Pheasant Coucal	12/1	Papua New Guinea
5468	White-crowned Koel	12/1	Papua New Guinea
5469	Papuan Mountain-Pigeon	12/1	Papua New Guinea
5470	Zoe Imperial-Pigeon	12/1	Papua New Guinea
5471	Dwarf Fruit-Dove	12/1	Papua New Guinea
5472	Beautiful Fruit-Dove	12/1	Papua New Guinea
5473	Pink-spotted Fruit-Dove	12/1	Papua New Guinea
5474	Wompoo Fruit-Dove	12/1	Papua New Guinea
5475	Great Cuckoo-Dove	12/1	Papua New Guinea
5476	Brown Goshawk	12/1	Papua New Guinea
5477	Pacific Baza	12/1	Papua New Guinea
5478	Forest Bittern	12/1	Papua New Guinea
5479	Brown Quail	12/1	Papua New Guinea
5480	Orange-footed Scrubfowl	12/1	Papua New Guinea
5481	Yellow-legged Brushturkey	12/1	Papua New Guinea
5482	Gray-headed Munia	12/1	Papua New Guinea

5483	Yellow-faced Myna	12/1	Papua New Guinea
5484	Black-backed Butcherbird	12/1	Papua New Guinea
5485	Orange-bellied Fruit-Dove	12/1	Papua New Guinea
5486	Peaceful Dove	12/1	Papua New Guinea
5487	Long-tailed Honey-buzzard	12/1	Papua New Guinea
5488	Willie-wagtail	12/1	Papua New Guinea
5489	Australasian Figbird	12/1	Papua New Guinea
5490	Rufous-banded Honeyeater	12/1	Papua New Guinea
5491	Fawn-breasted Bowerbird	12/1	Papua New Guinea
5492	Rainbow Bee-eater	12/1	Papua New Guinea
5493	Pied Heron	12/1	Papua New Guinea
5494	Torresian Imperial-Pigeon	12/1	Papua New Guinea
5495	Bar-shouldered Dove	12/1	Papua New Guinea
5496	Comb-crested Jacana	12/1	Papua New Guinea
5497	Masked Lapwing	12/1	Papua New Guinea
5498	Australasian Swamphen	12/1	Papua New Guinea
5499	Papuan Frogmouth	12/1	Papua New Guinea
5500	Australasian Grebe	12/1	Papua New Guinea
5501	White-eyed Duck	12/1	Papua New Guinea
5502	Hooded Munia	12/2	Papua New Guinea
5503	Blue-gray Robin	12/2	Papua New Guinea
5504	Stephanie's Astrapia	12/2	Papua New Guinea
5505	Superb Bird-of-Paradise (238)	12/2	Papua New Guinea
5506	Lawes's Parotia	12/2	Papua New Guinea
5507	Great Woodswallow	12/2	Papua New Guinea
5508	Loria's Satinbird	12/2	Papua New Guinea
5509	Buff-faced Scrubwren	12/2	Papua New Guinea
5510	Red-collared Myzomela	12/2	Papua New Guinea
5511	Smoky Honeyeater	12/2	Papua New Guinea
5512	Yellow-browed Melidectes	12/2	Papua New Guinea
5513	Archbold's Nightjar	12/2	Papua New Guinea
5514	Papuan Boobook	12/2	Papua New Guinea
5515	Black-billed Cuckoo-Dove	12/2	Papua New Guinea
5516	Ashy Robin	12/2	Papua New Guinea
5517	White-winged Robin	12/2	Papua New Guinea
5518	Ribbon-tailed Astrapia	12/2	Papua New Guinea
5519	Blue-capped Ifrita	12/2	Papua New Guinea
5520	Friendly Fantail	12/2	Papua New Guinea
5521	Regent Whistler	12/2	Papua New Guinea
5522	Black-breasted Boatbill	12/2	Papua New Guinea
5523	Spotted Jewel-babbler	12/2	Papua New Guinea
5524	Tit Berrypecker	12/2	Papua New Guinea
5525	Papuan Scrubwren	12/2	Papua New Guinea
5526	Large Scrubwren	12/2	Papua New Guinea
5527	Mountain Mouse-Warbler	12/2	Papua New Guinea
5528	Gray-streaked Honeyeater	12/2	Papua New Guinea
5529	Rufous-backed Honeyeater	12/2	Papua New Guinea
5530	Belford's Melidectes	12/2	Papua New Guinea
5531	Black-throated Honeyeater	12/2	Papua New Guinea
5532	Archbold's Bowerbird	12/2	Papua New Guinea
5533	Goldie's Lorikeet	12/2	Papua New Guinea
5534	Papuan Lorikeet	12/2	Papua New Guinea
5535	White-breasted Fruit-Dove	12/2	Papua New Guinea
5536	Chestnut Forest-Rail	12/2	Papua New Guinea
5537	Black-throated Robin	12/2	Papua New Guinea
5538	Brown Sicklebill	12/2	Papua New Guinea
5539	King-of-Saxony Bird-of-Paradise (238–239)	12/2	Papua New Guinea
5540	Mottled Berryhunter	12/2	Papua New Guinea
5541	Black Sicklebill	12/3	Papua New Guinea
5542	Rufous-naped Bellbird	12/3	Papua New Guinea
5543	Fan-tailed Berrypecker	12/3	Papua New Guinea
5544	Brown-breasted Gerygone	12/3	Papua New Guinea
5545	Mountain Swiftlet	12/3	Papua New Guinea
5546	Rufous-throated Bronze-Cuckoo	12/3	Papua New Guinea
5547	Lesser Melampitta	12/3	Papua New Guinea
5548	Black Sittella	12/3	Papua New Guinea
5549	Black-bellied Cicadabird	12/3	Papua New Guinea
5550	Crested Berrypecker	12/3	Papua New Guinea
5551	Mid-mountain Berrypecker	12/3	Papua New Guinea
5552	Plum-faced Lorikeet	12/3	Papua New Guinea
5553	Yellow-billed Lorikeet	12/3	Papua New Guinea
5554	Brehm's Tiger-Parrot	12/3	Papua New Guinea
5555	Gray Thornbill	12/3	Papua New Guinea
5556	Red-headed Myzomela	12/3	Papua New Guinea
5557	Orange-crowned Fairywren	12/3	Papua New Guinea
5558	Macgregor's Bowerbird	12/3	Papua New Guinea
5559	Sclater's Whistler	12/4	Papua New Guinea
5560	Slaty-chinned Longbill	12/4	Papua New Guinea
5561	Papuan Parrotfinch	12/5	Papua New Guinea
5562	New Guinea White-eye	12/5	Papua New Guinea
5563	Island Leaf Warbler	12/5	Papua New Guinea
5564	Lesser Ground-Robin	12/5	Papua New Guinea
5565	Fantailed Monarch	12/5	Papua New Guinea
5566	Dimorphic Fantail	12/5	Papua New Guinea
5567	Black Fantail	12/5	Papua New Guinea
5568	Varied Sittella	12/5	Papua New Guinea
5569	Yellow-bellied Longbill	12/5	Papua New Guinea
5570	Ornate Melidectes	12/5	Papua New Guinea
5571	Forest Honeyeater	12/5	Papua New Guinea
5572	Yellow-breasted Bowerbird	12/5	Papua New Guinea
5573	Fan-tailed Cuckoo	12/5	Papua New Guinea
5574	Rufescent Imperial-Pigeon	12/5	Papua New Guinea
5575	Wattled Ploughbill	12/6	Papua New Guinea
5576	Bismarck Crow	12/6	Papua New Guinea
5577	Purple-bellied Lory	12/6	Papua New Guinea
5578	Red-knobbed Imperial-Pigeon	12/6	Papua New Guinea
5579	Metallic Starling	12/7	Papua New Guinea
5580	Shining Flycatcher	12/7	Papua New Guinea
5581	Bismarck Munia	12/7	Papua New Guinea
5582	Latham's Snipe	12/7	Papua New Guinea
5583	Red-banded Flowerpecker	12/7	Papua New Guinea
5584	Long-tailed Myna	12/7	Papua New Guinea
5585	Varied Triller	12/7	Papua New Guinea
5586	New Britain Friarbird (240)	12/7	Papua New Guinea
5587	Ashy Myzomela	12/7	Papua New Guinea
5588	Red-flanked Lorikeet	12/7	Papua New Guinea
5589	Singing Parrot	12/7	Papua New Guinea
5590	Buff-faced Pygmy-Parrot	12/7	Papua New Guinea
5591	Blue-eyed Cockatoo	12/7	Papua New Guinea
5592	New Britain Kingfisher (240)	12/7	Papua New Guinea
5593	New Britain Dwarf-Kingfisher	12/7	Papua New Guinea
5594	Blyth's Hornbill (240–241)	12/7	Papua New Guinea
5595	Pied Coucal	12/7	Papua New Guinea
5596	Violaceous Coucal	12/7	Papua New Guinea
5597	Channel-billed Cuckoo	12/7	Papua New Guinea
5598	Finsch's Imperial-Pigeon	12/7	Papua New Guinea
5599	Knob-billed Fruit-Dove	12/7	Papua New Guinea
5600	Variable Goshawk	12/7	Papua New Guinea
5601	Black Honey-buzzard	12/7	Papua New Guinea

5602	Melanesian Scrubfowl	12/7	Papua New Guinea
5603	Australian Reed-Warbler	12/7	Papua New Guinea
5604	Spotted Whistling-Duck	12/7	Papua New Guinea
5605	Golden Masked-Owl (235–237, 239–242)	12/7	Papua New Guinea
5606	Moustached Treeswift	12/8	Papua New Guinea
5607	Island Monarch	12/8	Papua New Guinea
5608	Black-tailed Whistler	12/8	Papua New Guinea
5609	Sclater's Myzomela	12/8	Papua New Guinea
5610	Beach Kingfisher	12/8	Papua New Guinea
5611	Island Imperial-Pigeon	12/8	Papua New Guinea
5612	Nicobar Pigeon	12/8	Papua New Guinea
5613	Black-naped Tern	12/8	Papua New Guinea
5614	Black Noddy	12/8	Papua New Guinea
5615	New Britain Boobook (240)	12/8	Papua New Guinea
5616	Sharp-tailed Sandpiper	12/8	Papua New Guinea
5617	Sacred Kingfisher	12/8	Papua New Guinea
5618	Northern Fantail	12/8	Papua New Guinea
5619	Varied Honeyeater	12/9	Australia
5620	Australian Swiftlet	12/9	Australia
5621	Silver Gull	12/9	Australia
5622	Far Eastern Curlew	12/9	Australia
5623	Australian Pelican	12/9	Australia
5624	Magpie-lark	12/9	Australia
5625	Brown Honeyeater	12/9	Australia
5626	Double-eyed Fig-Parrot	12/9	Australia
5627	Bush Thick-knee	12/9	Australia
5628	Straw-necked Ibis	12/9	Australia
5629	Magpie Goose	12/9	Australia
5630	Gray Goshawk	12/9	Australia
5631	Mistletoebird	12/9	Australia
5632	Mangrove Robin	12/9	Australia
5633	Torresian Kingfisher	12/9	Australia
5634	Rose-crowned Fruit-Dove	12/9	Australia
5635	Green Oriole	12/9	Australia
5636	Chestnut-breasted Munia	12/9	Australia
5637	Crimson Finch	12/9	Australia
5638	Sulphur-crested Cockatoo	12/9	Australia
5639	Blue-faced Honeyeater	12/9	Australia
5640	Australian Kestrel	12/9	Australia
5641	Pied Stilt	12/9	Australia
5642	Royal Spoonbill	12/9	Australia
5643	Australasian Darter	12/9	Australia
5644	Green Pygmy-Goose	12/9	Australia
5645	Radjah Shelduck	12/9	Australia
5646	Forest Kingfisher	12/9	Australia
5647	Laughing Kookaburra	12/9	Australia
5648	Pale-yellow Robin	12/9	Australia
5649	Large-billed Scrubwren	12/9	Australia
5650	Graceful Honeyeater	12/9	Australia
5651	Noisy Pitta	12/9	Australia
5652	Australian Brushturkey	12/9	Australia
5653	Australian Magpie	12/10	Australia
5654	Great Bowerbird	12/10	Australia
5655	Pale-headed Rosella	12/10	Australia
5656	Galah	12/10	Australia
5657	Tawny Frogmouth	12/10	Australia
5658	Australian Hobby	12/10	Australia
5659	Pied Butcherbird	12/10	Australia
5660	Red-tailed Black-Cockatoo	12/10	Australia
5661	Blue-winged Kookaburra	12/10	Australia
5662	Apostlebird	12/10	Australia
5663	Olive-backed Oriole	12/10	Australia
5664	Rufous Whistler	12/10	Australia
5665	White-winged Triller	12/10	Australia
5666	Gray-crowned Babbler	12/10	Australia
5667	White-throated Gerygone	12/10	Australia
5668	Weebill	12/10	Australia
5669	Little Friarbird	12/10	Australia
5670	Brown Treecreeper	12/10	Australia
5671	Squatter Pigeon	12/10	Australia
5672	Double-barred Finch	12/10	Australia
5673	Noisy Friarbird	12/10	Australia
5674	Scarlet Myzomela	12/10	Australia
5675	White-gaped Honeyeater	12/10	Australia
5676	Yellow Honeyeater	12/10	Australia
5677	Red-winged Parrot	12/10	Australia
5678	Pacific Koel	12/10	Australia
5679	Little Bronze-Cuckoo	12/10	Australia
5680	White-faced Heron	12/10	Australia
5681	Brown Falcon	12/10	Australia
5682	Black-fronted Dotterel	12/10	Australia
5683	Red-kneed Dotterel	12/10	Australia
5684	Australian Bustard	12/10	Australia
5685	Maned Duck	12/10	Australia
5686	Banded Honeyeater	12/10	Australia
5687	Rufous-throated Honeyeater	12/10	Australia
5688	Bar-breasted Honeyeater	12/10	Australia
5689	Red-backed Fairywren	12/10	Australia
5690	Crested Pigeon	12/10	Australia
5691	Gray Teal	12/10	Australia
5692	Australasian Pipit	12/10	Australia
5693	Whistling Kite	12/10	Australia
5694	Eastern Yellow Robin	12/10	Australia
5695	Fairy Gerygone	12/10	Australia
5696	Lovely Fairywren	12/10	Australia
5697	Silver-eye	12/10	Australia
5698	White-browed Robin	12/10	Australia
5699	Spectacled Monarch	12/10	Australia
5700	Macleay's Honeyeater	12/10	Australia
5701	Dusky Myzomela	12/10	Australia
5702	Brown-backed Honeyeater	12/10	Australia
5703	Red-browed Firetail	12/10	Australia
5704	Gray Whistler	12/10	Australia
5705	Australian Kite	12/10	Australia
5706	Red-necked Crake	12/10	Australia
5707	White-throated Needletail	12/10	Australia
5708	Blue-faced Parrotfinch	12/11	Australia
5709	Gray Fantail	12/11	Australia
5710	Bridled Honeyeater	12/11	Australia
5711	Yellow-faced Honeyeater	12/11	Australia
5712	Scaly-breasted Lorikeet	12/11	Australia
5713	Victoria's Riflebird	12/11	Australia
5714	Yellow-spotted Honeyeater	12/11	Australia
5715	Spotted Catbird	12/11	Australia
5716	Brown Cuckoo-Dove	12/11	Australia
5717	Yellow-breasted Boatbill	12/11	Australia
5718	Brown Gerygone	12/11	Australia
5719	Black-necked Stork	12/11	Australia
5720	Black Swan	12/11	Australia

5721	Emu (245)	12/11	Australia
5722	Brolga	12/11	Australia
5723	Yellow-billed Spoonbill	12/11	Australia
5724	Pink-eared Duck	12/11	Australia
5725	Plumed Whistling-Duck	12/11	Australia
5726	Gray-headed Robin	12/11	Australia
5727	Eastern Whipbird	12/11	Australia
5728	Atherton Scrubwren	12/11	Australia
5729	Yellow-throated Scrubwren	12/11	Australia
5730	Tooth-billed Catbird	12/11	Australia
5731	Pacific Heron	12/11	Australia
5732	Common Cicadabird	12/12	Australia
5733	Pied Currawong	12/12	Australia
5734	Chowchilla	12/12	Australia
5735	White-browed Scrubwren	12/12	Australia
5736	White-cheeked Honeyeater	12/12	Australia
5737	Lewin's Honeyeater	12/12	Australia
5738	Eastern Spinebill	12/12	Australia
5739	Australian King-Parrot	12/12	Australia
5740	Topknot Pigeon	12/12	Australia
5741	Rufous-tailed Bush-hen	12/12	Australia
5742	Rufous Fantail	12/12	Australia
5743	Golden Whistler	12/12	Australia
5744	Bower's Shrikethrush	12/12	Australia
5745	Mountain Thornbill	12/12	Australia
5746	Fernwren	12/12	Australia
5747	White-throated Treecreeper	12/12	Australia
5748	Satin Bowerbird	12/12	Australia
5749	Golden Bowerbird	12/12	Australia
5750	Shining Bronze-Cuckoo	12/12	Australia
5751	Gray Shrikethrush	12/12	Australia
5752	White-naped Honeyeater	12/12	Australia
5753	Fuscous Honeyeater	12/12	Australia
5754	Gray Butcherbird	12/12	Australia
5755	Dusky Woodswallow	12/12	Australia
5756	Noisy Miner	12/12	Australia
5757	Pied Monarch	12/13	Australia
5758	Chestnut-breasted Cuckoo	12/13	Australia
5759	Tree Martin	12/13	Australia
5760	Large-billed Gerygone	12/13	Australia
5761	Fairy Martin	12/13	Australia
5762	Southern Cassowary (245)	12/13	Australia
5763	Pied Oystercatcher	12/13	Australia
5764	Jacky-winter	12/14	Australia
5765	Yellow Thornbill	12/14	Australia
5766	Yellow-rumped Thornbill	12/14	Australia
5767	Inland Thornbill	12/14	Australia
5768	Spiny-cheeked Honeyeater	12/14	Australia
5769	Yellow-throated Miner	12/14	Australia
5770	Superb Fairywren	12/14	Australia
5771	Red-rumped Parrot	12/14	Australia
5772	Greater Bluebonnet	12/14	Australia
5773	Cockatiel	12/14	Australia
5774	Little Corella	12/14	Australia
5775	Horsfield's Bronze-Cuckoo	12/14	Australia
5776	Zebra Finch	12/14	Australia
5777	Australasian Bushlark	12/14	Australia
5778	White-winged Fairywren	12/14	Australia
5779	Plum-headed Finch	12/14	Australia
5780	Diamond Firetail	12/14	Australia
5781	Rufous Songlark	12/14	Australia
5782	Hooded Robin	12/14	Australia
5783	Australian Raven	12/14	Australia
5784	Restless Flycatcher	12/14	Australia
5785	Little Woodswallow	12/14	Australia
5786	White-browed Woodswallow	12/14	Australia
5787	Masked Woodswallow	12/14	Australia
5788	White-plumed Honeyeater	12/14	Australia
5789	Little Lorikeet	12/14	Australia
5790	Wedge-tailed Eagle	12/14	Australia
5791	Speckled Warbler	12/14	Australia
5792	Eastern Rosella	12/14	Australia
5793	Western Gerygone	12/14	Australia
5794	Spotted Pardalote	12/14	Australia
5795	Black-chinned Honeyeater	12/14	Australia
5796	Brown-headed Honeyeater	12/14	Australia
5797	Yellow-tufted Honeyeater	12/14	Australia
5798	White-winged Chough	12/14	Australia
5799	Painted Honeyeater	12/14	Australia
5800	Striped Honeyeater	12/14	Australia
5801	Red-necked Avocet	12/14	Australia
5802	Hoary-headed Grebe	12/14	Australia
5803	Chestnut Teal	12/14	Australia
5804	Spotted Harrier	12/14	Australia
5805	Australian Shoveler	12/14	Australia
5806	Brown Thornbill	12/14	Australia
5807	Bell Miner	12/14	Australia
5808	Variegated Fairywren	12/14	Australia
5809	Wonga Pigeon	12/14	Australia
5810	Australian Masked-Owl	12/14	Australia
5811	Marbled Frogmouth	12/14	Australia
5812	Australian Owlet-nightjar	12/14	Australia
5813	Southern Boobook	12/14	Australia
5814	Russet-tailed Thrush	12/15	Australia
5815	Rose Robin	12/15	Australia
5816	Paradise Riflebird	12/15	Australia
5817	Australian Logrunner	12/15	Australia
5818	Regent Bowerbird	12/15	Australia
5819	Green Catbird	12/15	Australia
5820	Albert's Lyrebird	12/15	Australia
5821	Crimson Rosella	12/15	Australia
5822	White-headed Pigeon	12/15	Australia
5823	Red-browed Treecreeper	12/15	Australia
5824	Yellow-tailed Black-Cockatoo	12/15	Australia
5825	Buff-rumped Thornbill	12/15	Australia
5826	Little Wattlebird	12/15	Australia
5827	Red-capped Plover	12/15	Australia
5828	Pied Cormorant	12/15	Australia
5829	Collared Sparrowhawk	12/15	Australia
5830	Mangrove Gerygone	12/15	Australia
5831	Mangrove Honeyeater	12/15	Australia
5832	Spotless Crake	12/15	Australia
5833	Common Bronzewing	12/15	Australia
5834	Australasian Grass-Owl	12/15	Australia
5835	Little Raven	12/16	Australia
5836	New Holland Honeyeater	12/16	Australia
5837	Red Wattlebird	12/16	Australia
5838	Purple-crowned Lorikeet	12/16	Australia
5839	Black-tailed Native-hen	12/16	Australia
5840	Cape Barren Goose	12/16	Australia

5841	Scarlet Robin	12/16	Australia	5901	Strong-billed Honeyeater	12/20	Australia
5842	Striated Thornbill	12/16	Australia	5902	Yellow-throated Honeyeater	12/20	Australia
5843	Striated Pardalote	12/16	Australia	5903	Pallid Cuckoo	12/20	Australia
5844	Long-billed Corella	12/16	Australia	5904	Beautiful Firetail	12/20	Australia
5845	Brush Bronzewing	12/16	Australia	5905	Dusky Robin	12/20	Australia
5846	Musk Lorikeet	12/16	Australia	5906	Scrubtit	12/20	Australia
5847	Banded Lapwing	12/16	Australia	5907	Ground Parrot	12/20	Australia
5848	Little Grassbird	12/16	Australia	5908	Sooty Oystercatcher	12/20	Australia
5849	Striated Fieldwren	12/16	Australia	5909	New Zealand Fantail	12/21	New Zealand
5850	White-fronted Chat	12/16	Australia	5910	Gray Gerygone	12/21	New Zealand
5851	Fairy Tern	12/16	Australia	5911	Tui	12/21	New Zealand
5852	Banded Stilt	12/16	Australia	5912	New Zealand Pigeon	12/21	New Zealand
5853	Australian Crake	12/16	Australia	5913	Red-billed Gull	12/21	New Zealand
5854	Baillon's Crake	12/16	Australia	5914	Red-breasted Dotterel	12/21	New Zealand
5855	Swamp Harrier	12/16	Australia	5915	Variable Oystercatcher	12/21	New Zealand
5856	Australasian Gannet	12/16	Australia	5916	South Island Oystercatcher	12/21	New Zealand
5857	Stubble Quail	12/16	Australia	5917	White-fronted Tern	12/21	New Zealand
5858	Musk Duck	12/16	Australia	5918	New Zealand Storm-Petrel	12/21	New Zealand
5859	Blue-billed Duck	12/16	Australia	5919	White-faced Storm-Petrel	12/21	New Zealand
5860	Australian Shelduck	12/16	Australia	5920	Fluttering Shearwater	12/21	New Zealand
5861	Freckled Duck	12/16	Australia	5921	Buller's Shearwater	12/21	New Zealand
5862	Pacific Gull	12/16	Australia	5922	Flesh-footed Shearwater	12/21	New Zealand
5863	Little Penguin	12/16	Australia	5923	Parkinson's Petrel	12/21	New Zealand
5864	Gray Currawong	12/17	Australia	5924	Fairy Prion	12/21	New Zealand
5865	Rufous Bristlebird	12/17	Australia	5925	Cook's Petrel	12/21	New Zealand
5866	White-eared Honeyeater	12/17	Australia	5926	Red-crowned Parakeet	12/21	New Zealand
5867	Southern Emuwren	12/17	Australia	5927	Gray Noddy	12/21	New Zealand
5868	Singing Honeyeater	12/17	Australia	5928	Little Shearwater	12/21	New Zealand
5869	Hooded Plover	12/17	Australia	5929	North Island Saddleback	12/21	New Zealand
5870	Chestnut-rumped Heathwren	12/17	Australia	5930	New Zealand Bellbird	12/21	New Zealand
5871	Blue-winged Parrot	12/17	Australia	5931	New Zealand Kaka	12/21	New Zealand
5872	Black-faced Cormorant	12/17	Australia	5932	Weka	12/21	New Zealand
5873	Crescent Honeyeater	12/17	Australia	5933	South Island Takahe	12/21	New Zealand
5874	Forest Raven	12/17	Australia	5934	Brown Teal	12/21	New Zealand
5875	Satin Flycatcher	12/17	Australia	5935	Paradise Shelduck	12/21	New Zealand
5876	Olive Whistler	12/17	Australia	5936	North Island Brown Kiwi	12/21	New Zealand
5877	Gang-gang Cockatoo	12/17	Australia	5937	Black-billed Gull	12/22	New Zealand
5878	Little Eagle	12/18	Australia	5938	Wrybill	12/22	New Zealand
5879	Gilbert's Whistler	12/18	Australia	5939	Double-banded Plover	12/22	New Zealand
5880	White-browed Babbler	12/18	Australia	5940	African Collared-Dove	12/22	New Zealand
5881	Shy Heathwren	12/18	Australia	5941	New Zealand Grebe	12/22	New Zealand
5882	Red-capped Robin	12/18	Australia	5942	New Zealand Scaup	12/22	New Zealand
5883	Chestnut-rumped Thornbill	12/18	Australia	5943	Tomtit	12/22	New Zealand
5884	Crested Bellbird	12/18	Australia	5944	Fernbird	12/23	New Zealand
5885	Powerful Owl	12/18	Australia	5945	New Zealand Robin	12/23	New Zealand
5886	Brown Songlark	12/18	Australia	5946	Stitchbird	12/23	New Zealand
5887	Olive-tailed Thrush	12/19	Australia	5947	North Island Kokako	12/23	New Zealand
5888	Flame Robin	12/19	Australia	5948	Whitehead	12/23	New Zealand
5889	Pilotbird	12/19	Australia	5949	Rifleman	12/23	New Zealand
5890	Superb Lyrebird	12/19	Australia	5950	Western Corella	12/24	Australia
5891	Pink Robin	12/20	Australia	5951	Port Lincoln Parrot	12/24	Australia
5892	Black Currawong	12/20	Australia	5952	Black-faced Woodswallow	12/24	Australia
5893	Tasmanian Thornbill	12/20	Australia	5953	Rufous Fieldwren	12/24	Australia
5894	Tasmanian Scrubwren	12/20	Australia	5954	Redthroat	12/24	Australia
5895	Black-headed Honeyeater	12/20	Australia	5955	Rufous Treecreeper	12/24	Australia
5896	Yellow Wattlebird	12/20	Australia	5956	Slaty-backed Thornbill	12/25	Australia
5897	Green Rosella	12/20	Australia	5957	White-browed Treecreeper (244–245)	12/25	Australia
5898	Tasmanian Native-hen	12/20	Australia	5958	Little Crow	12/25	Australia
5899	Swift Parrot	12/20	Australia	5959	Chiming Wedgebill	12/25	Australia
5900	Forty-spotted Pardalote	12/20	Australia	5960	Crimson Chat (244)	12/25	Australia

5961	Splendid Fairywren	12/25	Australia
5962	Mulga Parrot (244)	12/25	Australia
5963	Bourke's Parrot	12/25	Australia
5964	White-fronted Honeyeater	12/25	Australia
5965	Southern Whiteface	12/25	Australia
5966	White-backed Swallow (246)	12/25	Australia
5967	Elegant Parrot	12/26	Australia
5968	Regent Parrot	12/26	Australia
5969	Carnaby's Black-Cockatoo	12/26	Australia
5970	Western Yellow Robin	12/26	Australia
5971	Western Spinebill	12/26	Australia
5972	Gilbert's Honeyeater	12/26	Australia
5973	Baudin's Black-Cockatoo	12/26	Australia
5974	Western Thornbill	12/26	Australia
5975	Yellow-plumed Honeyeater	12/26	Australia
5976	Blue-breasted Fairywren	12/26	Australia
5977	Red-capped Parrot	12/26	Australia
5978	Western Rosella	12/26	Australia
5979	Red-eared Firetail	12/26	Australia
5980	White-breasted Robin	12/26	Australia
5981	Western Wattlebird	12/26	Australia
5982	Red-winged Fairywren	12/26	Australia
5983	Crested Shrike-tit	12/26	Australia
5984	Painted Buttonquail	12/26	Australia
5985	Tawny-crowned Honeyeater	12/27	Australia
5986	Straw-headed Bulbul	12/27	Singapore
5987	Gray Nightjar	12/27	Singapore
5988	Ruddy-breasted Crake	12/27	Singapore
5989	Tanimbar Corella	12/27	Singapore
5990	Slender-billed Vulture	12/28	India
5991	Dark-rumped Rosefinch	12/29	India
5992	Rufous-breasted Bush-Robin	12/29	India
5993	Ludlow's Fulvetta	12/29	India
5994	Rufous-vented Yuhina	12/29	India
5995	Streak-throated Fulvetta	12/29	India
5996	Beautiful Sibia	12/29	India
5997	Yellow-throated Fulvetta	12/29	India
5998	Rusty-throated Wren-Babbler (253)	12/29	India
5999	White-naped Yuhina	12/29	India
6000	Yellow-rumped Honeyguide (253)	12/29	India
6001	Gray-cheeked Warbler	12/29	India
6002	Scaly-breasted Cupwing	12/29	India
6003	Nepal House-Martin	12/29	India
6004	Slender-billed Scimitar-Babbler	12/29	India
6005	Chevron-breasted Babbler	12/29	India
6006	Striated Yuhina	12/29	India
6007	Wedge-tailed Pigeon	12/29	India
6008	Black-faced Bunting	12/30	India
6009	White-tailed Rubythroat	12/30	India
6010	Marsh Babbler	12/30	India
6011	Jerdon's Babbler	12/30	India
6012	Spotted Bush-Warbler	12/30	India
6013	Baikal Bush-Warbler	12/30	India
6014	Pallas's Grasshopper-Warbler	12/30	India
6015	Paddyfield Warbler	12/30	India
6016	Tickell's Leaf Warbler	12/30	India
6017	Smoky Warbler	12/30	India
6018	Gray-sided Bush-Warbler	12/30	India
6019	Brown-cheeked Rail	12/30	India
6020	Swamp Francolin	12/30	India
6021	Baikal Teal	12/30	India
6022	Falcated Duck	12/30	India
6023	Bar-headed Goose	12/30	India
6024	Siberian Rubythroat	12/30	India
6025	Thick-billed Warbler	12/30	India
6026	Whistler's Warbler	12/30	India
6027	Spot-winged Starling	12/30	India
6028	Sapphire Flycatcher	12/30	India
6029	Rusty-bellied Shortwing	12/30	India
6030	Small Niltava	12/30	India
6031	White-throated Bulbul	12/30	India
6032	Scaly Thrush	12/31	India
6033	Chestnut-backed Laughingthrush	12/31	India
6034	Rufous-necked Laughingthrush	12/31	India
6035	Nepal Fulvetta	12/31	India
6036	Rufous-throated Fulvetta	12/31	India
6037	White-hooded Babbler	12/31	India
6038	Buff-chested Babbler	12/31	India
6039	Large Woodshrike	12/31	India
6040	White-cheeked Partridge	12/31	India
6041	White-winged Duck	12/31	India
6042	Silver-breasted Broadbill (255, 257)	12/31	India

INDEX

Big Year (*cont.*)
  world Big Years, 43, 45–47, 98–99,
    198–99
  and world records, 200–204, 206–8
  year-end acceleration of time, 233–34
The Big Year (film), 248
Bird Guide (Reed), 38
birding
  addictive nature of, 62–63
  author's interest in, 3–4, 21–22, 36,
    86, 92–93, 95–96, 207–8, 248
  bird vocalizations, 11–12, 13–14
  cryptic bird behavior, 57
  field guides, 48
  in the Information Age, 47–49
  and ornithology, 36–37
  rare bird chasing, 153–54
  shared passion of birders, 1, 5, 35,
    157, 179, 208, 256
  and world records, 200–204, 206–8
  See also checklists
Birding magazine, 42, 121
BirdingPal website, 31, 47, 113, 164, 170
Birding Without Borders blog, 119–20
Birds of America (Audubon), 37, 38
birds-of-paradise, 237–39
A Birdwatcher's Guide to Norway (Tveit), 158
Black-and-cinnamon Fantail, 227
Black-and-white Hawk-Eagle, 60–61
Black-and-yellow Silky-Flycatcher, 116
Black-bellied Bustard, 167
Black Bittern, 240
Black-capped Chickadee, 1
Black-capped Vireo, 145
Black-casqued Hornbill, 173
Black Skimmer, 60
Black-spectacled Brushfinch, 72–75
Black-throated Saltator, 60
Blue-headed Parrot, 58
Blue Jay, 146
Blue-mantled Thornbill, 81
Blyth's Hornbill, 240–41
Boateng, Yaw, 164, 166, 167, 174, 179, 181
Borneo, 237
Brazil, 51–65
Bright-rumped Attila, 126

Broad-tailed Grassbird, 203
Bronze Mannikin, 167
Bronze-tailed Starling, 185
Bronzy Inca, 95
Brown-backed Chat-Tyrant, 81
Brown Jay, 126
Brown Pelican, 153–55
Buenaño, Edison, 105–10
Buff-collared Nightjar, 139–40
bullet trains, 220–21
Burgos, Freddy, 23, 24, 25–29, 30–31, 32–35
Burj Khalifa, 201

Cahill, John, 131–32
California, 145, 149
Call Collect, Ask for Birdman (Vardaman), 45–46
Cameroon, 166, 187–88
Campbell, Oscar, 201–2
Canada Warbler, 126
Cape Coast, Ghana, 175–77
Cape Crombec, 191
Capellone, Monal, 237
Cape Petrel, 9–10, 16
Carolina Wren, 146
Caroline Islands Ground-Dove, 43
Carvalho, Guto, 52, 53
Catesby, Mark, 37
Cayuga Lake, 153–55
Chattering Cisticola, 180
checklists
  Clements Checklist, 14–15, 46, 199, 255
  English common names, 26
  global, 14–15, 46
  heard-only birds, 11–12, 13–14, 230–31
  IOC World Bird List, 14, 255
  Latin names, 26, 52
  list length *versus* birding expertise, 183–84
  no introduced birds (NIB), 13
  "stringers" and "stringing," 12
Chestnut-crowned Antpitta, 109
China, 215–16, 218
Chinspot Batis, 191

EQUATOR